Experience Psychology!

A LABORATORY GUIDE TO

PSYCHOLOGICAL SCIENCE

SECOND EDITION

Carolyn A. Buckley

Lafayette College

Easton, PA

Kendall Hunt
publishing company

Contributors to interior artwork, unless otherwise noted on the pages of this book, include the following
(with page numbers where their work appears):

Leremy (xiii, xiv, xvi, xviii, 1, 5, 10, 11, 17, 43, 51, 52, 54, 55, 56, 57, 79, 86, 95, 117, 121, 124,
126, 128, 129, 153, 162, 166, 172, 203, 207, 208, 233, 239, 240, 241, 242, 243, 275, 279, 280,
282, 286, 287, 288, and "About the author.")
Cherstva (xiv, xvi, 83, 89)
DrAndY (240, 241, 242)
blojfo (157, 159)
danleap (47, 83)
Anniris (15)
Cat_arch_ (128)
Ecelop (128)
HuHu (124)
momoforsale (84)
RedlineVector (xviii)
Zack Stock Photo (199)

NOTE: Some of these images were combined or modified slightly from the original artists' work.
I hope they can forgive me and are pleased with the results. (C. Buckley)

Cover image © Carolyn Buckley, with contributions from multiple other artists
(see cover image credits, page iv).

Kendall Hunt
publishing company

www.kendallhunt.com
Send all inquiries to:
4050 Westmark Drive
Dubuque, IA 52004-1840

Copyright © 2014, 2020 by Carolyn A. Buckley

ISBN 978-1-7924-4325-1

Printed in the United States of America

IN MEMORY OF

Rudy Kulmus,
who loved science

and Mom,
who loved words

Cover Art: *The Stuff of Psychology* designed by C. Buckley using artwork from 13 different artists.

The black and white swirl on the front cover was created by TheVector and extended to the back cover by C. Buckley. Figures represent a sample of human behavior, with hidden meanings everywhere. Look for the mundane activities of life, the things we do for fun, for sport, for thrills, for each other, for ourselves, and for love. Find the ways we interact with nature, escape from discomfort and better ourselves. Look for our relationships with animals, with food and water and with our phones, and find at least one way the 2020 pandemic has influenced family behavior. The author is also there working on the cover design, which could not have been completed without the incredible talent of several other artists. All are listed below with the images they created, as numbered in the key above. Special thanks to Leremy, who contributed 53 of the 74 stick figures on the cover. Small modifications to original artwork were made in some cases, marked by an asterisk(*).

1. Leaning (Michael D Brown)
2. Holding a Child (north100)
3. Cheering Others (AnnIris)
4. Bowling (Leremy)
5. Handwashing (Leremy)
6. Meditating (Leremy)
7. Zip-lining (Leremy)
8. Hiking (Leremy)
9. Motorscooting (Leremy)
10. Friending (Leremy)
11. Addicting (Leremy)*
12. Showering (Leremy)
13. Dancing (Leremy)
14. Playing Basketball (Macrovector)
15. Seesawing (Leremy)
16. Floorcleaning (Leremy)
17. Lampcleaning (Leremy)*
18. Coercing (Jovanovic Dejan)
19. Leaping (Leremy)
20. Washing (Leremy)
21. Tugging (Leremy)
22. Phoning (Leremy)
23. Achieving (RedlineVector)
24. Freestyling (AnnIris)
25. Skiing (Leremy)
26. Leaking (Leremy)
27. Cardplaying (Leremy)
28. Helping (Leremy)
29. Punching (Leremy)
30. Cooking (Leremy)
31. Cycling (Leremy)
32. Photographing (Leremy)
33. Crawling (AnnIris)*
34. Watering Flowers (Leremy)*
35. Boating/Parasailing (Leremy)*
36. Splashing (Leremy)
37. Swimming (Leremy)
38. Floating (Leremy)
39. Surfing (AnnIris)*
40. Being Me (Leremy)*
41. Succeeding (Leremy)
42. Carrying (Leremy)
43. Jumping (aelitta)
44. Graduating (Leremy)
45. Rope Climbing (Leremy)*
46. Schooling (Leremy)
47. Swinging (Leremy)
48. Making Magic (Leremy)*
49. Waving (aelitta)
50. Rushing (Leremy)
51. Stairclimbing (north100)*
52. Rock Climbing (Leremy)*
53. Flying (Leremy)
54. Toothbrushing (Leremy)
55. Testing (Leremy)
56. Strolling (aelitta)
57. Painting (Leremy)*
58. Saying Hello (north100)
59. Racing (Macrovector)
60. Riding (Leremy)
61. Raiding Refrigerator (Leremy)
62. Sneaking (Leremy)
63. Resting (Leremy)
64. Sliding (C Buckley)
65. Hunting (Leremy)
66. Marching (DrAndY)*
67. Following (DrAndY)
68. Being Family (Sudowoodo)*
69. Running (Leremy)
70. Fishing (Leremy)*
71. Scuba Diving (Serhiy Smirnov)
72. Staying Dry (Leremy)*
73. Parenting (Leremy)
74. Trick Cycling (AnnIris)

ACKNOWLEDGMENTS

This book would not have been possible without the perseverance and helpful feedback of so many students with whom I have worked over the past 20 years, including those at Northampton Community College, East Stroudsburg University, Lehigh University, and for the past 13 years, Lafayette College. It is my sincere hope that these pages will give new students of psychology what all of you have given me: a profoundly satisfying learning experience. You have been my inspiration and my professional source of joy and enthusiasm.

Thank you to the faculty of the Psychology Department of Lafayette College, Easton, PA, past and present, especially those who have contributed to the ideas in this book, most notably: Jessica Redding, Jeannine Pinto, and Ralph Barnes. Jessica, your kindness and willingness to try new things have been a blessing in my life, and I know you will be a great coordinator of future labs. Jeannine, you started it all and gave me the confidence to keep going. Ralph, the value of your ideas, discussions, and support cannot be overstated. And a thousand thank you's to all the wonderful Psychology Lab Assistants who have contributed so many thoughtful ideas and comments that have made this book better, especially Rachel Venaglia (so proud of you), Kim Gutjahr, Kara Enz, and... oh, this is a dangerous game, the list is too long. Thank you, PLAs! Thank you to Fabienne Duré and Rob Bouton for all kinds of support over the years, administrative, technical and emotional. Sincere thank you to Kendall Hunt Publishers, especially Rachel Guhin and Bob Largent for expertly overseeing the project. Sincere apologies to the KH Composition team for using so many stick figures from so many different artists throughout the book! Speaking of that, I want to thank Leremy, the artist whose self-proclaimed dedication to stick figures was the inspiration not only for the cover, but for this book's whole design. I hope Leremy and the other stick figure artists do not mind the liberties I took with their images and my stylus. A huge thank you to the developers who made that possible with their free, fabulous, and easy-to-use image editing software, Paint.net. Thanks also to Gijsbert Stoet at PsyToolKit.org, for his kind assistance, past and future, getting data collection programs up and running for student use. And of course, thank you to my family, who has endured seeing me wearing pajamas and a laptop more often than not for the past 6 months... Dave and Trudyann, your patience, support, and encouragement are the only reasons I ever accomplish anything. Rudy, thank you for introducing me to Paint.net and teaching me how to use it, and for your sense of humor and expert advice on how people younger than myself might interpret certain text passages. You are an amazing writer with more talent than you should be allowed to have before age 18. Tris and Caitlin, you inspire me. And last but not least, thank you to my Luna Petunia, my YodaBear, my Bellaluna. You are the furry light of my life, and I could not have survived this process without your soft brown eyes telling me when it was time to get some sleep, time to play, and time to settle in for more concentrated tippity-tapping.

Any errors or failures to properly credit ideas that may have originated with others reflect my own mistakes, absolutely unintentional. Please direct comments or concerns directly to the author at buckleyc@lafayette.edu. Your comments and suggestions for improvement are welcome and appreciated.

Trudyann Buckley, 2020. Used with permission.

TABLE OF CONTENTS

Module 3 — Summarizing Data and Generating Hypotheses.......................79

Module 4 — Correlational Research: Testing Relationships Between Variables

Module 5 — Experimental Research I: Testing Causal Relationships

Module 6 — Quasi-Experimental Research 199

PREFACE

AN OPEN LETTER TO STUDENTS

Dear Student of Psychology,

Before you begin the lab portion of this course, it may help to consider an important question. Circling the image that matches your answer will help you recognize your feelings and deal with them more effectively, so don't just point to one; actually circle it, and be honest with yourself. How excited are you about doing research in psychology?

Not one bit　　**Only a little**　　**Somewhat**　　**Moderately**　　**Mostly**　　**A lot**

This might seem obvious, but it's good to explicitly recognize: The further your answer falls toward the right, the easier it will be for you to learn a lot in this course. If your emotions fall to the left, this course will be more difficult for you, but you can still learn a lot, depending on how good you are at motivating yourself to do things you don't expect to enjoy. Of course, your answer might change as the semester proceeds, but it's good to know where you stand as you begin. You have signed up for a learning experience, and your attitude about that experience will play an important role in your success. This laboratory course focuses on building the scientific research skills that can produce the kind of content you are learning about in your psychology lecture textbook. To learn those skills, you need to actively practice them.

There's an old joke about a woman returning from work who asks her husband what he did all day at home. He replies, "I taught the cat how to do the dishes." "Really? Wow!" his wife says, as she goes to the kitchen. She returns a moment later and asks, "Why are the dirty dishes still in the sink?" Her husband replies, "I said I taught him. I didn't say he learned it."

That man could have been the best dish-washing teacher in the world, but for the cat to actually learn how to do dishes, it would have to pick up a dish at some point. The moral of the story, if there is one, is that many factors affect how much people learn, and teaching is just one of them. Practice is another. The goal of this book is to help students with diverse learning styles and interests practice doing research in psychology. My goal is for you to learn a lot, and I have tried to build in many opportunities to practice because that's one of the best ways to learn. But neither this book nor your professor can force you to take advantage of those opportunities.

I hope you will be excited to try doing research in psychology, and that your excitement will motivate you to learn as much as you can. For me, trying something out is the best, most rewarding part of learning any skill. Learning brings great joy to my life, especially when what I have learned becomes useful later on. May you find much in this book to bring you joy!

Sincerely,

Carol Buckley

April, 2020

INSTRUCTOR PREFACE

Teaching introductory psychology with a laboratory component can be challenging, but is well worth the effort. Why? Carl Sagan said it best:

> *"Science is more than a body of knowledge. It is a way of thinking; a way of skeptically interrogating the universe with a fine understanding of human fallibility."*

In less than 30 words, Sagan communicates the essence of science and calls out those of us who would present our discipline as 15 to 20 chapters of information. To be fair, most introductory psychology textbooks do include commentary on where that information came from and even exercises on how to think critically about it, but do we sometimes skip the critical thinking exercises and the commentary in favor of covering more information? This is understandable; there are standardized content exams to worry about. Add to that our excitement over sharing the findings of our discipline, which can be particularly useful for young adults just starting out in the world, and it is easy to see why our introductory students might be thinking less like scientists than like depositories for "a body of knowledge."

Psychology has invoked the scientific way of thinking to study our species since its emergence as a new discipline in the 1800s—who has a finer scientific understanding of "human fallibility" than psychologists? As in any introductory course, there is a large and diverse body of knowledge to impart, but could we do more to prepare future psychology majors for the way of thinking that this field demands, and to prepare nonscience majors for a life full of assorted information called "science?" Can we do a better job of teaching our students to systematically gather data, think skeptically, and critically evaluate the information they are given?

Introductory courses in the biological, chemical, and physical sciences have long accepted that *doing* science is a necessary step in learning science, and have made laboratory learning a priority. As a recognized hub science, it is time for psychology to provide an introductory experience that is on par with other sciences. We *can* do this. In fact, it could be argued that due to our disciplinary emphasis on how humans think, we have an *obligation* to more effectively model and teach the specific way of thinking that has built our knowledge base. This book is a response to that call.

Experience Psychology! offers a personally meaningful context for students to explore the philosophy of science and build scientific reasoning skills, like research design, data handling, and null hypothesis testing, without expensive equipment and without assuming any background knowledge in core scientific principles.

Lafayette College has been teaching Introductory Psychology as a natural science course with a laboratory component for more than 20 years. As coordinator of that program for over 12 years, I have learned much about what works and what does not, the level of scientific thinking that first-year students can achieve when given the opportunity, and how practice thinking like a scientist can help students develop intellectually and make more informed decisions about their course of study.

Annual rewrites of Lafayette's psychology lab course materials, many of which ended up in this book, have benefited from anonymous data provided by students, and I am grateful for their willingness to share their feelings about the book with me.

The "learning objective charts" included here have been included in previous versions throughout several years of rewrites, and the data they produced has made the writing clearer and the content more relevant and appropriate to students' background knowledge coming into the course. Each learning objective is labeled to match the Essays and Applications that help meet that objective, making it easy for instructors to decide what readings and projects to assign based on their own course goals. For more information on how learning objective charts can help you tailor your course and help your students learn, see item #3 in the Student Preface.

In short, *Experience Psychology! 2nd Ed.* combines years of practice and feedback into a laboratory guide for introductory psychology courses. Although this book could be used for an introductory methods course, it is not intended to provide comprehensive coverage of research methodology. Rather, it provides a strong foundation for students who will major in psychology, and first-hand experience in how science works for those who might never take another laboratory course. Research methods and statistical concepts are explained on a conceptual level, without reference to complex formulae or frequency distributions. The book introduces the fundamental principles behind testing ideas with data, primarily, the interpretation of statistical results based on probabilities. This is not a statistics book, and does not cover how to perform statistical tests, nor which tests to apply, beyond a very basic level. The main goal is to clarify factors that affect the trustworthiness of statistical information and the kinds of conclusions we can (and cannot) draw from various types of research.

Eight modules cover the following topics: (1) the philosophy of science and exploratory research; (2) descriptive research, conceptual variables and operational definitions; (3) summarizing descriptive data and generating hypotheses; (4) correlational research and probabilistic testing of relationships; (5) experimental research; (6) quasi-experimental research; (7) experimental designs that increase power; and (8) the interpretation and communication of scientific ideas.

The overarching design principle of this book is flexibility. Although the modules are placed in an intuitive order of increasing complexity, content stands alone as much as possible and referrals to other modules are provided when necessary, so that any number of modules may be covered in any order. Indexed glossaries with comprehensive definitions and multiple examples make it easy for students to quickly catch up on (or review) the meaning of terms from other modules.

Content within each module is covered in short (500 to 2,000 words) "Essays" covering important concepts in scientific thinking, along with multiple options for research projects that directly apply those concepts. The short-essay format allows you to prioritize and assign reading without complicated references to page numbers and sections that begin half-way down one page and end a third of the way down another page. Instead, simply assign "Essays 2.1 and 2.3." As with whole modules, every attempt was made to package each essay as stand-alone content with cross-referencing when necessary, which makes skipping some essays a practical option.

Research projects are optimized for groups of 15 to 40 students to discuss, collect data, and draw conclusions. Some projects give students room to formulate and test their own hypotheses. Rather than demonstrating known phenomena, the purpose of *Experience Psychology!* is to foster curiosity and to use a science attitude and basic research methods to test ideas. Projects can also stand alone for course flexibility. Teaching resources and helpful information for each research project are available online, and multiple-choice quiz questions will soon be available on the KHQ app to encourage student preparation for lab experiences.

For those who would like to introduce students to APA-Style standards of scientific reporting, **an "APA-Light" Style Guide is included.** Based on the 7th Edition of the *Publication Manual of the American Psychological Association,* "APA-Light" is a simplified version of the rules of presentation to be used as an introduction to standardized scientific reporting practices. The 7th edition of APA's *Publication Manual* is 428 pages. Students who major in psychology or other related fields will eventually learn how to use it to write APA-style reports, but it can be overwhelming to address all of the rules upon first exposure to reading and writing about psychology. The Style Guide in Appendix C gently introduces students to the most important content partitioning rules and to the detail-oriented mindset used in scientific reporting. There are many ways to accomplish this introduction, but this book is set up to assist with two basic approaches. One option is for students to use the "APA-Light" Style Guide to critique an unpublished sample manuscript (a poorly written lab report with questions to promote effective critiquing are included with the online teacher resources). Another option is for students to write a lab report on any research project, following the APA-Light Style Guide. These two options also work well in sequence.

Perforated pages allow students to work in groups or alone to produce standardized records of their research, apply proper terminology, draw appropriate conclusions, and share all of this with each other and with their instructor or a teaching assistant.

With a direct, engaging writing style, this book introduces the concepts behind quantitative psychology and probabilistic reasoning with minimal references to mathematical formulae. The goal is to conceptually prepare students who will major in psychology for core courses in statistics and research design. Perhaps just as important, students who do not major in science, but take introductory psychology for a core science credit, should leave this course with a high level of scientific reasoning skills, on par with or exceeding the best introductory science courses in other disciplines.

STUDENT PREFACE: INFORMATION THAT WILL HELP YOU LEARN MORE

Imagine an instructional science book where the author has used years of student feedback to continually improve the writing and make sure it is as clear as possible, enjoyable to read, and effectively teaches the concepts it sets out to teach. You are reading that book right now.

As with the purchase of a new phone, this book has several features that it may help to know about before you start using it.

1. **Number one in this list, in case you are considering purchasing a used book, is that the pages are perforated.** Some pages are meant to be written on and might be collected by instructors. If you are purchasing a used copy, check to make sure that all the pages are still in the book. Rather than count every page, it might be helpful to use the Table of Contents to check for pages that are labeled as "Lab Record Worksheets" and "Learning Objective Charts," as these are designed to be handed in. If those pages are not missing, you've *probably* got a complete copy.

And here are the more meaningful features that can directly affect how you learn:

2. **The modular format increases flexibility so that your instructor can assign readings to meet unique course goals.** The eight modules are like chapters, but with a more flexible order. Although they increase in complexity, they can be covered in any order, and some modules might be skipped, depending on your lab schedule and the course goals. If your instructor skips around, be aware that any new terminology you might have missed will be clearly defined with examples in the glossary of the module where it was introduced (which is easy to find—see item 4 below.) Every module has a tabbed glossary that explains all new terms with examples and page references so you can quickly and easily access the information you need to understand any reading assignment

Each module is made up of two sections: **Essays** and **Applications**.

Essays explain the concepts needed to develop a fundamental understanding of how psychological science works. They are short (500 to 2,000 words), as self-contained as possible, and provide information on a variety of topics related to the philosophy and practice of science. Instructors may decide to assign as much or as little reading as necessary to fit their course goals. Terminology is explained on a conceptual level, with enough detail to prepare you for advanced courses in research design, but not so much that you will become overwhelmed. This is not meant to be a comprehensive course in research methods, but will provide a strong foundation for students who decide to major in psychology. Statistical concepts are also explained on a conceptual level, without reference to complex formulae or advanced frequency distributions. This book introduces the fundamental principles of testing ideas with data: the interpretation of statistical results and how to maximize objectivity by making decisions based on probabilities. This is not a statistics course, and does not cover how to perform statistical tests, nor which tests to apply, beyond a very basic level. The main goal is to clarify factors that affect the trustworthiness of statistical information and the kinds of conclusions we can (and cannot) draw from various types of research.

Applications are hands-on research projects to give you practice applying the essay concepts. Each research project includes its own brief background, procedure, and lab record (worksheet). Some of the background information will overlap with other applications, but this is necessary to allow flexibility in course assignments and associated readings. Some background information will also overlap with typical lecture textbook content, which may improve your performance on lecture exams.

3. **Learning objective charts help you tailor your reading assignment to your own level of knowledge and skills.** Prechapter lists of what you should learn as you read are a common textbook feature that can help students prepare to read actively, and therefore remember more of what they read. Unfortunately, many students see these lists as redundant and time-consuming, and therefore do not read them. This book takes a different approach. Rather than a list of what you should learn, you'll see an interactive chart that is designed to help you assess your knowledge and skills both before and after reading and doing research.

   Two learning objective charts are included in every module: one before every set of Essays and one before every set of Applications. These charts include all the learning objectives for every essay or research project within that module. They are labeled so you'll know which ones apply to your reading assignment. It will only take about one minute (maybe two?) to consider the questions linked to your assignment and use the scale to rate how well you feel you can already answer them before doing the reading or the research, on a scale from 1 (I don't know how) to 4 (I know how to do this and/or have already done it). You don't have to answer any question; just think about whether you believe you *can* answer it correctly. There's no grading and no pressure. The goal is to give you control over where to focus your attention as you read. You are encouraged to skim quickly what you feel you already know (rated 4) in order to catch any misconceptions, and to slow down and actively look for the answers you don't already know (rated 3 or less). Students have reported that doing this metacognitive exercise (thinking about what they already know and/or still need to learn) helps them learn more from their reading because they are looking for answers. This *active reading* is much more effective than passive attempts to absorb information.

   The charts include space for you to return and reassess your knowledge after reading each section and/ or doing research. This is an excellent way to review, to formulate questions to ask in lab, and to prepare for quizzes and lab assignments.

   The charts might also be helpful to your instructors. They can be collected (anonymously) to provide data indicating what students already know coming into the class, and the extent to which students perceive that the readings and research are helping them learn.

4. **Unique, modular glossaries are conveniently located for optimum use as learning tools.** Rather than one large (and largely ignored) glossary in the back of the book, glossaries are located at the end of each module. These informative "teaching glossaries" include every bold, italicized term introduced in that module, its definition, references to essays, figures, and studies that can provide more information, and at least one example. In this second edition, glossary examples have been updated to increase personal relevance to students, including some references to pandemic situations, with which all students will be familiar.

   "Modular" means you can use them to check your understanding of the new terms in any module because they are grouped together alphabetically at the end of the module, and labeled according to the essays in which they appear. Terms that appear in a module but were introduced elsewhere are cross-referenced, so that you can quickly locate their full definitions and examples using the glossary tabs. And Appendix D provides a list of all key terms with the glossary numbers where they are defined, so any term can be looked up at any time, whether or not it appears in your current reading assignment.

5. **Skill-checks help you assess your understanding**. While reading, you will often find questions to check your understanding of the concepts and terms, with a list of correct answers to these questions in Appendix B. This second edition includes more skill-check questions for extra practice applying terms and understanding the most challenging concepts.

WHAT YOU SHOULD EXPECT TO LEARN IN PSYCH LAB

The laboratory portion of this course is designed to give you *hands-on experience with the science of psychology—and the psychology of science*. You'll learn how ideas in psychology are developed, scientifically tested, supported or refuted, and communicated; that is, how psychologists think. As you read about and discuss research and collect and interpret data, you will learn the basics in the art and practice of psychological science. Moreover, psychology is not unique among sciences, so you will also learn about the art and practice of science, in general.

You will complete several research projects on a variety of topics, most of which I hope you'll find interesting, but please don't think that this is all psychology has to offer! The field is so incredibly diverse that it would be overwhelming to cover even one-tenth of the topics that psychologists study. Instead, we focus on five basic *types* of research psychologists use: exploratory, descriptive, correlational, experimental, and quasi-experimental. These terms are applied in a categorical sense to describe the tools psychologists use, but it's important to realize that research in psychology does not always fit neatly into one category or another, and even the categories themselves are not mutually exclusive. This will become clearer as you do each type of research.

This course should help you become a more knowledgeable consumer of scientific information. The goal is not to turn you into a professional scientist, but to provide you with introductory-level knowledge and skills that can be applied to problems in psychology or any other science. By completing the research projects in this lab, you will gain a sense of familiarity with the processes used to gather the information you read about in your lecture textbook, in popular science magazines and newspapers, and on the Internet. You'll be better able to understand and critically interpret them. Whether this is your first college level science lab or your fifth, you should expect to learn new things about the philosophy and practice of science.

Although research in psychology often uses high-tech equipment and cutting-edge software to measure behavior and cognition, it is also possible to do research in this field using the stuff of everyday life—simple computers, cell phones, paper, and pencil. Freedom from complicated equipment means we can focus more of our attention on research design and the logic of hypothesis testing. This lab is about designing and interpreting logical research that addresses questions related to human behavior and the behavior of other animals. It's about creative problem-solving.

Even if you took a psychology course in high school, you can still expect this course to expose you to new ways of thinking about it and about other sciences. Because psychology has such a huge and diverse sphere of influence and applicability, learning the basic methods of psychological science can help you in many other walks of life, not the least of which is simply being a critical consumer of scientific information.

In conclusion, you should expect to learn something of value, regardless of your level of experience with psychology and/or other sciences. But doing so will require action on your part, as described in the next section.

THE BIGGEST CHALLENGES AND HOW TO NAVIGATE THEM

Some students find lab sciences very difficult; others find them very easy. The motivation level you feel (see "Open Letter to Students," page xiii) is a big factor, but not the only one. There are certain common challenges inherent in an introductory psychology course that lead some students to get lower grades than expected. Even those who have taken general psychology courses at other colleges and in high school sometimes struggle, but it is often for one of the four reasons listed below. Suggestions are included to help you meet these challenges and keep them from negatively affecting your grade.

Challenge # 1. **Terminology—not just memorization, but application!** There are about 600 terms in the glossary of most lecture textbooks, give or take a few. This book repeats some of those terms, but often adds technical details regarding their meanings and correct usage, and adds more new terms. Introductory Psychology is like an advanced language course. You have to be able to use the words in context, not just spit back their translations, flash-card style. You'll need to be "fluent" in the terminology and be able to recognize multiple examples of each term and provide your own examples.

Suggestion: The solution is to give yourself *time* to think about the course content. A good rule of thumb for all college classes is to set aside at least 2 hours outside of class for every hour in class, or 6 hours/week, for reading the textbook and studying. The average chapter is 16,000 words. The average college student reads textbooks at a rate of 240 to 300 words per minute, so reading a whole chapter of your lecture textbook should take about one hour. But you should not expect to absorb an entire chapter in one hour! To understand it at the level required, you should break it up into shorter sections, read each section multiple times, and think about it in contexts other than those presented in the textbook. While you may be able to do the assigned reading in about an hour per week, you will need another four or five hours to mentally process it (see Challenge #2). Most weeks, you will also need time outside of class to read this book and to do other reading and homework assignments for lab. The essays you will be assigned are generally short, and if you do the learning objective charts before and after you read, you can save time and focus your reading on the content you most need to learn.

Challenge # 2: **Overcoming poor study habits**. Many students start college with poor study habits. If this does not describe you, that's great—skip to the next challenge. But if you've ever read a textbook paragraph four times and still wondered what it was about, then remember this: The biggest challenge of any introductory course is to learn a lot of material in a very short time, and *if your mind is on other things, the pace will be frustrating and insufficient to get the grades you want*. Even with your mind on the reading, scraping a highlighter over things that seem important is not the best way to learn. It might help, but there are better ways. Cramming before exams is also a bad habit. Athletes do not reach peak performance by cramming all their exercise and training into a 5-hour session before a competition. Your ability to understand and apply new information is like a muscle that takes time to develop. If you've been successful this way before, imagine how much more successful you could be if you gave your understanding some time to develop!

Suggestion: To keep yourself focused, divide your study time into 20-minute sections with 10-minute breaks. You might think that would only encourage distraction, but the opposite is true. By taking on smaller sections of text, you increase the amount you retain, particularly if you read each small section *actively*. Knowing you will get a break soon can help you focus, and enjoying your break while you have it makes it easier to get back to work when the timer goes off. For this book, you can read actively by considering the objectives before you read and looking for the answers you don't already know. For most textbooks, you'll have to write the questions yourself. Here's how: (1) Choose a manageable section of text (usually 3 to 5 pages for a 20-minute study time). (2) Scan or survey the section to see what it's about. Read only the headings and bold-faced words (not their definitions) and look at the figures and their captions. (3) Based on what you've seen, write questions about the content. One way to do this is to turn headings into questions. For example, "Theories of Emotion" becomes "How many theories of emotion are there?" and "What are the theories of emotion?" and "Who proposed these theories of emotion?" (4) Read to find the answers to your questions. This will help you stay focused and remember what you read, and your memories will last much longer than if you had just highlighted important sentences. Lastly, before you stop reading a section of the textbook to take a break, take about two or three minutes to review your questions, your answers, and any additional information you picked up from the reading. Review the content without referring to the text, unless it's necessary to clarify a point. Once clarified, be sure you can review it without the text before you close the book and take your break. This technique, called SQ3R (Survey, Question, Read, Retrieve, Review), is best applied to small sections of reading, but can be applied to whole chapters. It is described in more detail in most introductory psychology lecture textbooks.

A quick note on highlighters and flashcards: Highlighters are more useful if you use them to highlight answers to your questions, rather than just painting everything that sounds important. Flashcards are useful, but there's a better way to use them: First, for convenience and to save paper and money, cut the cards into halves or thirds. Then put terms and definitions on separate cards, not front/back. Carry these small decks of cards around with you, and whenever you have a few minutes to kill, instead of taking out your phone, take out your cards and play matching games and organizing games. Pull out a card and then search for its match. Once you know the terms, pull two random cards and describe the similarities and differences between the terms. Any questions that arise as you try to do this can be added to the card and asked in class or looked up the next time you open your book. The more you can think about these terms relative to each other, the better you'll understand them and be able to distinguish between them on exams. Also your practice seeing both the terms and their definitions and examples at the same time will help you avoid that awful moment on a test where you can see the front of the flashcard in your mind's eye, but you can't recall what's on the back.

Challenge # 3: **Unlearning the stuff you thought you knew.** Psychology is a popular topic, often talked about in the media. Although thousands of popular books have been published that are categorized as "psychology," the appropriateness of that categorization is sometimes questionable. In spite of its popularity (or perhaps because of it), psychology is often misrepresented and misunderstood. People see it as a "soft science," implying that the rules of scientific thinking still apply, but that they are more flexible. This is just one of the many misconceptions about psychology. Misinformation makes it difficult to learn new content, since you have to actually let go of things you thought you knew. Learning is difficult enough without having to unlearn first.

Suggestion: Practice the science attitude presented in Essay 1.1. In this book and in your lecture textbook, you will often find evidence for the information (citations of research in psychology). You can almost always obtain the original research articles from your campus library or through interlibrary loan (super easy). In today's world of social and news media, finding the evidence behind information is a lot harder. In many cases, the evidence simply doesn't exist. Some of the things you think you know are probably not true! Science education is not just about learning facts. It is about learning how to determine the truth about the natural world through systematic analysis, attention and observation, while realizing that scientific truth is a dynamic construct. The only logical way to deal with this is to question everything and examine the evidence. Let go of that inner expert who keeps telling you that your knowledge is made up of facts, or even that your textbook is full of facts, and instead ask yourself "What's the evidence?" and, "What's the source of that evidence?" If you practice this way of thinking, you will soon find that old ideas are easier to replace.

Challenge # 4: **Phone addiction is a real thing.** It's also a real problem for college students in a lot of classes, not just lab. Most of us use our phone more than we realize. Hearing it buzz or seeing it light up is like hearing someone call our name, and that's hard to ignore. Some people check their phones habitually, without even realizing they're doing it. Using your phone in class is extremely distracting, not just to you, but to those around you who notice your behavior and think about it, instead of thinking about the research they are trying to do or the concepts they're trying to learn. If you can't control your phone use in situations where it is inappropriate, you might have an addiction. There is a free test you can take online to determine whether your phone use approaches or exceeds unhealthy levels: Go to virtual-addiction.com/smartphone-compulsion-test.

Suggestion: Sometimes you'll need your phone to help you collect data in lab (timers, apps, etc.), so leaving it home or turning it off might not be good options. But keeping your phone in an easy-access pocket, on the desk next to you, or in your lap virtually guarantees that it will be a distraction. The solution is to get in the habit of

"Yoohoo, the meeting's over"

taking your phone out of its normal, easy-to-retrieve location as soon as you arrive in any class. Put it somewhere you *cannot* easily access it. Backpack pockets with zippers work well, particularly if they are loud zippers, so you can't take out your phone without everyone else knowing about it. If you don't have a loud-zippered pocket, you can still leave your phone in some other part of the room. You can also trade phones with a classmate you trust. Learning to get along without the phone is an important skill, and someday, you're going to be glad you trained yourself to get through meetings without it.

Bonus Challenge (If you are asked to write a lab report): **Lab reports take time to write.** Writing clearly is not as easy as people think. Perhaps the number one reason why grades suffer when there is a lab report to write is that students do not give themselves the time (or, in some cases, must develop the skill) to proofread and revise their writing for clarity, and clarity is usually what distinguishes a grade of A from a B (or C) when it comes to lab reports.

Suggestion: If you want to improve your writing skills and earn an A on a lab report, you will most likely need to be more careful than you already are about how you write. You'll need to get into the habit of reading every sentence you write multiple times, preferably out loud, making sure each sentence has the exact meaning you intend to convey and no other meaning. The most popular text editing programs (MS Word, Adobe), now have a built-in read-aloud feature, so you can look at your own words and hear a (somewhat robotic) voice read them to you. This is an excellent way to catch errors! Practicing your own proofreading skills throughout the semester on lab records and other homework assignments will improve your grades and your writing. The first draft of your lab report should be completed long before it is due so that you can spend as much time as possible looking for ways to improve the clarity.

Module 1
The Science of Psychology

MODULE 1 LEARNING OBJECTIVES CHART

People who read this book will have widely varying levels of previous experience in psychology. Some of your classmates may have already done research in this field, while others never even thought of psychology as a science. To help you *avoid wasting time on knowledge and skills you already have,* each module of this book includes two charts like the one below: one for the essays on content and one for the projects designed to apply the content.

To save time when reading: Whenever you see a new chart, take a moment to read the learning goals related to the essays or research applications you plan to read (labeled in the first column). Check the boxes in the gray columns that reflect how well you already know each objective. For objectives you rated as "4,"

quickly skim those parts of the essays, just to make sure you know the material as well as you thought you did. If it looks different than expected, then you can slow down. For objectives that you rated less than "4," read those parts of the essays more carefully. Keep those questions in mind and actively seek answers.

This process is not only time-saving; it will also help you focus your attention where it is most needed. You'll remember more of what you read because you'll be mentally prepared and seeking answers, rather than passively reading and hoping the important information is what sticks to your brain. To make sure you've met the learning goals, come back to these charts and complete the white side after reading that section and/or doing the research.

ESSAY NUMBER	MODULE 1 ESSAY LEARNING OBJECTIVES	BEFORE READING				AFTER READING			
		I don't know how 1	I know a little about this 2	I know enough about this to guess correctly 3	I know how to do this and/or have already done it. 4	I don't know how 1	I know a little about this 2	I know enough about this to guess correctly 3	I know how to do this and/or have already done it. 4
1.1	What defines a science?								
1.1	Describe the basic elements of a science attitude.								
1.1	Critically discuss whether psychology is a science.								
1.1	Can one do science without reporting it? Why or why not?								
1.2	Describe the scientific method.								
1.2	Explain three common myths about the scientific method.								
1.1 1.2	Explain the difference between the scientific method and a "science attitude."								
1.2	List 5 different types of research used in psychology.								

		I don't know how 1	I know a little about this 2	I know enough about this to guess correctly 3	I know how to do this and/ or have already done it. 4		I don't know how 1	I know a little about this 2	I know enough about this to guess correctly 3	I know how to do this and/ or have already done it. 4
1.3	Do psychologists seek to verify ideas or falsify them? Explain.									
1.3 1.5	Explain and compare the goals of science as described by Karl Popper and Thomas Kuhn.									
1.3	Define confirmation bias and explain how it can affect scientific progress.									
1.3	Explain how to distinguish between science and pseudoscience and provide examples.									
1.3 1.5	Compare essentialist and operationist philosophies and tell why psychologists are operationists.									
1.3	Explain why scientists call the things they study "variables" and why it is necessary to "operationally define" variables.									
1.4	Describe in detail five types of research that psychologists do.									
1.4	Explain differences in the conclusions that can be drawn from each type of research.									
1.5	Describe the goals, methods and value of exploratory research.									
1.5	Discuss whether exploratory research is a science and why.									

Read the assigned essays and actively seek answers to any questions rated less than "4." Then return to this chart and complete the white half.

Now proceed to the chart for the applications section, read the objectives for your assigned research project, and complete the gray side of that chart.

ESSAY 1.1

IS PSYCHOLOGY A (HUB) SCIENCE?

"Science is more a way of thinking than it is a body of knowledge."

—*Carl Sagan*

For over 100 years, psychology has suffered repeated attacks by scientists and laypeople claiming that it is not a science. This field of study has been bullied and badgered for attempting to explain the inexplicable (e.g., consciousness), measure the immeasurable (e.g., love), and predict the unpredictable (e.g., the choices people make). Some of these complaints have come from psychologists themselves. William James, often called "the Father of American Psychology," wrote in 1892, "This is no science; it is only the hope of a science." Raymond Cattel, famous for his research on personality, wrote in 1965 that authorities in psychology have been known to "run in circles, describing things which everyone knows in language which no one understands." Paul Meehl, a well-known clinical psychologist, complained in 1978 that theories in psychology "… come and go, more as a function of baffled boredom than anything else…" (Ouch.) It is worth noting that Meehl won several awards for his outstanding scientific work in psychology. Clearly, these little quips are just attempts at humor in what is otherwise considered a rigorous scientific discipline, right? If not, then have the 40 years of scientific research since Meehl's comment finally closed the case?

No, the complaints continue, and have found their way into the popular press as well. A 2016 article in *Psychology Today* argued that psychology is not a science because it "lacks agreement from the experts about what it is and what it is about, what its foundational theories or even frameworks are…"[1]

Is that true? Or is a vocal minority of killjoy-scientists just trying to stir things up? Your journey as you learn about psychology and proceed through the essays, exercises, and research in this book will help you decide. The first step on the journey is to consider what science is.

Carl Sagan's quote is a good place to start. Science, at its core, is "a way of thinking," a way of understanding the natural world that is based on observations and logic combining to form evidence. It requires a value system that we'll call a "science attitude."[2]

The science attitude can best be achieved by following six pieces of advice, all of them about the way you think rather than what you know. This is not a complete list, but it covers the basic values that form the foundation of good scientific thinking:

1. Let go of your inner expert. This is important for two reasons: curiosity and humility. In general, experts are known for their answers, not their questions. But natural curiosity is the driving force behind a science attitude at *any* level of expertise. Letting go of your inner expert, regardless of your current level of knowledge, implies *a constant desire to learn more.* In the words of one highly accomplished cell biologist, "the desire to learn more is my reason for getting up in the morning."

Curiosity is easy and can even be fun, but humility is often difficult. It's natural to want to focus on what we know, rather than what we don't know. We also tend to overestimate what we know, especially in comparison to others. Take driving, for example. Research in psychology suggests that 80% to 90% of drivers believe themselves to be "better than average" at driving (Roy & Liersch, 2014). Clearly, 30% to 40% of drivers must be wrong about that because only about half can be above average.

Good scientific thinking works against this natural human tendency to believe we know more than we do. It requires mindful awareness that we are easily fooled, especially when explaining the behavior

---

[1] psychologytoday.com/us/blog/theory-knowledge/201601/the-is-psychology-science-debate. Bibliographic information on the sources cited in the Psychology Today article are also included in the References section of this book.

[2] Grammar sticklers might want to call it a "scientific attitude," as many textbooks and online articles do. But a "scientific attitude" sounds too similar to the "scientific method." They are not the same. More on that later.

of others. *We must humbly accept the possibility that we could be wrong about things.* For professional scientists, this is a vital part of their job description.

> *"The first principle is that you must not fool yourself and you are the easiest person to fool."*
> —Richard Feynman, Physicist

2. Be a persistent skeptic. Skepticism is often confused with cynicism, but is actually quite different. A cynic may stop at nothing to reveal unpleasantness, including selective attention to only those ideas that confirm the belief that unpleasantness exists. A skeptic (ideally) will stop at nothing to reveal the *truth* by searching for all available evidence with respect to a particular claim or idea. Contrary to popular opinion, skeptics are not "negative" people; they are truth-seekers. They don't accept ideas—even their own ideas—without observable evidence, gathered systematically. It is easy to be skeptical about things that do not fit in with our own view of the world. A science attitude also requires skepticism about things that do.

> *"Skepticism is the first step toward truth."*
> —Denis Diderot, French Philosopher

3. Be a careful, systematic observer. Systematic observation requires careful attention to details and logic, past ideas, how they were tested, and the results of those tests. Being systematic means building new knowledge with a plan that attempts to maximize objectivity, using a solid framework of logic and observation. It means being aware of potential biases in one's observations, and finding ways to minimize or eliminate those biases before observing. For example, one might casually observe a child playing, but a *systematic observation* would involve awareness and planning for the relevant factors that might affect either the child's behavior or one's own observations, like the child's environment and the time of day. Systematic observations produce descriptions of behavior that can be understood and replicated by others. Good record-keeping is part of this process, but so are careful planning and critical thinking.

> *"To acquire knowledge, one must study; but to acquire wisdom, one must observe."*
> —Marilyn vos Savant, American Columnist and Playwright

4. Be a critical thinker. All evidence is *not* created equally, and opinions are not evidence. Certain sources of scientific information (e.g., peer-reviewed journals) present stronger or better evidence than others because the work has been scrutinized by other scientists before publication. Critical thinkers are aware of the sources of evidence and upon what foundations and assumptions those sources are built. Some studies are funded by organizations with an interest in certain outcomes. Sometimes innocent biases and assumptions are built into the way a study is done, and may influence the results. Thinking critically means learning to assess the quality of the evidence, to recognize your own biases and assumptions, and to recognize and verify the characteristics of evidence that make it trustworthy.

> *"We are prone to let our mental life become invaded by legions of half truths, prejudices, and propaganda. ... The function of education, therefore, is to teach one to think intensively and to think critically."*
> —Martin Luther King, Jr., American Civil Rights Leader

5. Think logically, but with an awareness of emotions. Without question, a good science attitude relies heavily on logic. For example, if we take multiple measurements of two things called A and B, and observe that every time the value of A is high, B is also high, and when A is low, B is also low, then it is logical to conclude that we can simply measure A to predict the value of B, and vice versa. Another example: Imagine a closed system with only two movable objects called X and Y. You can manipulate X any way you want and then observe the effects on Y. If Y moves predictably whenever you move X, you can logically conclude that X affects Y. Such is the logic of scientific reasoning. The popular emphasis on the logic of science suggests that scientists do not allow emotion or intuition to affect their judgment, and to some extent, this is true. But research in psychology has found that emotion can play an important role in good decision making (e.g., see Kidwell et al., 2008). If you're a fan of vintage *Star Trek*, you might recall how Captain Kirk repeatedly demonstrated to his (Vulcan) First Officer Spock that making the best decision often requires accepting an emotional component to your assessment, particularly when evidence is sparse or unobtainable. Scientists strive to accumulate evidence so that we can rely less on our gut feelings, but we also recognize that those feelings are not the enemy, and can even be useful.

"Logic is the beginning of wisdom, not the end."
—Leonard Nimoy,
*Actor, Author, Photographer
(Spock in the Star Trek series)*

6. Be willing to share your ideas and observations publicly. This is one of the most important aspects of any science, because *science is a collective endeavor.* Scientific knowledge grows as a collection of ideas that are publicly available for scrutiny. Without clear and accurate communication of our ideas and the evidence for or against them, we do not give others the opportunity to consider the logic of our research or the validity of our conclusions. In short, *we are not doing science unless we publicly share our ideas and observations.* In general, contrary to the practice of some popular media, a scientific result should not be trusted unless it has been properly reported and scrutinized by other scientists, and even then, replication is needed.

"All scientists must communicate their work, for what is the point of learning new things about how the world works if you don't tell anyone about them?"
—Jim Al-Khalili, Physicist,
Author, Broadcaster

ADVICE FOR BUILDING A SCIENCE ATTITUDE

1 Let go of your inner expert (aspire to learn and be willing to accept that you could be wrong).
2 Be a persistent skeptic.
3 Be a careful, systematic observer.
4 Be a critical thinker, aware of sources, biases, and assumptions.
5 Think logically, first and foremost, but also recognize and weigh gut feelings.
6 Be willing to publicly share ideas and observations, because…

Science progresses collectively!

Keeping the science attitude in mind, let's revisit the debate: Is psychology a science? As a field of study, psychology definitely relies on a science attitude. But people often apply a science attitude to all kinds of problems; this does not make every problem a science. The attitude is necessary, but not sufficient.

Another frequently used indicator of science is the use of the *scientific method* (Essay 1.2), but that is also insufficient. Simply using the scientific method does not guarantee one is doing science. Furthermore, science can be done without the scientific method. Nevertheless, it is an important tool for most science, and the vast majority of research in psychology does use it.

What about the other complaints? Does psychology try to explain the inexplicable? No, research in psychology has definitely helped us understand consciousness, among other supposedly inexplicable subjects. Researchers in psychology have also discovered and shared whole volumes of information on love and other emotions that people have called "immeasurable" (they are not). And psychology has been used to predict, with better than random accuracy, how groups of people will behave. We can even provide probabilities regarding certain individual decisions.

So, as noted in that 2016 *Psychology Today* article, "If something looks like a science and acts like a science, then it likely should be considered a science." However, the author goes on to say that the problem is *not* that psychology doesn't look or act like a science. It does both, in addition to contributing massive amounts of information to our understanding of the natural and human world.

The complaint is that after more than 150 years of looking and acting like a science, psychology has no unifying theory of mind and behavior that can compare to the unifying theories of other sciences. Biology has evolution. Physics has the theory of relativity and quantum theory. Geology has plate tectonics. Chemistry has atomic theory and the periodic table of the elements. Psychology has… a lot of different theories of mind and behavior. The main complaint for those who say psychology is not a science is that we have failed to lump all our findings into any kind of core concept that explains or predicts enough future findings. This complaint is the byproduct of two simple facts: (1) *Psychology is diverse.* (2) *Psychology is complex.*

When I first began teaching introductory psychology over 20 years ago, my spouse was teaching an introductory astronomy course. As married couples tend to do, we debated who had the harder job: Teaching "the universe" in 14 weeks, or teaching "the mind and behavior" in 14 weeks. The universe is undoubtedly huge, but I argued that psychology wins due to the staggering diversity of questions it addresses. We never settled on a winner, but the popular science journal, *Scientific American* appears to be on my side. A 2002 editorial notes, "the natural universe, for all its complexity, is easier to understand than the human being." The authors went on

to say that if research on humans "seems mushy, it is largely because the subject matter is so difficult, not because humans are somehow unworthy of scientific inquiry."[3]

The mind and behavior are complex subjects. But it is not surprising, given our natural tendency to assume we know more than we do about people, that so many people think psychology is (or should be) simpler than it is.

Human behavior reaches into every corner of the inhabited world, plus most uninhabited corners, and even into space (e.g., Sannita et al., 2006). Add to that: Our studies are not limited to today's world, but also go back in time (comparative and evolutionary psychologists study animal behavior to learn how behavioral patterns, thinking, and planning evolved). The diverse list of topics psychologists study could easily fill this book. It is true: Psychology currently has no unifying theory, and it's possible it never will. Perhaps, instead, it should be thought of as a unifying science.

Consider that throughout all areas of study, from the sciences, mathematics and engineering to the humanities and the arts, there is one common thread—it is the human who does the studying. *Everything* human and nonhuman animals think, do, and feel can be studied by psychologists. This far-reaching applicability has made psychology simultaneously too complex for a unifying theory and too useful to ignore as a science.

But let's practice our science attitude. There is evidence that speaks to this claim. Boyack et al. (2005) examined thousands of journals publishing scientific research in all subjects, from aeronautics to zygotes. They used the *Science Citation Index* and *Social Science Citation Index* to create a list of 7,121 field-specific journals. Their computer algorithm then found over 16 million reference pairs (where researchers in one journal cited an article from another journal on their list). By linking these reference pairs into a network map, an image they called the "backbone of science" emerged (technically, it's more like the whole skeletal system of science). Their map shows how much each discipline relies on work from other disciplines as they formulate and discuss their own ideas. Seven subjects emerged as "hubs" in their map—areas of study that are frequently cited

---

[3] Editors. (2002). The peculiar institution. *Scientific American, 286(4)*, 8–9.

outside their own discipline. Psychology was one of the seven (Figure 1.1).

In summary, and somewhat ironically, psychology's diversity and complexity are simultaneously the reason we have no unifying theory to qualify as "a science" in the mind of critics, *and* the reason we are so incredibly useful as a science.

It is still possible that a unifying theory of mind is on the horizon. In the meantime, as you explore psychology and proceed through this book, practicing your science attitude and applying the scientific method, we encourage you to continue thinking about the extent to which this field of study belongs among the sciences.

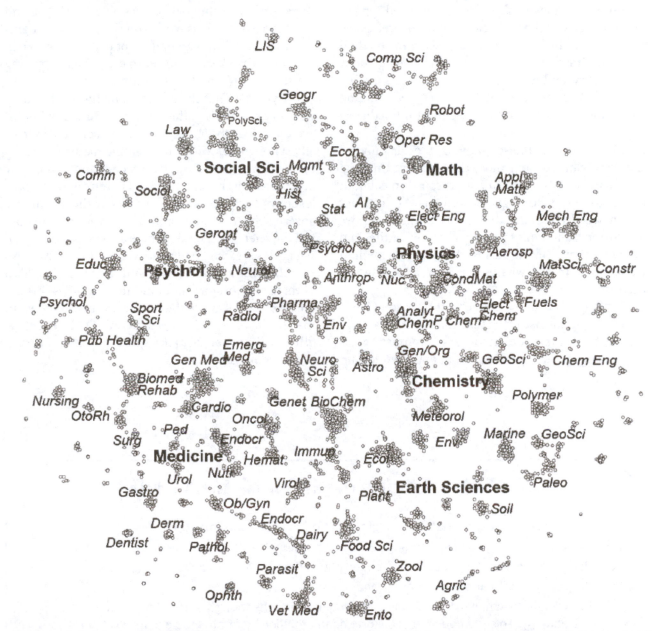

Figure 1.1   A cluster map of the areas of science covered in 7,121 journals listed in *Social Sciences Index* and *Science Citation Index.* Every small circle is a journal. Large fonts indicate that the topic is a hub, that is, an area of research with one of the top seven frequencies of co-citations with journals from other disciplines. Branches of psychology also appear two more times among the nonhub, frequently co-cited areas of science: experimental psychology, at the top middle of the map, between physics and general psychology, and applied/educational/clinical/developmental psychology, on the left edge, between Education and Public Health. (Figure reprinted with permission from Boyack et al., [2005], Figure 4).

ESSAY 1.2

THREE MYTHS ABOUT THE SCIENTIFIC METHOD

The *scientific method* is just one of the ways in which the science attitude can be applied. It is defined by the same five steps you've probably learned repeatedly since grade school (in case you need a refresher, they are listed in a box below). The scientific method is a useful framework for making objective decisions about reality, and we will refer to it and use it often in this lab. But before we do, there are three common myths about this method that we must immediately dispel.

Myth #1: That the scientific method is only for scientists. Not true, any more than creative thinking is only for artists. Any time a person thinks about a problem and takes a guess at an answer, tests out the answer by making direct observations, draws conclusions, and talks to others about what they did and what they think it means, the scientific method is essentially in use, whether or not that person is a scientist.

Myth #2: That the scientific method is completely objective and unbiased. The scientific method is a logical way to maximize objectivity and minimize bias as we try to figure out how things work in the world, and it is a powerful tool for everyone who uses it properly. But even when it is applied with perfection in mind, there is no such thing as perfect objectivity. You will learn more about bias when you study human cognition as part of your exploration of psychology. When you do, please keep in mind that everyone applying the scientific method is also human.

Myth #3: That the scientific method is the only way that scientists gather evidence. In many books, even some textbooks, science is presented as virtually synonymous with the scientific method, leading to misconceptions about the practice and philosophy of science. This book is designed to introduce the philosophy of science while you practice the techniques governed by that philosophy. This involves more than just the scientific method. There are five basic types of scientific research: *exploratory, descriptive, correlational, quasi-experimental,* and *experimental*. Two of them (exploratory and descriptive studies) do not follow the five steps of the scientific method shown in the gray box below. However, in order to be effective, *all of these types of research require the science attitude described in Essay 1.1.*

STEPS IN THE SCIENTIFIC METHOD

STEP 1: Identify a question, gather background information, and **think** about it.

STEP 2: Generate a hypothesis (an answer to the question that leads to a testable prediction).

STEP 3: Empirically test the idea (make observations that put the prediction to the test).

STEP 4: Analyze data and draw conclusions.

STEP 5: Clearly communicate everything above, including the thoughts from Step 1, for public scrutiny. This provides the "background information" that other scientists will think about as they take on Step 1. *Science progresses collectively!*

ESSAY 1.3

THE PHILOSOPHY AND PRACTICE OF SCIENCE

In Essay 1.1, we tried to describe the essence of science to address complaints from some people that psychology is not a science. We found that psychology not only looks and acts like a science (with our science attitude and heavy use of the scientific method), but that psychology also appears to be one of seven hub sciences, areas of study that most often contribute to research in other disciplines.

Here we will describe the philosophy of science, including the kinds of knowledge scientists seek and do not seek and why.

For the vast majority of modern history, people have tried to understand the natural world by deriving explanations based on logic and then verifying those explanations through observation. That was science. However, during the 20th century, largely due to the writings of the philosopher, Karl Popper, many people began to reconsider how they were going about doing science.

Popper wrote extensively about the difference between **verifiability** and **falsifiability**. He argued that verification—*confirming that one's ideas are correct through observation*—is not the best way to do science. Indeed, he saw verification as scientifically impossible. Any observation that seems to verify an idea might be limited to the instance in which the idea was tested. For example, we might propose that all fish have scales. To test our rule about the nature of fish through verification, that is, to confirm it, we would have to check every fish, even those we have not yet discovered. (There are more than 30,000 known species of fish!)

According to Popper, falsification—*testing one's ideas with the intent to show that they are wrong*—is the better way to do science. This makes a lot of sense. Logically, it takes far fewer observations to show that an idea is wrong—to find one fish with no scales—than to confirm that every fish has them. To improve our understanding of the natural world, falsification is definitely a more practical approach.

In addition, Popper argued that research and observations designed to verify ideas are inherently biased. In the 1960s, experimental research in psychology showed that humans are highly susceptible to **confirmation bias**, a tendency to only pay attention to

Image © Keystone/Staff/Getty

"Good tests kill flawed theories; we remain alive to guess again."

—Karl Popper (1902–1994)

observations that support their own ideas, while ignoring observations that contradict their ideas. By designing our research to show that an idea is true (rather than setting out to show it is false), Popper said that we are quite likely to fall prey to confirmation bias, and to miss instances in which the idea turns out to be wrong. We could spend 20 years confirming repeatedly that each species of fish we find has scales. Anything that looks like a fish but has no scales would be likely to be ignored, including the poor little zebra clingfish, which has no scales, but is definitely a fish (Figure 1.2).

For most scientists, ideas that cannot be tested for falseness are not considered science, and in practice, all good science should seek to find the flaws in our current understanding, and not set out to verify the scientists' ideas. The quote under Popper's photograph illustrates his point of view quite nicely. This is the general approach we will follow in this book.

Image © Levent Konuk, 2013/ Shutterstock, Inc.

Figure 1.2   Fish or not? If seeking to *verify* the idea that all fish have scales, this zebra clingfish might be ignored due to *confirmation bias*. In fact, it is a fish, and its discovery *falsifies* the idea that all fish have scales.

However, it should be noted that falsifiability as the acid test of what makes any endeavor scientific is not embraced by all scientists.

Thomas Kuhn, an MIT physicist and philosopher, argued that Popper's definition only applies to one kind of science, and the relatively rare kind, at that. Kuhn pointed out that defining science purely as the falsification of ideas requires that we discard ideas after they are falsified, and although this does happen, it is not common practice. Kuhn called science based on falsifiability "revolutionary" because, when applied properly, it results in the overthrow of established ideas. The rest of science he called "normal science." In normal science, when an experiment fails to support an idea, research methods, experimenter errors, or faulty equipment are more likely to be blamed for the negative results than an incorrect idea, particularly if that idea is largely accepted by the scientific community. Scientific ideas are more often *retested* than *rejected* after a failure to gain support.

Therefore, according to Thomas Kuhn, scientists spend most of their time working on the established ideas. We test our understanding of those ideas by designing research that we hope will produce the predicted results. Our studies are designed to add to the knowledge in our fields, helping us better understand how established theories can and cannot be applied, but generally not overthrowing them.

Kuhn's "normal science" is more like puzzle solving, and is not practiced according to Popper's strict criterion of falsifiability, but it remains science, nonetheless. Importantly, Kuhn was also concerned about confirmation bias, but saw it as just as likely to occur, whether one is attempting to falsify an idea or to solve a puzzle.

Kuhn's argument has merit. It would be expensive and time-consuming to toss out every idea the moment evidence against it arises, without any attempts to improve the quality of the evidence, if it can be improved. This means that part of doing science is figuring out the most likely reason why our observations did not match our predicted results, and scientists spend more time doing that than strictly trying to falsify ideas. However, if several experiments or experimental modifications continue to falsify an idea, most scientists will eventually revise that idea, or reject it and move on.

Just as the evidence from one scientific study showing support should not be taken as proof that an idea is absolutely true (more on this in other essays), one study that refutes an idea is not a good reason to trash the idea. Instead, our scientific understanding of nature progresses slowly, through the combined effort of many scientists and many observations. Shortly after the death of Thomas Kuhn, Vice President Al Gore summarized this point nicely in his MIT commencement address: "[Kuhn] showed how well-established theories

Image © Bill Pierce/Contributor/Getty

"Under normal conditions the research scientist is not an innovator but a solver of puzzles, and the puzzles upon which he concentrates are just those which he believes can be both stated and solved within the existing scientific tradition."
—Thomas Kuhn (1922–1996)

collapse under the weight of new facts and observations which cannot be explained and then accumulate to the point where the once useful theory is clearly obsolete."

Whether we see ourselves as falsifiers or puzzle-solvers, most scientists, including those who study psychology, agree that the goal of science is to better understand the natural world, both by putting our explanations to the test and by working out the details of those explanations through puzzle solving. We agree that each explanation of any behavior or phenomenon must be communicated clearly so that it can be scrutinized by others. Last but not least, we also agree that our ideas can and should change as new evidence is gathered. Scientists who refuse to modify their ideas in the face of mounting evidence that they should do so are, generally speaking, not successful, and theories that do not change when evidence mounts against them are not science.

Ideas that sound like science but do not change, despite logic and evidence against them, are called *pseudoscientific*. Astrology is a good example. Because it is based on observations of the sky, including charts reflecting the positions of the sun and planets relative to the stars at one's moment of birth, astrology sounds like it could be science. Even those who say it is "just for fun" tend to trust their horoscopes as though they were based on science. According to a recent article in *The New Yorker*, astrology is now a 2.2 billion-dollar industry in the United States.[4] The astrology app CoStar has been downloaded more than 3 million times since launching in October of 2017. This app and others like it almost always rely on zodiac maps that have been in use as predictors of everything from harvest time to shampoo time for roughly 4,000 years, give or take 500 (though advice on shampooing probably didn't appear until the 20th century). Unfortunately, those charts were wrong then, and they're wrong now, though for different reasons.

The ancient Babylonians who drew zodiac charts knew that the sun travels through more than 12 constellations, but they only included 12 in their charts, most likely in order to match their 12-month calendar, which was based on phases of the moon. Whatever their reason, they left out a 13th constellation called Ophiuchus,[5] so their charts were not an accurate representation of the zodiac.

Figure 1.3 The constellation Ophiuchus, shown here in a feeble attempt to make up for 4,000 years of being mostly ignored by astrologers.

Of course, our knowledge of the motions of stars and planets has grown considerably in the past 4,000 years. Among other things, we have discovered that the earth wobbles in its rotations. Our pole-to-pole axis moves about one degree around its circular wobble every 70 years, changing what we see as the position of the sun and planets relative to the constellations of the zodiac. Because of this, the International Astronomical Union (IAU) corrected the constellation boundaries (the dates between signs) for the zodiac in 1930, and righted another wrong by inserting Ophiuchus (Figure 1.3) where it belongs, between Scorpio and Sagittarius.

It is also worth adding that, contrary to nearly every zodiac chart used by today's astrology apps, the time that the sun spends passing through each constellation is not equal. It stays in Virgo the longest (45 days) and is in Scorpio for only about 7 days. So if you thought you were a Scorpio, odds are, you've been deceived. But you're not alone. Roughly 85% of people were not born under the sign they think they were, yet many people strongly believe that "their sign" determines their personality and affects their relationships. Despite anecdotal claims, there is absolutely no scientific evidence that the positions of the stars have any bearing on human personalities. To believe things that have no logical or observational support might be human nature, and people might find it helpful, comforting, or entertaining; there is nothing wrong with that. But it is important to realize that ideas and beliefs that do not change when evidence piles up against them are not science.

---

[4] Smallwood, C., (Oct. 28, 2019). Astrology in the age of uncertainty. *The New Yorker*.

[5] Pronounced **Oh**-fee-**oo**-kus.

Another notion that does not mix well with the philosophy of science is *essentialism*, which holds that the goal of trying to understand reality is to capture its "essence" with proper definitions. Like scientists, essentialists seek to explain the natural world, but their goal is to discover the ultimate, unchanging truth. Many people wonder about the meaning and purpose of life and the essence of love. These questions are fascinating and certainly worth discussing, but they are not the stuff of science.[6] Because psychologists study emotions and other topics about which essentialist questions are often asked, people commonly complain that despite years of research, psychology has never come up with satisfactory answers to these questions. What is love, after all, and what is the purpose of human life? Shouldn't psychologists know by now?

Researchers in psychology do not seek essentialist answers to our questions. Instead, we seek better understanding. Among other things, we study the biology of love and the ways in which being "in love" changes thoughts and behaviors. We also study how people find and define their own purpose in life, how society influences those definitions, and how belief in a purpose influences behavior. But finding one essential definition that will reflect an unchanging truth about our purpose as human beings is not a good scientific goal. Remember that ideas in science are understood to be subject to change with new evidence. Essentialist ideas are not.

Rather than essentialism, science uses an operationist approach. *Operationism* (also known as, *operationalism*) also seeks the truth about reality, but recognizes that the truth can change with new evidence. So instead of essential definitions, we seek good *operational definitions* (accurate, functional, and reliable ways to identify or measure things). The things we measure or identify, we call *variables* because they all vary in one way or another. When you stop and think about it, there is almost nothing in the known universe that does not vary (with a few notable exceptions, conveniently called "constants"[7]). Psychologists and other operationists put great effort into clearly communicating the operational definitions of the variables we study. This facilitates the collective process of science by allowing others to unambiguously check our findings. You'll read much more about variables and operational definitions in Module 2.

---

[6] While the philosophy of science itself is not essentialist, psychology can and does include the scientific study essentialist thinking, particularly developmental psychology, where researchers have described the age at which children begin to think of entities in their world as having an unchanging essence. So, essentialism itself is not science, but human use of it can be studied scientifically, just as spiritual faith itself is not a science, but the existence of faith and the factors that strengthen or weaken it can be studied scientifically.

---

[7] Constants like π, τ, λ, and the speed of light are used in mathematical equations. In neuroscience, τ and λ refer to the time constant and the space (or length) constant, respectively. These values affect the speed at which neurons can transmit information.

The Birth of Science

ESSAY 1.4

TYPES OF RESEARCH

In science, as in life, one's choice of words matters. Although most laypeople refer to any kind of scientific study as an experiment, psychologists reserve the word "experiment" for a specific type of research—one that tests whether a cause-and-effect relationship exists between two variables. Other types of research have different names, and although they might test ideas, they are not properly called "experiments." It is important to recognize the differences among the types of research because the ideas they test and the conclusions that can be drawn from each type are different. Big mistakes in critical thinking often happen when we draw conclusions that are inappropriate for the type of research used. General descriptions of the five types of research we will introduce in this book are described here and visualized in Figure 1.4.

Exploratory research has no specific goal or question, but seeks to explore the vast unknown, symbolized by the wavy line in Figure 1.4. There is no specific problem being addressed other than a desire to know more about some unknown subject. We still take a systematic approach, in that we have a plan for exploring and we take careful notes on our observations, but the point of exploratory research is to jump into the unknown. There is no purposeful manipulation or specific prediction, and no particular expectation of differences or relationships to be observed. The conclusion that can be drawn from exploratory research involves identification and description of an interesting and previously unknown variable. It is commonly accompanied by a call for more research.

When we have identified a variable of interest and want to examine it more closely, we often start with *descriptive research*. This means we carefully define it, then observe the extent of its variability by counting or measuring what we have defined, and then we share our observations. Our definitions can change as we observe and learn more, but unlike exploratory research, we know what we are looking for. Again, there are no expectations or specific predictions. Instead, events or behaviors are systematically observed and described quantitatively. The variable (symbolized by X or Y in Fig. 1.4) can be anything

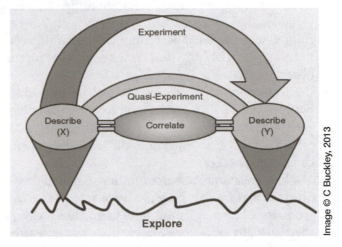

Image © C Buckley, 2013

Figure 1.4. Types of research. It may help to visualize the types of research as different ways of investigating a vast ocean of information that varies over time and space. Exploratory research happens in this unknown "ocean." We don't know what we will find, but we systematically search for new concepts. Descriptive research is when we isolate one or more specific things from this ocean to systematically observe up close and describe in detail. Correlational research examines changes in two or more things to test whether they vary together in some predicted way. Experimental research tests whether manipulating one thing affects another, and quasi-experimental research attempts to examine the same question, but in a more natural way, usually because we have no ethical or practical way of doing a true experiment. The lack of control in quasi-experimental research means the causal relationship is called into question (no arrow).

at all of interest (e.g., football game attendance, the number of toilet paper rolls used by the average American family, or how much time people spend on social media per week). The conclusion of descriptive research is a clear description of the variable (typically, how it varies), using the appropriate data summaries.

Note that for both exploratory and descriptive studies, conclusions are limited to exactly what was observed—no more, no less. We cannot draw conclusions about relationships between the observations with any degree of confidence. Why not? Because *if no relationship was predicted before observing, then no predictable relationship can be claimed to exist.* In other words, we did not use the scientific method, which is the only way to draw confident conclusions about predictable relationships between variables. Even when a relationship appears to emerge from descriptive data, we cannot claim that the relationship predictably exists. Likewise, no cause for the observations can be inferred.

In *correlational research* (symbolized by the link between X and Y in Fig. 1.4), at least two variables are systematically observed and described to test a *prediction* that changes in one will be associated with changes in another.

In correlational research, nothing is manipulated. The variables are only measured, just as they exist. All we do is make a prediction about them, then measure them, usually on a continuum. If, as the measured value of one behavior or event increases or decreases, the other also changes in a predicted direction, then we can conclude that the two are related, and knowing the value of one will give us some confidence in predicting the value for the other. For example, we might want to test the idea that our quarterback's passing performance (variable X) is related to attendance at the games (variable Y). Note that we must make a prediction *before* we look at the measurements, but if X does correlate with Y *in the predicted way*, we can conclude that these two variables are related. Based on our idea, we could predict that an examination of the records for the past two years will show the quarterback generally passing for more yards when there are more people in the stands. If the records show that the predicted relationship exists, then we have evidence to support our idea. Now, if a lot of tickets are sold for the next game, we can expect better performance from the quarterback than if ticket sales were low.

Note that we *cannot* conclude from our correlational research that being watched by more people *causes* the quarterback to pass more successfully. It is equally feasible that more people attend games when the opponent is weaker and there is a better chance of seeing a win. Or there might be some other explanation; our correlational data will not tell us anything about the *reason* these variables change together, only that they do. But this is still a useful conclusion because it increases our confidence in making

predictions based on that relationship. The predictions will not be perfect, but they will be better than guessing.

In *experimental research*, we test whether there is a cause-and-effect relationship between two variables. We do this by manipulating the cause and measuring the effect. For example, we might state that a particular type of training improves job satisfaction. To test that idea, we would manipulate the type of training provided (the cause, symbolized by X in Fig. 1.4): One group of workers would receive the training, while another group would not. Later, we would measure job satisfaction (the effect, symbolized by Y), perhaps by asking the workers in both groups to rate how satisfied they feel with their jobs. We then compare job satisfaction ratings for the two groups, predicting higher ratings in the trained group.

For a true experiment, the workers should be randomly assigned to either receive or not receive the training. If, instead, those who got training worked in a different building than those who did not, then any differences in job satisfaction could be due to other factors, such as different bosses, different morale, or different air quality in the two buildings. Randomly assigning individuals to either receive or not receive training would be the best way to assure that the two groups started out about the same, so the only difference between these groups is their training. If the groups then differ in job satisfaction, we can conclude that the training probably improves job satisfaction.

In *quasi-experimental research*, a cause-and-effect relationship is also stated, but for a variety of reasons, randomly putting individuals into different groups for comparison is not possible. This happens when we have no control over the variable of interest, like college major, for example. If a researcher predicts different behavior from math majors versus history majors, the researcher would have to assign people who are majoring in math to one group and those who are majoring in history to a different group for comparison. The participants in the study would determine which group they are in, not the researcher, because we cannot randomly assign people to major in a subject of our choosing.

Whenever researchers lack control over which participant goes into each group (i.e., when we cannot use a completely random procedure), a causal study becomes quasi-experimental. Often, this is for practical reasons unrelated to the variable we're trying to manipulate. Returning to our example of research on worker training, imagine that to comply with company regulations, we can only require workers with less than one year of experience to attend training, while workers who have seniority must be placed in the no-training group. We are still testing a cause-and-effect relationship (that training improves job satisfaction), and we can still control our variable of interest by providing training to one group and not providing it to the other. We still measure job satisfaction in both groups and predict higher satisfaction in the group that was trained. However, we cannot call this a true experiment because workers were not randomly assigned to their groups. The two groups will therefore start out with different levels of job experience, which could cause them to differ in other important ways, like age and level of job responsibility, and even pre-existing job satisfaction. Therefore, if we observe any difference in job satisfaction after training, we can only conclude that the difference *exists* between a group that was trained and a group that was not; we *cannot* conclude that the difference was *caused* by the training.

As the name implies, quasi-experiments are like experiments, but lack important characteristics (most notably, control over other variables) and therefore, they do not allow the researcher to draw a cause-and-effect conclusion. Figure 1.4 shows a link between X and Y, but no arrow because a quasi-experiment showing a difference between groups allows us to conclude that there is a link between X and Y (like correlational research), but we cannot conclude that X directly affects Y.

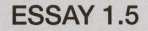

ESSAY 1.5

EXPLORATORY RESEARCH

Maybe you recall seeing children's science books from the *Little Explorers* series, designed to make science exciting and accessible to very young children. The author does this by reinforcing children's natural perception of science as exploration. The shift from being "little explorers" to thinking of science as a body of knowledge usually happens slowly and without notice, perhaps as we open science books full of facts rather than questions, or as we proceed through science classes that are packed with information to memorize, with too little emphasis on where that information came from. Learning what is already known is good and necessary; it helps us ask better questions about what we don't know. But it is also good and necessary to remember that the driving force of science is still exploration.

The term "*exploratory research*" applies to a certain kind of data-gathering, where there are no predictions and no preconceived ideas about what will be discovered. It does not follow the five steps of the scientific method. The main purpose is, as the name strongly implies, to explore; to see what can be seen; to find something that we didn't know existed.

Exploratory research is done with the goal of finding or generating possible new ideas and explanations, not *testing* existing ideas or explanations. From the inner space of anatomy to the outer space of astronomy, much of what we know began with this kind of exploration.

The lack of specific goals in exploratory research might seem nonscientific. It is not. Recall that science is a way of thinking: ever curious and always accepting the possibility of being wrong; skeptical; careful and systematic; thinking critically; and publicly sharing ideas and findings. Admittedly, with exploratory research, there is no possibility of being wrong about a prediction because there is no prediction. But the other characteristic ways of thinking are all essential to exploratory research. Curiosity, especially, is there in abundance.

One potential problem for exploratory research as a science is that it can easily flirt with **essentialism**. Those who want to explore "what love really is," so that they can define the "essence" of love are not doing science. But systematic explorations of reported reactions to being in love are science, especially when they are operationally defined, publicly shared, and critically evaluated. They can help us better understand what there is to know about love, and develop testable explanations for the things people report, like butterflies in the stomach or feelings of insecurity. Importantly, these explanations can change as new information is gathered. This is the stuff of science, and it can begin with exploratory research, perhaps in the form of interviewing people in love.

Another itchy notion in exploratory research, as a science, is Kuhn's definition of what scientists do: "puzzle-solving." Exploratory research often has no specific puzzle to solve. In practice, this type of research can feel like more like being in search of a puzzle than solving one. To appreciate the puzzle-solving aspect of exploratory research, we must think on a grander scale about a bigger puzzle: What knowable information is out there, waiting to be discovered? As with most human exploration, the goal of a scientist is not just to inform oneself about what's deep inside the forest or at the bottom of the ocean; it is to inform humankind. Yet again, we return to the notion that science, in its truest form, is a collective endeavor.

MODULE 1 RESEARCH LEARNING OBJECTIVES CHART

The chart below lists what you should expect to learn by reading the background information *and* completing each project in lab. As with the essay learning objectives, you should only complete the gray half of this chart for the project(s) your instructor assigns (as indicated in the first column on the left). Then read about the project to prepare for lab, but do not complete the white half of this chart until asked to do so in lab (after you've completed the research project).

STUDY NUMBER	MODULE 1 RESEARCH LEARNING OBJECTIVES	BEFORE READING				AFTER DOING PROJECT			
		I don't know how 1	I know a little about this 2	I know enough about this to guess correctly 3	I know how to do this and/ or have already done it. 4	I don't know how 1	I know a little about this 2	I know enough about this to guess correctly 3	I know how to do this and/ or have already done it. 4
1A	Explore and gain a sense of the diversity and complexity of research in psychology, and briefly describe research on two different topics.								
1A	List and explain the distinguishing characteristics of the five different types of research in psychology.								
1A	Given a brief explanation of research in psychology, identify the type of research and explain why it is that type.								
1A	Gain experience with peer reviews of scientific information.								
1B	Turn Internet advice into a testable claim, stated as a relationship between two variables.								
1B	Apply all the basic elements of a science attitude to information on the Internet.								
1B	Use the PsycINFO® database to find research on a specific topic in psychology.								
1B	List two ways to limit and two ways to expand a PsycINFO® search.								

		I don't know how 1	I know a little about this 2	I know enough about this to guess correctly 3	I know how to do this and/ or have already done it. 4	I don't know how 1	I know a little about this 2	I know enough about this to guess correctly 3	I know how to do this and/ or have already done it. 4
1B	Gather accurate information on the publication date of Internet information.								
1B	Defend an informed decision about the trustworthiness of a claim using a variety of evidence.								
1C	Give examples of how vision affects behavior.								
1C	Define and provide at least two examples of sensory transducers.								
1C	Distinguish between sensation and perception.								
1C	Explain how shape and/ or appearance relates to function for at least five parts of the human eye.								
1C	Use proper anatomical terms to describe the relative locations of parts of the eye.								
1C	List the parts of the eye, in order from the point where light enters to the transmission of signals to the brain.								

Now read about the project to prepare for lab. For any scores less than "4," keep those questions in mind as you complete the research project(s). Do not do the white half of this chart until after you've completed the assigned research project(s).

STUDY **1A**

A SIMULATION OF EXPLORATORY RESEARCH: IDENTIFYING TYPES OF RESEARCH

In this study, we'll try to simulate what it is like to explore the unknown without specific expectations. The world of psychology, as presented in your lecture textbook, will be your unknown. You'll browse through the chapters, looking for research on topics that interest you (i.e., observing). *As with all exploratory research, you will probably see things you've already seen or heard about before. Ignore those. To capture the spirit of exploratory research, look for the things you didn't already know about.*

As an example, let's assume you've never heard about the "Bobo Doll" studies conducted by Albert Bandura in the 1960s. You're skimming the chapter on learning and you come across a series of pictures that show a child beating the crap out of an inflatable doll. That's interesting. and maybe a little disturbing. Skim the text to find out more. To find an explanation of this research, you should look for citations: names and/or dates in parentheses, meaning the author is writing about someone else's work or idea. You find "(Bandura et al., 1961)",[8] and you read the surrounding text.

While reading, you learn that Bandura et al., allowed a small group of children to observe an adult who was kicking and punching an inflatable clown doll. Another group of children did not see that behavior. After a separate, mildly frustrating experience, the children in both groups were given an opportunity to play with the Bobo doll. Those who saw the adult model beat up on the doll were much more likely to do so themselves than the other children. This was one of the first studies of what is now called observational learning, a well-known phenomenon that, based on extensive research since then, raises real concerns about how violent video games, television, and movies affect aggression in young people.

After something is discovered in exploratory research, the next step is to identify and describe

it as accurately as possible and share that description so others may scrutinize your work. They might examine what you've described and see if they agree with your identification of it. In this simulation, you will try to identify whether the research you found is exploratory, descriptive, correlational, quasi-experimental, or experimental. Use the information in Essay 1.4, Figures 1.4., and 1.5, and the glossary of this module to help you decide and to justify your answer. Others will then look at the same research and see if they agree with your identification and explanation.

Note that your lecture textbook might not include all the necessary details to help you identify the type of research. For the Bandura study, the author probably won't mention that the researchers *randomly* split one larger group of children into the two smaller groups (those who saw the adult beat up the doll and those who did not), so that natural aggressiveness was probably about the same in both groups. In studies where two or more groups are compared and there is no *reason* to put any person into a specific group, you can assume for this project that the researchers used a randomizing procedure to assign groups. In general, the only time researchers don't follow this standard practice is when groups must be based on characteristics the researcher cannot control, like gender or age (see Essay 1.4).

Sample Answer: Bandura et al. wanted to study a possible *cause* of aggression in children, so it's likely to be either an experiment or a quasi-experiment. Because there was no reason to place specific children into one group or the other, we can assume they were randomly assigned to witness aggression or no aggression, so this is a true experiment.

Another way to identify the type of research is to focus on the methods, as shown in Figure 1.5. Because Bandura et al. wanted to test an idea (that children learn aggression from watching adults), this is not exploratory research. There were two variables (watching aggression and behaving aggressively), and

---

[8] Most psychology textbooks cite this seminal study. If yours does not, don't be concerned. This is just an example.

he predicted a relationship between them, so we can eliminate descriptive research. Children were separated in two groups that were treated differently on purpose, so this is not correlational. Bandura et al. had control over the formation of the two groups—there was no good reason to put a particular child in a particular group—so we can assume they were *randomly* placed in two groups. Therefore, this study was a true experiment.

Most research discussed in your lecture textbook will not be easy to identify. Due to the large volume of research that is presented, the authors might occasionally give you just the conclusions, and leave out the details on how those conclusions were reached. In cases like that, you can usually work it out based on the conclusion and the information in Essay 1.4. For this project, it's okay to guess at the details about how a study might have been done when no details are provided, as long as your details are logical and consistent with the researchers' conclusions. Remember that a science attitude still allows you to use your gut instincts when no better information is available. Your primary goal for this project is to practice applying what you have learned about the types of research, not to be perfect in your identification.

Here are some suggestions to help you find usable original research in your lecture textbook:

- [ ] Look for graphs that display data (bar charts, line charts, scatterplots) and read the figure captions. Citations (author names and/or dates in parentheses) usually indicate that the graph is showing the results of original research. You can also use the graph to help you determine what kind of research it is. Scatterplots usually show correlational data; bar charts are usually experimental or quasi-experimental data.

- [ ] If your lecture textbook has sections with featured research or critical thinking sections that describe research in detail, that might be another good place to look.

- [ ] Skim the text for citations. Look for key terms around the citations, like "studied," "examined," "investigated," or "reported." Look also for descriptions of how studies were conducted, rather than just conclusions describing what the results mean.

IMPORTANT NOTE: Unfortunately, the word "experiment" is often used as a lay-term to describe any type of research, and sometimes even textbook authors slip into this casual usage. Be forewarned that the use of the word does not guarantee that a study is a true experiment. At the introductory level, it is important to learn the correct terminology for different types of research (for reasons why, see the first paragraph of Essay 1.4).

1A PROCEDURE

1. Follow the advice above to find two examples of research in your lecture textbook that interest you and that you did not know about before. Use the lab record worksheet to record the studies you selected, and use Essay 1.4, Figures 1.4 and 1.5, and the Module 1 glossary to answer the questions about them. If you are working in pairs or groups, everyone should use the same two studies to complete the worksheet. One copy will be collected per group.

2. Complete the entire front page of the worksheet. Then tear it out and swap worksheets with a different student or group. Then use the information provided on the front to find the research that the first group wrote about. **Choose one** of their two studies and complete the questions on the back of the page, noting whether you agree or disagree with their answers and why.

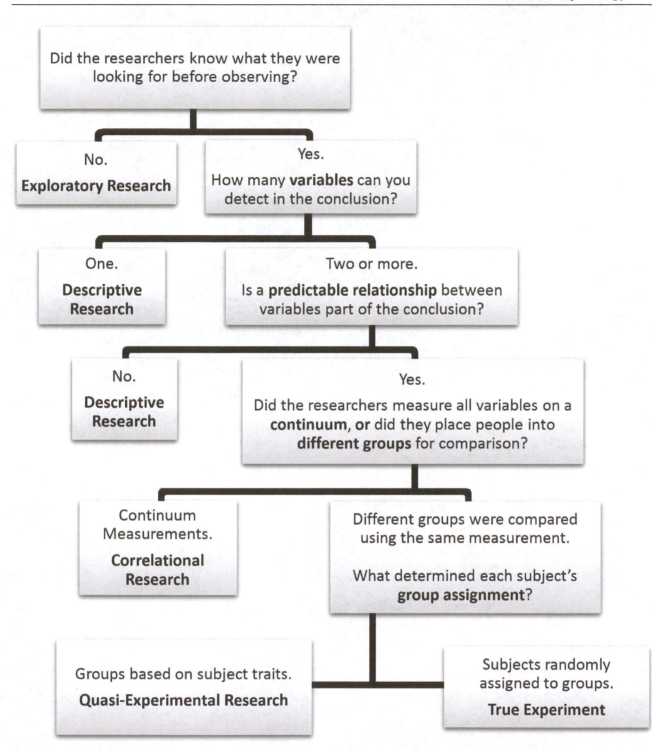

Figure 1.5 Decision tree for identifying types of research. Note that this is a simplified chart, and not all research will fit neatly into one of the five types described here. For example, studies with repeated measurements of the same participants in different conditions are not included, and some studies might use combinations of different types of research. Nevertheless, this is a good basic way to familiarize yourself with the elements of the different types of research covered in this book.

LAB RECORD WORKSHEET FOR STUDY 1A

IDENTIFYING TYPES OF RESEARCH

Group Members' Names: _____

First Study   Brief Topic: _____

Page # _____ (in your lecture textbook) Is this research shown in a figure or graph? Y / N

Researchers' Last Names: _____

Year of Publication: _____

Brief Description of the Research: _____

_____

_____

Type of Research (Circle one):

Exploratory   Descriptive   Correlational   Experimental   Quasi-Experimental

Explain WHY you think this study fits that type of research: _____

_____

_____

- -

Second Study   Brief Topic: _____

Page # _____ (in your lecture textbook) Is this research shown in a figure or graph? Y / N

Researchers' Last Names: _____

Year of Publication: _____

Brief Description of the Research: _____

_____

_____

Type of Research (Circle one):

Exploratory   Descriptive   Correlational   Experimental   Quasi-Experimental

Explain WHY you think this study fits that type of research: _____

_____

_____

REVIEWING GROUP: CHOOSE 1 OF THE ANSWERS ON THE BACK OF THIS PAGE TO EVALUATE BELOW.

Reviewing Group's Names: _____

Find the pages where the two studies on the front of this page are described in your lecture textbook. Decide which study you want to review.

Which answer are you reviewing?   (Circle one)   First Study   Second Study

Brief Topic: _____

Read about the research and consider\discuss the other group's answers.

Does your group agree or disagree with the research type that the other group circled?

We Agree   We Disagree

If you agree, give another reason why this research type was correctly identified:

_____

_____

If you disagree, then what type of research do you think best describes the study? (Circle one)

Exploratory   Descriptive   Correlational   Experimental   Quasi-Experimental

Explain WHY you think this study fits that type of research: _____

_____

_____

What type of conclusion was drawn in this research? (Check the one that fits best)

☐ Description of one or more variables with no predictions

☐ Predictable link between two or more variables

☐ Cause and effect: One variable directly affects another

Was that an appropriate conclusion, as far as you can tell?   Yes   No   Not Sure

Explain your answer: _____

_____

STUDY **1B**

PRACTICING A SCIENCE ATTITUDE:
"I SAW IT ON THE INTERNET, SO I KNOW IT'S TRUE."

Because psychologists study human behavior, and the Internet is full of advice on how to behave, our field of study is particularly susceptible to misinformation online. A solid science attitude helps weed out the misinformation and find the good stuff. This is not as easy as it sounds. Study 1B invites you to find online advice related to psychology and practice your science attitude as you examine assumptions and biases and look for scientific evidence for or against the claim.

Your first goal is to find some advice on the Internet. It should be written advice, not video, and not from a Q & A site like "Quora" or "Yahoo! Answers." If you've used the Internet for more than 5 minutes, you know this won't be difficult. Articles and blogs give advice on everything: What to say, what not to say, how to walk, talk, dress… the list is endless. Pick any piece of advice and state it as a claim. (What does the author claim will happen if you follow the advice?). For example, if the headline is "Six ways to get people to like you," and one of the ways is "Smile more," then the claim is that "Smiling increases likability." It is a statement of a causal (cause and effect) relationship; that is, changes in smiling *cause* changes in likability.

Put on your science attitude. Start by turning off the expert in your head. This is easier if you choose an advice topic about which you know little. Let go of your urge to give the author your own advice, and just focus on what the website is telling you. Consider all the information the author provides about the claim and the reasons behind it.

Second, you should be skeptical, focusing on the *truth* about the claim, not wishful thinking or cynicism. If it sounds like a miracle, that's probably wishful thinking. If it sounds like the stupidest thing you've read in years, that's probably cynicism. In both cases, you should either find different advice or resolve to know the truth, rather than setting out to prove your opinion is right.

Third, look for evidence—systematic observations that back up the claim. Did the author present any evidence for the claim, or just stories or hearsay? It's harder to assess the evidence if you feel strongly about a claim, one way or the other, as noted above. It might help to ask whether the claim should be true for a random group of strangers. What would you want to observe or measure in order to determine whether this claim is true for others, beyond simply asking for their opinions?

Fourth, think critically. If evidence is not included on the website, does the author provide links or bibliographic information to help you find the sources for the claim? Who sponsors the site, and do they have obvious reasons for wanting you to follow the advice? What are the author's qualifications to write on this subject? Does the author appear to have any underlying biases or make any assumptions?

Next, you'll be asked to dig up one piece of scientific evidence that either supports or refutes the claim, directly or indirectly. This will most likely require using your campus library's database services or another academic research engine. Although Google Scholar is easy to access and comprehensive, there are three good reasons to try your college or university library's resources instead: (a) Google Scholar includes many nonrefereed sources (sources that have not undergone careful scrutiny by scientists before being published); (b) filtering out irrelevant information can be difficult; and (c), unless it is linked to your campus resources, Google Scholar often suggests articles that charge fees for viewing or downloading.

Generally, your campus library databases will let you filter your findings to focus on refereed, relevant resources with full access, or they offer "interlibrary loan," which gives you access to articles from other libraries.

The fifth step in applying your science attitude to this claim is to think logically about the claim in light of all that information you've gathered, including any possible biases or assumptions made by the author *and* by you, as well as the scientific evidence.

Keep in mind that one scientific study is *not proof* of a claim, even if it supports it. Normally, you would want to find more research before deciding whether a claim is trustworthy. But considering all the evidence and information you have, do you trust the claim?

Lastly, be ready to discuss the claim, including your reasons for whether it should or should not be trusted. You will be asked to explain your reasons with logic and evidence, not opinions, and to cite at least one relevant scientific source.

GETTING STARTED WITH PSYCINFO®

The American Psychological Association has produced a searchable database containing nearly five-million records of research related to psychology from more than 2,500 journals published all over the world. The database, called "PsycINFO®," includes abstracts (one-paragraph summaries) for most articles, all indexed and searchable in a variety of ways including titles, keywords, content, author names, and even synonyms. Because there are many ways to search and a variety of filters, it can get a little overwhelming. But you don't have to use every feature to find it extremely useful.

Getting started is easy. The hardest part is probably finding the database among your library's resources, and even that is pretty easy. Go to your library's website and you're likely to find PsycINFO® among the links for research tools, research databases, or indexes (indices). If not, try using the search bar on your campus website or library's website. If you still can't find it, call your reference librarian and ask whether your library carries "PsycINFO®," and how to access it. Once you find it, you'll see that the main search page looks like a typical database search engine, but with more options.

Here are some tips for using PsycINFO® to find research articles related to the claims you might find on the Internet:

1) Start with the easiest thing: Type your claim into the search box and put quotation marks around it. This tells PsycINFO® that you only want records that include your exact words, in that order. (Without the quotation marks, you'll get a list of every record that uses any of your claim's words, in any order.) Click on "Search" and see what you get. You might find an exact match. If not, you'll get a message that says no exact matches were found, but you might also get some related results, thanks to "SmartText Searching," which analyzes the words and phrases in your quote and tries to match them to the most relevant results for you.

2) If any records do pop up, skim through the titles, and if one sounds like it will be related to your Internet claim, click on the title to read the abstract. (You may also ask PsycINFO® to show abstracts for all your records by clicking on "Page Options" and selecting "detailed," but this makes browsing titles harder if you have more than four or five records).

3) If the records you get don't seem related enough (or you don't get any), try a keyword search. It's best to use the variables in your claim. For instance, if the claim is that "Smiling increases likeability," type "smiling" in the first search bar and "likability" in the second one; then click search again to see what you get. Table 1.1 explains how to increase (expand) your search if you're not getting enough items, and how to decrease (limit) your search if you're getting too many items to handle.

4) When you find an article you want to read (based on the abstract) look for an html link or pdf link to the whole article. Immediate access will depend on which journals your library subscribes to, but there is also likely to be an ILL (Interlibrary Loan) link for articles your library doesn't have. Check with your reference librarian for more information.

Table 1.1 How to expand or limit a PsycINFO® database search.

How to expand your search (if you don't see enough records)	How to limit your search (if you see too many records)
☐ Truncate your search terms with an "*" For example, instead of "Smiling," use "**smil***" This will return all records that start with "smil," including smiling, smiles, smiled, smiley, smiler, and smilax (a type of flower).	☐ Change the Boolean operator to the left of a search box to "not" and type a term you do not want included there. ← For example: (based on example to the left) smil* NOT ▾ smilax
☐ Add more search terms, and change the Boolean operator to the left of each search box to "or." This will return all records that contain any of the search terms. You can also add search boxes to allow more terms by clicking on the "+" symbol.	☐ Add more search terms, and make sure the Boolean operator to the left of each search box says "and." This will return only records that contain all of the search terms you listed. You can also add more search boxes by clicking on the "+" symbol.
☐ If you have found a somewhat related record that is unavailable or not quite what you're looking for, click on the title for the detailed view of the record (with the abstract) and then click on an author name. This will return all works by that author, who might have done closely related work that your search terms did not pick up.	☐ Check the options in the left panel on the screen to filter your results. Click on "Source Types" and choose "Academic Journals" to eliminate books, dissertations, and other types of publications that are less likely to be as rigorously reviewed before publication. The left panel or the "advanced search" options can also limit records to a range of years of publication, peer-reviewed work, or and English language, among many other choices.
☐ In the Basic Search Options, make sure the boxes for "Apply equivalent subjects" and "Apply related terms" are checked. This will produce results that include synonyms of your search terms.	☐ Use the drop-down menu to the right of each search box to limit results to those in which the term appears in the Title only, or as a keyword only.

WARNING: An abstract alone is NOT good evidence for or against a claim, even if it sounds like the research directly supports or refutes that claim. Abstracts are severely limited in word count, so authors must leave out important details that almost always affect the quality and strength of the evidence. At this introductory level and for this study (1B), your professor might approve using information from an abstract to support or refute your claim, but you should be aware that this practice is unacceptable for advanced students of psychology and for professional science writers and researchers.

FINDING THE DATE A WEBPAGE WAS PUBLISHED

While some websites will include a date of publication near the author's name, many do not. It's worth carefully searching the whole page before you conclude that there is no date. Try bringing up a "find bar" (while on the webpage, hold the "ctrl" key and hit "F") and typing "20" into the find bar to see if any dates from this century show up anywhere on the page.

Even if there is no date, there is still a way to tell when something on the Internet was originally published. It's a bit clunky, but involves no source-code-searching and no browser extensions:

On the advice website you chose, go to the browser's address bar at the top, where the full url (address of the website) is located. Select and copy the entire url from the address bar. Open a new browser tab and type **inurl:** into the new address bar, then paste the address. The beginning of your new address should end up looking like the beginning of this one:

inurl:https://www.sciencefocus.com/nature/why-do-we-find-puppies-so-cute/

Hit enter. The original site should be the first result. If there is a date under it, like the one to which the arrow points in the image below, then you're done. That is the date it was published. If you don't see a date, then you must take one more step.

Your address bar will now show a much longer url with a lot of symbols mixed in. Click anywhere within that url to insert your cursor, then hold down your **right** arrow key to get to the end of the url. Leaving no spaces, type **&as_qdr=y15** at the end of the url and hit enter. You should now see a search result for your page with the date under it, like this:

www.sciencefocus.com › Nature ▾

Why do we find puppies so cute? - BBC Science Focus ...

Sep 14, 2018 - With their big, round eyes, button noses and large heads, puppies share many of the same physical characteristics as human babies. And like babies, as well as ...

1B PROCEDURE

This research can be done in pairs or groups of three, with one person being a recorder of the answers that the pair or group agrees upon.

1. Surf the Internet to find one website with advice on any topic of interest to you. The site can provide any number of pieces of advice. For example, it could be a whole article on why it's important to wash your hands, or it could be a blog on "65 ways to get your boyfriend or girlfriend to stop annoying you." It must be an article or blog, NOT a public Q&A forum like "Yahoo! Answers" or "Quora," and not a video.

2. Choose one piece of advice from the website and turn it into a claim. What does the author claim will happen if you follow the advice? Will you be happier? Richer? Liked by more people? Reword the claim clearly as a cause-and-effect statement. Remove "will" (this is not a prediction, it is a present-tense

claim). Also remove references to individuals, like "you," "one" or "a person." For example, instead of "Smiling will make people like you more," the claim would be, "Smiling increases likability."

3. Now dig deeper. Who owns/publishes the website, and/or who wrote the article? Use your browser's search engine to trace down that person or corporation's source of funding or find out the purpose or goals of the company. If it is an author's blog, unaffiliated with a company, try to find out more about the author. What is the author's educational background? For blogs, what companies or products are being advertised on the site?

4. Find out when the advice was published. Old advice is sometimes still good advice, but should be evaluated based on current trends and knowledge at the time it was published, which would make assessment more difficult. Make sure the advice you choose was published within the last year or two. (See "How to tell when a webpage was published," above.)

5. Go to your college or university's library webpage, find their psychology research databases, and look for one published research article that appears to either support or refute the claim. It may be direct or indirect evidence, but if it is indirect, you must explain the logic (in what way does it support or refute the claim?). It might be helpful to contact your reference librarian for assistance. Your professor will let you know whether you need to access the entire article or use the abstract.

6. Complete the lab record questions, either alone or with your group, as instructed.

LAB RECORD WORKSHEET FOR STUDY 1B
PRACTICING A SCIENCE ATTITUDE

Group Members' Names: _____

1. Chosen website address: _____

2. Claim: _____

3. Author of Claim: _____

4. Date of Claim: _____ (see above for how to find the date if it's not on the webpage)

5. Qualifications of Author (you might have to do a search to learn more about the person):

_____

_____

6. Evidence presented by the author (systematic, NOT opinion): _____

_____

_____

_____

7. Are there any advertisers on the website who might benefit from getting people to follow the advice?

If so, explain. _____

_____

8. How might you test this claim (for a random group of people)? _____

_____

_____

9. Reference information for related evidence (does not have to be a direct test, just related).

_____

Author's Last name, First initial. Repeat for all authors, up to 5.

(_____). _____
Year of Publication.   Article Title.

_____ , _____ , _____
Journal Title   Volume #   Page numbers

Attach a copy of the abstract for the article.

10. Discuss the claim either in writing or in a group. Do you trust the advice? Why or why not?

EXPLORATORY RESEARCH:
THE MARVELOUS MAMMALIAN EYE

Psychologists like to ask questions about behavior that most people never think to ask. For example, how does vision impact behavior? Let's just think about that for 10 seconds…

If you see your cell phone about to hit the floor, you'll reach out to grab it. When you see an obstacle in your path, you'll move it, or step over or around it. If you *don't* see an object that you want, you'll look around and maybe go looking for it. If you see an old friend raise a hand as though he's about to hit you, you might back away or high-five, depending on the expression you *see* on his face. In fact, if you think about it for a whole minute, you can probably come up with many more ways in which what you do is impacted by what you see (or don't see).

People who are fortunate enough to be able to say we have good vision don't often stop to think about *how much* of our behavior is influenced by visual input. Or, we tend to give all the credit to our brains for their ability to perceive and react to our world, rather than to our eyes for giving the brain the information it needs. But your brain processes and transmits information using electrochemical energy, not light. And the world around you is made visible by light energy, not electrochemical. Your brain lives in the dark, and cannot see by itself.

Your eyes act as **transducers**, turning light energy from your environment into electrochemical signals that your brain then interprets to form perceptions and control reactions. Thus, what we call "vision" is actually two processes, sensation and perception. **Sensation** is the process of transducing physical energy from the environment into the electrochemical energy the brain needs to process it. Sensory organs are transducers: Your eyes transduce light energy; your ears transduce the physical energy of sound waves; your skin transduces pressure. Your lecture textbook has detailed information on these and other sensory processes.

To study perception, one must also understand transduction (sensation) because without it there can be no perception. Indeed, without any transduction,

we would be disconnected from the reality that governs our behavior.

Our "data" for this study are not numbers or measurements, but pieces of information gained by careful observation. Our lab record will be a chart of our observations, rather than a comprehensive account of what we did. Our conclusions will most likely be information that is already well-documented and accepted by the scientific community, which has a standardized way of describing anatomical parts and locations. We will attempt to describe where the parts are relative to each other using some of this terminology.

Why does the terminology matter? Consider how you would describe the location of the eye's lens unambiguously. From the front of the eye, it appears to be in the center. From the side of the eye, it appears to be in the front. To further complicate matters, the terms "front" and "side" are not unambiguous, either. If someone is facing you, but looking sideways, is the front of the eye the part facing you, or the part facing sideways? Clearly, better terminology is needed to describe where things are. The terms you will use in this study are applicable to most anatomical descriptions, and are frequently used in neuroscience to describe the locations of brain parts or other nerve tissue.

Because this will be an exploratory study, we encourage you to ask a continuous stream of questions as you see the different parts of the eye. "What does that do?", "Why is it shaped that way?", "Why is it that color?", and "How is it connected to that other part?" would be good questions to ask yourself and your professor or lab instructor. Exploration is a big part of any science, including psychology, and in this study, we hope you will gain a sense of how psychologists have learned some of what they know, in addition to gaining some useful knowledge about how your brain gets its visual information (content for lecture exams!).

Image © Arisia, 2014. Used under license from Shutterstock, Inc.

PLEASE NOTE: You will be handling a piece of an animal that is no longer attached to the animal. This is not an unusual event; most humans and other omnivores (and all carnivores) eat animal parts. But some people are opposed to eating or even handling cooked or raw meat, and no one should be forced to do so. **If, for any reason, you feel that you cannot participate in this study, we ask that you do the following:** First, examine your reasons. If you are in true disagreement with the morality of this research, let your professor know immediately (**before lab meets**) so that a different assignment can be arranged for you. This will not affect your grade unless you fail to do the alternate assignment. If you feel that you might react physically, by getting ill or fainting, we ask you to consider watching a dissection, as students are often surprised by their lack of a physical reaction, or by how quickly they get over it. The same students often report being truly fascinated with what they get to see in this study. This is not an opportunity you are likely to have again. If you try and find that you physically cannot stay in the room to observe, another assignment will be arranged for you.

1C PROCEDURE

This will be an exploratory study of a sensory organ to learn more about how the sensation of vision is accomplished. The procedure below is for actual dissections. A video exercise is also available.

1. You will work in pairs or small groups. Ideally, at least one of you should be comfortable with the idea of dissecting, although no one need have any dissection experience.

2. Pay close attention as your instructor reviews safety information.

3. If available, obtain a lab coat, gloves, and goggles (if you don't already wear glasses). Even if you are just observing, you should wear all the protective clothing. You might accidentally be touched by someone wearing a dirty glove, and you probably don't want vitreous humor on your sweater. Or you might change your mind about wanting to be involved—that often happens.

4. Each group should obtain one pair of scissors, one scalpel, one pointer, and a dissection pan with a cow eye on it from your instructor.

5. DO NOT begin dissection! In order to keep our exploration systematic and not damage any parts that we will want to look at later, the entire class will perform the dissection in steps, exploring each part before moving on to the next. If you go ahead of the class, you might damage a part that is more interesting to see intact.

6. Your instructor (or a video) will demonstrate each step, starting with an examination of the extraocular muscles, and ending with the retina and optic nerve. Ask questions and make guesses about function as you examine the various forms. Discuss what the parts look like and where they are located relative to other parts, using the glossary of locational terms and examples that follows this procedure list. Also write the functions of each part. One person should be filling in the lab record as the dissection is happening. Do not wait until the dissection is complete to fill in the chart.

7. When the dissection and chart are complete, dispose of the parts as instructed in lab. DO NOT put organic waste in the trash bins, and DO NOT wash even small debris down the drain, as this will result in an expensive and disgusting clog.

8. Once your dissection pan is scraped clean (into the correct disposal bag), rinse the pan, rubber mat, and all equipment under HOT water and place them on a towel or rack to dry. DO NOT put wet tools into dissection boxes (they will rust).

9. Remove your gloves as demonstrated in lab and place them in the disposal bag with the organic waste.

10. Use paper towels, warm water, and a little soap to wash down your work area.

11. Wash your hands with soap and warm water.

12. Hand in one copy of your lab record, making sure all students' full names are on it.

LAB RECORD WORKSHEET FOR STUDY 1C

THE MARVELOUS MAMMALIAN EYE

Group Members' Names: _____

Parts	Relative location (e.g., "anterior to lens," "posterior to iris.")	Describe appearance	Describe function
Extraocular Muscles			
Cornea			
Aqueous Humor			
Pupil			
Iris			
Ciliary Body			
Lens			
Vitreous Humor			
Retina			
Tapetum (not in human)			
Optic Nerve			

GLOSSARY OF LOCATIONAL TERMS AND EXAMPLES

The following terms can be used to describe the location of any human anatomical parts, including the parts of the eye. As in the examples, these terms refer to the location of each part *relative to some other part*. Use the same approach in your lab record (e.g., the cornea is anterior to the lens).

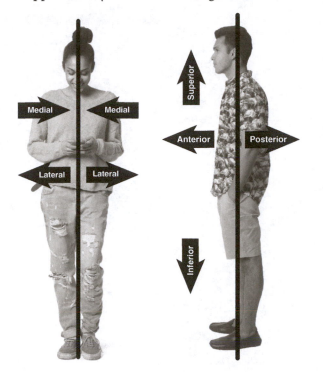

Anterior/Ventral: Closer to the face or belly.
  Examples: The tongue is anterior to the throat; the belly is ventral to the backbone.

Posterior/Dorsal: Closer to the back
  Examples: The ears are posterior to the cheeks; the shoulder blades are dorsal to the collar bones.

Lateral: Toward the sides
  Examples: The arms are lateral to the chest; the ears are lateral to the brain.

Medial: Closer to the vertical midline separating the left and right sides.
  Examples: The heart is medial to the lungs; the neck is medial to the shoulders.

Superior: Closer to the top of the head.
  Examples: The neck is superior to the chest; the chest is superior to the gut.

Inferior: Closer to the feet.
  Examples: The feet are inferior to the knees; the knees are inferior to the head.

ANATOMY OF THE HUMAN EYE

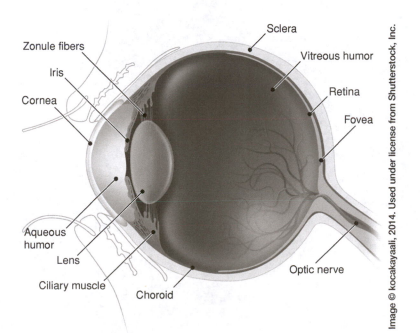

Image © kocakayaali, 2014. Used under license from Shutterstock, Inc.

MODULE 1 GLOSSARY OF TERMS AND EXAMPLES

Confirmation Bias: The tendency to focus on evidence that supports our ideas while ignoring evidence against our ideas.

Examples: (1) Politically biased reporting (e.g., when a journalist believes that the opposition's political party always lies, they might only report the lying and ignore evidence that the opposition sometimes tells the truth. In this case, the confirmation bias of the reporter can strengthen the confirmation bias of viewers. (2) Misanthropes tend to fall prey to confirmation bias quite easily, because social media stories of people and society being mean and awful are easy to find on the Internet, and stories of kindness can be easily avoided.

Where to find this term: Essay 1.3, Fig. 1.2

Correlational Research: A study that measures two or more things that vary (***variables***) with the goal of testing a predicted relationship between them.

Example: A review of correlational research on marriage shows that the more equity there is in a marriage, the higher the levels of satisfaction reported (Gray-Little & Burks, 1983). Note that this is not evidence that sharing responsibilities increases marital satisfaction. It could be that feeling more satisfied with a partner increases the likelihood of helping them, or that generally happy people are both more likely to feel satisfied *and* more likely to want to help their partners. No cause for satisfaction levels can be determined from correlational research.

Where to find this term: Essay 1.4, Fig. 1.4. See also Module 4.

Descriptive Research: A study that measures or identifies one or more things that vary (***variables***) with the goal of describing it (them) in some useful way.

Examples: A description of the number of retweets per hour for #genz combined with #tech. At the moment of this writing that number is 137. See https://ritetag.com/best-hashtags-for/genz for updates on descriptive hashtag data. Other examples of descriptive research include the percent of children who are allergic to peanuts, or the number of people who violate stay-at-home orders during a pandemic.

Where to find this term: Essay 1.4, Fig. 1.4. See also Module 2.

Essentialism: The philosophy that holds that the goal in trying to understand the natural world should be to understand the essential, correct, and unchanging meaning of everything in it. The idea is that everything has its own distinct and fixed essence that makes it what it is, and that's what we should try to understand.

Examples: (1) Gender essentialism is the belief that men are essentially different from women, in clear, understandable, and unchanging ways. (2) Cultural essentialism is the belief that every culture has its own fixed essence that distinguishes it from other cultures.

Where to find this term: Essays 1.3, 1.5

Experimental Research: A study designed to test a cause-and-effect relationship between two things that vary (***variables***). An experiment tests whether changing one variable causes changes in the other.

Example: Godden and Baddeley (1975) tested the idea that matching surroundings during learning to surroundings while recalling learned information improves memory performance. Whether or not the location matches between learning and recalling was one variable of interest (the cause). Memory performance was the other variable of interest (the effect). They manipulated the cause to observe the effect. Divers learned and later tried to recall lists while diving 10 ft under water and while sitting on a beach, sometimes matching learning and recall locations, and sometimes not. They recalled more words when the locations for learning and remembering matched than when they were different.

Where to find this term: Essays 1.3, 1.4, Fig. 1.4. See also Modules 5, 7 & 8.

Mod 1 Glossary

Exploratory Research: A study designed to systematically explore the unknown, without specific goals or predictions.

> *Example:* Recent research in neuroscience is using a new type of brain imaging technique called Diffusion Spectrum Magnetic Resonance Imaging (a type of MRI, often called DSI) that produces images of the neural fibers in the brain like never before. These images have led to the discovery of many new neural centers in the human brain—areas of concentrated brain activity during certain cognitive tasks that we did not previously know about, nor expect to find.
>
> *Where to find this term:* Essays 1.4, 1.5, Fig. 1.4, Studies 1A, 1C.

Falsifiability: The qualifying characteristic of any scientific idea. Every scientific idea must be falsifiable, meaning that it can be subjected to tests designed to show that it is wrong (whether or not the technology is available to do so). The more of these kinds of studies (tests) the idea withstands without being shown wrong, the more confidence we can have that the idea is right.

> *Example:* The idea that Santa Claus exists "in spirit" is not falsifiable. It cannot be tested and shown to be wrong. Any study that suggests that the spirit of Santa is not real could be dismissed by saying that the scientist "misbehaved," and therefore did not deserve to witness the spirit of Santa. The idea that Santa Claus is your dad, dressed in a red suit with white trim *is* falsifiable (if Dad and Santa are in the room at the same time, that idea is falsified).
>
> *Where to find this term:* Essay 1.3, Fig. 1.2

Operational Definition: Briefly, a working definition of a *variable*.

> *Examples:* See Module 2 Glossary
>
> *Where to find this term:* Essay 1.3. See also Module 2.

Operationism (Operationalism): The philosophy that holds that the goal of research should be to improve our understanding of reality by careful definition and observation of concepts and the relationships between them, while recognizing that this endeavor is imperfect and that the "truth" as we understand it may change with new information.

> *Examples:* Every scientific study described in this book and your lecture textbook takes an operationist approach.
>
> *Where to find this term:* Essay 1.3

Pseudoscience: A field of study that sounds scientific (borrows terminology or concepts from science and presents them as facts) but does not recognize the fundamental principle of science that ideas must change as evidence accumulates against them. Pseudoscientific ideas resist change regardless of evidence or logic against them.

> *Examples:* Climate change denial. The Flat Earth Society. Conversion therapy (attempts to change sexual orientation with therapeutic intervention).
>
> *Where to find this term:* Essay 1.3

Quasi-Experimental Research: A study that, like an experiment, manipulates something (A) that is expected to change something else (B), but does not randomly assign subjects or participants to different treatment groups, so that those groups often differ in important ways other than the purposeful difference being tested as a cause (A).

> *Example:* A study of the personality types of software designers examined how personality types "influence" decisions about chosen software design tasks (Capretz et al., 2015). While it is possible that personality types have a direct influence on these decisions, that conclusion cannot be drawn from their research because it was quasi-experimental. Participants were assigned to groups for comparison based on their responses to a personality inventory, which means the researcher had no control over who ended up in each comparison group. People cannot be randomly assigned to have certain personalities.
>
> *Where to find this term:* Essay 1.4, Fig. 1.4. See also Module 6.

Science Attitude: To be curious, unassuming, and eager to learn; to actively seek ways of learning more; to be aware of our own and others' built-in assumptions and biases; to reason logically, with an awareness of the impact of our emotions, and to share ideas publicly. Note that these are not the only traits composing a science attitude, just some of the most common and basic.

Examples: For a more complete list of the traits that make up a science attitude (with 20 attributes rather than 6), see: bestlibrary.org/sc9/2007/03/twenty_science_.html or google "Science Nine, 20 Science Attitudes."

Where to find this term: Essays 1.1, 1.2, 1.3, Study 1B

Scientific Method: One of the tools for doing science, this is a five-step way of trying to better understand the natural world: Learn, hypothesize, test, conclude, and share. A key step is the formulation of a hypothesis, which leads to predictions about what will be observed and observations that test those predictions.

Example: A scientist learns about possible contamination of her garden hose water and hypothesizes that a pathogen in her water supply is bad for her plants. She tests this by randomly watering some of her plants with the garden hose, and others with purified water. She predicts that the second group of plants will have fewer dead leaves, counts dead leaves on all plants after two weeks, and observes the same number of dead leaves in both groups. She shares this information with a friend, and suggests that the water is not contaminated, or if it is, it is not bad for her plants. The scientific method comprises all of this, including the interpretation of the findings and sharing of information.

Where to find this term: Essays 1.1, 1.2, 1.3, 1.4, 1.5 (but especially 1.2)

Sensation: The transduction of various forms of energy from the environment into electrochemical signals that can then be transmitted via neurons.

Examples: When light energy from the environment strikes the retina, specialized neurons in the retina (rods and cones) transduce the light into electrochemical energy and release neurotransmitter. Other neurons react to the neurotransmitter and send electrochemical signals via the optic nerve to the brain; When your hand touches a hot stove, the heat energy is transduced to electrochemical signals by specialized neurons in the skin, and that signal is transmitted to the brain and to the motor neurons that pass the signal to muscles to pull your hand away, even before your brain has processed the information.

Where to find this term: Study 1C

Systematic Observation: Observation with a clearly defined plan or system for gathering information.

Examples (systematic): *Exploration* of reactions to isolation by open-question interviews of a wide variety of people who have experienced prolonged isolation. *Description* of parent--child attachments by observing specifically defined behaviors indicating attachment or lack of attachment. *Correlation* of GPA from college records with number of high school math classes taken. *Experiment* on the effects of money on ratings of happiness that gives precise amounts of money to people who are randomly assigned to either receive the money or not, followed by surveys and comparisons of mood in the two groups. *Quasi-experiment* on the effect of parental status on video-game-playing enjoyment, where 30-year-olds are asked to play a video game and rate their enjoyment, and enjoyment ratings are then compared between parents and nonparents.

Examples (NOT systematic): Taking a piece of paper and a pencil outside, intending to write down the ways people behave. There might be some value in this exercise, but it could be made much more valuable with a systematic approach that involves planning and recording when to observe, for how long, where, whom, what to look for, etc.

Where to find this term: Essay 1.1, Study 1B

Transducer: Anything capable of turning one form of energy into another

Examples: A radio is a transducer because it turns electromagnetic energy into sound waves (an audio signal); a sensory organ (the ear) is a transducer because it turns sound waves into electrochemical signals that the brain perceives as sound.

Where to find this term: Study 1C

Variable: Briefly, anything that differs, changes, or can be made to change.
   Examples: See Module 2 Glossary
   Where to find this term: Essays 1.3, 1.4, Fig. 1.4, Study 1B. See also Module 2 Glossary.

Verifiability: The extent to which an idea can be shown to be correct. Although the term is often used loosely, this quality is no longer stressed in scientific research, since the real test of the truth of an idea is whether it resists being *falsified*, not whether it is verified. This is because it is infinitely more difficult to convincingly verify an idea than it is to convincingly falsify it.
   Example: In order to verify that a person (e.g., Abe Lincoln) is always honest, one would have to watch Abe in hundreds of different situations and verify that he is honest in all of them. To falsify the idea that Abe is always honest, one could set up just a few situations in which most people would be dishonest, and see whether Abe is honest in those situations. Putting the idea to the test (falsifying) means actively *trying* to show it is wrong, rather than looking for all the instances in which it is right (verifying).
   Where to find this term: Essay 1.3

"The limits of my language mean the limits of my world."
—Ludwig Wittgenstein (1889–1951),
Philosopher, Cambridge Professor

Module 2
Descriptive Research

MODULE 2 LEARNING OBJECTIVES CHART

ESSAY NUMBER	MODULE 2 ESSAY LEARNING OBJECTIVES	BEFORE READING					AFTER READING			
		I don't know how 1	I know a little about this 2	I know enough about this to guess correctly 3	I know how to do this and/ or have already done it. 4		I don't know how 1	I know a little about this 2	I know enough about this to guess correctly 3	I know how to do this and/ or have already done it. 4
2.1	Explain the purpose of descriptive research and provide at least two examples that illustrate its value.									
2.1	List and distinguish among three types of descriptive research.									
2.1	Describe two subtypes of descriptive observational research and give an example of each.									
2.2	Define and distinguish between the terms "conceptual variable" and "operational definition."									
2.2	List three ways that data from a descriptive study might be meaningfully summarized and give an example of each.									
2.2	Explain the difference between validity and reliability of an operational definition and explain how to improve each.									
2.3	Give at least two good reasons why self-report data must be interpreted cautiously.									

		I don't know how 1	I know a little about this 2	I know enough about this to guess correctly 3	I know how to do this and/ or have already done it. 4	I don't know how 1	I know a little about this 2	I know enough about this to guess correctly 3	I know how to do this and/ or have already done it. 4
2.3	Correctly define the term bias and explain how its meaning is commonly misinterpreted.								
2.3	List and give examples of five ways questions can be biased.								
2.3	Define social desirability bias and explain how it can be minimized.								

Read the assigned essays and actively seek answers to any questions rated less than "4." Then return to this chart and complete the white half.	Now proceed to the chart for the applications section, read the objectives for your assigned research project, and complete the gray side of that chart.

ESSAY 2.1

FUNDAMENTALS OF DESCRIPTIVE RESEARCH

Descriptive research is closely related to exploratory research (Essay 1.5), but has a different, more specific goal, which is to identify and provide a *systematic* description of a known behavior or phenomenon. Both descriptive and exploratory studies are idea-generators, not idea-testers. They do not fit neatly into the five steps of the scientific method because they are not designed to test predictions. In exploratory research, observations are directed at the unknown, but in descriptive research, the object of study is clearly defined.

For ease of discussion, we should first clarify the meaning of a word introduced in Essay 1.3 that is commonly used in all types of psychology research and in all other sciences. A *variable* is anything that differs from one instance to another, changes over time, or can be made to change. All of the topics—the behaviors, thoughts, feelings, events and characteristics—that are the subject of psychological science are variables. In fact, there is very little in the natural world that cannot be called a variable. Everything differs in some way from one person to another, over time, across cultures, or in different locations.[1]

Descriptive studies describe variables and how they vary. They give us high-resolution snapshots of the natural world, as though we are taking apart our surroundings to see the different pieces from previously unexamined angles, with the simple goal of describing reality in clear, meaningful, objective ways. Often, the information we collect through descriptive research leads to interesting, testable ideas that would not have occurred to us without first describing the variables involved.

Sometimes ideas generated from descriptive research lead to important technological advancements. If descriptions of the properties of stars, planets, and galaxies were not done first, astrophysicists could not calculate meteor trajectories or gravitational effects on satellite systems. Geneticists have used

descriptive studies to unveil the human genome, leading to advances in the identification and treatment of disease. The United States Census is a good example of large-scale descriptive research with important social, political, and economic applications (for more information on the economic uses of Census data, see "census.gov/programs-surveys/economic-census/guidance/data-uses.html").

Two excellent examples of ground-breaking descriptive research in psychology can be seen in human development research by Jean Piaget and animal behavior research by Jane Goodall.

Piaget observed children's responses to a variety of questions and problems like the one shown in Figure 2.1, and described identifiable stages in the development of human reasoning. Published in 1936, his descriptions have been critical to the development of more effective teaching strategies in early childhood education, and have formed the basis for a good deal of research in developmental psychology for almost 85 years. Anyone who studies human cognitive development, even at the most basic level, will learn about Piaget's work.

In another striking example of descriptive research that has changed world views, Jane Goodall was the first to describe nonhuman animals using tools. She watched in amazement as chimpanzees placed twigs and blades of grass into otherwise inaccessible spaces, waited patiently for insects to climb aboard, then carefully lifted the makeshift spoon to their lips and nibbled on the insects (Figure 2.2). Her descriptions shattered the illusion that the human ability to use tools—objects that help us achieve our goals—makes us special. Documented evidence now exists for tool use by many animals, from apes to insects. Perhaps the most entertaining example can be seen on video at youtube.com/watch?v=pvzOAnfzR90. Watch the whole 38 seconds of video to see why that animal is doing what it's doing. While some animal behaviorists argue that this is not tool use, others do label it as tool use because of the planning involved in collecting two pieces of something to serve one purpose. Scientists

---

[1] The only exceptions are physical and mathematical constants. See Essay 1.3, footnote 7.

Image © Kendall Hunt Publishing

Figure 2.1 Descriptive research by Jean Piaget. One of many questions Piaget asked of children: Two identical glasses containing the same amount of liquid were placed in front of each child (top image). A child watched as the liquid was poured from one of the two shorter glasses into the taller, narrower glass. In the bottom image, the child points to the glass that has "more liquid." Piaget described this level of reasoning as preoperational, because children were not yet able to perform "mental operations" on the objects in front of them. They did not mentally reverse the pouring of the liquid back into the wider container, and did not yet understand that a given quantity of liquid does not change with the shape of its container.

often disagree on the definitions of the concepts they study, and tool use is no exception. More on this in Essay 2.2.

Doing quality descriptive research is not as easy as it seems. The goal is not merely to describe, but to provide *systematic* descriptions, which means you need a plan that will include the goal of your study and a way of unambiguously identifying or measuring what you wish to describe. Descriptive studies fall into three broad categories based on their goals,

Image © Kjersti Joergensen/Shutterstockv

Figure 2.2 Because of descriptive research of Jane Goodall, we have long known that humans are not the only species to use tools to achieve goals.

which influence how the data are[2] collected. The three broad categories of descriptive research are: 1) case studies; 2) observational research; and 3) surveys.

(1) *Case studies* have a strictly defined goal, which is to provide a detailed, in-depth description of a single individual, institution, or event that is unusual or interesting. Any ethical means of data collection can be used, including careful observation by the researcher or observer; questioning the individual being studied or surveying individuals who represent the institution or event; as well as information from third-party observers or experts, such as a family member or doctor, event coordinator, or institutional advisor who has worked with the case being described. Regardless of the type of data collection, the focus of a case study always remains on the single entity being described. The results are not meant to be generalized, but case studies can lead to other types of research—often observational studies or surveys—that then produce more generalizable results.

---

[2] If the word "are" bothers you here, and you feel it should say "…data *is*…" try substituting "numbers" or "pieces of information" in place of the word "data." You would never say "numbers *is*…" or "pieces of information *is*…" In this context, "data" refers to numbers or pieces of information," so "are" is the grammatically correct verb. Numbers *are* collected. This common mistake is noted here because it is important to keep in mind when writing scientific reports.

(2) The goal of an **observational descriptive study** is to produce a description of at least one variable (i.e., how it varies within a context or population). Data are collected from the point of view of the observer using one of two techniques: **naturalistic observation**, so named because it occurs in a natural setting, without the knowledge of the people or nonhuman animals being observed, and **analog observation**, which occurs in a laboratory or contrived environment, such as a clinic, hospital, or research lab.

The choice to use naturalistic or analog observation can be a difficult one. Each approach has advantages and disadvantages. In **naturalistic observation**, described in more detail in Applications 2B and 2C, we aim to describe the variable (usually a behavior) as it occurs in nature. No interference or intrusion is allowed. This has the advantage of feeling more authentic because we are recording "real-world" behavior, presumably unaffected by our watchful eyes—it might reveal behaviors that would not be observed in a lab environment. The main disadvantage is that there are probably unknown outside factors influencing the behavior, and even the factors we know about cannot be controlled. Multiple hidden variables—moods and prior experiences and even air quality—could affect our measurements. Additionally, this way of collecting data requires patience. We must rely on our subjects to simply "behave" in a way that will contribute meaningfully to our data. Remember the old adage that "a watched pot never boils?" It's not true, of course, but it can sometime feel that way during naturalistic observation.

In **analog observation**, we can elicit behaviors by setting up situations that call for responses, then measure the variability in those responses. The behaviors we observe might lose some of that real-world quality, but we gain confidence in the accuracy of our measurements, as there are fewer outside factors that could impact our observations. One disadvantage is that analog studies usually cost more than naturalistic observation, unless they use a pre-existing setup. The bigger disadvantage is that we don't know how much real-world character is lost. We do know that people behave differently when they are aware someone is watching, and when they're in a laboratory environment. Laboratory researchers often admit to some artificiality in their measurements, suggesting that results should be "taken with a grain of salt," but how big is the grain? In most cases, it is probably very small, but we must admit that its true size is difficult to accurately assess.

(3) The goal of **descriptive survey research** is the same as observational research: "to produce a description of at least one variable (i.e., how it varies within a context or population)." The difference is that the variable of interest is measured from the point of view of participants, rather than the observers. Questions are presented electronically, on paper, or in a face-to-face interview, and participant responses provide the data. Survey researchers usually try to collect data from a sample of people who represent a larger group, with the goal of generalizing the information to the larger group. If the larger group is small enough, or the funding large enough, surveys sometimes question everyone, as with the US Census.

Because survey data come from the point of view of the participants rather than an observer, they are often called **self-report** data. The great advantage of self-report data is that they provide information on variables that cannot be directly observed, such as feelings, attitudes, memories, and internal reactions. The disadvantage is that participants are usually aware they are contributing to a data set, which can impact their responses. People tend to reply in ways that fit social norms, rather than risk being perceived as different. Some may not take questions seriously, and may give answers that are meant to make the researcher smile (ironically, these responses bring more frowns than smiles to researcher faces). Another caveat with any kind of self-report data is that the questions asked can sometimes influence the answers given (more on this in Essay 2.3 and Application 2D).

A final, but important note: The ways of collecting data used in all three types of descriptive studies are *not* limited to descriptive research. What distinguishes descriptive studies from other types of studies is their goal: *description*, not *comparison*. Please keep this in mind throughout the rest of this module: Observational and survey data collection methods are used in all the types of research shown in the top row of Figure 2.3. They are not unique to descriptive research, and will appear repeatedly throughout the rest of this book.

All three categories of descriptive research have made valuable contributions to our understanding of behavior, but case studies are typically only done when a unique case calls for a thorough description. The remainder of this Module will therefore focus on descriptive observational studies and surveys. Figure 2.3 places these terms into a meaningful context with the types of research presented in Module 1.

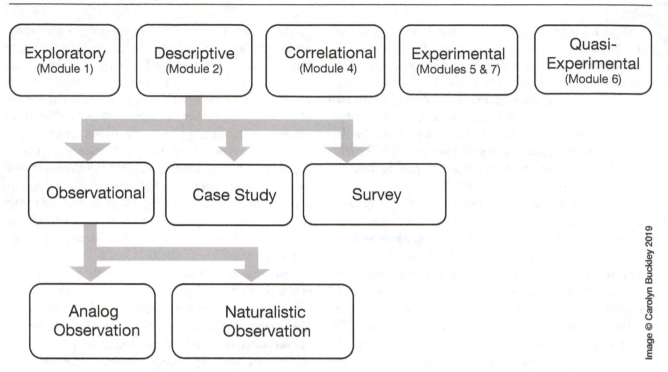

Figure 2.3   A summary of the types and subtypes of research. The top row shows the five main types of research. The middle row shows subtypes of descriptive research, and the third row shows the subtypes of descriptive observational research.

SKILL CHECK

(Answers in Appendix B):

1. Piaget's research was ___analog___, while Goodall's research was ___naturalistic___
    (naturalistic or analog?)   (naturalistic or analog?)

2. A researcher tests the idea that having an accountability buddy increases exercise. He asks 100 people how often they exercise and whether they have a friend who checks to make sure they are exercising. He places people into two groups: those who have such a friend, and those who do not. He then compares how much each group exercises. What type of research is this?

3. A clinician works with a patient who has a rare condition and writes a report detailing the patient's childhood, school experiences, work life, and family life, and how the condition impacts each of these. What type of research is this?

4. A teacher wants to test the idea that playing Minecraft increases creativity in children. She randomly splits her class into two groups. One group uses their computer time to play Minecraft, while the other group plays educational computer games of their own choosing. After three weeks of this, all children are given a creativity test. What type of research is this?

5. A researcher wants to test the idea that self-reported loneliness can be used to predict time spent on social media. She asks 100 college students to rate how often they feel lonely on a scale of 0 (never) to 10 (always), then looks at their phones to see how much time they've spent on social media apps over the past week. She compares these two measurements to see if they are related. What type of research is this?

ESSAY 2.2

CONCEPTUAL VARIABLES AND OPERATIONAL DEFINITIONS

In descriptive research, whether we're doing a survey or an observational study, our focus is on some variable of interest. It begins as an idea in your head—a concept. The *concept varies* among individuals, over time, or across situations, so we call it a *conceptual variable (CV)*. The CV is whatever we have decided to study. It can be a behavior (e.g., hand-washing; reactions to a bricked phone), a characteristic (e.g., enthusiasm for rock concerts; kindness), thoughts or feelings (e.g., perceptions of morality; happiness), or anything else, but it must always be a noun or noun-phrase, and must have variable qualities. The term *conceptual variable* is used in all types of research, but in this module, we'll focus on CVs in descriptive research.

In descriptive studies, the variable qualities of the CV are measured over time or across different people or situations to produce numbers (data). Those data[3] are then summarized to describe how that concept varies within or among situations or populations. The same conceptual variable can be measured in different ways to produce different data summaries. Typical data summaries describe the CV in terms of its *prevalence* (proportion of times it happens out of the total number of times it *could* happen), its *frequency* (the number of times it happens in a given period of time), or its *duration* (how long it lasts).

For example, if our conceptual variable is "enthusiasm for rock concerts," we can report on the proportion of all live concerts within a community that feature rock music (prevalence), or the total number of rock concerts in a single summer (frequency), or the total length of stage time that is devoted to rock concerts (duration). Another example: We can summarize data on "hand-washing" by observing everyone who uses a restroom and reporting the proportion who wash their hands afterwards (prevalence). Or, we can report the number of times hand-washing occurs within a given period of time (frequency), or the average length of time people spend washing their hands (duration).

Of course, before the data summary, we must first collect the data, and to do that, we need an *operational definition*—a functional way of identifying or measuring the conceptual variable. For instance, in the first (top) data summary of the skill check below, "reaction" was probably defined as "time spent staring at the phone." The middle summary used the definition, "instances of throwing the phone on the ground." You can easily guess the definition used in the third (bottom) summary.

Operational definitions are not always so simple to write or apply. For example, how would you define "hand-washing?" Does a quick rinse count, or must soap be used? Must the scrubbing continue long enough for the whole Happy Birthday song? Writing good, clear operational definitions is difficult, but it is crucial in science.

---

[3] Note that the word "data" in this context is a synonym for "numbers" and is therefore plural. One number would be called a "datum" or "data point."

SKILL CHECK

Summarizing reactions to a bricked phone. Draw a line from each data summary to the correct term for it. Answers are in Appendix B.

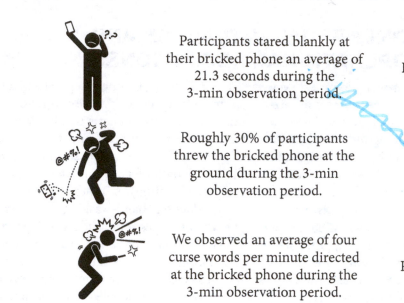

Participants stared blankly at their bricked phone an average of 21.3 seconds during the 3-min observation period.

Frequency

Roughly 30% of participants threw the bricked phone at the ground during the 3-min observation period.

Duration

We observed an average of four curse words per minute directed at the bricked phone during the 3-min observation period.

Prevalence

Consumers of scientific information and other researchers need to know *what* was observed and *how* so that they can assess the quality of the data. To get the best quality data, an operational definition needs both *reliability* and *validity.* These terms are often confused, so let's start with an example, then define them, then practice them.

Imagine you are traveling to outer space, and you've been severely warned to avoid the aliens when they are angry. Happy aliens are great, but you can be killed instantly by an angry alien. So alien anger is your conceptual variable.

You need a high-quality operational definition of alien anger so that you'll know when you see it. Assuming you can only use one of the two operational definitions below, which would you prefer?

Operational Definition A

An angry alien will have a somewhat sad posture, but a pleased-looking mouth, with alert, suspicious eyes and curious ears. It will also make some strange sounds, almost like an excited donkey or a European ambulance.

Operational Definition B

An angry alien will have a rounded, protruding backbone with drooping shoulders. Both corners of its mouth will turn up; the eyes will move left and right, and the ears will point straight up. It will make a two-syllable, "ee-aw" noise.

Imagine yourself using operational definition "A." What do a "sad posture," "a pleased-looking mouth," and "curious ears" look like? Will you recognize a sound that is "*almost* like an excited donkey?" What if you've never heard a European ambulance? Definition A depends heavily on experience and is therefore likely to be interpreted differently by different people. Definition B is more *reliable* because it uses only directly observable, easily identified traits. It would only take a second to spot a protruding backbone and ears pointing straight up, but you might be dead before you could figure out whether the alien's posture was "somewhat sad" or its eyes were "suspicious." Definition B has better *reliability*. That is, everyone who uses it will most likely agree on whether a particular alien is angry or not. Reliability is good, but it is not enough for everyone to agree on whether the alien is angry; they also have to be *correct*.

Validity refers to the accuracy with which the operational definition captures the true meaning of the conceptual variable. Like an expert archer, a valid definition hits the target at its center; it comprises the core of the CV. Valid definitions are therefore based on careful and comprehensive observation, often achieved through previous exploratory or descriptive research. For a valid operational definition of alien anger, we would need to observe calm aliens, and then irritate them and observe the differences. Pointy ears might be easy to spot consistently, but do these aliens ever point their ears when they're not angry? Are they ever angry without pointing their ears? Thankfully, most operational definitions in psychology can be validated without risking our lives.

For comparison, then, *validity* is about authenticity. A valid definition is what it says it is; it matches the meaning of the CV. Validity is demonstrated by the degree of overlap between the concept and its definition. *Reliability* is about consistency. A reliable definition steadfastly measures or identifies *something* (if it's also valid, that something is the CV). Reliability is demonstrated by consistency over time or across different observers. Reliable definitions are like reliable friends; undeviating, constant, unwavering… and sometimes wrong.

An operational definition can be *reliable* without being *valid*. A practiced archer, given an unbalanced bow, might repeatedly hit the target three inches above center. She is very reliable (always hitting the same area), but not very accurate (that area is not the center of the target).

Can an operational definition be *valid* without being *reliable*? Consider an archer whose arrows land in no predictable, consistent way; there can be no practical accuracy. The more unreliable the definition, the more measurements one would need to achieve any validity. It could take thousands of unreliable arrows aimed at the target to produce a trustworthy, valid (bullseye) average.

SKILL CHECK

The operational definition of "friendliness" is "instances of one person walking toward another person to within 2 feet." Is this definition reliable? Why or why not? Is it valid? Why or why not? Suggested answers are in Appendix B. The skill check in Table 2.1 offers more practice recognizing validity and reliability of operational definitions.

No matter how valid and reliable a definition is, it's almost never perfect. Researchers draw conclusions about conceptual variables, but they must use operational definitions to gather the data, and operational definitions are almost never exactly equivalent to the conceptual variables they measure. CVs are abstract: we have representations of them in our heads, and we know what they mean to us, but their edges can be blurry, and they might not mean exactly the same thing to someone else. There is no perfect definition of any CV that every scientist will agree with.

All this boils down to an important point about science that many people don't realize: *The quality of the evidence for any scientific claim depends on the validity and reliability of the operational definitions used to produce the data.* This is why clear communication is so critical to the interpretation and progress of science. If operational definitions are not reliable, the findings cannot be replicated. If they're not valid, the findings won't mean what we think they mean. In other words, proper interpretation of scientific findings requires some awareness of how the science was done.

SKILL CHECK

Table 2.1 shows some more examples of conceptual variables and possible operational definitions. Check the boxes that match your own opinion of each definition. Then think about how you could make each definition more valid or more reliable. This will be good practice for research Applications 2B or 2C.

Table 2.1   Some Examples of Conceptual Variables and Possible Operational Definitions

Conceptual Variable	Operational Definition	How valid is this definition?				How reliable is this definition?				Suggested Improvement to Operational Definition
		not at all	a little	moderately	perfectly	not at all	a little	moderately	perfectly	
Surfing Ability	Average duration of each ride over five rides									
Thrill-Seeking Behavior	Number of roller coaster rides over summer vacation									
Smoking Addiction	Number of cigarettes smoked in one day									
Consumerism	Average number of nonfood items bought per day									

ESSAY 2.3

SURVEYS AND SELF-REPORT DATA

Essay 2.2 introduces the challenge of writing clear operational definitions with good reliability and validity. As we move from measuring behaviors to measuring thoughts and feelings, it doesn't get easier. These things are difficult to observe, but not impossible. In your lecture textbook, you'll read about how cognitive psychologists use clever research techniques to indirectly observe conscious thoughts and feelings, and can even get the unconscious mind to show itself.[4] But these techniques are limited and not without some controversy. The most direct way to get information about thoughts and feelings, as well as behaviors that we can't observe, is to ask the person doing the thinking, feeling, and behaving. Survey research produces *self-report data*: that is, data that come from the point of view of the

---

[4] One controversial measure of subconscious thoughts is the "Implicit Associations Test (IAT)" Proponents of these tests claim that they measure subconscious biases and stereotypical beliefs, and prejudices. Though the evidence for an effect on decision-making is inconsistent, results from these types of studies do appear to reveal hidden biases, even among people who feel very strongly that they have no bias against any particular group. To learn more and take a variety of IAT's, go to "Project Implicit," at implicit.harvard.edu/implicit/takeatest.html

participants in the study, rather than the researcher's point of view.

Although surveys are common in many areas of psychology and economic research, information gathered in this way should be interpreted with caution. Asking a direct question may be easier, but it does not always produce better data. Participants might not tell the truth about their thoughts and feelings, especially when the truth is embarrassing or a lie would feel better and seems harmless. In health psychology, for example, participants might under-report problems to avoid having to undergo testing, or over-report problems to get attention.

Even honest people lie on questionnaires for various reasons, including but not limited to: "helpfulness" (they sometimes report what they think the researcher wants to hear); misplaced humor (they're trying to entertain themselves or the researcher with funny answers rather than the truth), simple human frailty (wanting to feel better about themselves or give the researcher a good impression), or fatigue or carelessness (often in the mistaken belief that the answers don't matter).

In some studies, people are given one or more stories to read, then asked how they would respond if they were in that story, or they might be asked to make decisions for characters in the story. Self-report data from these "vignette studies" can be extremely valuable, particularly in well-designed, true experiments. But again, these data must be interpreted with caution. Some people find it very difficult to imagine themselves in an unreal scenario, and participants might answer in ways that they honestly believe reflect the truth, when in reality, they would react differently.

Socially unacceptable attitudes like sexism and racism are particularly difficult to study with surveys because participants often give socially preferred answers when asked about gender or race, even when their answer is not what they are thinking or feeling. How many people would admit that they disagree with the statement, "Women should receive equal pay for equal work," even if, deep down, they honestly feel that women are not as good at certain jobs as men? And yet, the data show that many women do receive less pay for doing the same job, so some employers must feel that way. The failure to admit to this socially objectionable feeling produces data that reflect a *social desirability bias*: results do not reflect the respondents' true feelings, but instead reflect the feelings society deems "desirable."

The general term *biased* means that the data lean away from the truth about what we are measuring. It's a common misconception that bias only occurs when researchers actively try to lead respondents to answer in a particular way—most of us have seen political questionnaires that are clearly "biased," designed to get predetermined answers, rather than the truth. But bias is not always purposeful, and can describe data that either support or refute the researcher's claims.

Have you ever felt the frustration of trying to answer a multiple-choice question about yourself where none of the answers applied to you? Or two or more answers were equally truthful? Or your answer was "it depends…"? Chances are, those surveys were producing *biased* data. Poorly written questions can lead to data that *accidentally* lean away from the truth. They can support or refute the researcher's claims, but either way, the data are biased simply because they do not reflect the truth. Five common types of biased questions are listed below with examples.

(1) FORCED (LIMITED) CHOICES

Which statement describes your attitude toward children?

   a. Children are always wonderful, well-behaved, and sweet.
   b. Children are always terrible, obnoxious, and mean.

A question with only two choices generally leads to biased data. Assuming adult respondents are about equally drawn to each answer, the data would suggest that 50% of adults think children are always terrible (if true, human population growth would no longer be a problem). The truth about most adults' attitudes probably lies somewhere between one of the two choices. Consider the difference in the final report if we remove the forced choice and ask this question instead:

Which statement describes your attitude toward children?

   a. Children are always wonderful, well-behaved, and sweet.
   b. Children are always terrible, obnoxious, and mean.
   c. Children are sometimes wonderful and sometimes terrible.

Adding the last option would certainly decrease the number of respondents who choose either a or b. Most would probably choose c, and our final report might say that less than 5% or 10% of adults think children are always terrible or always wonderful, rather than 50%. So a question with comprehensive choices, covering all possible responses, leads to better, more accurate data.

(2) LEADING QUESTIONS

We all know that questions with wording designed to influence the respondents' thoughts or feelings can produce biased data. But this influence can be subtle or even unintended. Researchers' own attitudes can accidentally sneak into their questions without notice. For example, below is a survey question I wrote that started out biased. It was edited to remove the bias by removing a leading phrase ("exhaust-free"). Answer it yourself, but do it quickly, without too much thought:

I am happy about the increasing number of clean-air electric cars in the city.

1	2	3	4	5
Strongly Disagree	Disagree	Neutral	Agree	Strongly Agree

Unless you feel strongly about this issue, you probably answered at least a 3, even if you have some reservations about electric cars. Usually, the questions you see on surveys have undergone editing to remove bias, but sometimes, a little remains. It took several re-reads before I realized the question should have been written this way:

I am happy about the increasing number of electric cars in the city.

1	2	3	4	5
Strongly Disagree	Disagree	Neutral	Agree	Strongly Agree

The words, "clean-air" have become so closely associated with electric cars that I had to review the question several times before I noticed that they were leading words. When you're asking for the truth, watch out for adjectives in your question! If the noun can be clearly understood without them, take them out. The second question would provide less biased data on feelings toward electric cars.

(3) MAKING ASSUMPTIONS ABOUT RESPONDERS

What day of the week do you feel sad? _____

This question is biased because it assumes the responder is sad at least one day a week, and therefore traps responders into answering in a way that might not reflect their true thoughts or feelings. An unbiased way to ask the same question would be:

What day of the week, if any, do you feel the saddest? _____

Another example of assumption bias is the classic story of a lawyer cross-examining a witness with the question, "Have you stopped beating your wife yet, yes or no?"

(4) AMBIGUITY/LACK OF CLARITY

When was your first real kiss? _____

"Real" means different things to different people. Responses might vary from "two minutes after I was born," (a kiss from a loving parent), to somewhere in the teenage years (a romantic kiss). The word "when" is also ambiguous. Responses might include "when I fell in love," or "when I was in middle school." If the researcher is looking for the age at which people experience their first romantic kiss, a clearer (less biased) way of asking this question would be:

How old were you when you first kissed someone in a romantic way? _____

(5) COMPLEXITY

Cramming too much information into one question can lead to biased self-report data because the responder doesn't know which part of the question to answer. Consider the following example:

I plan to take the subway instead of driving and install energy-saving lights at home.

1	2	3	4	5
Strongly Disagree	Disagree	Neutral	Agree	Strongly Agree

If the responder agrees with part of the statement but not with the rest, an honest response becomes impossible. The following two questions should replace the one above:

I plan to take the subway instead of driving.

1	2	3	4	5
Strongly Disagree	Disagree	Neutral	Agree	Strongly Agree

I plan to install energy-saving lights at home.

1	2	3	4	5
Strongly Disagree	Disagree	Neutral	Agree	Strongly Agree

In summary, direct questioning is a valuable way to gather data for all kinds of research, including, but not limited to descriptive studies. In surveys, CVs are operationally defined by the questions we ask, and the answers, being from the point of view of the participants, should be interpreted with caution and critical awareness.

SKILL CHECK

In each of the examples of survey questions above, label the conceptual variable being measured and state the operational definition based on the unbiased version of the question(s). Answers in Appendix B.

"This is interesting... 70% of the respondents to our survey said they don't respond to surveys."

MODULE 2 RESEARCH LEARNING OBJECTIVES CHART

STUDY NUMBER	MODULE 2 RESEARCH LEARNING OBJECTIVES	BEFORE READING					AFTER DOING PROJECT			
		I don't know how **1**	I know a little about this **2**	I know enough about this to guess correctly **3**	I know how to do this and/ or have already done it. **4**		I don't know how **1**	I know a little about this **2**	I know enough about this to guess correctly **3**	I know how to do this and/ or have already done it. **4**
2A	Identify different types of research from summaries.									
2A	Given a research summary, identify the conceptual variables and their operational definitions.									
2A 2B 2C 2D	Discuss and improve the validity and reliability of operational definitions in published research (2A), in naturalistic observation (2B/2C), and in surveys (2D).									
2B	Considering college student behavior on campus, decide on your own conceptual variable and write a naturalistic operational definition for it.									
2B 2C	Create a logical, systematic, clear observational data collection sheet.									
2B 2C	Identify and clearly express the relevant details of your research method, including participants, materials, and procedure.									

		I don't know how 1	I know a little about this 2	I know enough about this to guess correctly 3	I know how to do this and/or have already done it. 4		I don't know how 1	I know a little about this 2	I know enough about this to guess correctly 3	I know how to do this and/or have already done it. 4
2D	Gain experience writing unbiased and biased survey questions and comparing them.									
2D	Witness differences in data due to intentional bias in survey questions.									

Now read about the project to prepare for lab. For any scores less than "4," keep those questions in mind as you complete the research project(s) Do not do the white half of this chart until after you've completed the assigned research project(s).

STUDY 2A

IDENTIFYING CVs AND OPERATIONAL DEFINITIONS IN PUBLISHED RESEARCH

Essay 2.2 reminds us that as consumers of science, we should be aware of the differences between conceptual variables and their operational definitions.

Imagine a survey researcher reports that she observed a high rate of enthusiasm for rock concerts in her community. When reading her methodology, we discover that she measured enthusiasm by counting the number of rock concerts in the month of December at every venue within 50 miles of the community. Is that a valid definition of enthusiasm for rock concerts (does *attendance* at those concerts matter)? Is it reliable (would the same "enthusiasm" occur if concerts were counted for May or June)? Could the operational definition be more reliable if concerts were counted for several months or a year?

In this project, you'll read about published research in psychology and try to identify the conceptual variables and their operational definitions. You'll be asked to consider the validity and reliability of these definitions and think about ways to improve them. It's also a good opportunity to practice identifying different types of research based on their method and the ideas they're testing, if any. You'll see one or more examples of four of the five types of research introduced in Module 1: descriptive, correlational, experimental, and quasi-experimental. Why won't you see an example of exploratory research with a conceptual variable and clear operational definition? If you're not sure, revisit Essay 1.2 (the answer is in Appendix B).

PROCEDURE 2A

SUMMARIES OF PUBLISHED RESEARCH

Read each of the four numbered research summaries below and answer the corresponding questions on the worksheet.

1. Previous studies (e.g., Coulter et al., 2018; Marshal et al., 2008) suggest that the LGBTQ (lesbian, gay, bisexual, transgender, queer) population experiences unusually high levels of substance abuse compared to the general population. To better understand why, **Puhl et al. (2019)** tested the relationships between substance abuse and several other specific social stressors in a sample of 9,838 LGBTQ teens. One primary variable of interest was "Weight-Based Victimization," or "WBV," which they measured in three ways: (1) "Have you ever been teased or made fun of by members of your family because of your body weight?" (yes or no) (2) "Have you ever been teased or made fun of by your peers because of your weight ?" (yes or no), and (3) How frequently were you "treated badly or teased by other students at school because of your weight?" This was answered on a 5-point scale from 0 (never) to 4 (very often). Substance abuse was measured using selected items from the Youth Risk Behavior Survey, including "... how many days in the past 30 days they had at least one alcoholic drink, five or more alcoholic drinks, used marijuana, and/or smoked cigarettes." A 7-point scale was provided, ranging from 1 (0 days) to 7 (all 30 days). Further coding of the responses was used (see the original article), but for this exercise, we'll stop there. The authors reported, "WBV was associated with increased odds of alcohol use, binge drinking, marijuana use, and cigarette use."

2. **Cramer et al. (2007)** examined the use of cell phones by college students while driving. Data collection took place in 2005 on a large university campus, where about 90% of nearly 30,000 students commuted to campus in privately owned cars, and the parking areas for students were separated from other parking and had their own exits. Trained observers watched college students leaving campus parking lots and recorded the drivers' apparent gender and use of a hand-held cell phone while driving, among other things. Out of 3,609 drivers in the final data set, 11% were using a hand-held phone while driving. Of those recorded as female ($n = 2,139$), 12.9% were using the phone, and of those recorded as male ($n = 1,470$), 8.6% were using the phone.

3. **James et al., (2018)** studied the effects of habitual caffeine consumption on cardiovascular responses to stress in a sample of 333 teenagers between 14 and 19 years of age. Participants responded to a question about how many glasses of each type of caffeinated beverage they drank per day, and their responses were converted to mg caffeine based on the types of drinks and their typical caffeine content. They were then placed into three groups based on caffeine consumption: low (less than 20 mg per day), moderate (between 20 and 120 mg per day), and high (greater than 120 mg). Among other things, cardiac output and peripheral resistance (pressure needed to push through arteries) were then measured as participants underwent psychosocially stressful conditions, including an on-camera mock job interview and a verbal math test. Those in the high caffeine consumption group showed slightly lower cardiac output and significantly higher peripheral resistance than those in the low or moderate caffeine consumption groups. Increased peripheral resistance may contribute to poor cardiovascular health later in life.

4. **Eskine et al., (2011)** tested the idea that "gustatory disgust" (having a bad taste in one's mouth) influences perceptions of moral behavior. While drinking liquid that was either bitter (Swedish bitters), or sweet (berry punch), or neutral (water), participants read stories about people engaged in socially unacceptable behavior, such as a student stealing a library book and a politician taking a bribe. After each story, they rated the immorality of the behavior on a scale from 1 to 100, with higher scores indicating greater perceived immorality. The researchers compared the average immorality ratings given by people who consumed each type of liquid, and found that those who drank the bitter liquid gave higher immorality ratings than those who drank the sweet or neutral liquids.[5]

---

[5] Ghelfi, et al. (2020) were unable to replicate this finding using a much larger sample across multiple labs.

LAB RECORD WORKSHEET FOR STUDY 2A
IDENTIFYING CVs AND OPERATIONAL DEFINITIONS IN PUBLISHED RESEARCH

Part 1: Identify the type of research, the CVs, and their operational definitions.

Puhl et al., (2019): What type of research is this? (circle one)

Descriptive   Correlational   Experimental   Quasi-Experimental

There are two major CVs in this study. What are they?

1. _____

2. _____

Briefly describe the operational definitions of those two CVs.

1. _____

2. _____

Cramer et al., (2007): What type of research was this? (circle one)

Descriptive   Correlational   Experimental   Quasi-Experimental

What was the primary CV of interest? _____

What was its operational definition?_____

_____

James et al. (2018): What type of research is this? (circle one)

Descriptive   Correlational   Experimental   Quasi-Experimental

There are two CVs in this study. One (the cause) is claimed to influence the other (effect).

Name the causal CV _____

Name the affected CV _____

Operational definition of the causal CV (how were the groups different?). _____

_____

_____

Operational definition of the affected CV (how was the effect of the difference measured?). _____

_____

Eskine et al., (2011): What type of research is this? (circle one)

Descriptive   Correlational   Experimental   Quasi-Experimental

There are two CVs in this study. One (the cause) is claimed to influence the other (effect).

Name the causal CV _____

Name the affected CV _____

Operational definition of the causal CV (how were the groups different?). _____

_____

Operational definition of the affected CV (how was the effect of the difference measured?). _____

_____

_____

Part 2: Critical thinking about validity and reliability: Choose ONE CV from each study.

1. **Puhl et al., (2019):** Chosen CV: _____

   Do you think the operational definition was *valid*? Circle your answer: Yes   No

   Why or why not? _____

   _____

   Do you think the operational definition was *reliable*? Circle your answer: Yes   No

   Why or why not? _____

   _____

2. **Cramer et al., (2007):** Chosen CV: _____

   Do you think the operational definition was *valid*? Circle your answer: Yes   No

   Why or why not? _____

   _____

   Do you think the operational definition was *reliable*? Circle your answer: Yes   No

   Why or why not? _____

   _____

3. **James et al. (2018):** Chosen CV: _____

   Do you think the operational definition was *valid*? Circle your answer: Yes   No

   Why or why not? _____

   _____

   Do you think the operational definition was *reliable*? Circle your answer: Yes   No

   Why or why not? _____

   _____

4. **Eskine et al., (2011):** Chosen CV: _____

   Do you think the operational definition was *valid*? Circle your answer: Yes   No

   Why or why not? _____

   _____

   Do you think the operational definition was *reliable*? Circle your answer: Yes   No

   Why or why not? _____

   _____

STUDY 2B

NATURALISTIC OBSERVATION OF COLLEGE STUDENTS

For this research project, you and a partner will decide on a conceptual variable that can be studied naturalistically on campus. For the observation to be naturalistic, your CV must be identified and measured without interfering in what you are observing. You'll write a naturalistic operational definition of the variable and get some experience trying to apply it with a data collection sheet you design. The experience you gain from your observations will help you improve the validity and reliability of your definition.

Depending on your course schedule and goals, you will then either summarize your data and report them to others in your lab for discussion, or wait until you've read Module 3 on types of data and how to summarize them, and then summarize the data from this study using what you learn from Module 3. Your instructor will let you know which approach to take.

When this research is done, you can use the data you collected to generate testable ideas (hypotheses) that could explain your observations or relate them to other observations. Module 3 provides more information on summarizing data and generating hypotheses.

Image © Yuriy Rudyy/Shutterstock.com

HOW TO CHOOSE A CV AND WRITE A NATURALISTIC OPERATIONAL DEFINITION

Think for a moment about all the things people might be doing on campus while you are in psych lab. For example, depending on the weather and the time of day, they might be eating, studying, driving, walking, slack-lining, or having a snowball fight. Think also about the characteristics of students on campus. They might be dressed up or wearing pajama pants; prepared for the weather or not; wearing school logos or not. They might appear in a hurry or not; attentive to their surroundings or not... etc.

To do this research, you'll have to decide on what you want to study. That will be your conceptual variable, and it must be a noun or noun-phrase that can vary across individuals, over time, or in different places. For example, the CV for "studying" would be "studying behavior." For dressed up or dressed down, it might be "clothing appearance." The point is, you will be observing some*thing*, so you should express it as a noun or noun-phrase. For naturalistic research, the variability must be identifiable or measurable without interference.

You must also consider the ethics of your observations and be sure to adhere to strict ethical guidelines, which require that we do not cause potential stress to others without the consent of the person being observed. Asking people for permission to watch them would obviously interfere with their behavior, so your study would not be naturalistic if you have to ask for consent.

Because you will not have the consent of the observed, it is therefore your responsibility as a researcher to make sure you do not cause any stress. This means you may not observe behaviors that are personal (like bathroom behavior), or stress people out by noticeably watching them for any longer than about 5 to 10 seconds, depending on the situation and whether or not your own behavior, as an observer, is noticeable.

To decide on a conceptual variable (CV), it might help to brainstorm (with your research partner) a list of common behaviors for the time of day, then choose something from the list. Your CV can also be some characteristic of a more general behavior. For example, you might have "eating behavior" on your list, but if you think a little deeper, there are several aspects of eating that can be described separately, like hunger, haste, nutritional awareness, or social interaction while eating. These can be operationally defined by the amount eaten or purchased, the number of chews per bite, the proportion of healthy foods on the plate, or the amount of time spent talking versus eating, respectively.

Writing an operational definition for your CV is more challenging. Four pieces of advice:

1) Make sure it is something that can be directly observed, not inferred. For example, an operational definition of studiousness might be the number of books each person brings into the library, or number of times each person looks away from their book during a 10-second period (people who are studying can be watched for a little longer than others, as they are less likely to notice). While it may seem more valid to measure the amount being learned, that is not directly observable without interference, and is therefore not a good naturalistic operational definition. (If you were allowed to use a survey or analog observation for this study, the amount learned while studying would probably be a more valid definition of studiousness than your naturalistic operational definition).

2) The observations you plan to make must be stated in quantifiable terms. Note the difference between "looking away from work" and "the number of times people look away from their work." Or compare "people looking away from work" to "the number of people who look away from work." Which definition gives the reader the clearest indication of what you would observe, count and record? Also consider which is the better indicator of any particular behavioral characteristic of individuals: Measuring the characteristic itself in multiple individuals, or counting the number of people who show the characteristic? When the behavior of interest can be directly measured, it is preferable to do that, rather than to count people, because each person may display any level of the behavior.

3) Don't expect your operational definition to be perfect. It must match, as well as possible, the conceptual variable, but there will inevitably be complications. There may be aspects of the CV that are not captured by your definition. For example, sometimes studiousness does not involve books. But if you expand your

definition to include those studying on computers, it might become difficult to determine whether students are studying or web-surfing. Your definition should be like a net that captures as much as you can of the meaning of the conceptual variable, without catching a lot of other stuff that has nothing to do with your CV.

4) For maximum reliability of your definition, remove all ambiguity. The fewer different ways a definition can be interpreted, the more reliable it will be. For instance, consider trying to apply this definition of attention to surroundings: "the number of times each person looks up while walking across campus." "Across campus" will mean different things to different people. Instead, be specific: "the number of times each person looks up while walking from the library steps to the bus stop." Anyone who does not take this path would not be counted, but for those who do, the measurement would be more reliable. Leaving definitions open to interpretation decreases reliability.

IMPORTANT: *You should not make predictions* about what you will observe. You can (and should) record other data that are of interest to you and might be related to your conceptual variable, like the apparent gender identity of each person you observe, or their location while being observed, or whether they had their phones out or were wearing backpacks (even if that is not your CV). But remember that you are not setting out to test relationships, so you should not even predict that relationships exist. The goal of descriptive research is to *describe* as objectively as possible. Having a specific prediction may bias the way you observe (more on that in other Modules).

PROCEDURE 2B

This will be a naturalistic observational study of college students. More information on how and when to summarize the data you collect will be provided by your lab instructor.

1. You and a partner will agree upon a conceptual variable of interest, and each of you will independently write an operational definition for that variable.

2. Get together and discuss your operational definitions, decide on your best, and revise as needed using the advice described on the previous pages. Remember that you can NOT interact in any way with the people you observe (e.g., smiling or saying hello to see how friendly they are would not be *naturalistic* observation). Once you have agreed on a CV and its operational definition, turn to the lab record worksheet for Studies 2B/2C, located after the procedure for Study 2C.

3. Discuss where and how the conceptual variable can be measured using your definition. You should have answers to these questions before you seek approval of your project:
   - Location for your observations? (Be precise—where will you stand/sit?)
   - Participants? (How will you decide who should be included and excluded?)
   - How will you avoid being noticed while observing and/or recording?

4. Design a data collection sheet, being sure to include these important elements: (1) Date and Time of Day, (2) Location, (3) Names of Observers, (4) Conceptual Variable, (5) Operational Definition, (6) A table for checking off or writing down *quick symbols* to record your observations, and (7) (if you use symbols that are not obvious) include a key somewhere on the datasheet. **Sample data sheets are shown in Figure 2.4.**

5. Upon approval of your data sheet by your instructor, leave the classroom to make your observations as a pair. Pay close attention to your assigned return time and make sure you are back in lab on time. You may travel anywhere within a 5-minute walking radius. The total length of time for your observations will be given to you when your work is approved (usually about 25 to 30 minutes).

6. When you return from your observations, complete the first part of your lab record worksheet, up to the dotted line. Fill in all relevant details of your data collection *procedure*, as indicated on the lab record worksheet. Go back to the participants section of the worksheet and fill in relevant information from your observations (include the number and general description of the people you observed).

7. Check with your instructor regarding whether you should (a) summarize your data and complete the rest of the lab record worksheet (beyond the dotted line), or (b) wait to complete the rest of your lab record worksheet until after reading Module 3 on how to summarize data.

A

Time: 3:15 pm to 3:45 pm   Date: Sept 4, 2017
Observer Names: Shelly Scientist, Robin Researcher
Location: Lafayette College "Quad" (in front of Fannon)
Conceptual Variable: Extroversion
Defined as: For people who are walking alone, the number and type of social interactions they have with other people who walk within sight and within 10 feet from them (other pedestrians).

Subject #	Apparent Gender		Behavior (✓ = yes)				
	Subject	Pedestrian	Smile	Wave	Words	Contact	None
1	M	M		✓			
2	F	F	✓		✓		
3	F	F					✓
4	F	M	✓				
5	M	M				✓	
6	M	F	✓				
⋮	⋮	⋮					
⋁	⋁	⋁					

B

Time: 3:10 to 3:40pm   Date: Jan 30, 2018
Observer Names: Steve Scientist, Rick Researcher
            (no relation to Shelly or Robin)
Location: Lafayette College Early Learning Center
Conceptual Variable: Parental Affection
Defined as: Duration of parent-child hugs, hand-holds, or hand-resting-on-child contact over 10-second observation periods.

Parent-child Pair #	Apparent Gender		Seconds of Contact (out of 10 sec.)			
	Parent	Child	Hug	Hand-Hold	Hand-Resting	None
1	F	F	8		0	2
2	F	M		6	2	2
3	M	M	6			4
4	F	M			3	7
5	F	M			5	5
6	M	F				10
7	M	M	3	2		5
⋮	⋮	⋮				
⋁	⋁	⋁				

Figure 2.4   Sample data collection sheets for naturalistic observation measuring extraversion (A) and parental affection (B). Some information may seem redundant with the lab record worksheet, but this is necessary in case the data sheet and lab record get separated. A data collection sheet may be rendered useless if it doesn't include the CV and operational definition, time, date, location, and observers.

STUDY 2C

NATURALISTIC OBSERVATION: APPLYING AND REFINING OPERATIONAL DEFINITIONS

Writing a good operational definition takes time, particularly if you've never done it before. A good way to decrease that first-time stress is to try applying someone else's operational definition and then try to improve that definition based on your experience using it. For this application, your instructor will provide a conceptual variable along with a few operational definitions. As a pair, you will choose your operational definition from among those provided, then go out on campus for 25 to 30 minutes to measure your conceptual variable using your chosen definition. When you return, you'll reflect on how to improve its validity.

PROCEDURE 2C

1. Your instructor will assign a conceptual variable and a few operational definitions to choose from. As a pair, choose one of the definitions to use.
2. Copy the CV and its operational definition verbatim onto the lab record worksheet for study 2B/2C, which starts on the next page.
3. Continue with steps 3 through 7 for Procedure 2B.

Image © Cartoonresource/Shutterstock

"I have this creepy feeling that I'm being observed."

LAB RECORD WORKSHEET FOR STUDY 2B OR 2C
NATURALISTIC OBSERVATION

Name: _____ Partner's Full Name: _____

A complete LAB RECORD is NEEDED when you have to write a LAB REPORT!

LAB RECORD: A full set of research notes, including everything described in brackets on the left side of this worksheet.	LAB REPORT: A *formal* communication of your research and how it fits into the big picture. You will not write a lab report on this research, but the brackets on the right illustrate where all of the lab record information would appear in a lab report.

Purpose

Purpose: *To identify a conceptual variable of interest, design a way of measuring/observing it in a naturalistic setting, report and evaluate our results.*

Combine with background literature, rationale, hypothesis (if there is one) and study design to write **Introduction**

Variable(s)

Conceptual Variable (CV): _____

Operational Definition: _____

_____

_____

Participants (general descriptions of the people you observed, including all characteristics relevant to your conceptual variable, plus number and approximate age of participants):

Subjects

_____

_____

Materials (only describe things that are NOT obvious. Pencil, paper, data sheet are obvious):

Materials

_____

_____

Procedure for data collection: Be thorough and specific! For example, where did you go? How many observers? How long did you observe (each person?) (in total?)? What day/ time? How did you keep from being noticed? How did you decide whom to observe? Exactly what did you record and how? Were there any ambiguous or unclear measurements? How did you decide whether to count them (or how to count them?) Try to describe **_all relevant aspects_** of your observation. _____

Method Section

_____

_____

Procedure

_____

If necessary, use an extra sheet of your own lined paper to complete the Procedure section. THEN STOP HERE. Follow instructions given by your instructor regarding when to do the next page. _____

Data Handling

Data handling: Describe how you will summarize the data you collected. Will you calculate totals? (Total of what?) Percentages? (Percent of what? Out of what total?) Means? (What will you average?). The calculations you describe will produce the numbers in the Results section. For example, "*We will calculate the percent of people on their phones out of all people observed.*" Notice: There are no numbers in that example, and there should be no numbers in your answer here... It is a description of HOW you will calculate your results from the data you collected, not what results you got. _____

_____

_____

Second variable of interest: What other variable will you use to summarize the data and how? For example, "*We will then categorize people as either carrying or not carrying a backpack and calculate the percent on their phones out of the total number of people in each category.*" Again, no numbers, just a description of what you plan to do with your numbers:

_____

_____

Results

Results: Write the summary of the data (answers to the calculations you described in the data handling section). Use <u>sentences</u> <u>with numbers in them</u> to *meaningfully* summarize the data. Report on your conceptual variable first; then write the results for your second variable of interest. _____

_____

_____

Breakdown based on a second variable: _____

_____

_____

Discussion

Discussion: Rate the validity of your operational definition and explain your answer:

1	2	3	4	5
Not at all Valid	A little Valid	Somewhat Valid	Mostly Valid	Perfectly Valid

Why did you choose that rating? _____

_____

Write a new operational definition of your CV that is *more valid*. It does NOT have to be naturalistic! It might be more valid if it is *not* naturalistic! If the increased validity is not very clear in your new definition, explain it.

_____

_____

Write a testable hypothesis about **your CV**. Use the information in Essay 3.5 to help. Your hypothesis may be correlational or cause-and-effect. It should be a logical idea that can be tested. Reading the examples in the box in Essay 3.5 will make this a lot easier!

STUDY 2D

WRITING SURVEY QUESTIONS AND VISUALIZING BIAS IN SELF-REPORT DATA

Designing good, unbiased questions is a skill that comes with practice. The purpose of the following research application is to provide an opportunity for you to learn about your classmates and to practice designing questions and gathering and summarizing descriptive survey data, and to see how the wording of questions can influence final reports. This project is based on the information in Essay 2.3.

PROCEDURE 2D

1. The class will discuss and decide on several topics of interest to most students. Examples might be environmentalism, study habits, athleticism, or music-listening preferences.

2. The class will break up into groups. Each group will be assigned a topic and asked to come up with an unbiased question on the topic. The questions may be open-ended (one-or two-word answers only) multiple choice, Likert-type (questions that provide a scale, e.g., from 1 to 5, where 1 = strongly disagree and 5 = strongly agree), or any other type. Questions should be handed in immediately upon completion.

3. The group will then be randomly assigned a type of bias from the list of five types in Essay 2.3, and asked to rewrite their original question in a way that exemplifies that type of bias. It must be a question measuring the SAME conceptual variable as your original, unbiased question. This will work best if it is as similar as possible to the original, except for the bias. When it's complete, hand it in immediately.

4. Your instructor will type all the questions into a single questionnaire that will be made available to all students, either on paper or electronically.

5. All students will answer the questions anonymously, and summary statistics will be computed either instantly or for the next week's lab.

MODULE 2 GLOSSARY OF TERMS AND EXAMPLES

Analog Observation: Observational research done in a laboratory setting.

    Example: Gibson and Walk's (1960) visual cliff was a laboratory apparatus used to measure the ability to detect depth. It was used to test the depth perception of many animals, and eventually to test human babies to determine the age at which depth perception develops. Another good example of analog observation is a study by Skolnick and Bloom (2006) titled, "What does Batman think about Spongebob?" They examined children's understanding of reality and fantasy by asking them questions about how fantasy characters perceive each other, within and between fantasy worlds. This resembles survey research, but is better described as analog observation because they talked with the children and showed them cards with images to identify which characters they knew, and then questioned them about how those characters would interact. Surveys would involve asking all participants the exact same set of questions to collect data.

    Where to find this term: Essay 2.1, Fig. 2.3, Study 2B

Biased: Reflecting something other than the best measure or estimate of the truth; leaning or leading away from the truth. A biased question causes the responder to give an answer that does not reflect his or her true thoughts or feelings, whether intentionally or not.

    Examples: Biased marketing researchers tend to write biased questions about the products they represent to get higher ratings of those products from consumers. As an exaggerated example, "To what extent do you agree with the statement that this beautiful, wonderful, life-saving product is worth buying for this super-low price?" Another example of bias is this limited choice political question, "Do you agree with this candidate's policies, yes or no?" The truth is more likely to be "some of them."

    Where to find this term: Essay 2.3, Study 2D

Case Study: In-depth research focusing on one entity (e.g., one person, one family, one social organization, one animal, one business) that usually has some interesting or unusual characteristic.

    Example: H.M. was a patient who underwent brain surgery to remove certain areas of his brain as a treatment for severe epilepsy. The epilepsy was cured, but he displayed fascinating changes in his memory functions, which were studied intensely for many years after the surgery. He died in 2008, at which point his real name was revealed. Read more about him online by typing this article title into your search bar: "H. M., an Unforgettable Amnesiac, Dies at 82"

    Where to find this term: Essay 2.1, Fig. 2.3

Conceptual variable (CV): Something of interest, such as an event, characteristic or behavior, singled out for study. CVs are usually given broad labels that can mean slightly different things to different people.

    Examples: anger, height, quality of education, happiness, intelligence, friendliness…

    Where to find this term: Essays 2.2, 2.3, Studies 2A, 2B, 2C, and most other studies in this book.

Data Handling: Describes *how* the data were summarized (not the actual data, but what you did with them in order to summarize them).

    Examples: Assume you measured anger by counting the number of times people shouted.

    - If you simply counted frequency of shouting, your data handling would say that you "calculated the total number of times the behavior occurred during the observation period," or, "reported the sum of all instances of shouting."
    - If you wanted to report the prevalence of shouting, your data handling would say that you "calculated the proportion [or percent] of students who shouted out of all those observed." To report proportion, you divide the number of participants who shouted by the total number of participants observed, and to get percent, multiply that by 100.
    - If you quantified certain aspects of a variable, such as durations, distances or sizes, you will most likely compute an average (or "mean"). For example, "we calculated the mean duration of the shouts."

    Where to find this term: Lab Record for Studies 2B or 2C

Descriptive Research: A study that measures or identifies one or more conceptual variables with the goal of describing it (them) in some useful way. Descriptive research can be an observational study, survey, or case study.

> *Examples:* User data from social media sites describes the number of hours they spend on the apps (analog observation if participants give consent to let researchers look at their phones, naturalistic observation if researchers have access to user data without users' knowledge). A marketing survey describes customer attitudes toward a particular product (survey). A clinician describes an interesting patient in great detail (case study).
>
> *Where to find this term:* Essays 2.1, 2.2, 2.3, Fig. 2.1, 2.2, 2.3, Studies 2A, 2B, 2C, 2D.

Duration Data: Numbers that describe how long something lasts from beginning to end.

> *Examples:* Studies of drug effects often consider the duration of those effects. Studies of social media habits often describe the duration of app use.
>
> *Where to find this term:* Essay 2.2

Frequency Data: Numbers that describe how often something occurs in a given period of time.

> *Example:* Clinicians often attempt to modify undesired behaviors using frequency data. They monitor how often a person engages in an undesired behavior over a given period of time, such as the number of cigarettes smoked per day, to observe the effects of therapy on smoking behavior. Keeping track of frequency data during smoking cessation therapy can help determine the effectiveness of the therapy.
>
> *Where to find this term:* Essay 2.2

Naturalistic Observation: Research that observes behaviors or events in their natural settings, without interference or manipulation.

> *Examples:* Most field studies of animals start with naturalistic observation, as researchers sit quietly and observe animal behavior, recording the frequencies of carefully defined behaviors without interference in order to learn about the natural behavior of the animal. People-watching at an airport *could* be naturalistic observation if certain conceptual variables were first operationally defined and then counted or measured, such as hugging behavior, sign-holding behavior, or restroom-searching.
>
> *Where to find this term:* Essay 2.1, Fig. 2.3, Studies 2B and 2C

Operational Definition: A way of defining a conceptual variable so that it can be identified and/or measured. Or, defining a variable in terms of the operations used to identify and/or measure it.

> *Examples:* Anger might be operationally defined as…
>
> 1) a furrowed brow combined with tight pressing together of the lips in a straight line or the corners of the mouth angled downward.
>
> 2) any instance of yelling directed at another person or object.
>
> 3) for an operational definition of alien anger, see Essay 2.2.
>
> *Where to find this term:* Essays 2.2, 2.3, Studies 2A, 2B, 2C, 2D, and most other studies in this book.

Observational Descriptive Study: A type of research designed to describe some conceptual variable from the point of view of an observer, by systematically observing it. The variable can be observed as it exists in nature (*naturalistic observation*) or in a laboratory setting (*analog observation*).

> *Examples:* See *Naturalistic Observation* and *Analog Observation*
>
> *Where to find this term:* Essay 2.1, Fig. 2.3

Prevalence Data: Numbers that represent how many times a behavior or event happens out of all the possible times it could happen.

> *Example:* Beaver and Barnes (2012) counted drunk driving convictions among people who had twins who had also been convicted of drunk driving, and found that having an identical twin who had already been convicted of drunk driving was associated with a higher prevalence of drunk driving convictions than having a previously convicted fraternal twin.
>
> *Where to find this term:* Essay 2.2

Reliability: The consistency with which an operational definition can be applied by different observers and/or at different times. Reliable definitions are clear and unambiguous. To improve the reliability of an operational definition, ask yourself, "How can I remove any ambiguity from this definition?"

   Examples: A reliable operational definition of a smile might be "curving the corners of the mouth upward." By this definition, a smile is easily identified and fairly unambiguous. A less reliable operational definition of smiling might be "the expression of pleasure." There are as many ways to interpret this definition as there are ways to express pleasure, only some of which involve smiling (e.g., clapping and even crying tears of joy).
   Where to find this term: Essays 2.2, 2.3, Studies 2A, 2B, 2C

Results: The *summarized version* of the data. This does *not* include **raw data** (see Module 3 glossary) unless they are being used to stress a point or as an example. Results are obtained from procedures described in the **data handling** section of a lab record or lab report. Results should be reported in full sentences that summarize what was observed using numbers. See Module 3 for more information.

   Example (correct): "Of the participants observed ($N = 43$), 20% shouted at least once during the 30-minute observation period."
   NOT an Example (incorrect): "Participant 1 shouted once. Participant 2 did not shout. Participant 3 shouted…" (These statements report "raw data," not Results, and should not be included in the Results unless they are used to stress a point or as an example.)
   Where to find this term: Lab Record for Studies 2B, 2C, and most other Lab Records in this book.

Self-Report Data: Numbers or information gathered from the point of view of the participant in a study, rather than from the researcher's observations. Usually collected using a questionnaire or interview.

   Examples: The answers to these two questions would produce self-report data:
   1) Please state your age, in years: _____ .
   2) Do you feel informed right now? (circle one): Yes   No   Not Sure
   Where to find this term: Essays 2.1, 2.3, Study 2D

Social Desirability Bias: The under-reporting of socially unacceptable attitudes and behaviors based on self-report data due to the tendency of responders to choose socially acceptable or preferred (desirable) answers to questions.

   Example: Voter exit polls can reflect social desirability bias, particularly if opposition to an idea or a candidate has been kept quiet due to threats or fear of retaliation.
   Where to find this term: Essay 2.3

Systematic: Having a clearly defined plan or system for completing a task (see Systematic Observation, Module 1 Glossary).

   Examples (systematic): Exploration of solar storms by observing the sun at regular intervals and measuring size and temperature of sunspots; Description of parent–child attachments by observing specifically defined behaviors indicating attachment or lack of attachment; Comparing GPA from college records with number of high school math classes taken, from high school transcripts; Studying the effects of money on ratings of happiness by giving precise amounts of money and surveying mood.
   Examples (NOT systematic): People-watching without a plan. Birdwatching without a plan or guide. Trying to recall something you saw a while ago, but really can't remember well. Doing a so-called "experiment" where you just try something new without background knowledge, plans or predictions. Note that while this is a perfectly acceptable common use of the word "experiment," it is not the correct scientific meaning.
   Where to find this term: Essay 2.1, Studies 2B, 2C

Validity: The *accuracy* of an operational definition as a measurement of a conceptual variable. A valid operational definition is one that captures the actual meaning of the conceptual variable. To improve the validity of an operational definition, ask yourself, "What can I do to make a better match between what I am trying to measure and what I am actually measuring?"

Examples: If the conceptual variable is intelligence, a valid operational definition might be "the average speed with which a person solves 10 puzzles testing logic, spatial, and mathematical reasoning." A less valid operational definition might be "average speed with which a person adds, subtracts, multiplies and divides 10 random pairs of single digits." Note that both definitions are very specific and would probably yield fairly consistent results for any one person at different times (that is, both are *reliable*), but the first is probably more *valid* because it does a better job of capturing the actual meaning of intelligence, which is more than just speed in arithmetic.

Where to find this term: Essay 2.2, Studies 2A, 2B, 2C

Variable: Anything that differs, changes or can be made to change.

Examples: Color of the sky (during sunset, cloudy, etc.); age; environmentalism (from person to person or over time); the color of carpeting (from room to room or over the years); Presidents; Ice cream flavors; Activity; TV programming; Netflix charges; Exercise; Gym equipment; Clothing; Pixar movies; Toe nail clippers (and clippings); Dinner menus; Airplane ticket prices; How much you miss home; How boring you find this list of examples; How much you love your pets; How many pets you have... (This list could go on forever.)

Where to find this term: Essays 2.1, 2.2, 2.3, Studies 2A, 2B, 2C, 2D, and most of the rest of this book.

Module 3
Summarizing Data and Generating Hypotheses

MODULE 3 LEARNING OBJECTIVES CHART

ESSAY NUMBER	MODULE 3 ESSAY LEARNING OBJECTIVES	BEFORE READING				AFTER READING			
		I don't know how 1	I know a little about this 2	I know enough about this to guess correctly 3	I know how to do this and/or have already done it. 4	I don't know how 1	I know a little about this 2	I know enough about this to guess correctly 3	I know how to do this and/or have already done it. 4
3.1	Provide two examples of "raw data"								
3.1	Define and give examples of a research sample and a research population.								
3.1	Given a description of how data were collected, label the sample as a convenience sample or a random sample and explain why.								
3.2	Correctly identify examples of categorical, ordinal, interval, and ratio data.								
3.2	Give an example of a Likert Scale question.								
3.2	Explain the differences in the amount of information provided by nominal, ordinal, interval, and ratio data.								
3.2 3.3	Given a type of data (nominal, ordinal, interval or ratio), describe one good way to summarize the data.								
3.3	When summarizing interval or ratio data, explain when it is best to use a mean and when one should use a median.								
3.3	Describe two ways of expressing how much the scores vary in an interval or ratio data set.								

		I don't know how **1**	I know a little about this **2**	I know enough about this to guess correctly **3**	I know how to do this and/ or have already done it. **4**		I don't know how **1**	I know a little about this **2**	I know enough about this to guess correctly **3**	I know how to do this and/ or have already done it. **4**
3.4	Enter and sort data and calculate means and SDs using MS Excel or Google Sheets.									
3.5	Define the word "hypothesis."									
3.5	Explain why descriptive data that lead to a new hypothesis cannot be used as evidence for that hypothesis.									
3.5	Explain the difference between a correlational and a cause-and-effect hypothesis and provide an example of each.									
		Read the assigned essays and actively seek answers to any questions rated less than "4." Then return to this chart and complete the white half.					Now proceed to the chart for the applications section, read the objectives for your assigned research project, and complete the gray side of that chart.			

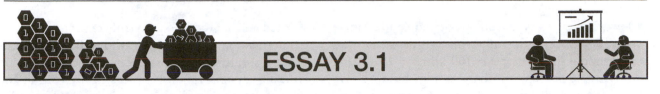

FROM RAW DATA TO MEANINGFUL SUMMARIES

Every scientific endeavor is an attempt to better understand the truth about the natural, physical world (or universe). In psychology, the reason we make observations is to determine the truth about the mind and behavior. Multiple observations are needed because they will be a better representation of the truth than just one observation. But it would be confusing and overwhelming to present data from multiple observations individually. Instead, data must be summarized into a concise, understandable statement that accurately reflects the meaning of all the data.

If you collected data as directed in Application 2B, 2C, or 2D, those check-marks or numbers or answers to survey questions were an attempt to describe the truth about some conceptual variable (CV). That information is called *raw data*, the numbers directly produced by observations (and survey responses). The data may eventually be used to generate testable ideas (hypotheses) describing or explaining relationships between the things we observed, but before that can happen, the raw data must be summarized in an accurate and meaningful way. This module will present an introduction to the process of raw data handling.

This will not be an exhaustive list of all the ways that data can be summarized. Instead, we will focus on the basic information and skills needed to meaningfully summarize a small data set. We will then see how a data summary can lead to a hypothesis and define two types of hypotheses that differ in how they are tested. Although you might use your descriptive data from Module 2 to learn terms and practice skills, it is important to keep in mind that these basic data-handling skills are also necessary in all other types of research covered in this course. A basic understanding of these terms and procedures is increasingly valuable in our data-driven culture.

When summarizing and reporting data, the goal is to clearly express as much *relevant, meaningful* information as you can regarding your observations with as few words and numbers as possible. It's important to think about what the reader needs to know to critically evaluate your report. Missing important details can render a data summary nearly useless. Consider this report:

> *Over a 30-min period, we observed 15 people using their cell phones as they walked across campus.*

The first problem is that there is no meaningful context in which to consider the number 15. Is that a lot of people using cell phones for a 30-min period? If 150 people were walking across campus, seeing only 15 with cell phones suggests that they are not commonly in use (only 10% of those observed had phones). If just 15 people walked across campus during those 30 min, then 100% were using phones. Switching to percentage would improve the report, but still leaves out important information:

> *Over a 30-min period, we observed that 10% of people walking across campus were using their cell phones.*

Does that tell you everything you need to know? If you don't see what's missing, consider a different example:

> *Over a 30-min period, 100% of the people observed in a gym were walking with a limp.*

To read that one-sentence report with a science attitude, you need to know the total number of people observed in the gym. If only two people were observed, the fact that both (100% of those observed) were limping is not that meaningful. Maybe they were playing basketball together and collided. But if 50 people were observed, and 100% were limping, that calls for a meaningful explanation. Maybe the equipment in that gym is dangerous, or the "gym" is actually a physical therapy site for people with leg injuries.

When summarizing with a percent, the number of observations is critically important information. We will call that number "N." Usually, a capital N refers to all the people observed in a single study, and a lowercase n refers to a subset of people in a single study. For example, a study with four days' worth of observations might have $N = 100$, with $n = 25$ on each day. There are exceptions to these rules, but we'll save them for a more advanced class in statistics. Case studies, as defined in Module 1, like the fascinating story of Phineas Gage (the man who had a 3-foot-long iron rod pass through his brain and lived to tell about it) are often called "N of 1" studies because they are based on observations of just one person.

Better evidence for or against ideas can be found in studies with a much higher N. The more observations in our study, the more we can trust those observations to represent the real behaviors of a population. The research *population* is the larger group of people about whom the researcher wishes to draw conclusions. Returning to the data summary examples about cell phone use (the first two (italicized) examples above), let's assume the researcher wants to describe typical cell phone use on campus. The population would then be the set of all college students who walk across campus, day after day. As it would be impossible to study the whole population of all those students, a research *sample* is selected.

If the sample consists of everyone who happens to be walking across campus during preset, convenient observation periods, it would be called a *convenience sample*, because the people who are included in the study are only those who are (conveniently) walking across campus while the researcher watches. Convenience samples are chosen at the researcher's discretion, not randomly.

A *random sample* is one in which every member of the population has an equal chance of being selected for the study. To get a truly random sample of the population of all students who walk across campus, we would have to select our participants using an arbitrary and random process, unrelated to the time of day or day of week that they would be walking across campus. With a *random selection* process, every person in the population has an equal chance of being selected to be in the sample, regardless of their personal characteristics such as class schedules. Convenience samples are obviously much easier to obtain, and are more often used in research than truly random samples.

Coming back to our cell phone example, then, critical readers will want to know the value of N. Thus, the best way to report the data would be:

> Over a 30-min period, we observed that 10% of people walking across campus (N =150) were using their cell phones.

This way of reporting provides all the relevant information for the critical reader to understand the meaning of the data. Also recall that the goal in reporting data is to summarize observations *meaningfully* and *concisely*. By simply inserting "(N = 150)" immediately after the description of the sample that was observed, in this case, "people walking across campus," we add important information in the most concise way. But this is just one example of a summary, specific to *prevalence* data (Module 2). There are many ways to summarize data, and the best way to summarize depends on the type of data collected.

ESSAY 3.2

THE BEST DATA SUMMARY DEPENDS ON THE TYPE OF DATA

Over a 30-min period, we observed that 10% of people walking across campus (N = 150) were using their cell phones.

Read the italicized data summary above again and consider how cell phone use was operationally defined to produce the summary. Apparently, researchers observed 150 people walking across campus and placed them into two different categories: either they were using a phone or they were not. Each person in the study contributed one data point, and that data point was a label: Phone User or

Non-Phone User. There was no measurement, just a category placement. We therefore call these observations *categorical data* (or *nominal data*). Other examples of categorical data would be the number of students majoring in Math, Science, English, or History; or the most popular favorite colors. The best way to summarize categorical data is to report either the frequency (number of observations) in each category or the percentage or proportion within the category out of the total observed. The italicized summary of data on cell phone use above is a good example of how to summarize categorical data in percent form.

Another way of collecting data is to rank observations in some meaningful order, such as first, second, third place, and so on. We do this every time we watch a race or talk about college football rankings. In psychology research, people are often asked to rank their choices in a list. This produces *ordinal data*, meaning that the single data point contributed by each observation is a place holder relative to other observations. Ordinal data points are not measurable amounts. Knowing which runner came in first and which runner came in second does not tell us how fast either runner completed the race, nor whether they were very close at the finish-line or 50 m apart. Ordinal data simply give each observation a rank relative to other observations. These data can be summarized by reporting the *median* (middle) ranking within any ordinal data set, but it must be remembered that the amount of difference between any two rankings cannot be determined from the data. An example of an ordinal data report would be:

When college students (N = 15) were each given 10 music videos to rank from most-liked to least-liked (with 1 being the top rank), the median rank for Lady Gaga's original video of "Bad Romance" was 6, whereas the median rank of an a cappella version of the same song by the group "On the Rocks" was a 3.[1]

This summary indicates that students more often gave the "On the Rocks" video a rank closer to the top,

while Lady Gaga's original version was more often ranked toward the bottom half of the list of songs. Yet, the 3 and the 6 do not tell us how much more liked the a cappella version was, any more than race results tell us how close the race was.

Where nominal data provide a count for each observation, and ordinal data provide a place for each observation relative to other observations, *interval data* provide a numeric measurement of value for each observation. These measurements allow meaningful comparisons of the values for different observations. IQ and SAT scores are good examples of interval data. Each observation contributes a number (IQ or SAT score) that gives that observation a meaningful value. Unlike ordinal data, the difference between two interval measurements has a real, quantifiable meaning.

Two important points must be made clear about the types of data presented so far. First, the amount of information obtained from a single observation decreases as we shift from interval to ordinal to nominal data. Imagine a sample of 3 people who take an IQ test. Person A scores 112; Person B scores 140; and Person C scores 111. These *interval* data tell us that B has a much higher IQ than A or C, and that A and C do not differ much in IQ. We can convert these data to *ordinal*: Instead of 112, 140, 111, the same observations would be 2, 1, and 3 for persons A, B, and C, respectively (second, first, and third place scores in comparison to each other). But in going from interval to ordinal data, we have lost information. Our reader can no longer tell how much higher B's score was, compared to A and C. We could also convert these interval data to *nominal* data by categorizing them as "scores over 115" (B) and "scores under 115" (A and C), but we lose even more information. Now the reader can't even tell that A scored slightly higher than C.

The second important point refers to interval data: These measurements do not include a true value of zero[2] and therefore are not fraction-friendly. That is, interval data cannot be meaningfully divided or multiplied. For example, a person who has an IQ score of 160 is not "twice as smart" as a person with an IQ of 80. Interval data will not allow for that kind of comparison. A jump of 5 points is still a jump of 5 points, whether a score goes from 95 to 100 or 100 to

---

[1] These data are completely made up. Lady Gaga's video would probably be ranked higher (it has over one billion views on YouTube). But I happen to like the spoofy, relaxed YouTube video of it by On the Rocks (the 4/23/10 version).

[2] A true value of zero means that "0" on the scale indicates a complete lack of whatever is being measured. There is no valid score of "zero" on an IQ test.

105. Interval scores can be added and subtracted and the differences can be compared. But scores cannot be expressed as fractions or products of other scores. Fahrenheit temperature is another good example of interval data: A temperature of 0°F is not a complete lack of heat (Fahrenheit temperatures can go below 0.) Furthermore, if it's 25°F outside, it is not five times as hot as 5°F. It is simply 20° warmer.

Ratio data include a possible score of zero, which would indicate a complete lack of whatever is being measured. Therefore, ratio scores can be multiplied and divided. Annual salary is a good example of ratio data. With no job (or a volunteer job), salary is zero. A job that pays $50K per year is twice the salary of a job that pays $25K. Notice that interval comparisons can still be used for ratio data: To make a mathematical comparison to our IQ data above, an increase from 95K to 100K is the same amount of money as an increase from 100K to 105K.

There is a blurred line between ordinal and interval data that we should also address here. A typical survey question might use a *Likert scale*,[3] where participants are asked to what extent they agree or disagree with a statement and are given a scale from 1 (strongly disagree) to 4 (strongly agree). Data collected with a Likert scale are often summarized as interval data because they provide a kind of "measurement" for each observation. However, some researchers would argue that the measurement is not truly quantifiable, and therefore should not be summarized as interval data.

People who respond to Likert scale questions are merely selecting the best option from a range of choices, not providing a measurement of their actual thoughts or feelings. It's like showing someone four different bikes and asking, "Which bike do you like best?" Giving people choices and asking them to pick the best automatically produces ordinal data, not interval data.

The conundrum is that there is no easier way to numerically express the answer to the question we really want to ask, which is "How much do you like this particular bike?" Even when we ask, "On a scale of 1 to 10, how much do you like this bike?" we are still technically providing choices from which people select the best. On such a scale, can we always claim that the difference between 8 and 10 has the same value as the difference between 4 and 6, even though both are 2-point differences? Some would say no. But most psychologists, economists and others who use Likert scales for data collection would argue that it depends on the context of the question, and many peer-reviewed journals publish research that treats these data like interval data.

In conclusion, the same CV can usually be measured multiple ways, limited only by our imagination. Ratio data are slightly more informative than interval data, but are generally very difficult to achieve, and are typically summarized using the same simple calculations described in Essay 3.3 for interval data. Nominal and ordinal data can be summarized quite simply, as described above, but interval data and ratio data require more information to summarize them meaningfully. Essay 3.3 details why this is the case and how to summarize interval (or ratio) data.

---

[3] The "Likert Scale" question type was named for the person who invented it, Rensis Likert. Although it is often pronounced as "like`-urt," Rensis actually pronounced his name as "lick`-urt."

ESSAY 3.3

SUMMARIZING INTERVAL (AND RATIO) DATA

Interval and ratio data are quite similar and are generally handled the same way for data summaries. For simplicity, therefore, this essay focuses on interval data. Please know that the information being presented also applies to ratio data.

Interval data are usually summarized with an arithmetic average (add all the scores and divide by the number of scores), or with a median, which is simply the middle score when all scores are listed from lowest to highest. The raw data will determine which

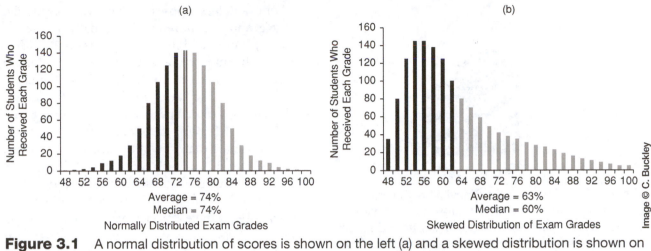

Figure 3.1 A normal distribution of scores is shown on the left (a) and a skewed distribution is shown on the right (b).

summary is more appropriate. The arithmetic average (mean) is used to summarize interval data when the measurements look "normal" (Figure 3.1a). That is, the majority of the scores are close to the average, with about the same number of measurements above the mean as below. Loosely defined, this is a normally distributed data set. A median is more often used when the data are skewed (Figure 3.1b). A *skewed* data set has considerably fewer scores above the average compared to below it, or vice versa.

When reporting means, readers also need to know about *variability*. Even in measuring the length of a piece of rope, perfect precision is nearly impossible. Measuring human behavior is obviously more complicated! There will always be some variability when behaviors are measured. The *amount* of variability is critical information. To understand why, imagine a child has a fever and you're using an electronic thermometer to see what her temperature is. To get the true temperature, you take a reading three times and calculate an average. Suppose the three readings are 98, 101, and 104. The average is 101, but the temperatures vary by as much as 3 degrees from the average.

Would you trust that the correct temperature was actually 101? For comparison, suppose readings only deviate from the average by one tenth of one degree, such as 100.9, 101, and 101.1. The average is still 101, but now you instinctively trust that average more. The lower variability is the reason for that trust. Whenever an average is reported, skeptical readers will always want to know how much the measurements vary around that average, so that they will know how much they can trust that average.

From now on, we'll call the average a "*mean*," to use the preferred term, and with every mean we report, we will always report an estimate of the variability in the measurements. There are several ways to report variability. The simplest is the *range*. Range can be expressed by reporting both the lowest and the highest score (e.g., the range of the first set of temperatures, two paragraphs above, was 98 to 104; for the second set of temperatures, the range was 100.9 to 101.1). You can also report the range more concisely with just one number, equal to the difference between the highest and lowest score (e.g., 104 minus 98 equals a range of 6). A range of 6 is greater variability than the range of 0.2 for the second set, meaning you can trust the mean more in the second set. However, range is not commonly used in scientific literature because there are better and more informative ways to express variability, one of which is the standard deviation.

Standard deviation (*SD*) is a number that reflects exactly what the name implies: a standardized calculation of the deviations from the mean (i.e., differences between each measurement and the mean of all the measurements). The SD is a way of expressing how closely bunched the numbers in a set are around their mean. The *range* can only tell you how far apart two scores are, the lowest and the highest. The rest of the scores could be anywhere between those two. Calculating a standard deviation allows you to estimate where *most* of the scores are, relative to the mean. You will learn the formula to calculate a standard deviation by hand in more advanced courses. Here, we will focus on how to interpret the SD. Essay 3.4 shows you how to get MS Excel to calculate an SD for you.

Image © C. Buckley

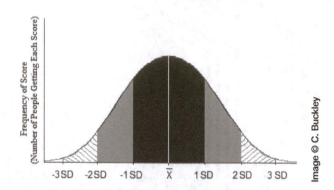

Figure 3.2   The standard deviation (SD) tells how much the scores in a data set differ from the mean of the whole set ($\overline{X}$). In a *normally distributed* data set, 68% of the scores fall within 1 SD of the mean (black area under curve); 95% of scores fall within 2 SD of the mean (black plus gray areas); and 99% of scores fall within 3 SD of the mean (black, gray and scored areas). Less than 1% of the scores will fall in the white areas, more than 3 SD from the average of the data set.

In simplest terms, the smaller the SD, the closer the majority of the measurements are to the mean, and the more we can trust the mean as an estimate of the truth. But the SD is much more useful than that. In a normally distributed set of measurements (randomly taken from a large population), we can estimate that most (about 68%) of the measurements will fall within 1 SD above or below the mean. Almost all (about 95%) of the measurements will fall within 2 SD of the mean, and all but 1 out of 100 will fall within 3 SD of the mean (Figure 3.2).

For example, suppose creativity was measured in a large group of children with normally distributed creativity scores, and the mean score was 25 with an SD of 4. This means that about 68% of the children scored between 21 (25 minus 4) and 29 (25 plus 4). Doubling the SD to 8, we can also estimate that 95% of the children scored between 17 (25 minus 8) and 33 (25 plus 8). Tripling the SD gives us 12, so we can further estimate that 99% of the scores are between 13 (25 minus 12) and 37 (25 plus 12). This utility makes SD a preferred measure of variability.

Knowing how to interpret the SD is quite practical: Suppose you take a proficiency exam for a job you really want, and you score a 47. You ask the examiner: Is that a good score? Yes, she says; the mean is 40 and the SD is 2. Now you can easily determine how 99% of the people who take this test score on it. Start by tripling the SD ($2 \times 3 = 6$). Subtracting 6 from the mean gives you 34, and adding 6 to the mean gives you 46, so 99% of the people who take this exam probably score between 34 and 46. By this measure, your score is exceptionally high.

In conclusion, summarizing data is a matter of knowing what type of data you have and presenting all the important aspects of the data set in a concise and meaningful way (Table 3.1). Microsoft Excel can be used to calculate all these data summaries, and many others. Several of them, you probably already know how to calculate by hand. After a brief skill check, we will focus on how to manage and summarize data in Excel.

Table 3.1   Reporting data summaries

Type Of Data	Report Summary	Also Report
Categorical (nominal)	Frequency, percentage	N (with percent)
Ordinal	Median	N
Interval (normally distributed)	Mean	N, SD
Interval (not normally distributed)	Median	N

SKILL CHECK (ANSWERS IN APPENDIX B)

1. What would a data set look like if its SD = 0 and its range = 5?
   a) All the scores in the data set would be the same.
   b) All the scores in the data set would be in the shaded regions of Figure 3.2.
   c) It is impossible to have a data set with an SD of 0 and a range of 5.

2. A normally distributed, large sample from the "American Time Use Survey" (2012) found Americans (ages 15 & up) watch an average of 2.8 hr of TV per day. If the standard deviation was 0.4 hr, how many hours of TV would about 68% of Americans probably watch per day?
   a) between 0.4 and 0.8 hr
   b) between 2.4 and 3.2 hr
   c) between 2.0 and 3.6 hr
   d) between 3.2 and 3.6 hr

ESSAY 3.4

SUMMARIZING DATA WITH MS EXCEL (AND GOOGLE SHEETS)

Microsoft Excel is a data handling (spreadsheet) tool that easily calculates percentages, means, medians, modes, and standard deviations (among many, many other things, including advanced statistics). It can do any calculation you ask for, most of them with shortcut formulas like the ones described in Box 3.3. Excel can also be used to create charts and other kinds of data summaries with tremendous flexibility in design, including the option to save chart designs for use with other data sets.

As of this writing, Google Sheets can do many of these things, but not at the same level nor with the same fluidity or transferability that MS Excel can do them. Nevertheless, Google's spreadsheet functions are improving every day, so by the time you read this, their app might be as good or better than Excel (not likely, but possible). Either way, it is a good idea to learn how MS Excel works because most of what you learn will also apply to other spreadsheet apps (including Google Sheets) with only minor adjustments.

The main advantage of Google Sheets is that it is currently free. Another advantage (simultaneously a disadvantage) is that it automatically saves everything you do. So while you won't need that pesky extra click to save your work now and then, you will have the near-constant worry that data may have been accidentally deleted (with sorting and data management, this happens more often than you might expect). Once you break a file, it's yours to keep.

There is a work-around to ease your worries, and it's a good habit to get into whether you're working in Excel or Google Sheets. As soon as all your data are entered in the spreadsheet, always, without exception, save a backup copy of your original data set, and do nothing to that copy unless something terrible happens to the spreadsheet you're working with. That's when you're going to need the copy. There are few things you can do in science that are more frustrating than losing data. Without a backup of your original data sheet, Google Sheets' autosave feature is a terrible thing waiting to happen.

In the balance, then, it is probably best to learn how to use Excel, and that will be our primary focus in these instructional boxes. However, given that not everyone has access to Excel, instructions will be included for Google Sheets, when the instructions differ and/or the feature is critically important.

Students taking this course will probably have varying levels of experience using MS Excel or Google Sheets (GS). For this reason, Excel and GS instructions are given here in separate, labeled boxes. If you already know how to enter data and do simple calculations in Excel or GS, skip Box 3.1. If you already know how to select continuous and discontinuous sets of data from a spreadsheet and how to sort data numerically and alphabetically, skip Box 3.2. Box 3.3 explains how to calculate a percentage, a mean, and an SD. Those who have never used MS Excel or GS should read all three Boxes and follow along using MS Excel or GS on a computer. Because new versions of Excel are released every few years, please persist through minor differences in appearance that may occur between these instructions and the version you are using. The basic steps will be very similar whether you are using a PC or a Mac, and regardless of versions.

BOX 3.1   Entering Data & Simple Equations & Creating Backup Sheets

Open MS Excel (or Google Spreadsheets, hereafter called "GS") and choose the option to *open a blank workbook* (Excel) or a blank "spreadsheet" (GS). Before computers became so common, the term "spreadsheet" meant a single paper with a grid for organizing information – what both Excel and GS now call a *sheet*. Because a "sheet within a workbook" is more intuitive than a "sheet within a spreadsheet," these instructions will always use the term *workbook* to describe a data file, whether it's in Excel or GS.

Like a paper notebook, a *workbook* can have multiple *sheets*; electronic mini-files within a file. You can access different *sheets* within the same workbook by clicking on tabs at the bottom of the Excel or GS window. Just like a paper notebook, this allows you to keep all related data in one place, so you can conveniently view, copy paste, etc., from one sheet to another without opening or saving any new files.

A *sheet* is a grid of rows (horizontal) and columns (vertical). Rows are identified by numbers going down the left side, and columns are identified by letters going across the top. Each box created by the intersection of a column and row is called a cell, and cells are named using column and row letters and numbers, respectively. In Figure 3.3a, the number 4.5 is in the cell that would be named B3.

Figure 3.3a is a sample sheet in which data have been entered showing the number of hours of Netflix watched per day by 10 different people. To recreate the data set on your own computer, click on each cell, type the contents of that cell, and hit <enter>. Open an Excel or GS file now and try it!

Every time you hit <enter>, Excel or GS will automatically move you to the next cell down (or over, depending on your settings – down is the default).

Every cell is like its own document with a tiny (but expandable) writing space. One click on a cell starts a new writing space within that cell. There is one notable exception; the = sign can affect what your next click does, as described in Box 3.3. But ignoring that for now, if you click once on a cell and something is already in that cell when you begin typing, Excel and GS will automatically replace the old cell contents with whatever you type. *This is one reason why backup copies of original data sets are so important: It is extremely easy to accidentally type over something without realizing it.*

To *edit* the contents of a cell without completely erasing it, you must double-click inside the cell. This will produce an insertion cursor, which allows editing just like any normal text document. To erase everything in a cell, click on it once and hit backspace or delete. When strange things happen that you didn't want, click on everyone's best friend, the undo button at the top of the screen: ↰ in Excel or ↰ in GS. If that doesn't work, your cursor might be in editing mode. If so, hit <enter> to finish the edit, even if it's not what you wanted. Then click the undo button and the cell will revert to its previous content.

Due to Excel's advanced autoformat features, you might type **1.5**, hit <enter>, and see "Jan 5." You might have accidentally typed **1/5**, which Excel interpreted as a date rather than a number. It will now auto-format that cell as a date. Typing over the date won't fix the problem; Excel will politely interpret every attempt as another date. The undo button is the best way to fix these problems. Just keeping clicking on it until the cell goes back to the default format

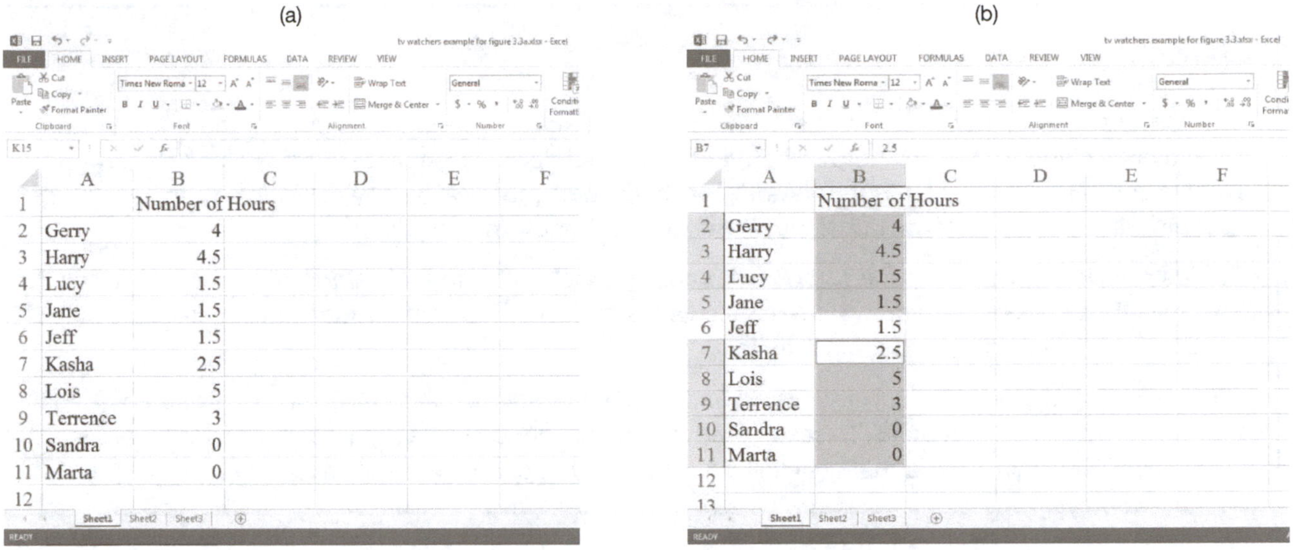

(a)

(b)

Figure 3.3   MS Excel spreadsheets with data samples for practice. Used with permission from Microsoft Excel

---

BOX 3.1, continued

If you have typed in all the information on a sheet and it looks like the one in Figure 3.3a, great! Now let's get into the good habit of *creating a backup of your data* before we do anything else. In Excel (not GS), right-click on the "Sheet 1" tab at the bottom of the window. Select "Move or Copy…" and in the dialog box that pops up, click on the box next to "Create a copy." Excel gives you the option to place your copy in the same workbook or copy it to a new or different workbook, which can be very useful, but you'll want a copy within this workbook, so just click "OK" and a new sheet will be added to your workbook with the exact same content and formatting as Sheet 1. If you right-click on the new tab, you can select "Rename" and call it "backup." In GS, left-click on the arrow next to the "Sheet 1" tab and select "Duplicate." Rename it the same way.

Now click on the original Sheet 1 tab with a smile in your heart, knowing you can do whatever you want with the original sheet. Your data are safe and easily accessible if something goes wrong.

Note: If cell B1 only shows part of the phrase "Number of Hours," this is because there is something (maybe even just a space) entered in cell B2. To fix this, you can either click in cell B2, hit <delete> or <backspace>, then <enter>, or you can widen the column. Widening the column is better, particularly if you have something typed in cell B2 that you want to keep visible.

To widen a column, place your cursor on the line between the letters at the top of that column and the next (in this case, the line between B and C). When you see a double-pointed arrow, your cursor is in the right spot. Double-click, and the column to the left of the line will automatically adjust its width to show all the text in its longest entry. There are other ways to adjust column width, but this is the easiest. You can also drag the double-pointed arrow to manually adjust width, or give excel precise column widths with the "Column Width" option that pops up if you double-click on any column letter.

Another option is to just accept that even though the whole phrase is not showing, Excel or GS is storing the whole phrase for you in that cell. Verify this by clicking on cell B1 and looking at the "formula bar" at the top of the screen. It's a text-entry bar just above the column letters and to the right of "f_x". If you have clicked on cell B1, the formula bar will show you all the contents of that cell, even if the complete phrase doesn't show on your sheet.

BOX 3.1, continued

The formula bar will become your next-best friend in Excel or GS (second only to the undo button). It always tells you what is inside a selected cell. This is important because *what the cell displays and what is actually in the cell are not always the same thing.* If you click on any cell with a formula in it, the formula will show in the formula bar, but the *answer* will show in the cell.

To illustrate, let's type a simple equation (a formula) in a cell. Every formula *starts* with an equals sign (=). This tells Excel or GS that you want it to calculate something. Remember that while a cell is selected, anything you type will go into the cell as text.

Click cell E4 and type **= 2 + 2**. Hit <enter>. Cell E4 will now say "4" and cell E5 will be selected. (Recall that every time you hit <enter>, Excel and GS will move your cell selection down or over by one cell.) Click in cell E4 again. The formula bar will say "= 2 + 2" but cell E4 will still say "4."

BOX 3.2 Selecting and Sorting Data

If you skipped Box 3.1 because you already know how to enter data, create simple formulas, and back up your data, please open Excel or GS now on a computer and recreate the data in Figure 3.3a. Then follow along in this box to learn how to select and sort data. To manage data, we have to select the cells containing the data we want to manage. Left-clicking once in any cell selects *only* that cell, but we want to select multiple cells at the same time.

Multiple adjacent cells are unfortunately called a "range," not to be confused with the *range* that expresses the variability in a data set. To select a range of cells with a mouse, left-click and drag from the beginning to the end of the selection. If you have a track pad, this can be difficult, but there is an easier way: Left-click at the beginning of your range, then hold down the <shift> key and click on the end of your range. The selected cells will turn blue or gray to show that they are selected, but one will remain white (or have a dark border around it in GS). Any typing you do while multiple cells are selected automatically goes into the white (or dark-bordered) cell.

To select cells that are not adjacent to each other, hold down the control key (command key on a Mac) while making separate selections. Try it now. Select cells B2 through B5 and B7 through B11 in one selection. It should end up looking like Figure 3.3b. Cell B6 is white because it has not been selected. Cell B7 is white and/or has a darker border because it is part of the selected set, and anything you type at this point will go into cell B7.

Excel's superpowers include the ability to sort, summarize, and make charts from the information in multiple cells (numbers or text) quickly and easily.

Sorting data is one of Excel's most useful features (and that is saying something!). To sort the set of data in order from those who watched Netflix most to least:

> Select all the data, including names, by left-clicking on A1 and dragging to B11 (or clicking A1 and holding t he shift key while you click on B11). Make sure you include BOTH columns (A and B) in your selection in order to keep names linked to the correct data. Note that your selection should also include the "header" or label for the data set, "Number of Hours."

BOX 3.2, continued

In the Data tab at the top of the screen, click on "Sort" (or "Sort range" in GS). A dialogue box will open.

Check the box for "My data has headers" (or "Data has header row" in GS) to tell Excel or GS that the top row is a label, not data. Using the drop-down menu labeled "Sort By," choose "Number of Hours."

In Excel only, using the drop-down menu labeled "Order," choose "Largest to Smallest," and click "OK." In GS, there is no "order" menu, so just click on "Z → A" (GS translates this into largest to smallest for numbers). Your data will instantly rearrange from most to least hours spent watching Netflix. The names in column A should rearrange themselves to stay with their corresponding data. If they don't, then undo everything, or go to your backup copy, make another backup copy, and start over. Then go back to the first step above ("Select all the data"). Make sure you select BOTH columns, A and B.

Try sorting the data alphabetically by name, or from smallest to largest number of hours. When you feel comfortable with the sorting feature, click the "undo" button repeatedly to return the data to their original order before proceeding to Box 3.3. Or start over by making another copy of your backup sheet.

BOX 3.3 Summarizing Data: Formulas & Calculations

The instructions in this box use the data sheet shown in Figure 3.3a. Please open Excel or GS and either recreate that sheet or use the copy you created in Box 3.1 or 3.2. If you're not sure how, refer to Box 3.1.

Excel and GS have built-in formulas for a wide variety of data summaries. If your data are in one column, a calculation can be performed in Excel (but not GS) without even having to select the range of cells containing the data. Simply click on the first cell beneath your column of data cells, choose a formula, hit <enter>, and excel will provide the answer! Note that as of this writing, GS does not do this.

An example in Excel: To calculate the mean number of hours watching Netflix for the data in Figure 3.3a, click in cell B12, then go to the top of the screen and click on the "Formulas" tab. Look for the "AutoSum" option to the left. Click on the small triangle near the word "Autosum" to see a list of built-in formulas. Select "Average" from the list. Then hit <enter>. To borrow an old Southern phrase, Excel gives you the average "faster than green grass through a goose."

GS will calculate an average, but it takes a few more clicks. Start by clicking in cell B12. Then go to the "insert" tab and click on "Function." Choose "Average" from the list, and GS will fill in a formula for average that will look something like this: **=AVERAGE(|...)**. The vertical line in the parentheses will be a blinking cursor. Now select the range of cells B2 through B11 (all the cells with the numbers you want to average). They will automatically go into the formula. Hit <enter>, and cell B12 will display the average number of hours spent watching Netflix.

Recall from Essay 3.3 that whenever you report a mean, you must report the standard deviation (SD) along with it. Excel and GS can calculate the SD: Click on the cell where you want the SD to appear and type **= stdev(**. After the open parenthesis, select the range of cells with the data (B2 through B11) and hit <enter> (as with the formula for an average, you don't need the closing parenthesis). The SD of the cells you selected will appear in the box. Important note: Excel and GS have a built-in SD options so that you don't have to type out "=stdev(" but there are two different formulas to calculate SD that will give you two different answers! Be careful...

BOX 3.3, continued

For the standard deviation of a *sample*, either type **=stdev(** or select stdev.s (or stdevs in GS). Do not choose stdev.p (or stdevp in GS). The "p" stands for "population," which means the formula is slightly different (it provides an estimate of the *population* SD, not the *sample* SD). You'll learn more about that in a statistics course.

It is also possible to type a formula of your own to "manually" calculate the sum (or average, or anything else) for any set of cells. Recall from Box 3.1 that clicking on a new cell starts a new writing space, and that typing = in any cell starts a formula or calculation. If you type = into a cell, then click on a new cell, Excel (and GS) will automatically enter the contents of the new cell (symbolized by the cell label) into your formula. In other words, typing = tells Excel that the next cell you click should be entered into a formula. As an example, let's use cell D10 to calculate the sum of cells B3, B5, and B7:

> Click on D10 and type = . Excel is now ready for you to enter a formula.
>
> Click on cell B3. Notice in the formula bar that Excel enters "B3" after the = sign.
>
> Type + and then click cell B5.
>
> Type + and then click cell B7.
>
> Hit <enter>, and the sum of cells B3, B5, and B7 will appear in cell D10. (It should be 8.5.)

You can also sum any set of cells by typing **= sum(** and then selecting each cell you want to add, using the control key as described in Box 3.1 to select nonadjacent cells. Try that in cell D11. Hit <enter>, and you should have the same answer in cells D10 and D11. Thus, you can use built-in formulas or you can type out formulas to perform any mathematical calculation you want on the content of any cells.

Let's calculate a percentage using a custom formula. From our Netflix-watching data set, we have already calculated the total number of hours watched by three people, Harry (B3), Jane (B5), and Kasha (B7). What percentage of that total time was contributed by Harry, who watched for 4.5 hr?

To get the answer:

> Type = in the cell where you want the answer (any blank cell).
>
> Click B3, as this contains the part of the total that we want to translate into a percentage.
>
> Type / (the symbol for "divided by").
>
> Click on the cell containing the total (either D10 or D11).
>
> Type ***100** to convert the proportion into a percent. (Excel uses * as a multiplication symbol.)
>
> Hit <enter>. Excel returns the percentage of time that Harry contributed to the total watched by all three people. (About 53%! Harry should probably watch less Netflix.)

Playing with Excel's features is the best way to learn what it can do. Next time you have a set of numbers to add for any class or project, type them into Excel or GS instead of a calculator. When working with larger data sets, it's much easier to find and fix mistakes in a spreadsheet than on a calculator!

ESSAY 3.5

GENERATING AND TESTING HYPOTHESES

In trying to understand the natural world, it is not enough to merely describe conceptual variables. Often, the more interesting and important questions lie in the relationships between those variables. Descriptive or exploratory data, once summarized, can inform our guesses about these relationships, and those guesses are called hypotheses (singular: hypothesis).

It is important to note that the same data used to *generate* a hypothesis <u>cannot</u> be used as *evidence for* that hypothesis. Descriptive data might suggest a pattern, and that pattern might make you think that something is true. But if you never predicted that pattern, it could just be random coincidence. The only way to know whether a pattern is predictable is to predict it first, then test the prediction. Maybe while you were watching students walk across campus, more females were using phones than males (or vice versa). That makes you think: Maybe phone use is related to apparent gender. This would be your hypothesis, but you do not have *evidence* to support it! Not yet! You would have to state that idea, make a prediction, *then* collect *new* data to test the prediction (or examine data you have not yet seen).

The human mind is very good at spotting patterns. Often, they are no more than accidental happenings, like finding a potato chip shaped like a dog. One observation does not allow you to generalize to all the chips in the bag. Nor does observing a surprising or unique relationship make it generalizable to a broader population. You can't know whether any observed relationship is predictable until you test it. Let's say while you're watching students walk across campus, most of the people you identified as female had their phones out, while few of the people you identified as male had phones out. This suggests that a relationship might exist between apparent gender and phone use, but no generalizable hypothesis has *evidence* unless some unique event is predicted based on that hypothesis, and

subsequent observations then fall in line with the prediction. Why?

To test a hypothesis, we have to turn to the scientific method, and the steps of the scientific method must be followed *in order* (see Essay 1.2 for a refresher of the steps). This requires that a hypothesis logically leads to a prediction that must be made *before* evidence for or against the hypothesis can be examined. Even if a descriptive study shows 100% of the people using phones were female (or male), that still does *not* count as evidence for the hypothesis that gender is related to phone use. One would have to predict before the observations that there will be more females (or males) using phones, *then* properly collect the data. *To test a hypothesis, predictions must precede observations*. If this seems repetitive, it's because it is a very common mistake in logic to make an observation and call it evidence for a hypothesis without ever having predicted it. In Modules 4 through 8, you'll be testing research hypotheses, so all this will become clearer.

But before we test any hypotheses, let's clarify our definition of the word and distinguish the two main types.

People often use the word "hypothesis" to describe any idea, but a scientific hypothesis is not just any idea. The popular definition of a hypothesis as "an educated guess" is sadly lacking in clarity. A guess about what? If a performer at a fair guesses your age based on your style of dress, that's an educated guess, but is it a hypothesis? If so, it is an extremely limited one, and not very useful. A better, more specific definition would be that a *hypothesis* is a declaration of a testable relationship between two or more conceptual variables. A hypothesis may be one of two types, correlational or causal. These are defined with examples in the box below. Notice that the CVs are exactly the same for each example with the same number; only the words describing the type of relationship are changed from a correlational relationship to a causal relationship.

Correlational Hypothesis—Declares that a relationship exists where changes in one conceptual variable are associated with changes in another, so that a score for either variable can be used to predict the score for the other (within a limited range, depending on the strength of the relationship). Some examples:

1. The desire to own a pet rat <u>is related to</u> experience watching *Ratatouille*.
2. Smoking <u>is linked to</u> heart disease.
3. Happiness <u>increases as</u> time spent in nature increases.
4. Purposeless Internet surfing <u>is correlated with</u> depression.

These hypotheses would be tested with **correlational research** (see Module 1 glossary and all of Module 4).

Cause-and-Effect Hypothesis (Causal Hypothesis)—Declares that a relationship exists where changes in one conceptual variable (the cause) directly influence changes in the other (the effect). Some examples:

1. Experience watching *Ratatouille* <u>increases</u> the desire to own a pet rat.
2. Smoking <u>causes</u> heart disease.
3. Happiness <u>is increased by</u> spending time in nature.
4. Purposeless Internet surfing <u>leads to</u> depression.

These hypotheses would be tested with **experimental research** (see Module 1 glossary and Modules 5, 7 & 8).

Notice that the conceptual variables in these hypotheses are the same for corresponding numbers—only the proposed relationship between them changes from correlational to causal. Go back and forth between correlational example 1 to causal example 1. Do the same for examples 2 and 2, etc., reading just the underlined parts, and focus on the difference in meaning between a correlational and a causal hypothesis. This difference is extremely important, as it determines not only the type of research that should be used to test the hypothesis, but also the conclusions that can be drawn from that research.

Also notice that going from correlational to causal increases the specificity of the relationship. Take example #4. The correlational statement can be true without the causal statement being true. Surfing the Internet is related to depression, but that does not mean that it *leads to* depression. Maybe depression leads to more Internet surfing. Or maybe both are caused by intense boredom or quarantine conditions. A relationship can exist without being a causal relationship. However, if the causal hypothesis is true (if surfing the Internet *does* lead to depression), then by default, the relationship must exist—Internet surfing and depression must be correlated.

All cause-and-effect relationships between variables are, by default, also correlational, because changes in the cause will always be correlated to changes in the effect. However, the opposite is not true: *Correlational evidence does not support a cause-and-effect relationship.*

To test correlational hypothesis #4, we need only measure hours spent surfing the Internet and depression scores on a survey to test the prediction that increases in one will be linked to increases in the other. To test *causal* hypotheses #4, a researcher would have to randomly place people into different groups: One group could be asked to surf the Internet for 5 hr/day, while another group would be asked to not surf at all. Everyone would then be asked to take the survey measuring depression to test the prediction that those who surf will have higher depression scores than those who do not. In either case, correlational or causal, we only have evidence for the hypothesis if our observations match our predictions.

MODULE 3 RESEARCH LEARNING OBJECTIVES CHART

STUDY NUMBER	MODULE 3 RESEARCH LEARNING OBJECTIVES	BEFORE READING				AFTER DOING PROJECT			
		I don't know how 1	I know a little about this 2	I know enough about this to guess correctly 3	I know how to do this and/ or have already done it. 4	I don't know how 1	I know a little about this 2	I know enough about this to guess correctly 3	I know how to do this and/ or have already done it. 4
3A	Explore a real data set reflecting living conditions all over the world and see multiple real-world examples of conceptual variables and their operational definitions.								
3A	Sort a data set using MS Excel or Google Sheets.								
3A	Isolate variables and calculate means and SDs using Excel or Google Sheets.								
3A	Generate logical correlational and cause-and-effect hypotheses from descriptive data summaries.								
3A	Witness preliminary examples of proper APA formatting to report descriptive Results and Discussion.								
3B	Gain experience with random selection to produce a random sample.								
3B, Pt 1	Witness and explain the effects of sample size on estimates of the population mean.								
3B, Pt 2	Explain the effects of sample size on estimates of the population SD.								
3B, Pt 3	Practice critical consideration of the important steps in testing a hypothesis.								

		I don't know how 1	I know a little about this 2	I know enough about this to guess correctly 3	I know how to do this and/ or have already done it. 4		I don't know how 1	I know a little about this 2	I know enough about this to guess correctly 3	I know how to do this and/ or have already done it. 4
3B, Pt 3	List three important elements of a mathematical comparison that are needed to determine whether two populations differ.									

Now read about the project to prepare for lab. For any scores less than "4," keep those questions in mind as you complete the research project(s). Do not do the white half of this chart until after you've completed the assigned research project(s).

STUDY **3A**

SUMMARIZING DATA WITH MS EXCEL OR GOOGLE SHEETS & GENERATING HYPOTHESES

The United Nations Development Programme (UNDP) works with governments, financial organizations, and private organizations in many countries around the world to monitor and improve the quality of life for all people. As part of their mission, they collect and report descriptive data on conceptual variables (CVs) related to quality of life all over the world. For about 200 countries, they report on education CVs like average years of schooling per adult and primary school student/teacher ratios; health CVs like fertility and mortality rates and availability of physicians; economic CVs like GDP (Gross Domestic Product) and GNI (Gross National Income), the labor force, and cell phone and Internet access; and social factors including gender inequality, homicide and suicide rates, and prison populations.

In an excellent example of the power of data to change lives, UNDP's mission is to define and measure human development in terms that go beyond economic indicators to include quality of life. They use their data to calculate a Human Development Index (HDI) that is a composite score for each country along three dimensions: life expectancy/health, knowledge/education levels, and standard of living. The UNDP uses this index to rank the countries from highest to lowest HDI. They make this information publicly available for governments and agencies working to improve lives.

The data set provided to you will include a subset of 40 countries. It was produced by ranking all the countries in the original data set according to their HDI, then splitting the data into "quartiles," that is, four subsets of countries ranked in the bottom 25%, between the 25th and 50th percentile, between the 50th and 75th percentile, and above the 75th percentile. Ten countries were then randomly selected from each subset to create a sample of 40 countries representing the entire range of human development. The only nonrandom selection was the United States, which was purposefully included in order to provide a meaningful reference point for American students.

A variety of conceptual variables reported by the UNDP are included in the data set, but not all of them. If you would like to learn more about the quality of life around the world, please do some exploratory research at the UNDP general website: undp.org or go direct to their data sets at hdr.undp.org/en/data. Other wonderful websites with fascinating human data include the Google Public Data Explorer (easily found by googling that title), the World Values Survey (worldvaluessurvey.org), and the Pew Research Center (pewresearch.org).

Your lab instructor will provide a subset of UNDP data as an MS Excel or GS file. You will be asked to produce simple data summaries for any two CVs that interest you in order to practice sorting and summarizing data. You'll also be asked to generate correlational and cause-and-effect hypotheses related to the data set. Table 3.2 shows the conceptual variables that could be included in your data set along with their operational definitions.

Table 3.2   UNDP Sample Data Set in Excel/GS, Conceptual Variables and their Operational Definitions

Conceptual Variables in Alphabetical Order (After HDI)	Operational Definition
Human Development Index (HDI)	*A composite index measuring average achievement in three basic dimensions of human development—a long and healthy life, knowledge, and a decent standard of living.*
Adolescent Birth Rate	Number of births to women ages 15–19, per 1,000 women ages 15–19.
Current Health Expenditure	Spending on healthcare goods and services, expressed as a percentage of GDP. It excludes capital health expenditures such as buildings, machinery, information technology and stocks of vaccines for emergency or outbreaks.
Government Expenditure on Education	Current, capital and transfer spending on education, expressed as a percentage of GDP.
Gross National Income (GNI) per capita	Aggregate income of an economy generated by its production and its ownership of factors of production, less the incomes paid for the use of factors of production owned by the rest of the world, converted to international dollars using PPP rates, divided by midyear population.
Homicide Rate	Number of unlawful deaths purposefully inflicted on a person by another person, expressed per 100,000 people.
Hospital Beds	Number of hospital beds available, expressed per 10,000 people.
Income shares (%)	Percentage share of income (or consumption) is the share that accrues to indicated subgroups of the population (Poorest 40% and Richest 10%)
Infants Lacking Immunization Against DPT	Percentage of surviving infants who have not received their first dose of diphtheria, pertussis and tetanus vaccine.
Infants Lacking Immunization Against Measles	Percentage of surviving infants who have not received the first dose of measles vaccine.
Internet Users	People with access to the worldwide network.
Justification of Wife Beating	Percentage of women and men ages 15–49 who consider a husband to be justified in hitting or beating his wife for at least one of the following reasons: if his wife burns the food, argues with him, goes out without telling him, neglects the children or refuses sexual relations
Labor Force Participation Rate	Proportion of the working-age population (ages 15 and older) that engages in the labor market, either by working or actively looking for work, expressed as a percentage of the working-age population.
Life Expectancy at Birth	Number of years a newborn infant could expect to live if prevailing patterns of age-specific mortality rates at the time of birth stay the same throughout the infant's life.
Maternal Mortality Ratio	Number of deaths due to pregnancy-related causes per 100,000 live births.
Mean Years of Schooling	Average number of years of education received by people ages 25 and older, converted from education attainment levels using official durations of each level.

Mobile Phone Subscriptions	Number of subscriptions for mobile phone service, expressed per 100 people.
Mortality Rate, Adult	Probability that a 15-year-old will die before reaching age 60, expressed per 1,000 people.
Mortality Rate, Infant	Probability of dying between birth and exactly age 1, expressed per 1,000 live births.
Mortality Rate, Under-five	Probability of dying between birth and exactly age 5, expressed per 1,000 live births.
Physicians	Number of medical doctors (physicians), both generalists and specialists, expressed per 10,000 people.
Population Using at Least Basic Drinking-Water Services	Percentage of the population that drinks water from an improved source, provided collection time is not more than 30 min for a round trip. This indicator encompasses people using basic drinking water services as well as those using safely managed drinking water services. Improved water sources include piped water, boreholes or tube wells, protected dug wells, protected springs, and packaged or delivered water.
Population Using at Least Basic Sanitation Services	Percentage of the population using improved sanitation facilities that are not shared with other households. This indicator encompasses people using basic sanitation services as well as those using safely managed sanitation services. Improved sanitation facilities include flush/pour flush toilets connected to piped sewer systems, septic tanks or pit latrines; pit latrines with slabs (including ventilated pit latrines); and composting toilets.
Population with at Least Some Secondary Education	Percentage of the population ages 25 and older that has reached (but not necessarily completed) a secondary level of education.
Prison Population	Number of adult and juvenile prisoners—including pretrial detainees, unless otherwise noted—expressed per 100,000 people.
Rural Population with Access to Electricity	People living in rural areas with access to electricity, expressed as a percentage of the total rural population. It includes electricity sold commercially (both on grid and off grid) and self-generated electricity but excludes unauthorized connections.
Share of Seats in Parliament	Proportion of seats held by women in the national parliament expressed as a percentage of total seats. For countries with a bicameral legislative system, the share of seats is calculated based on both houses.
Suicide Rate	Number of deaths from purposely self-inflicted injuries, expressed per 100,000 people in the reference population.

3A PROCEDURE

Open the UNDP data file provided by your instructor, using MS Excel or Google Sheets, at your instructor's request. Do NOT attempt editing or data management in the HTML (viewing) format. The file must be downloaded either in Excel or GS in order to do this assignment.

1. Using Table 3.2, decide on two conceptual variables that interest you. Fill in the answers on the Lab Record for Study 3A, indicating your choices and their operational definitions.

2. Follow instructions in Box 3.1 to create a backup *sheet* (NOT a backup workbook) of the data before you do anything else. When you're done, you should have a "backup" tab at the bottom of your workbook window, in addition to your original sheet with all the same data.

3. Once you have a backup sheet, go back to the original sheet and delete all columns except your chosen CVs.

4. Use the instructions in Box 3.1 (if needed) to sort the countries by HDI Rank, from best to worst. Remember that rankings are like race results—the *lowest* numbers are the *best* rankings.

5. Use the information in Box 3.3 (Essay 3.4) to calculate the requested means and standard deviations and insert them into the APA-Style Results section in your Lab Record. Create your own formulas to calculate differences as requested.

    a. DO NOT USE A CALCULATOR. The main goal of this assignment is to practice using a spreadsheet to manage data. You already know how to use a calculator. You might be asked to submit your Excel or GS file electronically so that your instructor can see the formulas you used. This will allow better feedback on what went wrong, if anything does.

    b. If data are missing for any of the top 10 or bottom 10 ranked countries for your CV, then you should count the top or bottom 10 countries WITH DATA, rather than averaging fewer than 10 countries.

6. Read the APA-Style "Discussion" and answer the questions as instructed in that Discussion. Do not use HDI rank as one of your CVs for your new hypotheses.

"Let's shrink Big Data into Small Data... and hope it magically becomes Great Data."

Image © Cartoonresource/Shutterstock

LAB RECORD WORKSHEET FOR STUDY 3A

USING MS EXCEL/GOOGLE SHEETS, SUMMARIZING DATA, AND GENERATING HYPOTHESES

Name: _____

Follow instructions in the Procedure for Study 3A.

Your conceptual variables: 1) _____

2) _____

Operational definitions (included in the file – scroll to the bottom)

1) _____

2) _____

The section below is a sample Results section for a lab report. The content of the sentences is awkward because your actual CV's are not mentioned by name, but the sentences are meant to show two different ways of correctly *formatting* reports of means and SD's, with proper headings, line spacing, abbreviations and italicizing.

Results

Variable 1

The mean for the countries with the best 10 HDI rankings was _____ ($SD =$ _____), while the mean for those with the worst 10 HDI rankings was _____ ($SD =$ _____). The difference in means for the top-ranked versus bottom-ranked countries was _____, and was not statistically tested.

Variable 2

Countries with the best 10 HDI rankings had a different score on this variable ($M =$ _____, $SD =$ _____) than countries with the worst 10 HDI rankings ($M =$ _____, $SD =$ _____). The difference was not statistically tested, and was equal to _____.

Discussion

A normal Discussion section of a lab report would look like this in terms of its heading and line-spacing (evenly double-spaced), but it would talk about the meaning of the results in plain language. Often, when the research is descriptive in nature, as this UNDP report would be, the author(s) will use part of the discussion to present new correlational or causal hypotheses. Let's do that here. Think about other conceptual variables that might be related to the UNDP CVs you chose. Look at the examples of correlational hypotheses in Essay 3.5. Then write two *different* correlational hypotheses on the lines below. Write one correlational hypothesis for each UNDP variable you chose, and relate it to any other conceptual variable. In each case, the correlated variable should NOT be another UNDP variable. For example, if one were to choose the UNDP variable "Mean Years of Schooling," a correlational hypothesis might be "Mean years of schooling is related to parent involvement in education." Write your two correlational hypotheses here:

1) _____

2) _____

Now think about what might *cause* either of your UNDP variables to increases or decrease, or what effect one of your UNDP variables might have on some other (non-UNDP) variable. For example, one might hypothesize that "Parent involvement in education increases the mean years of schooling." For examples of causal hypotheses, see Essay 3.5. Write a <u>cause-and-effect</u> hypothesis that uses one of your UNDP variables and some other (non-UNDP) variable on the line below. Your causal hypothesis may use the same CVs as either of your correlational hypotheses, but does not have to.

_____

SAMPLE SIZE AND ESTIMATES OF THE TRUTH

How much can you trust a sample of measurements to reveal the truth about a whole population? You can probably feel, on a gut-level, that a large sample of measurements will provide a better estimate of the truth than a small sample. But how much better do our estimates get as the sample size increases? This imaginary "research" is designed to provide first-hand experience with the answer to this question, without requiring you to leave the lab to collect data.

Your lab instructor will provide a bucket of beads. Each bucket represents the population of people about whom you would like to generalize based on a sample. Each bead represents a person in that population who might be randomly selected to participate in your study—a member of your research sample. In other words, each bead that you select will simulate a *person* whose behavior you are measuring. The actual behavior doesn't matter, but it will be more interesting if you decide on a behavior you'd like to measure as a class (e.g., the number of words correctly recalled from a list, or the number of unmatched socks produced by each load of laundry the person does . . . the real meaning of the numbers can be anything).

Once your class agrees on a behavior of interest, you must also agree on point values for each color of the beads in your bucket. These point values will simulate measurements for each participant in your sample. For example, if you're measuring the number of unmatched socks people produce per laundry load, you can assign a blue bead a score of 1 sock, a red bead = 2 socks, green = 3 socks, and so forth. After the class agrees on the imaginary measurement that each color will represent, fill in the white boxes below with that information.

Imaginary behavior of interest: _____

A	B	C	D
Color of Bead	Point Value (imaginary measurement)	Actual Frequency (%) (= number of beads of this color for every 100 beads in the bucket)	Predicted Total Value of beads per 100-bead sample (= Column B × Column C)
Expected (True) Mean (= total of column D/100) $\longrightarrow$			

3B PROCEDURE

Your lab instructor will tell you the actual frequencies of each of the different colored beads in your bucket for Column C, and from that, you can calculate what the expected mean score should be.

To collect data:

1. Pairs of students will take samples of various sizes (listed in the charts below) from their populations and record the data for each sample.

2. The person pulling the sample should close his/her/their eyes or turn away from the bucket while selecting and counting out beads.

3. Each bead you select is a measurement of your variable. Record the measurement in the correct data table designed for the sample size you selected. SHORTCUT: Although you should imagine that each bead is a separate person in your study, you don't have to record the score for each bead independently. Since participant numbers are arbitrary, you can just count the number of beads of each color and write that score as many times as there are beads of that color in your sample. For example, if blue beads represent a score of 4, and you have 10 blue beads, you should write in a score of "4" 10 times, for 10 participants of your sample.

4. After you pull a sample of five beads and record your data, return all the beads to the bucket and mix them before pulling your next sample (10 beads). Always remember to return your beads to the bucket and mix them up before you take your next sample.

5. Write the possible values for the measurements under the x-axis (lowest to highest, evenly distributed in units along the x-axis).

6. When all samples are done, your instructor will ask for the means for sample size of 5 from each pair of students and these will be plotted on the scatterplot. Recreate the instructor's scatterplot on your own lab record. The instructor will then ask for mean for sample size 10 from each pair, and these will be plotted, etc., until the means obtained for all sample sizes have been plotted on the Lab Record for Study 3B.

7. Answer the questions on Part 1 of the Lab Record, after the scatterplot. There are two additional parts to the Lab Record for this study, designed to take cover more advanced, but related, concepts. Your instructor might assign those records or might not, depending on the course goals and time availability.

DATA COLLECTION SHEET FOR STUDY 3B

Sample Size: **5**	
Participant #	Measurement
1	
2	
3	
4	
5	
Mean >>	

Sample Size: **10**	
Participant #	Measurement
1	
2	
3	
4	
5	
6	
7	
8	
9	
10	
Mean >>	

Sample Size: **25**	
Participant #	Measurement
1	
2	
3	
4	
5	
6	
7	
8	
9	
10	
11	
12	
13	
14	
15	
16	
17	
18	
19	
20	
21	
22	
23	
24	
25	
Mean >>	

Sample Size: **35**	
Participant #	Measurement
1	
2	
3	
4	
5	
6	
7	
8	
9	
10	
11	
12	
13	
14	
15	
16	
17	
18	
19	
20	
21	
22	
23	
24	
25	
26	

(continue)

Sample Size: **35** (continued)	
Participant #	Measurement
27	
28	
29	
30	
31	
32	
33	
34	
35	
Mean >>	

Sample Size: **50**	
Participant #	Measurement
1	
2	
3	
4	
5	
6	
7	
8	
9	
10	
11	
12	
13	

Sample Size: **50** (continued)	
14	
15	
16	
17	
18	
19	
20	
21	
22	
23	
24	
25	
26	
27	
28	
29	
30	
31	
32	

Sample Size: **50** (continued)	
33	
34	
35	
36	
37	
38	
39	
40	
41	
42	
43	
44	
45	
46	
47	
48	
49	
50	
Mean >>	

Modified by C. Buckley

LAB RECORD WORKSHEET FOR STUDY 3B SAMPLE SIZE AND ESTIMATES OF THE TRUTH

PART 1: ESTIMATES OF THE POPULATION MEAN

Name: _____

The lab instructor will ask for means from each research team (pair of students) so that you can plot those means on the scatterplot below. Before you begin, write the lowest bead value near the left end of the x-axis. Then distribute the values as evenly as possible along the x-axis so that the highest value ends up near the right corner. For example, if the lowest bead value was 5 and the highest value was 25, your x-axis would look like this:

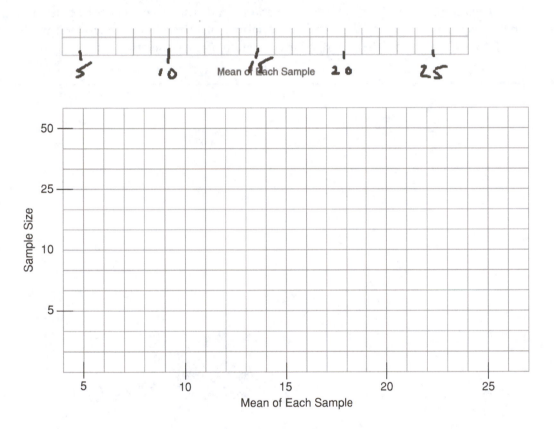

After data are entered in your scatterplot, answer the following questions based on the plot:

If you had chosen beads without closing your eyes or looking away, would you still have random samples?
Circle: Yes   No   Explain _____

_____

The population has one true mean, as calculated on your original values table. Our samples are taken as a way of estimating that true mean. Use your own words to explain how sample size affects our ability to estimate the true mean: _____

_____

All other things being equal, given the mean of a set of data, which mean would you trust more: one that was based on 10 participants, or one based on 100 participants? Circle one: 10   100

In your own words, explain why.

_____

LAB RECORD FOR STUDY 3B
SAMPLE SIZE AND ESTIMATES OF THE TRUTH

PART 2: ESTIMATES OF THE POPULATION SD

In Part 1 of this lab record, you reported that the size of a sample affects how much you can trust the sample's mean to reflect the true mean of the population. Do larger sample sizes also provide better estimates of the amount of variability within the true population?

Remember that there is one true SD that describes this population. Your instructor (the Creator of the population of beads) can tell you what the true SD is.

As with a mean, each sample you take from the population can be used to estimate the true variability in the population. Below is a graph showing the standard deviations of 11 randomly generated samples of various sizes, from $N = 5$ to $N = 500$, where the true standard deviation of the population was 1.70.

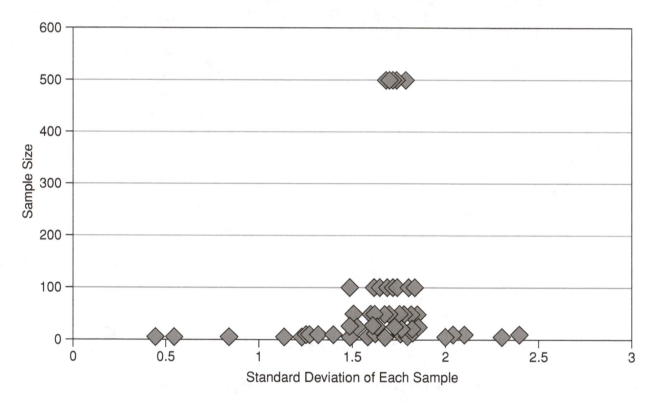

What do you notice about how the size of the sample affects our estimates of the true variability?

_____

All other things being equal, given the mean and SD of a set of data, which SD would you trust more to reflect the real variability within the population (circle one): $N = 3$ or $N = 500$

In your own words, explain why.

_____

_____

LAB RECORD FOR STUDY 3B
SAMPLE SIZE AND ESTIMATES OF THE TRUTH

PART 3: DETECTING DIFFERENCES BETWEEN POPULATIONS

Suppose you were given two new buckets of "bead-people," and you wanted to know whether the populations differed in terms of some behavior of interest. For example, imagine you gave advice to the bead people of Bucket A on how to keep their socks together in the laundry, and now you want to test the hypothesis that following your advice leads to fewer sock losses.

If your hypothesis is true, then you would predict that the bead-people of Bucket A will lose fewer socks in the laundry than the Bucket B bead-people. In other words, the mean score for the beads you pull from Bucket A will be lower than for Bucket B.

Imagine the buckets are real populations with thousands of people in each. Below is a list of statements about the steps one might take and the things one might consider in order to test the hypothesis and its associated prediction. Some are good ideas, and some are bad ideas and/or would not help you test the hypothesis. Identify the good ideas with "G" and the bad or useless ideas with a "B."

_____ 1. Select a small sample (about five bead-people) from each bucket.

_____ 2. Select a large sample (about 100 bead-people) from each bucket.

_____ 3. Make sure you select your samples to include beads of every color for variability.

_____ 4. Use a completely random selection process, regardless of variability in your samples.

_____ 5. Calculate the means for each sample.

_____ 6. Compare each mean to the number of beads in the bucket it came from.

_____ 7. Compare the difference between the means of your two samples.

_____ 8. Consider the variability around the means in your samples.

_____ 9. Compare the actual variability for each population to the sample SDs.

_____ 10. Compare the actual means for each population to the sample means.

Given what you've read about reporting means in Essay 3.3, your responses to questions in Parts 1 and 2, and the statements you selected as good ideas above, which three good ideas would be *most* important and directly applicable to your decision about whether the two bucket populations are different from one another? (Circle the numbers to show your answer):

1	2	3	4	5
6	7	8	9	10

Module 5 will provide more specific information on detecting differences between data sets.

MODULE 3 GLOSSARY OF TERMS AND EXAMPLES

Categorical Data: Data that tell how many observations fit one or more defined categories or groups.
  Examples: The numbers of students in each fraternity and sorority on campus would be categorical data. Counting the number of students who are athletes and nonathletes produces categorical data. A report of the number of cars of different colors passing through an intersection would also be presenting categorical data.
  Where to find this term: Essay 3.2, Table 3.1

Cause-and-Effect Hypothesis (Causal Hypothesis): A statement that declares a relationship between two conceptual variables whereby changes in one variable cause (lead to, affect, influence, increase or decrease...) changes in the other variable.
  Examples: Drinking heavily leads to poor judgment. Smoking causes cancer. A positive attitude leads to greater happiness. Study habits affect grades. Friendliness toward others increases friendliness received.
  Where to find this term: Essay 3.5, Study 3A, Modules 5, 6, 7 & 8.

Convenience Sample: A group of people or events chosen for study based on their availability.
  Example: If one wishes to know more about the challenges faced by elderly people in a particular community, the population would consist of all elderly people in that community, and a convenience sample of those people might be chosen by visiting local nursing homes and retirement homes, and asking people who are over age 65 if they would be willing to participate in the study. This is not a random sample because each elderly person in the community does not have an equal chance of being selected for the study (e.g., those who live independently would not have a chance of being selected). Compare to definition and example for *random sample.*
  Where to find this term: Essay 3.1

Correlational Hypothesis: A statement that declares a predictable relationship between two conceptual variables whereby knowledge of a datum for one variable provides information about the datum for the other variable (datum = 1 data point).
  Examples: Shoe size is related to height (given a person's shoe size, one can predict a range for that same person's height). Precipitation is related to barometric pressure. Total revenue generated by arcades is related to interest in computer science educational programs.
  Where to find this term: Essay 3.5, Study 3A. See also Module 4.

Experimental Research: See Module 1 Glossary and Essay 1.4. See also Modules 5, 7 & 8.

Hypothesis: A sentence that declares or implies a relationship between two conceptual variables.
  Examples: See Correlational Hypothesis or Cause-and-Effect Hypothesis.
  Where to find this term: Essay 3.5, Studies 3A and 3B (Part 3). See also Modules 4, 5, 6, 7, & 8. Note that many introductory psychology textbooks are unclear about the difference between a "hypothesis" and a "prediction," and sometimes use them as synonyms. They are NOT synonyms, as explained in Essay 4.4 and Figure 4.5.

Interval Data: Numbers that represent consistent, measurable amounts, where the difference between any two measurements can be quantified and compared meaningfully to the difference between any other two measurements.
  Examples: Exam scores are interval data (the difference between a 95 and a 90 is the same as the difference between an 85 and an 80, in terms of the number of points earned). Shoe sizes are also on an interval scale.
  Where to find this term: Essays 3.2, 3.3, Table 3.1

Likert Scale: A way of quantifying opinions, thoughts or feelings by asking people to rate their responses to statements or questions on a numeric scale, where low numbers represent one extreme and high numbers represent the opposite extreme.

    Example: Rate your level of agreement with this statement:

        This is a clear example of a Likert-Scale question.

1	2	3	4
Strongly Disagree	Disagree	Agree	Strongly Agree

    Another example: How much do you rely on glossary examples to learn terminology?

1	2	3	4	5
Not at All	Minimally	Moderately	Heavily	Very Heavily

    Where to find this term: Essay 3.2

Mean: The arithmetic average of a set of numbers. The mean is often used as a way to summarize the "real" value of most of the scores in a data set, or as an estimate of the true score of the population from which the set of numbers came.

    Example: The mean of 8, 9, 10, 11, and 22 is equal to the sum of 8, 9, 10, 11, and 22 divided by 5, which equals 60 divided by 5, which is equal to 12. Note that this is a *skewed* data set because the mean is higher than four out of the five numbers in the set. Therefore, the *median* would be a better estimate of the true score for this data set.

    Where to find this term: Essays 3.3, 3.4, Figures 3.1, 3.2, Table 3.1, Studies 3A, 3B, Box 3.3

Median: The middle score when all scores in a data set are ranked from lowest to highest. The median is sometimes used to summarize the "real" value of most of the scores in the data set, or as an estimate of the true score of the population from which the set of numbers came.

    Example: The median of 8, 9, 10, 11, and 22 is equal to 10, because there are two scores lower than 10 and two scores higher than 10. The sample is not normally distributed, so the median is probably a better estimate of the true score of the population that these numbers came from than the *mean*.

    Where to find this term: Essays 3.2, 3.3, 3.4, Figure 3.1, Table 3.1

Nominal Data: See *Categorical Data*

Ordinal Data: Numbers that represent rankings of observations relative to other observations. Ordinal data do not provide information about an individual alone, only relative to others, and only in terms of order.

    Examples: Class rankings among graduates are ordinal data. We know the order (Valedictorian first, Salutatorian second, etc.). However, the difference between Valedictorian and Salutatorian cannot be quantitatively compared to the difference between the Salutatorian and the third-ranking graduate. Another example would be a taste-test, where three or more drinks are compared and ranked from best to worst taste as 1, 2, and 3.

    Where to find this term: Essay 3.2, Table 3.1

Population: The larger group of people or events about which a researcher wishes to draw conclusions. Usually, the population is too large to study every individual within it, so we choose a sample of individuals from the population to study.

    Examples: When advertising executives study the way children react to a new toy, they use a small group of children, but wish to generalize the results to the way most children will respond to the toy. The population consists of all the children to whom the toy will be marketed.

    Where to find this term: Essays 3.1, 3.3, Studies 3A, 3B, Box 3.3

Mod 3 Glossary

Prevalence: See Module 2 Glossary, Essay 2.2

Random Sample: A group of people or events chosen for study based on some arbitrary condition that is unrelated to the variable of interest or mathematically random process, whereby every person or event belonging to the population has an equal chance of being selected for the sample.

> *Example:* If one wishes to know more about the challenges faced by elderly people in a particular community, the population would consist of all elderly people in that community, and a random sample might be chosen by going through an alphabetical listing of all community members over age 65 and selecting every tenth person for the study.
>
> *Where to find this term:* Essay 3.1, Study 3B

Random Selection: The process by which a *random sample* is chosen from a population. Random means that every member of the population has a mathematically equal chance of being selected.

> *Examples:* To randomly select people from the population of all the residents of a community, a researcher might contact every 100th home with a registered address. To randomly select from the population of all college students at a particular university, a researcher might use a random number generator to select from student ID numbers, or choose every 50th name from the student directory.
>
> *Examples of NOT random selection:* Going to homes on a particular street or in a particular neighborhood of the community to select participants, or putting out a campus flyer asking for volunteers for a study (only those who see the flyer and want to volunteer will be in the study).
>
> *Where to find this term:* Essay 3.1, Study 3B

Range: A way of expressing the amount of variability in a set of scores. In any set of scores, the range is the difference between the highest and lowest scores.

> *Example:* The range of the data set 8, 9, 10, 11, and 22 is equal to the difference between 22 and 8. The range of this sample could be expressed as "8 to 22," but we usually represent range with one number that is the difference between the high and low score (in this case, 14).
>
> *Where to find this term:* Essay 3.3

Ratio Data: Numbers that represent quantified values for each observation, where (1) differences between observations are measurable and can be compared meaningfully (i.e., one difference can be said to be greater than another), (2) differences can be added, subtracted, multiplied and divided without losing meaning, (i.e., differences can be halved or doubled meaningfully, and (3) a true zero exists on the scale, representing the complete lack of whatever was being measured.

> *Examples:* In a study on smoking, people are asked how many cigarettes they smoke per day. Abe smokes 60, Bek smokes 20, and Cardan smokes 10. The numbers of cigarettes smoked per day are ratio data because (1) We can quantify and compare differences and say that the difference of 40 cigarettes between Abe (60) and Bek (20) is much greater than the difference of 10 cigarettes between Bek (20) and Cardan (10). (2) The differences can be multiplied/divided accurately: The difference between Abe and Bek is four times the difference between Bek and Cardan. And (3) A true zero is possible (that would be a nonsmoker).
>
> *Where to find this term:* Essays 3.2, 3.3

Raw Data: The information recorded during observations. These data can be *categorical, ordinal, interval,* or *ratio*.

> *Examples:* In a study on pet preferences, people are asked whether they prefer cats, dogs, or other pets. Each person's answer places them in a category and provides one raw data point (categorical). A restaurant critic describes all the restaurants in one town and ranks them from best to worst. Each restaurant's rank is raw data (ordinal). In a study on motivation, people are asked questions that measure how motivated they feel to go to work. The motivation scores for each individual in the study are raw data (interval). In a study on smoking, people are asked how many cigarettes they smoke per day and at what age they started smoking. The answers for each individual are raw data (ratio).
>
> *Where to find this term:* Essays 3.1, 3.3

Sample: A subset of a population, assumed to represent that population in terms of the conceptual variable of interest. The sample should be as large as possible and randomly selected in order to best represent the population.

> *Example:* If one wishes to know more about the challenges faced by elderly people in a particular community, the population would consist of all elderly people in that community (too many to interview). Those who are included in the study would be a sample.
>
> *Where to find this term:* Essay 3.1, Study 3B

Skewed: Describes a data set where a great majority of the numbers are either above or below the *mean*. This happens when one or a few numbers in the set are either much higher or much lower than the rest of the numbers in the set.

> *Example:* A single very high number (compared to all the other numbers in the data set) can increase the mean so that it is much higher than most of the numbers in the data set, so the mean does not truly represent most of the numbers. The mean of 2, 3, 4, 6, 12, and 1000 is about 171. Five out of six of the numbers in the sample are way below the mean, and one is way above. These data are skewed. Also see examples for *mean* and *median*.
>
> *Where to find this term:* Essay 3.3, Fig. 3.1b

Standard Deviation (SD): A way of expressing the variability in a data set. The standard deviation is a standardized measure of the differences (deviations) between each number in a data set and the mean of the set. In a large, normally distributed data set (see Fig. 3.1a), the standard deviation allows us to estimate where 68%, 95%, and 99% of the scores fall. Sixty-eight percent of scores fall within one SD above or below the mean, 95% fall within two SD, and 99% fall within three SD of the mean.

> *Examples:* "The average child will eat 1,500 peanut butter sandwiches before he/she graduates from high school." (Source: National Peanut Board, nationalpeanutboard.org.) The National Peanut Board does not offer complete descriptive statistics on their website, but if, for this example, we assume that the SD is 300 sandwiches, then 68% of children would eat between 1,200 and 1,800 peanut butter sandwiches before they graduate from high school, 95% of children would eat between 900 and 2,100, and 99% of children would eat between 600 and 2,400 peanut butter sandwiches. It takes an average of 540 peanuts to make a 12-oz jar of peanut butter. This is much easier to accurately measure than the number of sandwiches eaten per child over several years, so the SD is probably much smaller. A reasonable guess is about 25 peanuts (approximately half an ounce). This would mean that 68% of 12-oz peanut jars contain between 515 and 565 peanuts. About how many peanuts would you find in 95% of all 12-oz jars? 99%? The answers are upside down at the bottom of this page.
>
> *Where to find this term:* Essays 3.3, 3.4, Box 3.3, Fig. 3.2, Table 3.1

Variability: How much the scores in a data set differ from the mean. The greater the variability, the less we can trust the mean as an indication of the most representative score in the sample or as an estimate of the true mean of the population from which the data points came. There are several ways to express variability, but two of them are discussed in this module: see *range* and *standard deviation*.

> *Example:* In measuring friendliness of workers at a fast-food chain, the manager records the percentage of time spent smiling per customer being served. She finds employees smile an average of 50% of the time per customer, but there is variability: One employee never stops smiling (he smiles 100% of the time) whereas another smiles just 2% of the time. The range is from 2% to 100%, or 98%. However, those measurements are unusual, and the SD is only 10%, so most of the employees smile between 40% and 60% of the time (assuming the measurements were normally distributed).
>
> *Where to find this term:* Essay 3.3, Study 3B

Module 4
Correlational Research: Testing Relationships Between Variables

Variable X   Variable Y   Variable X's Sister   Variable X's Brother-in-law

X & Y's Son   X & Y's Daughter   X & Y's Nephew and Niece

MODULE 4 LEARNING OBJECTIVES CHART

ESSAY NUMBER	MODULE 4 ESSAY LEARNING OBJECTIVES	BEFORE READING				AFTER READING			
		I don't know how **1**	I know a little about this **2**	I know enough about this to guess correctly **3**	I know how to do this and/ or have already done it. **4**	I don't know how **1**	I know a little about this **2**	I know enough about this to guess correctly **3**	I know how to do this and/ or have already done it. **4**
4.1	Define and discuss the goals and value of correlational research.								
4.1	Recognize and distinguish between examples of positive and negative correlations.								
4.1	Discuss the direction and relative strength of correlations from scatterplots and correlation coefficients.								
Box 4.1	Use MS Excel or Google Sheets to produce a scatterplot with a trendline.								
4.2	Given a correlational research hypothesis, provide the corresponding null hypothesis.								
4.2	Explain the meaning of the term "significant correlation" and the role of probability in making objective decisions about whether or not a correlation is "significant."								
4.2, Box 4.2	After correlational data have been collected and summarized as a correlation coefficient, describe three steps used to decide whether the data support the research hypothesis.								

		I don't know how 1	I know a little about this 2	I know enough about this to guess correctly 3	I know how to do this and/ or have already done it. 4		I don't know how 1	I know a little about this 2	I know enough about this to guess correctly 3	I know how to do this and/ or have already done it. 4
4.3	Explain the meaning of "spurious correlation" in two different ways.									
4.3	Explain how "third variables" and "bidirectionality" play a role in the consideration of new, causal hypotheses from correlational findings.									
4.4	Distinguish between a hypothesis and a prediction in terms of conceptual variables and operational definitions.									
4.5	Give at least two good reasons why scientists are careful *not* to use the word "proof" when discussing the evidence from one study for or against a research hypothesis.									
4.5	Distinguish between a hypothesis and a theory.									
		Read the assigned essays and actively seek answers to any questions rated less than "4." Then return to this chart and complete the white half.					Now proceed to the chart for the applications section, read the objectives for your assigned research project, and complete the gray side of the *research* learning objectives chart.			

ESSAY 4.1

CORRELATIONAL RESEARCH MEASURES RELATIONSHIPS

In Modules 2 and 3, we operationally defined and measured conceptual variables, summarized them quantitatively, and generated new hypotheses about relationships between them. We now turn to how these hypotheses can be tested, beginning with correlational research. A *correlational hypothesis* declares that a predictable relationship exists between two conceptual variables. As explained in Essay 1.3, finding evidence for a hypothesis is not a matter of verifying or confirming it, but of putting it to the test. To test whether a relationship exists, we have to predict its direction and then measure its direction and strength. If our measurements match our prediction, we will have evidence to support the existence of a relationship.

Consider the correlational hypothesis, "*Musical talent increases with artistic talent.*"[1] Assuming we can quantify musical and artistic talent, this relationship can be tested by first predicting that people who score high for musical talent would also tend to score high for artistic talent (in other words, both variables should change dependably in the same direction). We would then measure both variables for each individual in a group of people, then determine the direction and strength of the association between the two variables within that group. If our observations are in line with our prediction, we have evidence in favor of the hypothesized relationship.

Correlational research is similar to descriptive research, but instead of describing conceptual variables in isolation, we test and describe the pattern of the relationship between pairs of data: As one measurement changes, what happens to the other? Like descriptive studies, correlational studies cannot test whether one variable causes changes in the other, but can be used to generate good ideas for *new* cause-and-effect hypotheses that can be tested with subsequent experiments.

The data we collect through correlational studies can be visualized and summarized with a *scatterplot*, a graph that shows, for each participant in our study, the value of both variables with one dot. For example, to test the research hypothesis that SAT scores are related to GPA, we would record both scores for each participant in our study (a group of college students). Our scatterplot would show SAT scores on one axis (x-axis or y-axis) and GPA on the other axis, and we would plot a single dot for each student on the graph where his or her SAT score and GPA intersect.

A *positive correlation* occurs when low values for one variable are associated with low values in the other variable, and high values in one are associated with high values in the other. Using our SAT/GPA example, Figure 4.1 shows the scores for each variable, matched for every student. Dots show where each student's SAT score and GPA meet. Because low SAT scores tend to be associated with low GPAs, and high SAT scores with high GPAs, the dots are all included within an oval (shaded area) from the lower left to the upper right of the scatterplot. The predictability of

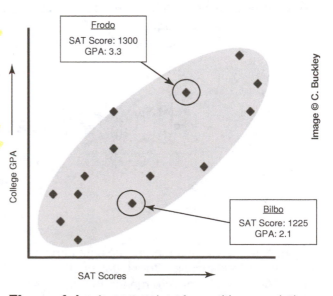

Figure 4.1 A scatterplot of a positive correlation.

---

[1] Notice the difference between "increases *with*" and "increases." The first is a correlational hypothesis; the second is a causal hypothesis. For more Information, see Essay 3.5.

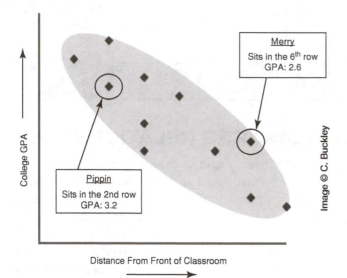

Figure 4.2   A scatterplot of a negative correlation.

this relationship means that our correlational hypothesis has resisted falsification. *Both variables change dependably in the same direction.* We now can predict, given a student's SAT score, the range for that student's GPA. Our predictions will not always be correct, but the existence of a correlation can greatly improve our accuracy in predicting GPA from SAT scores, and vice versa. However, we cannot conclude that getting a high SAT score *causes* one to get high grades in college.

A *negative correlation* occurs when **low** values in one variable are associated with **high** values in another variable. Figure 4.2 is a scatterplot that shows imaginary data comparing seat choice to GPA. The pattern suggests that if students are allowed to choose, sitting a great distance from the front of the classroom is associated with having a low GPA, whereas sitting

in a lower-numbered row (1 or 2) is associated with having a high GPA. Plotting the points for every student where each student's seat choice and GPA meet produces a pattern of dots that are all included within an oval (shaded area) from the upper left to the lower right of the scatterplot. If we had predicted this relationship before seeing these data (and if these data were real), we could conclude that as the distance one sits from the front increases, GPA tends to decrease. In this case, *both variables change dependably in opposite directions.* But remember that correlational studies do not imply cause-and-effect relationships. We could not conclude that professors assign grades based on seating choices! However, if these data were accurate, then it would make sense to test that cause-and-effect hypothesis with a true experiment (see Module 5).

Scatterplots help us visualize the strength of a correlation. Imagine a straight line drawn lengthwise through the middle of the shaded oval, a *regression line* for the data points, also called a line of best fit. If the dots were all close to a sloping regression line, the shaded area would be a skinny, cigar-shaped, sloping oval, indicating a strong relationship (the dots show little variation from a consistent relationship). Rounder ovals and flat (horizontal) regression lines show weaker relationships, and shaded areas that look more like circles than ovals tell us that there is no relationship at all. But visually estimating how round the oval appears or how much the line slants is not a good way to measure the strength of a relationship. Instead, we use correlation coefficients.

A *correlation coefficient* is a single number that serves as a measurement of the strength of a relationship (Fig. 4.3). It only takes a few mathematical steps

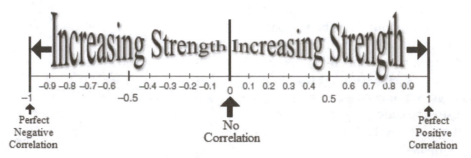

Figure 4.3   Correlation coefficients can vary from −1 to 1. The closer the coefficient is to −1 or 1, the stronger the relationship. Correlation coefficients in the middle of the scale, closer to zero, are weaker relationships. A coefficient of zero means that there is no predictable relationship between the two variables, while coefficients of -1 and 1 indicate equally strong, perfect correlations.

to calculate a correlation coefficient for any two sets of numbers (e.g., SATs and GPA scores). You will learn how to do this in more advanced courses in psychology or statistics. For this course, you only need to know how to interpret a correlation coefficient: 0 represents no relationship at all. Positive coefficients represent positive correlations, up to a maximum (perfect) positive correlation of 1. Negative coefficients represent negative correlations, getting stronger as one approaches a perfect negative correlation of –1. Coefficients above 1 or below –1 are mathematically impossible.

The *strength of a correlation* is shown by the absolute value of the correlation coefficient. The direction of the relationship, positive or negative, does not affect how strong, useful, or important it is. A correlation coefficient of 0.70 is equal in strength to –0.70, and would be equally useful in describing any relationship, given the same number of data points on the scatterplot.

While perfect correlations (–1 and 1) are mathematically possible, they are not likely in practice. A perfect correlation would mean that knowing the value of one variable would tell us precisely the value of the other. Many factors impact behavior, making this level of natural association between any two behavioral variables extremely unlikely.

BOX 4.1 Creating Scatterplots in MS Excel or Google Sheets (GS)

Open MS Excel or GS and recreate the spreadsheet shown to the right. To make a scatterplot of the relationship, select all the cells containing labels and data (click on A1, then hold the <shift> key and click on B13). Click on the insert tab at the top of the screen, then "Scatter," then the icon in the top left corner (which looks like a scatterplot). You now have a scatterplot. GS has the same "Insert" tab, but you might have to use the "Chart Editor" and scroll down to select "scatter chart" (see below).

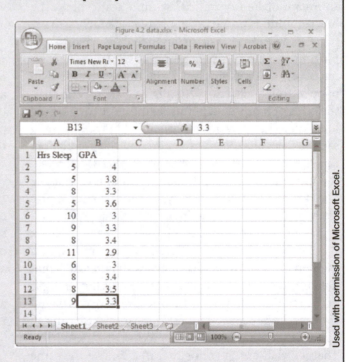

To get a regression line in Excel, click on the scatterplot to select it. A "+" appears next to the graph. If you click anywhere outside the scatterplot, the "+" will disappear. Click "+" and select "trendline" from the drop-down menu. In GS, you might automatically get a different type of chart (line or column). To switch to scatterplot, you need to open the "Chart Editor." If it doesn't pop up on its own when you select the chart, click on the three vertical dots in the upper right corner of your chart and select "Edit Chart." In the Chart Editor box, in the "Setup" tab, click on "Chart Type" and scroll down to "scatter graph." To get a trendline in GS, use the "Customize" tab in the Chart Editor box and click on "Series." Then scroll down and click the box for "trendline."

Excel and GS always graph the left-column variable on the x-axis and the right-column variable on the y-axis. In Excel, you can label your x- and y-axis with the "+" tab by selecting "Axis Titles," then typing in your labels for the "Primary Horizontal Axis" and the "Primary Vertical Axis." GS is one step ahead here and will automatically label your axes. What does your scatterplot suggest about the relationship between the number of hours of sleep and GPA in this imaginary sample?

ESSAY 4.2

INTRODUCTION TO OBJECTIVE (ODDS-BASED) DECISION MAKING

Our goal in measuring the strength of a relationship between two variables is to test the hypothesis that they are predictably related. If we collect the data and see that they are not, then we have falsified our hypothesis. But how will we know, when we look at a scatterplot of our data, whether it shows evidence for a predictable relationship or just a bunch of dots that happen to look sort of close to a sloping line (especially when you squint and tilt your head to the left)?

In most cases, evidence for or against a relationship cannot be "eyeballed" from a scatterplot. The human mind is prone to apophenia, a tendency to see patterns where none exist (apophenia is what makes playing the cloud-shape game possible). When we have only a few data points, the odds that they will happen to fall close to a sloping line are greater than the odds of *many* data points falling close to a sloping line. But as you may have learned in Study 3B, a small sample is less likely to truly represent the population. So we try to use the largest sample we can, but when there are many data points, our tendency is to imagine lines where none exist. Clearly, we can't make objective decisions about relationships based on scatterplots and regression lines alone. There is a better way.

The correlation coefficient, calculated with a mathematical formula[2], condenses all our scatterplot data into a single number that represents the strength of the relationship (Fig. 4.3). Once we have calculated the correlation coefficient for our sample, we can ask ourselves a simple question: "What are the odds?" That is, what are the odds that in a sample the same size as ours, we would observe a correlation coefficient at least as strong as ours, *if in fact these two variables are completely unrelated in the population*?

It is important that we imagine ourselves in a world where the two variables are, in fact, unrelated, and our research hypothesis is wrong. Why? Because, we know that *when there is no predictable relationship between two variables* measured within a population, the correlation coefficient for that population is theoretically zero (see Fig. 4.3). We also know that in such a world, if we repeatedly take random samples from that population, the mean of all the correlation coefficients of our samples will be zero, but each sample will vary, and rarely, just by chance, we will get samples with strong correlation coefficients, even though there is no predictable relationship in the population. (If you don't believe this, think about the odds of guessing the winning lottery numbers. It's unlikely, but it happens all the time because so many people buy tickets.)

Here's where scientists get really clever: *As long as we know what the correlation coefficient is in a population (e.g., if it is zero)*, we can determine the probability of observing any other coefficient in a sample taken from that population.[3] Scientists use these probabilities to decide whether they have evidence for their research hypothesis.

All this is to say that once the data are collected and their relationship is summarized as a correlation coefficient, making an objective decision about whether the data support our research hypothesis becomes a three-step process, grounded in probabilistic reasoning. Of course, nothing is perfectly objective, but using probability makes our decisions much less subjective.

The three steps to make an objective decision about the evidence for or against a research hypothesis are as follows:

1. **Assume the null hypothesis is true.** That is, assume your research hypothesis is wrong. This may sound a bit pessimistic, but as explained above, it is an essential first step. "Null" = nothing = bupkis = nada = zilch. The ***null hypothesis*** claims that no relationship exists. This is an

---

[2] You will learn how if you take a basic statistics course. In the meantime, MS Excel and Google Sheets have built in formulas that will calculate the correlation coefficient for you.

[3] You'll learn how these probabilities are determined in a more advanced statistics course. For now, it is enough to know that they can only be determined if we assume we know the correlation coefficient in the real population. That generally only happens when there is no relationship, and the coefficient must be zero.

either-or view of reality: Either the *research hypothesis* is true and the relationship exists, or the *null hypothesis* is true and it does not. In the world where the *null* hypothesis is true, if we repeatedly attempt this study and take many random samples and measure their correlations, they will vary, but the mean correlation coefficient for all our attempts will be zero. We need to know that in order to take the next step.

2. **Considering the size of the sample, determine the *p-value*.** The *p*-value is the probability of producing the observed result *in the world where the null hypothesis is true* (i.e., there is *no* relationship). For a correlational study, we must ask ourselves, "If there is no relationship between these two variables in the population from which we drew our sample, what are the odds that a sample of this size would, just by chance, produce a correlation coefficient like the one we observed? What are the odds that a scatterplot like ours would have just 'happened', despite these two variables being completely unrelated?" Those "odds" are called the *p-value* (or "probability value.")

3. **Apply a decision rule.** Knowing the *p*-value, we can now make a decision based on one simple rule: If the *p*-value is *less* than 5%, or ".05" we have evidence for our *research* hypothesis. Why? Because a *p*-value "less than point-zero-five" means that in a world where the null hypothesis is true, our observations would have a less-than-1-in-20 chance of happening. In other words, we observed a much stronger relationship in our sample than we should have if the population's relationship is truly zero. If it's so unlikely to see such a strong correlation coefficient when the null hypothesis is true, then the null is probably not true, which means we probably live in the other reality: The one where our research hypothesis *is* true.

Stated another way, a sample correlation coefficient that has a less-than-1-in-20 chance of happening when a random sample is drawn from a population where no real relationship exists is evidence that a real relationship probably *does* exist in the population. We will call this sample's observed relationship "statistically *significant*," meaning that our observations support our *research* hypothesis. Remember that this is an either-or decision about reality: either there is no relationship, or there is one. If our observations are very unlikely when there is *no* relationship, we can conclude that there probably *is* a relationship.

These three steps (**the words in bold, underlined type**) form the basis for most (though not all) hypothesis testing in psychology and other natural sciences, not just correlational studies. We will apply this "probabilistic reasoning" to all our future research projects, whether we are testing correlational or causal hypotheses.

BOX 4.2 Probabilistic Reasoning

Many students have trouble working with the three-step decision process just described. If it's all perfectly clear for you, ignore this box. If it seems a little foreign or confusing to you, consider this: Everyone (including you) makes probabilistic decisions like this every day. Imagine a decision to buy an expensive item. You want this item desperately and you think it is worth the money [that's your research hypothesis]. But you don't really want to spend that money unless you're sure, so the conversation in your head might go something like this: "Okay, let's assume for now that it's not worth the money [you're assuming the null hypothesis is true]. Let me ask some friends who've tried it and see what they say [you're collecting data to test the null hypothesis]. Turns out, everyone you ask loves it. Now ask yourself: What are the odds that everyone would say they love it if it's really not worth the cost? [That's your *p*-value]. Pretty unlikely, right? So... [you're about to apply a decision rule based on your very low *p*-value]... You're going to reject the idea that it's not worth the cost, and go out and buy it [reject the null hypothesis in favor of the research hypothesis]."

(continued on next page)

BOX 4.2, continued

Here's another example, this time where you would *not* reject the null hypothesis: "This guy is being super friendly toward me; maybe he likes me [research hypothesis]. I'd like to ask him out, but what if I'm wrong? Let's assume he doesn't like me [assuming the null hypothesis is true]." Ask a few of his coworkers how friendly he is toward strangers [collecting data to test the null hypothesis]. Turns out, he's a really friendly person toward everyone, even his enemies. Assuming that he doesn't like me, what are the odds he would be so friendly toward me? Those odds are high, since he's nice to everyone [a very high *p*-value]. So... [apply the decision rule] ... I can't reject the idea that he does not like me. Better hold off on asking him out [no evidence for the research hypothesis]. If you're really thinking like a scientist, you might then say, "If he does something *really* unlikely under the null, like sing a love-song outside my bedroom window, that would have a much lower *p*-value, so then I could reject the null in favor of the idea that he *does* like me, and ask him out." But of course, if you ever do ask him out, you won't want to put it in those terms.

ESSAY 4.3

INTERPRETING CORRELATIONS

Imagine that we have just observed a statistically *significant* relationship (we observed a correlation coefficient in our sample that was less than 5% likely to occur if the population's correlation coefficient is actually zero). How should we interpret that?

Of all the mistakes made by the popular media (and even by some scientists!) as they interpret significant correlations, the most common and bothersome is the use of the word "effect" when describing the observed relationship. *Correlation does not imply causation.* A significant correlation means that two variables were *measured* and found to vary together in a predicted pattern. The factors that may have *caused* the variables to end up as they did were not tested. Nothing was purposefully changed (manipulated) to see how it affected anything else. It is therefore inappropriate to conclude that a cause-and-effect relationship exists when interpreting a correlation.

To borrow a phrase from the classic movie *Stripes*, when we see a significant correlation, we should "treat it like a UFO sighting." We saw something, so we're pretty sure it exists, but we don't know where it came from; no reason for its existence can be inferred from the data.

It is also a mistake to interpret **spurious (accidental) correlations**[4] as evidence for a relationship that was never predicted. You've heard the old phrase, "Things happen." In correlational research, we could add "...and sometimes they happen together."

Accidental correlations can pop out of an analysis of exploratory or descriptive data, where no prediction was made before the data were analyzed, but certain variables happen to be correlated. If you're looking hard enough and measuring enough different things, you can find many things that happen together for no apparent reason.

---

[4] This explanation uses the Oxford English Dictionary definition of spurious: "Superficially resembling or simulating, but lacking the genuine character or qualities of, something; not true or genuine; false, sham, counterfeit." (OED Online. March 2020. Oxford University Press. oed.com, accessed May 18, 2020). As per Haig (2003), spurious correlations are held to be those that are not valid because of an error in statistical interpretation (in this case, the failure to predict), though Haig might call the example provided here a "nonsense correlation." Regardless, the failure to state the predicted correlation before examining the data affects the authenticity of the probabilistic evidence for a relationship. The American Psychological Association defines "spurious correlations" as identical to the third variable problem. See note 5.

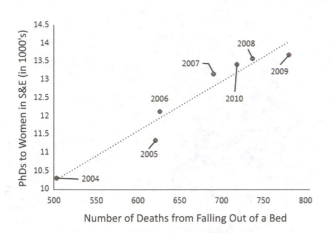

Figure 4.4   Between 2004 and 2010, the number of people who died each year from falling out of a bed was highly correlated with the number of PhDs granted to women in science and engineering, $r(6) = .97$. (Note that the y-axis is expressed in thousands, e.g., 11.5 = 11,500 PhDs). Source: tylervigen.com, a website devoted to the discovery of spurious correlations. Explore it for fun! You can select from among thousands of variables to see how they correlate. Have fun coming up with new hypotheses to explain the correlations... just remember that you have *no evidence* for your new hypotheses! (see text).

Figure 4.4 shows a "statistically significant" correlation between the number of PhDs granted to women in science and engineering (in thousands) and the number of people who died each year from falling out of bed! The correlation coefficient for the seven data points from 2004 to 2010 is a staggering .97! Using probabilistic reasoning, a correlation this strong is extremely unlikely in a world where there is, in fact, no relationship between these two variables: The p-value is less than .0004! *This is precisely why we must predict first, then examine the data that test our specific prediction.*

The "spurious correlations" website is a beautiful demonstration of what can happen when we simply sift through data, looking for patterns. When there are thousands of variables, potentially forming hundreds of thousands of relationships, we are virtually guaranteed to find relationships that have a less-than-1-in-20 chance of happening. Even very strong correlations of .97 with probabilities of less than 4 in 10,000 will appear frequently, just by accident, if hundreds of thousands of coefficients are searched. Because this correlation was never predicted, there is no evidence of future predictability between these two variables,

despite the "statistically significant" correlation. If, for some strange reason, you want to claim that fatal bedroom accidents are related to the academic advancement of women, you may do so, but you must first come up with a logical explanation for the relationship, then find new data to support your claim.

Provided that an observed relationship was hypothesized and predicted *before* examining the data, and keeping in mind that a significant correlation does not tell us anything about *why* the two variables are related, correlational research can be very useful! Having evidence for a hypothesized relationship allows us to predict the approximate value of one variable when we know the value of the other, which can be extremely useful—like predicting sales from website visits or a medical prognosis from a patient's mental health record.

Beyond its usefulness for making predictions, correlational research is often a starting point from which to generate new hypotheses to explain what we saw. Two variables might be correlated because they are both influenced by some other variable (often called a **third variable**[5] explanation). For example, the negative correlation between seat choice and GPA (Fig. 4.2) might be due to a third variable like motivation to do well. Such motivation might affect where a student sits (in front, to minimize distractions, or in back, which would make it easier to get away with texting during class). Motivation might also directly increase GPA (by increasing overall effort). These third variable explanations form the basis for new hypotheses that can then be tested with experiments.

Another possible explanation for a correlation is that changes in one of your two variables directly caused changes in the other. In generating such new hypotheses, it is important to remember the **bidirectionality** of correlations: If two variables (A and B) are correlated, A might cause B, or B might cause A.

---

[5] Many scientists and scientific organizations, including the American Psychological Association, define spurious correlations as those that can only be explained with third variables. This does not contradict the definitions of spurious correlations and third variables given in this essay. For instance, the data shown in Figure 4.4 could fit either definition of a spurious correlation ("accidental" *or* "only explainable with third variables"). Perhaps an increase in women pursuing PhDs led to both: more PhDs granted to women *and* more people falling out of bed because they fell asleep sitting up, working late into the night. Arguably, some third variable explanations might stretch the imagination.

The correlation itself does not give us a clue. Based on the data in Figure 4.2, we could form the new hypothesis that having a high GPA causes one to feel like the stereotypical "good student," and therefore to sit in the front. Or we could hypothesize that sitting in the front makes it easier to hear and follow directions, thereby causing increased GPA. Because of bidirectionality, the observation that two variables are predictably related can form the basis for two new causal hypotheses: A affects B, or B affects A.

While tests of hypotheses generally develop from correlational research to experimental, sometimes correlational research is done after a cause-and-effect relationship has already been tested and supported with laboratory research. This is a good way of checking to see that the findings from lab research can be applied outside the lab. *If two conceptual variables are shown to be causally related in lab research, the same two variables should correlate in the real world.* If they do not, the generalizability of the lab results is called into question. For example,

"Bad news. We've discovered a negative correlation between the number of CEOs and company profits. The next step is an experiment..."

an experiment showing that inhaling cigarette smoke causes cancer in laboratory rats would be less meaningful if smoking and cancer were not significantly correlated in humans.

ESSAY 4.4

HYPOTHESIS VERSUS PREDICTION: A CRITICAL DISTINCTION

Don't let the brevity of this essay fool you. The difference between a hypothesis and a prediction might seem trivial, but it has important implications for critically evaluating research. These will become clearer in the next essay and in the Applications section of this Module.

So why a separate, tiny essay on the difference between a hypothesis and a prediction? Two reasons: These terms are commonly used as synonyms, so it's likely you'll have to unlearn something you thought you knew. They are *not* synonyms. Second, realizing this difference and keeping it in mind throughout the course and throughout your life will improve your science attitude.

Research hypotheses declare relationships between conceptual variables. They can be interpreted broadly and tested in different ways to improve our understanding of the natural world. In order to test

any hypothesis, we must operationally define the conceptual variables so that we can measure them (and, in the case of an experiment, manipulate them).

Predictions are statements about what will happen in each correlational, experimental, or quasi-experimental study we do. Predictions are based on our own operational definitions of the conceptual variables in the hypothesis. If our predictions become our results, and if the operational definitions in our study are valid and reliable, the hypothesis will become the conclusion.

Because our operational definitions are never perfectly valid or perfectly reliable (see Essay 2.2) they are *not identical* to the conceptual variables in our hypothesis. The less valid our definitions are, the closer we get to claiming one thing and testing another.

The essential differences between hypotheses and predictions are explained with an example in Figure 4.5.

IF...	VS.	THEN...
HYPOTHESIS		**PREDICTION**

	HYPOTHESIS	PREDICTION
What is it about?	Conceptual Variables	Operational Definitions
What is it?	A broad statement about a relationship between conceptual variables	A test of the hypothesis. A specific statement about what will happen if the hypothesized relationship is true.
How is it worded?	In the present tense: "A relationship <u>exists</u> between two conceptual variables."	In the future tense: "Something specific <u>will</u> happen."
Provide an example?	"Cursing is related to the amount of television watched." (This is a correlational hypothesis.)	"The number of F-bombs used in a 5-min talk on an emotional topic will increase with the number of hours of TV-watching over the previous 7 days (self-reported)."
Explain the example?	Cursing is a conceptual variable that can be defined in many ways: Should the listener matter? The topic? Which words count as curses? TV-watching is a CV that can also be defined different ways. Self-reported hours watching TV will produce different data than using an automated timer on the TV that counts hours used.	The above operational definitions of cursing and TV-watching are the ways we have selected to test the hypothesis. If these measurements turn out as predicted, we will have support for our hypothesis, not proof, partly because we only tested the hypothesis in one, very specifi way.

Figure 4.5 Distinguishes between the terms "hypothesis" and "prediction." Note that the common practice of calling a hypothesis an "if-then" statement is somewhat misleading. Technically, the hypothesis is the "if" part. What happens in the experiment (the predicted result) is the "then" part. For example, If traveling increases social tolerance (hypothesis), then people who have traveled outside their native country will have higher social tolerance scores than people who have not (prediction).

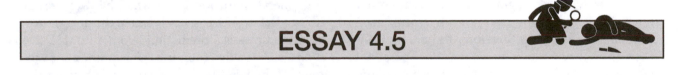

ESSAY 4.5

EVIDENCE IS NOT "PROOF"

If you've watched TV in the United States for longer than 10 min, you've probably heard a claim that something or other was "clinically proven." The phrase is so overused that it seems to have lost its meaning, if it ever had one. "Clinically proven" generally refers to the results of randomized, controlled trials, where the conclusion is a three-step, probabilistic decision, as explained in Essay 4.2 (and again, as applied to experiments, in Essay 5.4).

Always remember: One scientific study does not *prove* that a hypothesis is correct (or incorrect). If we accept that the word "proven" means "established as truth," then it may be possible to establish the truth in mathematics, through logic and deductive reasoning, but not in science, where we use inductive and probabilistic reasoning. In science, we infer from evidence, based on observations. Using a science attitude, we recognize that the truth can change with new observations. Scientists must always accept the possibility that they could be wrong about things, which makes them very uncomfortable claiming that they have "established the truth," or "proven" a hypothesis to be "true" or "correct" based on one study.

If a few uncomfortable scientists are not good enough reason to avoid a word, there are plenty of other good reasons to avoid saying we have "proof," presented here and throughout this book. We'll begin with two reasons related to what you already know about psychological science.

First, as shown in Figure 4.5, there is a critical difference between a hypothesis and a prediction. A hypothesis, which claims a relationship between conceptual variables, can only be *indirectly* tested by first operationally defining those variables, then testing the relationship using the measurements dictated by those operational definitions. Essay 2.2 explains why operational definitions are almost never perfect and can lack validity or reliability. **The strength of the evidence for any hypothesis depends on the validity and reliability of the operational definitions for the conceptual variables**. It is certainly possible to obtain statistically significant results with operational definitions that are not valid. This is partly why science must be a collective process and must be communicated clearly: to allow others to critically evaluate the validity and reliability of our operational definitions and to replicate our findings.

Recall, for example, the hypothesis that grades are related to where students sit in their classrooms (from Essay 4.3). If grades are defined as "the average of the first semester's grades," that might lead to a very different result than defining grades as "the final grade for one class." There might be a significant correlation between grades and seating arrangements in one class, but not in others.. Therefore, it would be unwise to claim that one study, using specific operational definitions, establishes the truth about a hypothesis.

A second good reason for not claiming proof of a hypothesis based on one study is that decisions about evidence are based on p-values, meaning they are based on *the odds of getting the observed result under the assumption that the null hypothesis is true*. If that likelihood is very low (less than 5%), then we reject the null hypothesis (it's probably not true) and claim evidence for our research hypothesis. But there is still a chance (albeit less than 5%) that the null hypothesis *is* true, and we just happened to get very unusual results. We can

never be 100% sure that what we observed wasn't just a lucky accidental sampling of data that happened to fit our prediction. Unlikely things *do* happen, although rarely. So, **based on our probabilistic (odds-based) decision-making process, there is always a small chance that we were wrong to reject the null hypothesis in favor of our research hypothesis.** Therefore, we cannot call our hypothesis "established truth."

Another good reason we shouldn't claim one study "proves" a hypothesis has to do with the design of the study and will be discussed in other modules.

Meanwhile, two more essential points must be made: First, just because we don't claim to have *proof* of our hypotheses **does not mean that scientific evidence is any less useful or important, or that it should be dismissed.** Evidence is still evidence; it is much better than guessing. Second, when a general, broad hypothesis explains multiple observations and is repeatedly supported by many different studies, as is the case with evolution, for example, it reaches the status of *theory*.

The National Academy of Sciences defines a *theory* as "a comprehensive explanation of some aspect of nature that is supported by a vast body of evidence."[6] So saying something is "just a theory" is actually saying that it is "just" an idea that explains a lot and has been repeatedly tested and supported by tremendous amounts of research. Often, when people say "… but it's just a theory," the preceding idea was not a theory at all. As in: "I have this idea that whenever I'm watching football and my boyfriend says that the quarterback never fumbles, that causes the quarterback to fumble on the next play, but it's just a theory." No, it's not. Calling it a theory contributes to the general confusion about what that word means. It's a causal hypothesis, easily tested the next time the boyfriend makes a prediction about a fumble. Even if one such "study" supports the hypothesis, it is not *proof* of the hypothesis, and still doesn't come close to a theory.[7]

In conclusion, whether you major in psychology, some other science, or a nonscience field, it will be useful to know how to evaluate the strength of scientific evidence. Our work so far suggests that asking the following critical questions can help you decide whether

---

[6] nas.edu/evolution/TheoryOrFact.html

[7] This example may or may not be the reason I'm not often invited to superbowl parties.

to trust a scientific conclusion, and may help you to be a wiser, more comfortable consumer of science.

☐ How valid and reliable are the operational definitions used by these researchers?

☐ How many observations (participants) were included in the study?

☐ How much variability was there in the measurements?

☐ How strong was the reported relationship?

☐ How likely was this result, assuming the authors of this study were wrong about their research hypothesis?

☐ Do other studies support the same hypothesis, with different research designs and different operational definitions?

MODULE 4 RESEARCH LEARNING OBJECTIVES CHART

STUDY NUMBER	MODULE 4 RESEARCH LEARNING OBJECTIVES	BEFORE READING				AFTER DOING PROJECT			
		I don't know how 1	I know a little about this 2	I know enough about this to guess correctly 3	I know how to do this and/ or have already done it. 4	I don't know how 1	I know a little about this 2	I know enough about this to guess correctly 3	I know how to do this and/ or have already done it. 4
4A	Explain how what we know about handedness can be used to learn more about lateralization of brain functions like language.								
4A 4B 4C	Gain practical experience with anonymous inventory and survey data collection techniques.								
4A 4B 4C	Clearly express the difference between your hypothesis and your prediction and describe why the difference is important for interpreting evidence.								
4A 4B 4C	Create a scatterplot with a regression line in either MS Excel or Google Sheets.								
4A 4B 4C	Draw conclusions regarding the strength and direction of the relationship between two variables based on a scatterplot and correlation coefficient (provided).								

		I don't know how 1	I know a little about this 2	I know enough about this to guess correctly 3	I know how to do this and/ or have already done it. 4		I don't know how 1	I know a little about this 2	I know enough about this to guess correctly 3	I know how to do this and/ or have already done it. 4
4A 4B 4C	Practice creating complete research records with all the information needed to write a report (essential introductory, method, results, and discussion information pertaining to your own research).									
4B 4C	Compose a correlational hypothesis and provide a rationale.									
4B	Explain how testing multiple hypotheses or predictions with one data set can impact the strength of the evidence for odds-based conclusions.									
4C	Explain order effects in data collection and how they can be avoided with counterbalancing.									

Now read about the project to prepare for lab. For any scores less than "4," keep those questions in mind as you complete the research project(s). Do not do the white half of this chart until after you've completed the assigned research project(s).

STUDY **4A**

ANXIETY SENSITIVITY AND HANDEDNESS:
IS THERE A RELATIONSHIP?

The average human brain has about a hundred trillion synapses. That's roughly 500 times as many sites for interneuronal communication *in one human head* as the number of stars in our galaxy. Jeremy Harper, the current world record holder for the fastest out loud counting, needed 3 months of 16-hr days, nonstop, to count to one million. To count every synapse in one human brain at Jeremy's world-record pace would require 750,000 years. Your brain is incredibly complex.

As you read this, many synapses in your own head are active right now, allowing you to see these words and comprehend their meaning, and begging you to stop reading for a moment to marvel over their very existence. Your brain is the ultimate cooperative system, with different areas at least partially devoted to different tasks, and the whole brain functioning as one unit. Although different areas of the brain have different functions, complex thoughts and behaviors are not isolated in any one brain structure. Even a simple task like reading the word "laughter" out loud, or actually laughing out loud, involves multiple brain regions.

We have much to learn about this complicated network of specialized areas, overlapping functions and individual differences. In addition to new and exciting functional magnetic resonance brain imaging techniques, psychologists have other, less expensive ways to investigate which areas of the brain are involved in different thoughts and behaviors, and we can use what we know to find out more, as we will in this correlational study.

For example, we can start with the knowledge that the right side of your brain controls voluntary

Image © abandsb/Shutterstock, modified by C Buckley

movement on the left side of your body, and the left side of your brain controls movement on the right side of your body. This is called **contralateral motor control**, and it is true for all human brains, due to the organization of the cranial nerves. We also know[8] that for about 95% of right-handed people and about 70% of left-handed people, the left side of the brain is mostly responsible for basic language functions (understanding and producing words).

---

[8] The truth, as usual, is more complicated than that, but the generalization is useful for this demonstration. For more information, see Knecht et al. (2000) and Villar-Rodríguez et al. (2020).

Are you among the 5% of right-handers or 30% of left-handers whose right hemisphere is more involved in language? You can use what we know about contralateral motor control to find out in less than 3 min.

Begin by going to clickspeedtest.info/mouse-test (a website designed to help gamers improve their clicking speed). Set the timer on the website to 30 s (10 s is usually not enough to see an effect). In silence, without thinking about anything else, click as fast as you can with your left hand for the whole 30 s and record your number of clicks in the table below (in the box labeled "1"). Then pick up some good reading material (I recommend anything related to psychology). Restart the timer, and again click as fast as you can, but this time do it while reading aloud. Record your number of clicks in the correct space (labeled "2"). Repeat these steps with your right hand (record clicks in boxes "3" and "4"). Then calculate the differences in clicking speed as shown in the table.

	# of Left-Hand Clicks	# of Right-Hand Clicks
While silent	1	3
While reading aloud	2	4
Difference	#1 – #2 =	#3 – #4 =

Which difference is larger, left or right? If your clicking speed *difference* is much greater for your right hand than for your left, you probably process language on the left side of your brain, like most of us. If you get the opposite pattern, you might be someone who processes language on the right side of your brain or on both sides. But remember: One round of data collection is not sufficient to "prove" either of those conclusions.[9]

Still, it is fun to see what happens. The neuroanatomy behind this test of brain lateralization is explained in the caption to Figure 4.6.

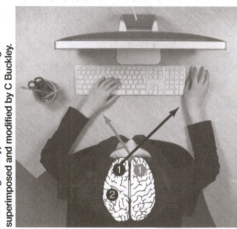

Girl at Computer Image © Glovatskiy/Shutterstock; Brain Image © Myper/Shutterstock Images superimposed and modified by C Buckley.

Figure 4.6   Language and motor control. Contralateral control via the cranial nerves means that for everyone, the right hemisphere of the brain controls the left side of the body (gray circle 1 and gray arrow) and the left hemisphere of the brain controls the right side of the body (black circle 1 and black arrow). For most people (not everyone), basic language functions are controlled by the left cerebral hemisphere (black circle 2). That's why most people who try to mouse-click with their right hand while speaking will slow down their clicking rate: The left side of the brain is doing two tasks at once (black circles 1 & 2). The same people can click faster with the left hand while speaking because they're using opposite sides of the brain (gray circle 1 and black circle 2), so the tasks are less likely to interfere with each other.

[9] If you do the four tasks in the order they are numbered, there is a methodology problem that might also explain the bigger difference for your right hand than for your left. Can you spot it? This is called an **order effect**, defined in Study 4C and Essay 7.4. If you'd like to see whether an order effect played a role, take another 3 min to repeat the task, but this time start with your right hand. Do you get the same result?

These observations, which have been replicated many times, support the hypothesis that in most people, the left side of the brain is more strongly associated with basic language production than the right side. It's a good example of how evidence regarding lateralized functions of the brain can be gathered without any expensive equipment.

We can also gain information about differences in function for the two sides of the brain by examining whether those functions or thought patterns are correlated with handedness, which we know is lateralized. If a particular cognitive ability or thought pattern is correlated with handedness, that would suggest that the ability or the thought pattern is also lateralized. The thought pattern we'll be examining in this research is anxiety sensitivity. It is not the same as general or social anxiety. Instead, anxiety sensitivity is the awareness of, and sensitivity to, one's own bodily signals when one is anxious. It can best be defined as "the fear of fear" (Reiss et al, 1986), because it measures *how we react* when our body sends us signals that are associated with fear or anxiety.

In this study, we will test the *correlational hypothesis* that **handedness is related to anxiety sensitivity.**

Usually, a correlational hypothesis declares a specific direction for the relationship (positive or negative—in this case, we should declare whether left handedness or right handedness is correlated with anxiety sensitivity). However, we'll wait until after we collect data (but before we analyze the data) to discuss that. You will be a participant in this study, and it's poor research practice for participants to know exactly what is expected. People will respond differently when they know what behavior is anticipated. This is usually unintentional, or arises out of a desire to help, or sometimes a desire to overcorrect for one's knowledge. We will therefore discuss the direction of the relationship in lab, rather than explain it here.

APPLYING RESEARCH TERMINOLOGY

This is a good place to practice the correct application of the terms *hypothesis* and *prediction*. Our operational definition of handedness will be the average score on a Handedness Inventory (HI), and our operational definition of anxiety sensitivity will be the average score on the Reiss—Epstein–Gursky Anxiety Sensitivity Inventory (ASI), a 16-item questionnaire (Reiss et al, 1986). A brief version of our *hypothesis* is stated in bold two paragraphs above. Our *prediction* is that the scores on the handedness inventory will be correlated with the scores on the ASI. Note the difference between the CV "*handedness*" and its operational definition, "*the score on a Handedness Inventory.*" This essential difference between a hypothesis (stated in terms of conceptual variables) and a *prediction* (stated in terms of the operational definitions) reminds us yet again that our evidence is not absolute "proof" of our hypothesis. If the evidence *could* be said to "prove" anything, it would be limited to proving the predictions, not the hypothesis. In a well-designed study, of course, evidence for the predictions is also strong evidence for the hypothesis, but good critical thinkers are always aware of this subtle difference (see Fig. 4.5).

4A PROCEDURE

This will be a correlational study examining the relationship between handedness and anxiety sensitivity. The specific hypothesis (i.e., the direction of the relationship) will be discussed in lab after data are collected, but before the data are graphed, summarized or analyzed.

1. Complete the Anxiety Sensitivity Inventory (ASI). Take your time and answer each question independently and honestly. Cover your answers, as this information may be personal.

2. Read all instructions on the Handedness Inventory (HI). If anything is unclear or you have any questions, ask! Chances are, if you have a question, others want an answer, too!

3. If materials to perform the tasks are set up at stations around the room:

   Go to any available station (or your assigned starting station). Read the instructions on how to do the first task posted at that station, then *perform the task ONCE, one-handed, as instructed*. Then switch hands and do it ONCE with the other hand. Then switch back and repeat one more time with each hand, for a total of two times with each hand, alternating. Then try to make a good decision about which hand is more COMFORTABLE performing the task. Accuracy and neatness do *not* matter, only comfort counts. Record your ratings on the inventory, then read the instructions for the next task and repeat. You do not have to do the stations in order.

   If no materials are set up around the room:

   Mime each activity at least twice with each hand. Alternate the hand you use. Pretend to perform the task ONCE, then switch hands and pretend ONCE with the other hand. Switch and repeat at least one more with each hand. Continue alternating hands as many times as needed (no less than twice) to make a good decision about which hand feels more comfortable performing the task. Record your ratings on the inventory.

4. Calculate your HI score by adding all your positive ratings and subtracting all your negative ratings, then dividing by the total number of ratings on the HI.

5. Calculate your ASI score by adding all your ratings and dividing by the number of ratings on the ASI.

6. To assure confidentiality, you will be secretly and randomly assigned an ID number (on the front page of your ASI). DO NOT TELL ANYONE YOUR NUMBER. Write it in the appropriate space on the HI, so that your ASI and HI scores may be matched without compromising your anonymity.

7. Record/submit your HI and ASI scores as instructed by your professor.

8. After everyone's data have been submitted and entered into a spreadsheet, the class will discuss the hypothesis in more detail, make specific predictions, and THEN look at the data to see if they support the hypothesis. Complete the Lab Record Worksheet based on that information.

LAB RECORD WORKSHEET FOR STUDY 4A

ANXIETY SENSITIVITY AND HANDEDNESS

Name: _____

Purpose *To examine a potential relationship between asymmetry (lateralization) of the brain's motor control and anxiety sensitivity. This could contribute to our understanding of whether anxiety sensitivity might be a lateralized thought pattern.*

Hypothesis *Handedness and anxiety sensitivity are related, such that sensitivity to anxiety can be predicted by degree and direction of handedness.*

We measured two variables for each participant. The conceptual variables were:

1. _____

2. _____

The operational definition of the first variable was _____

The operational definition of the second variable was _____

Prediction (If the hypothesis is true, will happen in our study, specifically? This should always be written in terms of the operational definitions): _____

_____

Method

Participants Describe the people who participated in data collection and provide relevant characteristics. Were they all students? Approximate age? How many left-handers, right handers, and ambidextrous? Etc. How many people participated in data collection, but were dropped from the analysis due to past hand injuries or for other reasons? _____

_____

_____

_____

_____

Materials (describe the Anxiety Sensitivity Inventory and the Handedness Inventory)

_____

_____

_____

_____

_____

_____

_____

_____

_____

_____

_____

Procedure (How were data collected? What instructions were given to all participants for each inventory?)

_____

_____

_____

_____

_____

_____

_____

_____

_____

_____

_____

_____

Data Handling Describe how individual HI and ASI scores were calculated.

_____

Describe what was compared to what and how (to look for a correlation).

_____

Results

The correlation between handedness scores and anxiety sensitivity scores was (*positive   negative   flat*), and was (*significant   not significant*), $r(_____) = _____$, $p \boxed{} _____$.   (circle one)
(circle one)   (fill in < or =)

Discussion

What can you conclude? _____

_____

GENERATING AND TESTING A CORRELATIONAL HYPOTHESIS

For some fascinating spurious correlations, go to

http://www.tylervigen.com/

Image © Fenton one/Shutterstock

Any two conceptual variables can be declared to be related to one another. One might declare, "Walking speed is related to hair length." This would be a correlational hypothesis, although seemingly illogical. The hypothesis that walking speed is related to *leg* length seems more likely to find support. However, if we consider that males might, on average, have longer legs, then a predictable link between walking speed and hair length becomes a logical hypothesis because males often have shorter hair. The point is that some correlational hypotheses might seem illogical until *third variable* explanations are given full consideration. However, we do not simply throw together any two conceptual variables with no reason at all for their proposed relationship. There should be a logical rationale for every research hypothesis, whether or not it is immediately obvious to others.

For this research, your team will be given a set of cards with conceptual variables on them. After discussing possible relationships between these CVs, you'll come to a consensus and write a correlational hypothesis for any two of them. You'll need a *rationale* for your hypothesis. That is, you must be able to logically make the case that the two CVs you chose are correlated. On the backs of the cards, survey-based operational definitions of the variables will help you decide on the direction of the relationship (which often depends on how CVs are defined). The survey

questions might also cause your group to rethink whether the relationship exists, in which case you may choose a new pair of CVs, if you wish. This group discussion should help clarify the wide range of operational definitions that are possible for any one CV, and the importance of valid and reliable operational definitions to test relationships between CVs. Once you finalize your hypothesis, you'll use the lab record worksheet to record the CVs and their operational definitions, then write a specific prediction based on your hypothesis.

We will collect data from everyone in the lab and enter them into one Excel or Google Sheets document. Groups will then use that document to produce scatterplots of their data while your professor runs a correlational analysis for each group. Your group will be provided with the results for the test of your hypothesis, and will informally present your study to the rest of the class.

For this research project, several hypotheses will be tested in your lab with one data set. Therefore, before you begin, it is worth considering how that affects the strength of your evidence, should you find support for your hypothesis.

Recall from Essays 4.2 and 4.5 that every odds-based decision we make has an accepted chance of being wrong. A less-than-5% chance of something happening means it could still happen up to 5%

of the time. It may help to think of our decision as one roll of a single die with 20 sides. If we only roll it once and predict that it will land on a 13, for example, our guess is probably going to be wrong, but there is still a 5% chance we could *accidentally* guess right. If we predict that it will be a 13 or a 14, then we have greater odds of accidentally being right. Predict a 13, 14, 15, 16, or 17, and you now have a 25% chance of being right. The more predictions we make for one roll of the die, the greater our chances of accidentally guessing right (more on this in Appendix A).

We must never forget that significant results might have accidentally turned out the way they did, even with no actual relationship between the variables, and that the more predictions we make with the same data set, the more likely that is to happen. This is yet another good reason not to speak of "proof" when drawing conclusions from your research, particularly when there are multiple predictions being made from the same data.

Remember that significant relationships provide *evidence to support* ideas. They do not *prove* that the ideas are true.

*Happens every time someone uses the word
"prove" in a scientific report.*

Image © Cartoonresource/Shutterstock

PROCEDURE 4B

This research will involve one or more correlational studies examining the relationships between conceptual variables of your choosing. In small groups or as a class, you'll be given a set of variables from which to choose, along with an operational definition for each CV in the form of a survey question.

1. Lay the deck of cards out on a desk or large surface area so that everyone can see them. Discuss possible relationships among the variables. Without looking at the definitions on the back, come to a consensus on at least three pairings that you think are likely to show three separate correlations.

2. Decide on the best pair (most likely to be correlated and most interesting to the group) and flip the cards over to see the survey questions that will be used to measure those two variables. Given those operational definitions, discuss the likelihood of a correlation and its direction (positive or negative). If the definitions change the way you were thinking about the variables so that they are now less interesting or less likely to correlate, discuss why that is. Then move on to the second-best pair your group selected and repeat this discussion. Continue until you find a pair of CVs with operational definitions that your group finds interesting and worth testing.

3. Enter the CVs and their operational definitions on your lab record worksheet (you will find it after Study 4C).

4. Hand in the cards you selected, keeping them separate from the other cards.

5. Your professor will randomize the order of the selected cards with their operational definitions and present the survey questions to the class one at a time. Use the data sheet on the back of this page to record your answers. To maintain anonymity and the accuracy of the data, do not discuss your answers with anyone else, and keep them covered as you record them.

6. When all survey questions are complete, tear out your data sheet, fold it over to keep your anonymity, and hand it in. You may then work on remaining lab record questions or take a short break, while your professor enters the data into an Excel or Google Sheets spreadsheet.

7. Either the whole class will examine and discuss each correlation together, or you will be asked to create a scatterplot of your data with a regression line while your professor runs the statistical analyses.

8. After analyses are available, complete the lab record and, if time allows, present your findings to the class. Ideally, your presentation should include the hypothesis and its rationale, the prediction, then a display of your scatterplot along with your results (correlation coefficient and p-value), and a conclusion, including a suggested explanation for why the results turned out as they did (if significant, offer a new causal hypothesis with a rationale, and if not significant, offer a suggested explanation). Take a picture of this paragraph so that you may refer to it after you hand in your data sheet.

STUDY 4B DATA SHEET

PLEASE ENTER ALL DATA HONESTLY AND AS ACCURATELY AS POSSIBLE.

TO MAINTAIN ANONYMITY: COVER YOUR ANSWERS. FOLD WHEN COMPLETE.

DESCRIPTIVE TERMS FOR MEASUREMENTS
(HIGHLIGHTED WORD/S ON EACH SURVEY QUESTION)   DATA

1. _____   _____

2. _____   _____

3. _____   _____

4. _____   _____

5. _____   _____

6. _____   _____

7. _____   _____

8. _____   _____

The lab record worksheet for studies 4B and 4C is the same and can be found after the procedure for Study 4C.

NOMOPHOBIA AND SOCIAL ANXIETY

Are you nomophobic? You're about to find out. The term "nomophobia" came out of a study commissioned by the United Kingdom Postal Service and is probably one of the best labels for a psychological condition ever invented. It stands for "no-mobile-phone phobia," meaning fear or anxiety associated with the separation from or inability to use one's mobile phone.

The past 20 years have seen a huge increase in cell phone use all over the world. Between 2000 and 2015, the number of phone subscriptions increased from 10% to 97% of the world's population (ICT Data and Statistics Division, 2015). One might argue that given the usefulness of cell phones and social pressure to own one, it is completely normal and even quite rational to feel attached and dependent upon our cellular devices. But when the attachment becomes so strong that it is maladaptive and mentally unhealthy, it can be called an addiction.

Mobile phone addiction resembles drug addiction in several ways: People can build tolerance, increasingly needing more and more contact with their phones to feel comfortable; they can experience difficult cravings and emotional and physical withdrawal symptoms upon separation; they often have difficulty controlling their use of the phone, even when using it could be dangerous (e.g., while driving) or is wildly inappropriate (e.g., at funerals and while supervising small children in public places); other obligations, sleep, relationships, and enjoyable recreation may be ignored in favor of time spent looking at the phone; and attempts to discontinue or limit the use of a phone are too often unsuccessful.

Unhealthy mobile phone dependency is growing in all age groups, but it appears to be growing the fastest among young adults and college students. Csibi et al., (2019) studied problematic phone dependency in over 1,600 individuals representing age groups from 3 to 11 years up to 50+ and reported that the highest level of addictive behaviors occurred in young adults, aged 20 to 34. Interestingly, the second most vulnerable age group was 3- to 11-year-olds.

Social anxiety is defined by the American Psychological Association as "fear of social situations in which embarrassment may occur (e.g., making conversation, meeting strangers, dating) or there is a risk of being negatively evaluated by others (e.g., seen as stupid, weak, anxious)."[10] The world of social media, though rich with social contact and communication benefits, is also a high-risk environment for confrontations with strangers, widespread public embarrassment, and negative evaluations on a public platform.

Like phone use, the prevalence of social anxiety has been growing in recent years, and its prevalence among college students is high, ranging from 10% to 40% depending on how prevalence is measured (self-reports yield higher prevalence rates than clinical diagnoses). Is social anxiety positively correlated with phone addiction? In other words, are the same people who are susceptible to phone addiction also susceptible to social anxiety? Or is nomophobia an unhealthy response to the healthy tendency to thrive in a social environment? In other words, are the same people who are susceptible to phone addiction *less* likely to experience social anxiety (more comfortable meeting strangers and less worried about public embarrassment or negative evaluations)? If so, we would expect a negative correlation between nomophobia and social anxiety.

These questions can be addressed with a correlational study. For this research, either your whole class or small groups will discuss these alternative research

---

[10] APA Dictionary of Psychology, https://dictionary.apa.org/ retrieved May 18, 2020.

hypotheses and come to a logical consensus on which hypothesis should be true. The whole class will then contribute to a data set, taking two surveys (provided by your instructor[11]), one on phone addiction and one on social anxiety. Your prediction regarding the direction of the correlation will depend on your group's or class's consensus.

Two important considerations for this research:

First, if we are not careful, **order effects** might bias our data. If, for example, people feel sensitive about their score on the phone addiction survey, they might overestimate their discomfort in social situations. Or if they score high in social anxiety, they might unconsciously compensate by aiming for low scores on phone addiction. Order effects occur when a response to one research situation influences the response to another. The best way to avoid this is to **counterbalance** the order in which participants complete the surveys. Therefore, half of the students in your class will do the phone addiction survey first, then the social anxiety survey, while the other half will do the two surveys in the opposite order (more information on order effects and counterbalancing can be found in Module 7, Essay 7.4).

Second, although elevated levels of addiction and anxiety may be fairly common experiences for college students, they are personal information. In order to respect everyone's privacy, we will use anonymous data collection techniques.

---

[11] Available with the teaching resources accompanying this book.

4C PROCEDURE

There are just two simple steps to data collection:

1) If you are asked to complete your surveys online, use an "incognito" window to protect your privacy. In Google Chrome, click on the three vertical dots in the upper right corner of your browser window and select "New incognito window." If you complete them on paper, be equally private and cover your answers. When you submit your data to your instructor, be sure to hand them in *face-down* or *folded* so that your scores do not show, and do not include a name or any other identifying information. You should also use blue or black ink or a pencil to maintain anonymity. (As much as your instructor might enjoy seeing a variety of ink colors on homework assignments, an anonymous survey is not the place for them.)

2) After compilation of the results by your instructor, you might be asked to create a scatterplot (see Box 4.1 for help if needed). Use the information provided by your instructor to complete the lab record worksheet.

LAB RECORD WORKSHEET FOR STUDY 4B OR 4C

Your Name: _____ Other group members: _____

_____

Purpose *To examine the correlation (if any) between two conceptual variables.*

Hypothesis:

_____

_____

Rationale (Logically explain why you think these two variables should be related):

_____

_____

Conceptual variables:

1. _____ 2. _____

Operational definition of the first variable: _____

_____

Operational definition of the second variable: _____

_____

Prediction Draw (roughly) what you expect the scatterplot to look like (Label your axes!)

Prediction (circle one):   Negative Correlation   Positive Correlation

Method

Participants (quantity and description, including any traits that may have influenced the data they provided):

_____

_____

_____

_____

Materials (Here you would be describing the survey/s, but we'll skip this step for this record.)

Procedure (Describe how raw data were collected):

_____

_____

_____

_____

Data handling (Describe any calculations that were performed on the raw data in order to summarize or compare them): _____

_____

_____

Results

The correlation was *(positive   negative   flat)*, and was *(significant   not significant)*, r(_____) =
_____, p [_____] _____.
                  (circle one)   (circle one)
         (fill in < or =)

Discussion

Did your results support the research hypothesis (circle one)?   Yes   No

<u>Answer only ONE of the next two questions (based on your results)!</u>

<u>If results supported the hypothesis</u>, suggest an explanation for the correlation—could this be a cause-and-effect relationship, or is there a third variable that might have influenced both of your variables?

_____

_____

<u>If results did not support the hypothesis</u>, suggest an explanation for the lack of a correlation.

_____

_____

MODULE 4 GLOSSARY OF TERMS AND EXAMPLES

Bidirectionality: The notion that if we propose a new causal hypothesis for an observed correlation between any two variables (A and B), we have no way of knowing which variable would be the cause and which would be the effect. Changing A *could* cause changes in B, or changing B *could* cause changes in A.

    Example: If musical performance is positively correlated with math scores, two direct, causal relationships are equally plausible: learning how to play music increases attention to numbers and math, OR, practicing math makes learning music easier. Our correlational data tell us nothing about which of these is the better explanation (indeed, both might be wrong–see *third variable*.

    Where to find this term: Essay 4.3

Cause-and-Effect Hypothesis (Causal Hypothesis): See Essay 3.5, Module 3 Glossary

Contralateral Motor Control: "Contra" = opposite; "lateral" = side. This term refers to the way each cerebral hemisphere of the brain (left or right) controls voluntary muscle movement on the opposite side of the body.

    Example: Using Electrical Stimulation of the Brain (ESB) during brain surgery, doctors can stimulate an area of the motor cortex in the right cerebral hemisphere and observe the patient's left arm move.

    Where to find this term: Study 4A.

Correlation Coefficient: A number between -1 and $+1$ representing the strength of a correlation between two variables, derived from data representing multiple pairs of measurements of those two variables. The absolute value of the coefficient reflects the strength of the relationship, and the sign of the coefficient reflects whether the relationship is direct (positive) or inverse (negative).

    Examples: Ratings of happiness and the number of times people smile might have a correlation coefficient of .85, while ratings of happiness and the number of times people punch someone else in the face might have a correlation coefficient of $-.85$. Ratings of happiness and the number of times people use the word "the" would probably have a correlation coefficient close to 0.00.

    Where to find this term: Essays 4.1, 4.2, 4.3

Correlational Hypothesis: A testable statement declaring that two conceptual variables are predictably related to one another, so that the value of one can be used to predict the approximate value of the other (within a range).

    Examples: The number of new pregnancies increases with the frequency of power outages within the last month across different locations. Belief in astrology is related to extroversion. Individualism is negatively correlated with the frequency of mask use during a pandemic. (These examples are made up, untested hypotheses.)

    Where to find this term: Essays 3.5, 4.1, Studies 3A, 4A, 4B, 4C

Correlational Research/Study: A study designed to measure two conceptual variables in matched pairs of measurements, in order to test the hypothesis that they are predictably related to each other.

    Example: Sherman and Flaxman (2001) measured average annual temperatures in different locations around the world and the amount of hot spices used in traditional recipes at those locations (climates and recipes were matched by location) to test the hypothesis that use of hot (bacteria-killing) spices is positively correlated with the intensity of heat experienced in a given climate.

    Where to find this term: Essay 4.1

Counterbalancing: A way of correcting for *order effects* by presenting conditions or response opportunities to different participants in different orders. The goal is to balance the different orders across all participants so that each response has equal opportunities to affect and be affected by other responses.

    Example: In a study measuring self-reported weight and body satisfaction, the researcher is worried that responses to the weight question might affect responses to the body satisfaction question, and vice versa, so half of the participants are asked their weight first, then rate their body satisfaction, while the other half rate body satisfaction first, then give their weight.

    Where to find this term: Study 4C, but see also Essay 7.4, Module 7 Glossary

Negative Correlation: A relationship between two conceptual variables such that as one increases, the other decreases.

> **Example:** Squirrel population size and chipmunk population size at a single food source are negatively correlated. The more squirrels you see, the fewer chipmunks you are likely to see.
>
> **Where to find this term:** Essay 4.1, Figure 4.2

Null Hypothesis: A statement that voids (nullifies) a **research hypothesis**. It simply says that the research hypothesis is NOT true.

> **Examples:** A research hypothesis might say that two variables, X and Y, are positively correlated. The null hypothesis would be that X and Y are not correlated. If the research hypothesis is that X and Y are negatively correlated, the null hypothesis would *still* be that X and Y are not correlated. If a scientist hypothesizes that there is a cause-and-effect relationship between X and Y, the null hypothesis would be that there is no cause-and-effect relationship.
>
> **Where to find this term:** Essays 4.2, 4.5, Box 4.2

Order Effect: When multiple data points are collected from the same participants, and exposure to information that is part of data collection affects subsequent data collection.

> **Example:** To test the hypothesis that loving relationships are correlated to overall happiness, participants are asked how happy they feel on a scale from 1 to 10 and how many loving relationships they have in life. For people in an unhappy mood, being reminded of that might make it harder to recall all the people they love. Or, having trouble recalling the number of people one loves might make one feel unhappy. The resulting correlation might be due to the effect of the *measurement* of one variable on the *measurement* of the other, rather than any natural relationship between the two variables. In this case, **counterbalancing** might not help, and a better approach would be to insert a period of time between measurements.
>
> **Where to find this term:** Study 4C, but see also Essay 7.4, Module 7 Glossary

p-value (probability value): The probability of getting whatever result we got (e.g., a particular correlation coefficient), assuming the **null hypothesis** is true. If the p-value is very low, the null hypothesis is probably not true, meaning the alternative (our **research hypothesis**) is supported. If the p-value is high, the odds of getting our results under the null hypothesis are high, so we can't reject the null hypothesis, and we have no support for the alternative (research hypothesis).

> **Example:** A researcher notices that whenever her college's football team does well, their basketball team also does well. She tests the research hypothesis that the football team's success is positively correlated with the basketball team's success. Going back 20 years, she compares the number of wins for both teams each year. If the **null hypothesis** (that the football team's success is not at all related to the basketball team's success) is true, the correlation coefficient should be zero. But she calculates a correlation coefficient of 0.43, and the **p-value** (odds of getting a coefficient that strong by chance when it should be zero) are just 0.02, or 2%. She therefore rejects the null hypothesis, and claims support for her research hypothesis. She can now offer better predictions about the basketball team's success at the end of each football season.
>
> **Where to find this term:** Essays 4.2, 4.5, Box 4.2, and throughout the rest of this book.

Positive Correlation: A relationship between two conceptual variables such that as one increases, so does the other.

> **Example:** Height and shoe size are positively correlated: Taller people wear larger shoes.
>
> **Where to find this term:** Essay 4.1, Figure 4.1

Prediction: A statement about what will be observed in a study (the expected results), based on the operational definitions of the variables being studied and assuming the research hypothesis is true.

> **Example:** To test the **research hypothesis** that intelligence and income are positively correlated, one might operationally define intelligence as "IQ score" and income as "self-reported annual salary." The **prediction** would be: "IQ scores will be positively correlated with self-reported annual salary." A similar study was done by Zagorsky (2007).
>
> **Where to find this term:** Throughout this book, but defined and distinguished from a hypothesis in Essay 4.4 and Fig 4.5.

Regression Line: In correlational research, a straight line through the points on a *scatterplot* that is as close as possible to the maximum number of data points. The slope of the line and the average closeness of the data points to the line tell us about the strength and direction of the relationship between the variables, which are represented on the X and Y axes.

   Example: (below)
   Where to find this term: Essays 4.1, 4.2, Study 4B, Box 4.1

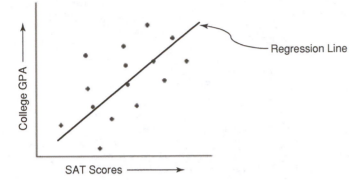

Regression Line   Each point on the scatterplot represents the X-score (SAT) and Y-Score (GPA) for one individual student.

Research Hypothesis: A sentence that declares or implies a testable relationship between two or more conceptual variables. The relationship can be correlational or cause-and-effect (see Essay 3.5). Compare to *null hypothesis*.

   Examples: See *correlational hypothesis*, *cause-and-effect hypothesis* (Essay 3.5, Module 3 Glossary).
   Where to find this term: Essays 4.1, 4.2, and throughout the rest of this book.

Scatterplot: A graph showing the relationship between paired measurements of variables (for example, height and weight), with the value of one variable on the X-axis and the value of the other on the Y-axis. One point is drawn for each pair of measurements at the point on the graph where the X-value and the Y-value intersect.

   Example: The image in the example for *a regression line* shows a scatterplot for GPA and SAT scores.
   Where to find this term: Essay 4.1, Figure 4.1, 4.2, and 4.4, Box 4.1

Significant: Refers to a research finding (observed data) that would happen less than 5 times out of 100 data samples if the null hypothesis is true. Significant *positive or negative correlations* allow us to reject the null hypothesis and conclude that we have evidence to support a *correlational hypothesis*.

   Example: A study by Deary et al., (2004) predicted a significant positive correlation between IQ scores at age 11 and at age 80. They had records for over 500 participants whose IQ had been measured at age 11 and again at age 80. The correlation coefficient was + .66. The correlation is *significant* because if IQ scores at age 11 and age 80 were completely unrelated, the chances of seeing a correlation coefficient of .66 for that many participants would be less than 5%. Therefore, we can reject the null hypothesis, and claim evidence for the hypothesis that IQ in childhood is related to IQ in late adulthood.
   Where to find this term: Essays 4.2, 4.3, 4.5. See also Module 5.

Spurious Correlation: A statistically significant correlation between two variables that either (1) is not genuine support for the predictable relationship because errors were made in analyzing the data (such as a failure to predict the relationship), or (2) (APA definition) is only explainable using a *third variable*.

   Examples: For definition (1), according to tylervigen.com, annual per capita cheese consumption is significantly correlated to the number of lawyers in Hawaii from 2000 to 2009 ($r = .98$!). For definition (2) the positive correlation between elementary students' grades and their height. While the reason for this correlation is not immediately obvious, it could be due to a third variable: A nutritious diet.
   Where to find this term: Essay 4.3, Study 4B

Strength of a Correlation: The predictability of the relationship between two variables, based on measurements of both variables. The strength of a correlation is indicated by the absolute value of the ***correlation coefficient***.

    Example: To test the hypothesis that the number of books read correlates with the size of one's vocabulary, Study A asks people to self-report how many books they read each week and the approximate size of their own vocabulary. Study B observes people for several weeks to see how many books they read per week, on average, and then measures vocabulary with an objective test. Researchers in Study A observe a correlation coefficient of .09, while Study B produces a correlation coefficient of .39. Study B shows a stronger correlation (see below).

    Where to find this term: Essay 4.1

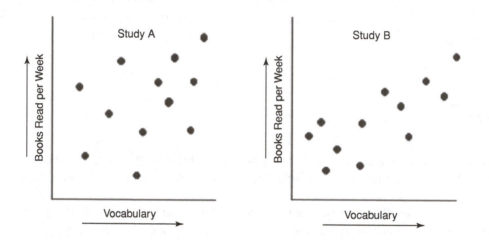

Theory: A unifying idea that explains multiple observations and has evidence to support it from multiple perspectives. A theory also suggests many testable predictions. In order to be called a "theory," an idea must be applied, tested and supported from multiple perspectives, such that there is wide agreement among scientists that it is true or at least plausible.

    Examples: The Schachter–Singer Theory of Emotion, presented in most introductory psychology textbooks, posits that emotions are derived from an assessment of our physiological state and an interpretation of our surroundings in combination. While the direct evidence for this theory is mixed, it has led to many predictions, and many neuroscience studies on how the brain processes and labels emotions.

    Where to find this term: Essay 4.5

Third Variable: Any variable that *could* influence both conceptual variables in a correlational study, and therefore cause the two variables to correlate. While correlational researchers often measure multiple conceptual variables and test for multiple relationships among them, a correlational study cannot positively identify a "third variable" as a cause for any observed relationship, since all variables are simply measured, not manipulated.

    Examples: A researcher tests the hypothesis that illness and hand washing are negatively correlated by secretly observing hand washing of employees in a company restroom and comparing that to the number of sick days each employee claims at work. She finds a significant negative correlation. This could be explained by general laziness (people who are lazy might be less likely to wash their hands AND more likely to call in sick, even if they are not actually sick). Laziness would be considered a possible ***third variable***.

    Where to find this term: Essay 4.3, Study 4.3

Module 5 Experimental Research I: Testing Causal Relationships

MODULE 5 LEARNING OBJECTIVES CHART

ESSAY NUMBER	MODULE 5 ESSAY LEARNING OBJECTIVES	BEFORE READING				AFTER READING			
		I don't know how 1	I know a little about this 2	I know enough about this to guess correctly 3	I know how to do this and/ or have already done it. 4	I don't know how 1	I know a little about this 2	I know enough about this to guess correctly 3	I know how to do this and/ or have already done it. 4
5.1	Compare the goals and methods of experimental research to correlational research.								
5.1 5.2	Explain the roles of manipulation, control, and measurement in an experiment.								
5.1 5.2 5.3	Given a simple two-group experiment, identify the independent, dependent, extraneous, and confounding variables.								
5.2	Identify the *levels* of the independent variable in a two-group experiment and correctly apply the terms "experimental group" and "control group."								
5.2	Define and contrast the terms representative sample, random selection, and random assignment.								
5.3 Box 5.1	Other than the number of observations, name two factors that contribute to the measurement of a difference between two groups.								

		I don't know how **1**	I know a little about this **2**	I know enough about this to guess correctly **3**	I know how to do this and/ or have already done it. **4**		I don't know how **1**	I know a little about this **2**	I know enough about this to guess correctly **3**	I know how to do this and/ or have already done it. **4**
5.3 Box 5.1	Explain why variability is so important when comparing two sets of numbers, and correctly apply the term "measurement error."									
5.3	Explain the meaning of the term "significantly different"									
5.4	Describe the three-step process for making objective decisions about experimental results.									
5.4	Describe what a p-value tells you about the results of an experiment.									
5.4	Explain why scientists do not claim that one experiment "proves" a hypothesis, in terms of the role of probability.									
5.4	Explain the meaning of the term "significantly different."									
		Read the assigned essays and actively seek answers to any questions rated less than "4." Then return to this chart and complete the white half.					Now proceed to the chart for the applications section, read the objectives for your assigned research project, and complete the gray side of the *research learning objectives chart*.			

ESSAY 5.1

THE LOGIC AND ANATOMY OF EXPERIMENTATION

In Module 4, we tested a correlational hypothesis by collecting data on two variables and summarizing the strength of their relationship as one number—a correlation coefficient (the observed result). We then applied a three-step, probabilistic decision-making process where we (1) assumed the null hypothesis was true and (2) examined the odds of getting the observed result under that assumption, and (3) if those odds were extremely low, we rejected that null hypothesis in favor of the research hypothesis.

The logic behind this decision-making process will be the same for experimental research. We will again summarize our data with a single number. Rather than representing the strength of a correlation, the number we calculate to summarize our data (our observed result) will represent *how much two sets of scores differ from one another*. We'll call it a "*t*-ratio" (it is also called a "*t*-test" or a "*t*-statistic"). More detail on where a *t*-ratio comes from will be provided in Essays 5.3 and 5.4. First, let's discuss what it looks like and how it's used.

A *t*-ratio is just one of several ways to quantify the difference between two sets of numbers, and it cannot be applied to every experiment—the correct statistical test depends on the type of data. But a *t*-ratio applies in many experiments, so we'll use it here as a conceptual example of how these decisions are made. Like a correlation coefficient, the value of *t* can be positive or negative, and the larger the *absolute value* of *t*, the bigger the difference between two sets of scores.[1] But unlike a correlation, *t* is not limited to the range from −1 to +1.

Once we have calculated the value of the *t*-ratio for our data, we will follow the same three steps outlined in the first paragraph of this essay. The logic of the statistical decision regarding support for the hypothesis is identical, but the design, goals, and conclusions of experimental research are different from correlational studies.

Experiments are the only type of research that can test cause-and-effect relationships. Doing so requires **manipulation** (of the cause), **control** (of other variables), and **measurement** (of the effect). The logic of experimentation is best explained with an analogy: Assume you have been given, absolutely free, a sound system with *amazing* speakers. There's only one catch: It has no labels on the buttons. No problem . . . you can figure out what each button does and label them yourself. Logically, all you have to do is push or turn one button (manipulation) while making sure the other buttons stay still (control) and listen for changes in the sound quality (measurement). Repeating this process for each button would eventually tell you what all the buttons do. Pushing more than one button at a time would be useless because you couldn't determine which button was causing the resulting differences in sound quality. "One button at a time" is the way science progresses, particularly with true experiments. Where correlational research often considers multiple variables simultaneously, experiments work best when the cause and effect are isolated for study. In the simplest experiments, we *directly manipulate* one variable (the hypothesized cause) and we *measure* another (the hypothesized effect) while maintaining *control* over everything else that might also influence the effect (keeping those other variables the same).

The terminology associated with experimentation can also be demonstrated using our sound system analogy (Fig. 5.1). For each button, we hypothesize a cause-and-effect relationship between moving the button and sound quality, where the button is the cause and the sound quality is the effect. Each hypothesis is tested with an experiment having its own independent variable, dependent variable, and extraneous variables. The conceptual **independent variable** is the hypothesized cause, which we manipulate (by setting the button to "low" or "high"). The conceptual **dependent variable** is the hypothesized effect, which we measure (sound quality).

---

[1] You might be wondering how you can arrive at a "negative difference." The numerator of the t-ratio is the difference between means, so the sign of the t-ratio will depend on whether you subtract the mean of Group A from the mean of Group B, or B from A. Either way, the absolute value of the difference is the same.

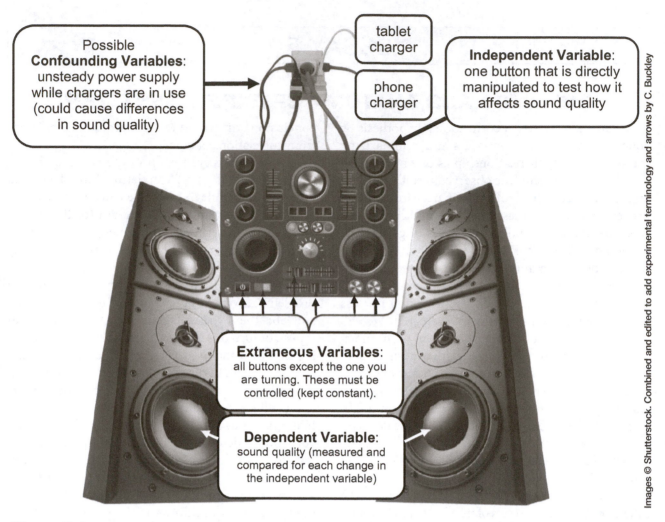

Figure 5.1   Terminology of experimentation, as applied to a stereo with no labels on the buttons. See text for explanation.

Other factors that could also cause changes in sound quality, which we must control or try to keep constant, are called *extraneous variables* (the other buttons, the power source, etc.). Any extraneous variables that are NOT controlled (like power drains due to chargers) can become *confounding variables* if they happen to change at the same time we turn the knob, because they can also affect sound quality and would confuse the results of our experiment. We do our best to **avoid confounding variables by keeping all extraneous variables constant.**

A true experiment with two groups will produce two sets of scores (or measurements) one set for each group. We design an experiment so that if our research hypothesis is true, we should observe a difference between those two sets of scores. The t-ratio allows us to quantify that difference. We'll explain how in Essays 5.3 and 5.4. First, let's take a closer look at how to design a true experiment.

ESSAY 5.2

MANIPULATION AND CONTROL

That heading might sound nasty, but in true experiments, manipulation and control are essential. It's easy when you're dealing with an unlabeled sound system (Fig. 5.1), but when you're trying to unravel the mysteries of human thought and behavior, manipulation and control get much more complicated. Extraneous variables are everywhere (not just in the power supply or on the face of the stereo); some are completely hidden, and even those we know about can be much harder to control. Nevertheless, as we manipulate our independent variable to see its effect, we are challenged to find the extraneous variables and control them, or they can become confounding variables and interfere with that effect.

Consider this simple hypothesis: *Exposure to classical music improves children's math performance.* Before we go on, note that you can easily determine the conceptual independent and dependent variables for an experiment. Recall the definition of a hypothesis: It is a claim regarding a relationship between two conceptual variables. Therefore, both conceptual variables are stated in the hypothesis.

SKILL CHECK (answers in Appendix B)

In the hypothesis above, what is the conceptual independent variable? _____

What is the conceptual dependent variable? _____

What might be one extraneous variable? _____

To test this hypothesis, we *could* expose a group of kids to classical music each day, then measure the effect on math performance with a test. But if they get high scores, would that support the research hypothesis? This would be like turning an unlabeled stereo button to high, then turning on the stereo for the first time and thinking, "That's all about the bass." Would you immediately take out your permanent marker and label that knob "bass?" Or would you try turning that button down first to make sure the bass decreases? Remember, it's a permanent marker…

To test the hypothesis that classical music improves children's math performance, we would have to directly manipulate exposure to classical music the same way we would manipulate the stereo button (i.e., compare high to low). Our experiment would have two **levels of the independent variable** (two levels of exposure to classical music). These can be thought of as our operational definition of exposure to classical music: One group listens for three hours per day, and a second group does not. The group that gets classical music is called the **experimental group**, and those who get no music are in the **control group** (also called the comparison group). Our conceptual **dependent variable** is math performance, and it can be measured (operationally defined) by the score on a math test given to all children in both groups.

The **extraneous variables** in this experiment consist of everything that could affect scores on the math test (except exposure to classical music). Things like age and grade level are easy enough to control by keeping them the same for both groups. But what about IQ, motivation to succeed, enjoyment of math, and attention span? These extraneous variables have the potential to affect scores on our math test, but it would be difficult, maybe even impossible, to control all of them.

Instead of trying to directly control them, we will use a process called **random assignment**. Each child will be assigned to either the classical music group or the no music group using some truly random process, such as the flip of a coin. With random assignment, each child in the study has an equal chance of ending up in either group, thereby making it quite likely that things like IQ and enjoyment of math will be distributed about evenly between the two groups. Based on probability theory, the larger the groups, the more effectively random assignment will even out any extraneous variables between the groups. Random assignment is one of the most common techniques used by psychologists to control extraneous variables.

But why use a coin flip? Wouldn't it be easier to just assign the first 20 kids who show up for our experiment to the classical music group, and the rest to the control group? Although it might seem like people show up "randomly," it's quite likely that the first participants who show up will be the most enthusiastic; they might do better on the math test for that reason alone. If we used this way of setting up groups, enthusiasm would be a **confounding variable** (something other than the independent variable that could cause a difference between groups when we measure the dependent variable). We would be stacking the odds in favor of supporting our research hypothesis because the most enthusiastic people would have a better chance of getting into the classical music group. But we are trying to *test* our hypothesis, not *verify* it. Truly random assignment would require that each participant has an equal chance of being placed in one group or another. Therefore, coin flips or some other genuinely random process should be used to assign participants to groups. One might also use an alternating assignment, where the first participant is assigned to Group A and the next to Group B, then A, then B, and so forth. This would not be truly random, but it would create a better match between groups in terms of their enthusiasm levels (more on this in Module 7).

The issues of control and the design of the **control group** are critical to experimentation. Without the control group, of course, we would have no way of knowing what math performance would have been like without the music. But that's just the beginning of the control issue.

The conclusions one can draw from an experiment depend heavily on the treatment of the control group. Suppose we found that the kids exposed to classical music scored much higher on our math test than the control group. Could we conclude that

classical music improved math test scores? Yes, but only compared to no music at all. It is possible that listening to *any* music might improve math performance, compared to no music. To be able to say that it is the classical nature of the music that makes a difference, we should design our experiment with another comparison group that hears a different type of music, but as more comparison groups are added to a single experiment, results become more difficult to interpret. We could address this question by repeating the whole experiment several times with different types of music, but each experiment takes time and money and requires participants, who are usually volunteers. This problem illustrates the creative, problem-solving aspect of doing science; our goal is to design experiments that get the best information in the simplest way with the fewest participants.

Another control issue is the *selection* of those participants. Whether we're doing descriptive, correlational, or experimental research, we want participants in our study to accurately represent the **population** about whom we wish to draw conclusions. That is, we want a **representative sample,** and the best way to get one is by **random selection**, because that is how we produce a **random sample**. Mathematically, the larger a random sample is, the better it will represent the population it is drawn from. But regardless of sample size, random selection from the population assures that no single person has a greater chance of being included in the study than anyone else from that population.

This is not an easy task. To be truly random, we must use a criterion for selection that is completely free of any influencing factors. Asking for volunteers is not random (only those who are interested in participating will be part of our sample). Asking "random people on the street" is not *truly* random either (those who stay indoors most of the time would have no chance of being selected). Instead, we should use a lottery-style drawing that includes everyone in the population, or select every person whose social security number ends with zero, or every 50th entry in a phone book. Unfortunately, in practice, random selection is not the norm. People tend to voluntarily sign up for experiments, so that helpful people generally have a greater chance of being included than others. Although there is some disagreement about this among scientists, in most cases, it doesn't noticeably influence the results, depending on the topic of research. Nevertheless, *researchers and others with a science attitude should always be aware of how the sample selection process might impact the results of a study.*

Random selection is often confused with *random assignment*. Random selection is the first step in the data collection process. It is a process by which we *select* participants for our study from the larger population and it helps us control how well our sample represents that population. Random assignment occurs *after* the selection process. It is how we *assign* our participants to the experimental and control groups (i.e., to different levels of the independent variable), and it helps us control extraneous variables. Random selection is used for descriptive, correlational, and experimental research, whereas random assignment only applies to certain types of experimental research (those with different people in different groups, like the Applications in this Module).

SKILL CHECK: DESIGN YOUR OWN EXPERIMENT

Imagine you want to test this hypothesis: *Offering ice cream at a dining hall increases the dining hall's popularity.* Answer the following (suggested answers in Appendix B):

LEVEL 1 (DIRECT APPLICATION) QUESTIONS:

1. What would be the conceptual independent variable? _____

2. What would be the conceptual dependent variable? _____

3. What might be one extraneous variable? _____

LEVEL 2 (CREATIVE THINKING) QUESTIONS:

4. How many levels of the independent variable would you use? _____

5. Describe your levels of the independent variable. _____

_____

6. How would you measure the dependent variable? _____

_____

LEVEL 3 (ADVANCED APPLICATION) QUESTIONS:

7. What would be the operational definition of your independent variable? _____

_____

8. What would be the operational definition of your dependent variable? _____

_____

Now that we know the terminology and basics of designing a simple experiment, let's return to the question of how to interpret the results. If our causal research hypothesis is true, then two groups of people who experience different levels of the independent variable should have different scores for the dependent variable. Essay 5.3 discusses how we can detect the difference in scores.

ESSAY 5.3

MEASURING DIFFERENCES BETWEEN GROUPS

This essay is not about how to do a *statistical analysis*. There are no mathematical formulas. Instead, the focus is on building a conceptual understanding of how scientists quantify the difference between two sets of numbers. Our goal here is not to teach statistics or data analysis, but to prepare psychology students for future courses in statistics and research design, while also helping all other students who complete this course become more informed consumers of science.

Suppose someone in your class claims that drinking ginseng tea while studying helps her retain information. Most of the class has developed a strong science attitude by now, so they want evidence. Your professor points out that this is a testable hypothesis: *Ginseng improves memory performance.* She recommends that each student who wants to know whether ginseng improves memory should do an experiment. In reality, these experiments would require approval from an Institutional Review Board (IRB—more on that in Module 8), but for the sake of this explanation, we'll pretend this assignment was IRB-approved. Here is the assignment that students were given:

Find 20 friends who all like tea and are not allergic to ginseng. Use random assignment to split them into two groups. Ask each participant to memorize a list of 40 words by studying the list for 5 min, but give 10 people a 12-oz cup of tea with ginseng (Group G) while they study, and give 10 other people a 12-oz cup of the same brand of tea, but with no ginseng (Group NG). Keep track of who gets ginseng, but do not tell the participants. After studying, all participants should play a video game for 5 min, then try to recall as many of the words as possible. Record the number of words correctly recalled by each participant and calculate the mean for each group. Based on your research hypothesis (that ginseng improves memory) predict that the group that got ginseng (Group G) will recall more words than the group that got no ginseng (Group NG).

Image © Dearnles for sale/Shutterstock

SKILL CHECK: Answers in Appendix B

Before you read on, try labeling the

✓ Conceptual *independent variable,*
✓ Conceptual *dependent variable,*
✓ *Operational definitions* of each, and
✓ A few *extraneous variables* in this experiment.
✓ Also state the *null hypothesis*. (See Module 4 glossary for definition and examples of null hypotheses.)

Since the assignment was optional, and fairly labor-intensive, only the most ambitious and curious students in the class completed it. Table 5.1 shows the *raw data* collected by four ambitious students. Their names are Nia, Kiri, Shawn, and Antonio. Each student got a different outcome for the same experiment.

If we only look at the means for the number of words recalled in Nia's experiment, it's pretty clear that the ginseng group (G) recalled more words than the no-ginseng group (NG). Nia's experiment would **support** the hypothesis that ginseng improves memory. Note that it would **not** "prove" the hypothesis is true. Maybe something happened that only affected the people in Group NG (a major distraction in their testing room might have interfered with their memory). Or maybe Nia assumed volunteers would show up "randomly," so she put the first ten people into the experimental group and the last ten into the control group (she didn't use truly random assignment). The more enthusiastic helpers, who showed up first, might have put more sincere effort into the memory test, while those who showed up late might not have tried at all to memorize the words. Although we do our best to assure that the independent variable is the only systematic difference between the groups, other systematic differences (confounding variables) can happen. *The possibility of undetected confounding variables is another good reason why you should think of the results of one study as evidence rather than proof* (see Essay 4.5 for other reasons).

Let's look at Kiri's data. The mean is less than one point higher for Group G than for Group NG. This is not a convincing outcome. Even if she had treated both groups exactly the same (i.e., if everyone in her study had the exact same tea), we would expect to see *some* difference in their ability to recall the lists. They are two different groups of people, after all. Is a less-than-one-point difference enough to support our hypothesis? Probably not, but let's reserve judgment for now.

Interestingly, Shawn and Antonio both observed the exact same means for their ginseng and no-ginseng groups (23.4 and 18.1 words remembered, respectively). In both experiments, the difference between the means for the two groups (5.3 words) seems to suggest that maybe ginseng improved memory, but there was some overlap; the lowest scores with ginseng are lower than the highest scores without ginseng. So how do we know when two sets of numbers are different *enough* to support our hypothesis?

Just as in correlational research, where we had a single number that summarized the strength and direction of the relationship (the correlation coefficient), *we need a single number to summarize the amount of difference* between the two sets of scores for each group.

At first glance, it might seem like the difference between the means of each group would be the best way to summarize how any two sets of numbers differ from one another. By that measure, Shawn's and

Table 5.1 Results of Four Repetitions of the Ginseng Experiment, Performed by Four Different Students. Each Student had 20 Different Participants in Their Experiment.

	Nia's Data		Kiri's Data		Shawn's Data		Antonio's Data	
	G	NG	G	NG	G	NG	G	NG
Number of words correctly recalled by each participant	40	2	19	15	13	10	2	3
	38	1	15	19	19	12	4	16
	38	0	19	18	21	13	15	11
	36	3	21	16	23	15	21	15
	39	5	10	12	25	17	23	17
	40	2	21	20	25	18	25	18
	30	4	15	21	25	21	31	20
	35	6	24	20	26	22	35	24
	40	1	15	12	27	24	39	29
	39	2	14	13	30	29	39	38
Averages →	37.5	2.6	17.3	16.6	23.4	18.1	23.4	18.1

Antonio's experiments would provide equally strong evidence for the ginseng hypothesis. But take a closer look at their data. Means can be deceiving! Notice the *variability*—how much the scores within each group differ from the mean of that group.

Variability matters. Imagine a small town of 100 people below the poverty level, with each person making just $15,000/year. If a famous actor who was born there decides to pay his Mom (who still lives there) $2 million/year to make her special-recipe pancakes for him once a year, the mean income in that town would suddenly be about $35,000/year. Imagine a nearby town where everyone actually makes $35,000/year. Before the lucrative pancake job, the difference between mean incomes in these two towns was $20,000/year. After, if we ignore variability and just compare means, we would conclude that one plate of pancakes suddenly erased a $20,000/year difference in incomes. Meanwhile, 99% of the population of the poorer town is still in extreme poverty. When we're talking means, variability *really* matters.

The difference in means matters, too, but as discussed in Module 3, the mean is an incomplete statistic without some measure of variability beside it. Therefore, when calculating a single number that represents the actual difference between two groups, we must consider both, the difference between means and the amount of variability in each data set.

Almost nothing in life can be measured with perfect precision. Chemists and physicists, when they measure the rates of chemical reactions or the magnitude of a force, must accept some degree of *measurement error*, although at the introductory level, they don't often emphasize the uncertainty of these measurements. Measurement error creates variability. Psychologists must pay careful attention to this because measurements of cognition and behavior are, by nature, imprecise. Even if we could measure memory performance with perfect precision, it would vary from one individual to another, regardless of the similarity in treatments of individuals. So many factors influence cognition and behavior that it is impossible to measure them without some error. Even the instruments for measuring our variables can vary a lot. Therefore, psychologists, like all scientists, accept variability as a natural part of science. We can't get rid of it, but we can minimize it.

One very important way to minimize error is to take multiple measurements and calculate an average. This is why, in the ginseng experiment, the professor recommended 10 participants (i.e., 10 measurements) in each condition (with ginseng and without). Experiments in psychology measure the same thing repeatedly in each condition in order to get the best estimate of its true value in that condition. The more measurements we can get, the more we can trust the mean as an estimate of the true score. Ideally, the ginseng experiment should have had at least 20 or 30 participants in each group, but practical considerations often make our samples smaller than we would like. Regardless of the number of participants, there will always be some with higher or lower scores on our measurement than the *true* value for the population (whatever that may be), so we must understand how variability affects our objective decisions.

To answer this, let's return to the results obtained by Shawn and Antonio. Note that they each got the exact same means, but they differed in the amount of variability in their scores. Essay 5.4 Spoiler Alert: One of these two students observed a big enough difference in scores between his two groups to support the research hypothesis; the other did not. First, let's examine how their results differed.

Table 5.2 shows their raw data with the scores rearranged from lowest to highest within each group. For Shawn's experiment, Group G's scores ranged from 13 to 30 (a difference, or range, of 17 points), and Group NG's scores ranged from 10 to 29 points (a 19-point range). If you calculate the ranges for

Table 5.2 Two Outcomes with the Same Means, with Raw Data Rearranged to Show Variability.

	Shawn's Data		Antonio's Data	
	G	**NG**	**G**	**NG**
	13	10	2	3
	19	12	4	6
Number	21	13	15	11
of words	23	15	21	15
correctly	25	17	23	17
recalled	25	18	25	18
by each	25	21	31	20
participant	26	22	35	24
	27	24	39	29
	30	29	39	38
Averages →	**23.4**	**18.1**	**23.4**	**18.1**

Antonio's experiment, you should get 37 for Group G and 35 for Group NG. The greater range indicates greater variability in each of the two sets of scores for Antonio's experiment, which makes those means less meaningful—less trustworthy—than the means for Shawn's experiment.

A comparison of these two outcomes is useful because the differences between means are equal, so we can see the effect of variability on the evidence. The difference between Shawn's means (5.3 words) is *stronger evidence* for the research hypothesis than the difference between Antonio's means (also 5.3 words), because the means are more trustworthy in Shawn's experiment. Although the *means* are the same, the actual difference between all the Group G scores and all the Group NG scores in Shawn's study is considered greater than in Antonio's study, simply because of the greater variability in Antonio's measurements. An increase in variability decreases the absolute value of the *t*-ratio, which is the value we calculate to measure the amount of difference between groups.

Box 5.1 explains how the difference between means and the variability contribute to the value of *t*. But the bigger picture here is that the absolute value of *t* can be used in the same way we used the correlation coefficient—to determine the likelihood of getting our observed result when the null hypothesis is true. That decision is explained in Essay 5.4.

BOX 5.1   The *t*-ratio: A Measurement of Difference

For our experiment on ginseng tea, we want to compare the scores in Group G to those in Group NG in order to arrive at a single number that represents the amount of difference between the two sets of scores. We'll call this number "*t*."[2] **Three factors affect the value of t: (1) the number of scores in each set, (2) the difference between the two means, and (3) the variability in each set of scores.** The impact of the first factor, the number of scores, can be most easily understood with a simple rule from Module 3: The more scores there are in a sample, the more you can trust the sample to tell the truth about the whole population. The other two factors can best be understood as a "signal-to-noise ratio," where the difference between the means is the signal, and the variability is the noise. As shown below, the value of *t* will increase as the difference between the means of the two groups increases, but a lot of variability in the scores will decrease *t*:

$$t \text{ can be thought of as a signal-to-noise ratio} \begin{cases} \text{The difference between the averages of the two groups} \leftarrow \text{SIGNAL} \\ \hline \text{The variability among the scores in each set} \qquad \leftarrow \text{NOISE} \end{cases}$$

The bigger the difference between means, the louder the signal, and the easier it is to detect the difference (just as ¾ is larger than ¼, a bigger numerator leads to a higher value of *t*). The greater the variability in the scores, the louder the noise, and the harder it is to detect the signal (just as ¼ is less than ½, a bigger denominator leads to a smaller value of *t*). Don't forget that the number of scores in each set plays a role as well, but in our four attempts at the ginseng experiment, we have the same number of scores in every set, so we can more easily focus on the signal-to-noise ratio and how that affects our calculation of the difference between groups (the value of *t*). Here are the actual values of *t* for the four imaginary outcomes of our ginseng experiment:

For Nia's Experiment, $t = 30.11$
For Kiri's Experiment, $t = 0.41$
For Shawn's Experiment, $t = 2.20$
For Antonio's Experiment, $t = 0.99$

---

[2] For this experiment, t is a two-sample, independent t-test, which you will learn how to do if you take a statistics course.

Compare these *t*-ratios to the pairs of averages you see for each student's experiment in Table 5.1. Nia's data produced a very high value of *t*, and Kiri's data produced a very low value, as we would expect, because *t* represents the amount of difference between Group G scores and Group NG scores. Note that even though Shawn and Antonio collected data with the exact same averages for G versus NG participants, the value of *t*—the estimated difference between the sets of scores in Group G and Group NG—is larger for Shawn's data, just as we would expect, because there was less variability in the scores for Shawn's participants than there was for Antonio's participants. Less variability equals less noise, which equals a lower number in the denominator of the t-ratio. So the same signal (the exact same difference between means) leads to a higher *t* in Shawn's experiment than Antonio observed. It's the same idea we introduced in Module 3: More variability = less trust in the means. If we can't trust the means, we can't trust the difference between them, either!

ESSAY 5.4

OBJECTIVE (ODDS-BASED) DECISION MAKING IN EXPERIMENTAL RESEARCH

In Essay 5.3, we learned about the *t*-ratio, the number we calculate to summarize the amount of difference between two sets of numbers. It's not the only way to summarize differences, and it can't be used with some types of data, but it is one of the most common. Just as we did with a correlation coefficient in Module 4, we will use our observed *t*-ratio to make an objective decision about whether our data support our research hypothesis.

If you read Module 4, the graphics below should look familiar. Going back to our experimental research hypothesizing that ginseng improves memory, we must decide whether *significantly* more words were recalled by people in the ginseng group than the control group. **Note that a *significant difference* does NOT mean an important difference.** It is merely a statistical term that reflects unlikely odds of getting the results we got if the null hypothesis is true. To make our decision, we'll use the same three-step decision-making process we used in correlational research:

1. **Assume the null hypothesis is true.** That is, assume your research hypothesis is wrong. The experimental research hypothesis states that there is a causal relationship between two variables, so we must begin by assuming there is no causal relationship. For the hypothesis that ginseng improves memory, the null hypothesis declares that ginseng does NOT improve memory. In a world where this null hypothesis is true, if we repeat our whole experiment many times with random selection and random assignment, our *t*-ratios will vary, but the mean *t*-ratio for all our attempts will be zero.

2. **Considering the size of the sample, determine the *p*-value.** Recall that the p-value is the probability of producing our observed result in the world where the null hypothesis is true. For an experiment, we will ask ourselves, "If there really is no difference in memory between a group given ginseng and a group given no ginseng, what are the odds that two groups with this many people would, just by chance, score as differently as they did on our memory test? What are the odds of observing our value of *t* when comparing two random sets of people who should not differ?" Those odds are called the *p*-value.

3. **Apply a decision rule.** Knowing the *p*-value, we can make a decision based on one simple rule: A difference that has a *p*-value less than

Step 3

.05 (a less-than-5% chance of happening when the null hypothesis is true) supports our research hypothesis. In other words, a difference between our groups that is so large that it would have happened by chance less than 1 time out of 20 repetitions of this experiment *when, in reality, no difference exists,* counts as evidence that a real difference probably *does* exist. We will call this probable difference a *"significant difference,"* meaning that our data can be used as evidence to support our research hypothesis.

You might be wondering why we have to assume the *null* hypothesis is true. Wouldn't it make more sense to assume the *research* hypothesis is true, and then calculate the probability of getting the observed results? That way, results that are unlikely would falsify the research hypothesis. But there is a really good reason we can't do that: If we assume a research hypothesis is true, what should the *t*-ratio be? Would it be 3? 4.5? 18.64? There is no way of knowing. If we don't know the *real* difference between groups that should be caused by our manipulation, we can't figure out the probability of getting the difference we observed. By assuming the null hypothesis is true, we know exactly what the difference between groups should be: zero. That information is absolutely required in order to figure out the probability of getting our observed results (the *p*-value).

Although in theory, the null hypothesis states that the difference between groups *should* be zero, in reality, the difference will *not* always be exactly zero. Remember that any two groups in an experiment are two randomly chosen samples from the same population. They are still different people, and will probably be at least a little bit different. But if they're *large* samples of people, they usually won't be *very* different. To test the null hypothesis statistically, we'll assume a difference of zero. We are using

exactly the same logic when testing for a significant difference as we used to test for a significant correlation: Our decision is still based on the *p-value*, the probability of getting our observed results when the difference should be zero.

Let's apply objective decision-making to our ginseng experiment. Table 5.3 shows the statistical results from each ambitious student's research. In each case, statistical formulas have been applied to arrive at *t*-ratios and *p*-values for each student's experimental results.[3] Nia observed a huge difference in word recall between her two groups, represented by the *t*-ratio of 30.11. If there really is no effect of ginseng on memory, the odds of observing a *t*-statistic as large as Nia observed are crazy small... if the null hypothesis was true, this would happen only eight times in one quadrillion replications of this experiment!

Based on Nia's data, we would conclude that the null hypothesis is probably wrong; ginseng probably improved memory. Of course, eight times out of a quadrillion, we would be wrong to draw this conclusion, because a difference at least this large is likely to occur by chance that often. Although one study does not prove the hypothesis is true, if Nia followed good experimental procedures and got these data, then we might consider upping our consumption of ginseng tea while studying.

The other students had more realistic data. Assuming the null hypothesis is true, the chances of getting a difference as large as Kiri observed are actually pretty good—about 69%. So Kiri's data give us no reason to reject the null hypothesis. A difference as large as Shawn's is quite unlikely when the null is true—chances are only about 4 out of 100. So if ginseng does not improve memory, Shawn's data probably would not have happened. Shawn would therefore reject the null hypothesis in favor of the research hypothesis that

---

[3] These probabilities also depend on the number of participants in each group (in this case, there were 10). They were calculated using the "Data Analysis" feature on MS Excel.

Table 5.3 Statistical Results from Four Attempts at the Same Experiment (raw data in Table 5.1)

	Value of *t*	*p*-value
Nia's data	30.11	0.00000000000000787
Kiri's data	0.41	0.689
Shawn's data	2.20	0.041
Antonio's data	0.99	0.335

ginseng does improve memory. Due to the huge variability in Antonio's data, a difference like his is likely to be at least that large (given that ginseng does not affect memory) about 34 times out of 100: likely enough that we could not reject the null hypothesis based on Antonio's data. His study would lead to the conclusion that ginseng did not improve memory.

In summary, by general consensus among scientists,[4] **"significance" means that if the null hypothesis is true, your observations would have occurred by chance less than 5 times out of 100**. This also means that when p is greater than 0.05, we have no basis for rejecting the null hypothesis; the differences we observed were "too likely" under the null hypothesis (even if $p = 0.06$!). So Nia and Shawn found support for the research hypothesis, but Kiri and Antonio did not.

It is now worth revisiting one of the reasons that significant correlations or differences should be taken as **evidence** for the research hypothesis, **not proof.** Rejecting the null hypothesis means that there is still a chance (albeit a small one) that the results we observed *did* happen by chance, even though the null hypothesis was actually true. For every "successful" experiment, scientists know that there is a chance we could be wrong when we reject the null hypothesis in favor of our research hypothesis.[5] We accept this because we know that it is a small chance—less than 5%. **Our statistical evidence does not prove that a real difference exists; it only shows that the lack of a real difference is very unlikely.**

---

[4] This "consensus" may differ depending on other factors you will learn about in a statistics course. In the meantime, it is sufficient to accept 5% as the standard maximum p-value to reject the null hypothesis.

[5] Scientists are so aware of this chance of being wrong, they even have a name for it: Type I Error.

MODULE 5 RESEARCH LEARNING OBJECTIVES CHART

STUDY NUMBER	MODULE 5 RESEARCH LEARNING OBJECTIVES	BEFORE READING				AFTER DOING PROJECT			
		I don't know how 1	I know a little about this 2	I know enough about this to guess correctly 3	I know how to do this and/ or have already done it. 4	I don't know how 1	I know a little about this 2	I know enough about this to guess correctly 3	I know how to do this and/ or have already done it. 4
5A	Give examples of perceptual adaptation, perception–action coupling, and a perceptual aftereffect.								
5A	Explain how perceptual adaptation can combine with perception–action coupling to produce a perceptual motor aftereffect.								
5A 5B 5C	Collect experimental data and interpret an analysis (provided) to draw conclusions about whether the hypothesis was supported.								
5A 5B 5C	Practice creating complete research records with all the information needed to write a report (essential introductory, method, results, and discussion information pertaining to your own research).								
5A 5B 5C	Apply the terminology of experimental research in an example of research in which you are a participant.								

		I don't know how 1	I know a little about this 2	I know enough about this to guess correctly 3	I know how to do this and/ or have already done it. 4	I don't know how 1	I know a little about this 2	I know enough about this to guess correctly 3	I know how to do this and/ or have already done it. 4
5A 5B 5C	Gain experience with random assignment from the perspective of both a researcher and a participant.								
5B	Explain the meaning of the term "linguistic determinism" and compare it to the Linguistic Relativity Hypothesis.								
5C	Gain experience with mindfulness practice and learn about some of the many ways of mindfulness appears to improve lives.								

Now read about the project to prepare for lab. For any scores less than "4," keep those questions in mind as you complete the research project(s). Do not do the white half of this chart until after you've completed the assigned research project(s).

STUDY **5A**

To experience a visual aftereffect: Cut out the shape below on the dotted line and glue or tape it to a piece of paperboard or cardstock. Push a pin or thumbtack through the center from behind. Spin the image smoothly and continuously while staring at the center (without looking away from the center at all!). Do this for about 45 s. Then look *immediately* at the man on the boat and see what happens.

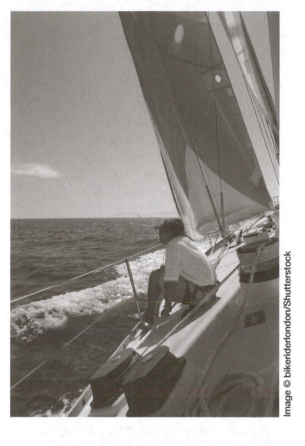

Image © bikeriderlondon/Shutterstock

Image © casejustin/Shutterstock

LOCATION OF PERCEPTUAL MOTOR AFTEREFFECTS

Have you ever been on a boat or cruise ship for an extended period? When you first got off the boat, you might have still felt the gentle rocking of the waves, as though your brain didn't get the memo that you were back on land. This strange feeling is called a *perceptual motor aftereffect,* and it is due to the interplay of two different processes, perception–action coupling and perceptual adaptation. *Perception–action coupling* is a concise way of saying that we move our bodies in ways that accommodate what we sense in our environment. This coordination of muscle movements with perceptual

information is demonstrated in the picture above by the man's ability to stay on the boat. As his brain perceives the tilt and sway of the boat, it sends signals to the muscles of his body to coordinate their activity, leaning back when the boat tips forward, and vice versa (lucky for him!). Perception–action coupling is probably the most underappreciated way that your brain takes care of your body. It is happening all the time, all day, every day, and we completely ignore how amazing it is. Each time you reach for a pencil to jot down a note, perception–action coupling is guiding your movements.

The space to the left is blank so that you can cut out the image on the back of this page without cutting any text. Don't cut off the boxes above! But do cut out the spiral and try the visual after-effect! (which wears off in a few seconds).

Perceptual adaptation is a change in how we perceive reality. We generally assume that the way we do this is solid, unchanging; our eyes and ears and brains accurately and consistently detect reality. But is that a correct assumption? The answer is no. An accurate perception of reality starts with **sensation**, which is the process by which sensory organs transduce energy from our environment into electrochemical signals that the brain can understand. **Perception** is the interpretation of those signals, that is, the interpretation of sensory information. During **perceptual adaptation**, the way we interpret that information *changes*. As sensory input repeats itself, we begin to perceive it differently. We adapt to it. A **perceptual aftereffect** occurs if our adaptation is no longer correct when the old information *stops* repeating. Perceptual aftereffects demonstrate that something about the sensation/perception process changes during repetition, causing us to misinterpret reality when the repetition stops. Why does this happen?

In order to interpret what one is seeing (or hearing, or touching), the brain must extract information from the stimulation it receives. Information comes in the form of differences, not sameness. For example, compare the two boxes at the top of this page. The left box contains more information because there are more differences in color, pattern, and shapes. Sameness is not only boring; it lacks information.

To get the most information out of our environment, our brains are specialized to detect differences, and not waste time on sameness. If a stimulus remains the same, like the background noise at a party, we adapt to it by raising our voices to be heard. We don't keep asking ourselves, "Is there a lot of noise?" so we can adjust our own volume each time we speak. We simply get used to speaking louder. It is not until a difference happens—the room suddenly goes quiet (usually just as we are saying something peculiar or embarrassing)—that we perceive the new sensory information about the lack of background noise, usually too late to save our dignity. But most of the time, perceptual adaptation is great; it helps us focus on important information by allowing us to put "sameness" on autopilot.

Dark adaptation is what happens as your eyes adjust to dim light. Your perception of the amount of light changes as you spend more time in a dim room, even though the actual amount of light in the room (that is, the light energy being transduced by your eyes into electrochemical signals) does not change. Where is dark adaptation happening? Where is the mechanism that allows you to see more clearly? Are your *eyes* transducing light energy more effectively, sending more information to the brain? Or is your *brain* becoming more sensitive to very low levels of incoming sensory information, perhaps getting better at interpreting it? Let's use the logic of scientific reasoning to figure this out:

Next time you wake up in the middle of the night, look around in the dark. If you've been asleep for a while, you will be maximally dark-adapted, so you should see well enough to identify some items in the room. Close or completely cover one eye (but do not put pressure on it). Turn the light on to expose the other eye to a bright room for a few seconds; then turn it off. Using just the eye that was exposed to the light, the room will be very dark. But if you close that eye and open the other, the room will immediately brighten without turning on any lights.

Practically speaking, this means that if you just use one eye and keep the other one closed or covered, you can turn on the bathroom light at night (useful for improved aim or to make sure the seat is down). You can then turn off the light and use the eye that was closed (which is still dark-adapted) to see very well on your way back to the bed, so you won't trip on a cat toy or stub your toe.

This observation supports the hypothesis that dark adaptation happens in the *eye* rather than in the *brain* (the causal hypothesis that a change in the eye causes the adaptation). If dark adaptation meant your *brain* was changing, getting more sensitive to signals from the eyes, then briefly exposing one eye to light would ruin dark adaptation entirely—your whole *brain* would lose its ability to see in the dark. So when the lights go out things would be very dark no matter which eye you use. Since this does not happen, and the eye that was *not* exposed to light remains dark-adapted, we can conclude that dark adaptation is happening in the eye itself.

APPLYING RESEARCH TERMINOLOGY

If you haven't read the preceding paragraphs about dark adaptation, you should do that now and make sure you understand how the evidence supports the hypothesis that *dark adaptation happens in the eye rather than in the brain.* In this research, we are going to use the same logic to address the question of what causes perceptual motor aftereffects. There are two possible hypotheses: Either the brain miscommunicates only with the specific muscles that are used during adaptation, or the brain as a whole adapts and then miscommunicates with the whole body. We will test the research hypothesis that *perceptual motor aftereffects are a matter of specific brain-to-muscle communication changes, rather than changes in the way the brain communicates with the whole body.*

It may be difficult to spot the conceptual variables in this hypothesis unless we reword it as a direct statement about cause and effect: *Specific brain-to-muscle miscommunication causes a perceptual motor aftereffect.* We have not changed the meaning of the research hypothesis, only the order of the words so

that the cause and effect are clearer. With the cause-and-effect statement, we can now more easily identify the conceptual independent and dependent variables. Our conceptual independent variable is the cause: "specific brain-to-muscle miscommunication," and the conceptual dependent variable is the effect: "a perceptual-motor aftereffect." If we thought the changes that cause aftereffects were located in the brain, we would hypothesize that general brain-to-body miscommunication causes perceptual motor aftereffects.

To test our research hypothesis, we will randomly split the class into two groups, A and B. All participants will complete three phases of data collection. First, you'll measure your baseline accuracy throwing a bean bag at a target. Second, everyone will then put on prism glasses that shift your visual field to the left and complete an adaptation phase, tossing the bean bag while wearing the glasses. When you first put them on, your throws will be off-target, but using perception-action coupling, your throws will generally get more accurate. Eventually, you'll be able to hit the center line four times in a row while wearing the prism glasses. This is perceptual adaptation at its best: Repeated sensory input tells you that everything in your environment must be further to the right than it appears, and your brain adjusts to this repeating stimulus and modifies your behavior accordingly. The third phase is testing: You will take the glasses off and toss the bag three times.

Everyone will do phases one and three, baseline and testing, with the same arm. Those in Group A will use the same arm for all three phases, but those in Group B will switch to their other arm during phase two, adaptation, then switch back to their baseline arm for testing. Our goal is to measure the change in accuracy between baseline and testing when the adaptation occurred with the same arm (Group A) or a different arm (Group B).

During the adaptation period, we are manipulating the independent variable (*the specific brain-to-muscle communication*) with two levels: For Group A, the specific brain-to-muscle communication

pathways that are tested for aftereffects *are involved in adaptation* because they are using the same arm for all three phases. For Group B, the specific brain-to-muscle communication pathways that are tested for aftereffects *are NOT involved in adaptation* because Group B will switch arms for adaptation, then switch back for testing (Fig. 5.2). So if our hypothesis is true, we predict that people in Group A will experience a larger change in accuracy than those in Group B.

For this experiment, as for all experiments, we will have to control **extraneous variables**, such as the level of adaptation attained while wearing the glasses and which arm is used for baseline and testing (dominant or nondominant). We'll do our best to avoid **confounding variables**, although you might notice one or two, if you think about it afterward. If these terms are not clear, review the information on experimental research in Essay 5.1, read the definitions and examples of these terms in the Module 5 Glossary, and/or ask your instructor for help.

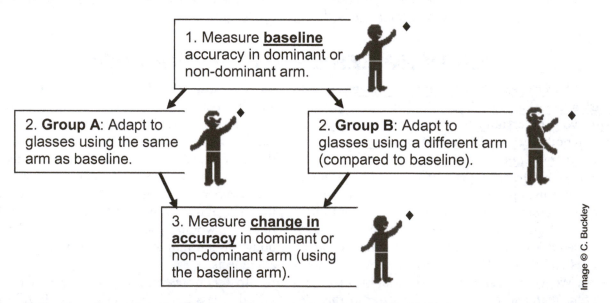

Image © C. Buckley

Figure 5.2   Experimental design for the perceptual adaptation study. (1) Both groups start by measuring their tossing accuracy. (2) Then both groups put on glasses and toss until adaptation occurs. Group A always uses the same arm for all three phases; Group B switches arms during adaptation, then goes back to the baseline arm for testing. (3) Both groups test the change in accuracy for the same arm they used during baseline.

PROCEDURE **5A**

1. Watch the instructor demonstrate proper data collection technique. Your instructor will also assign your pair to use either Data Sheet 1 OR Data Sheet 2. Do not attempt to use both.

2. Work in pairs. One person in your pair should tear out the data sheet from this textbook and put it on your clipboard with the correct side facing up. You only need one data sheet for your pair, and you will use EITHER Data Sheet 1 OR Data Sheet 2. You do not need both. The purpose of having two different data sheets is to control the extraneous variable of which arm (dominant or nondominant) is used for baseline and testing. Half of the class will use their dominant arms, and half of the class will use their non-dominant arms. This is NOT the independent variable because half of each will be in Group A and the other half will be in Group B. In this way, we are evenly distributing this variable (arm dominance) across both the experimental group (A) and the control group (B).

3. Decide who will be Participant A and who will be Participant B. While A tosses, B is the Experimenter, and while B tosses, A is the Experimenter. Each pair takes one clipboard with the correct data sheet facing up, one pair of prism glasses, one beanbag, and a pen or pencil. Take these things to a target station.

4. General rules for tossing and measuring: Tosser stands with toes on the launch mark (Fig. 5.3A). Starting with the appropriate throwing arm as instructed on the data sheet, toss the bag, aiming for the red X on the target. The Experimenter records where the bean bag lands during Phase 1 and 3 (Fig. 5.3B). IMPORTANT: Tosser must STAY at the launch mark for ALL tosses, NOT retrieve the bean bag. After each toss, the Experimenter must WALK the bag back to the Tosser and PLACE IT IN THE SAME HAND FROM WHICH IT WAS THROWN. Do not throw the bag back, not even gently. If the Tosser has to use the other hand to catch the bag, he/she might adapt using those muscles.

5. Participant A Tossers will ALWAYS use the same arm, for all three phases. To control for the extraneous variable of hand dominance, half of Participant A Tossers will use their dominant arm (Data Sheet 1) and half will use their nondominant arm (Data Sheet 2) for all tosses.

   a. **Measure baseline accuracy:** The Experimenter (B) measures the horizontal displacement (horizontal distance between the target and the landing place) for each of 10 tosses.

   b. **Adapt to left-shifted visual field:** Tosser (A) puts prism glasses on. Using the SAME arm, complete 25 tosses with no measurements, then keep tossing until at least *four in a row* land touching the

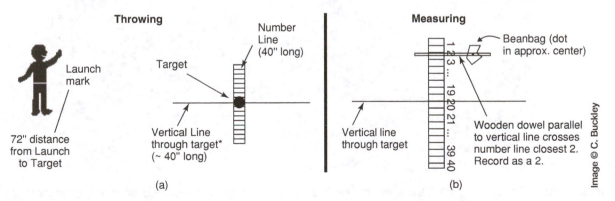

Figure 5.3 **(a)** Target station, showing where the Tosser should stand and the target station distances. **(b)** To record tossing accuracy, use a straightedge (wooden dowel or imaginary line) going through the approximate center of the beanbag, parallel to the vertical line (vertical from the perspective of the person throwing the beanbag). Record the whole number closest to the point where the parallel line crosses the number line. We are only interested in horizontal tossing accuracy.

vertical line (up to a maximum of 20 additional tosses, 45 total). **After** the first 25 tosses, the Experimenter (B) starts counting and records the number of additional tosses required to get 4 in a row, up to 20.

   c. **Measure accuracy after adaptation:** Tosser (A) takes off the glasses and then tosses three times with the same arm. Experimenter (B) records horizontal displacement of those 3 tosses.

6. Switch roles. Participant A becomes the experimenter, and B becomes the Tosser.

7. Tosser (B) will use the dominant arm (Data Sheet 1) OR nondominant arm (Data Sheet 2) for baseline tossing as instructed on the data sheet, then use the OTHER arm for adaptation, then go back to the baseline arm for testing.

   a. **Measure baseline accuracy:** The Experimenter (A) measures the horizontal displacement (horizontal distance between the target and the landing place) of each of 10 tosses.

   b. **Adapt to left-shifted visual field:** Tosser (B) puts prism glasses on (adaptation phase). Switching arms to the one NOT used for baseline, Tosser (B) completes 25 tosses with no measurements, then keeps tossing until at least four in a row land touching the vertical line (up to a maximum of 20 additional tosses, 45 total). **After** the first 25 tosses, the Experimenter (A) starts counting and records the number of additional tosses required to get 4 in a row, up to 20.

   c. **Measure accuracy after adaptation:** Tosser (B) takes off the glasses and switches arms, back to the same arm used during baseline, then tosses three times. Experimenter (A) records the horizontal displacement of those 3 tosses.

8. Return to the lab and calculate your mean accuracy before and after adaptation as demonstrated by your instructor. Then calculate your change in accuracy by subtracting your baseline mean (mean of first 10 tosses) from your postadaptation mean (mean of last three tosses).

9. Hand in your data and work on the lab record worksheet while awaiting results. Then discuss the results and complete the lab record worksheet.

© worldclassphoto /Shutterstock.com

Bonus Info: His Eyes Can See Better than Yours. The animal pictured above is spectacular in full color, and can see better than any human can. It has the ability to detect 12 different wavelengths of color (we can only detect three: red, green, and blue). It can also see in stereo with just one eye (we need two). To see this beauty, even with your own (limited) visual system is still quite impressive. For full color video and more fascinating facts about them, see Ze Frank's *True Facts about the Mantis Shrimp* at youtube.com/watch?v=F5FEj9U-CJM Warning: NSFW. There is some mild "adult language" in this video.

DATA SHEET 1 FOR PARTICIPANT A(DDD) AND B(DND)

Participant A(DDD) Name:_____ ← Tosser

Experimenter B(DND) Name:_____ ← Measurer

A DOM DOM DOM	PHASE 1 BASELINE Measure baseline accuracy. Record measurements.	PHASE 2 ADAPTATION Wear your prism glasses!		PHASE 3 TESTING Remove prism glasses. Test your tossing accuracy. Record measurements.
Trial	DOMINANT ARM	DOMINANT ARM	Trial	DOMINANT ARM
1		Toss 25 times, no measurements.	1	
2			2	
3		After 25 tosses, start trying to get 4 in a row touching the vertical line (maximum of 20 additional tosses, 45 total). When the participant gets 4 in row, go to Phase 3. Tally number of *extra* tosses needed to get 4 in a row.	3	
4				SWITCH ROLES (TOSSER AND MEASURER) AND COMPLETE THE SECOND HALF OF THIS DATA SHEET BELOW.
5				
6				
7				
8				
9				
10				
	GO TO PHASE 2.	GO TO PHASE 3.		

Participant B(DND) Name:_____ ← Tosser

Experimenter A(DDD) Name:_____ ← Measurer

B DOM **NON** DOM	PHASE 1 BASELINE Measure baseline accuracy. Record measurements.	PHASE 2 ADAPTATION Wear your prism glasses **and switch arms**!!		PHASE 3 TESTING Remove prism glasses and **switch arms again.** Test your tossing accuracy. Record measurements,
Trial	DOMINANT ARM	NONDOMINANT ARM	Trial	DOMINANT ARM
1		Toss 25 times, no measurements.	1	
2			2	
3		After 25 tosses, start trying to get 4 in a row touching the vertical line (maximum of 20 additional tosses, 45 total). When the participant gets 4 in row, go to Phase 3. Tally number of *extra* tosses needed to get 4 in a row.	3	
4				YOU'RE DONE. ENTER YOUR DATA IN MS EXCEL OR GOOGLE SHEETS.
5				
6				
7				
8				
9				
10				
	GO TO PHASE 2.	GO TO PHASE 3.		

DATA SHEET 2 FOR PARTICIPANT A(NNN) AND B(NDN)

Participant A(NNN) Name:_____ ← Tosser

Experimenter B(NDN) Name:_____ ← Measurer

A NON NON NON	PHASE 1 BASELINE	PHASE 2 ADAPTATION		PHASE 3 TESTING
	Measure baseline accuracy. Record measurements.	Wear your prism glasses!		Remove prism glasses. Test your tossing accuracy. Record measurements.
Trial	NONDOMINANT ARM	NONDOMINANT ARM	Trial	NONDOMINANT ARM
1		Toss 25 times, no measurements.	1	
2			2	
3		After 25 tosses, start trying to get 4 in a row touching the vertical line (maximum of 20 additional tosses, 45 total). When the participant gets 4 in row, go to Phase 3.	3	
4				SWITCH ROLES (TOSSER AND MEASURER) AND COMPLETE THE SECOND HALF OF THIS DATA SHEET BELOW.
5				
6				
7				
8		Tally number of *extra* tosses needed to get 4 in a row.		
9				
10				
	GO TO PHASE 2.	GO TO PHASE 3.		

Participant B(NDN) Name:_____ ← Tosser

Experimenter A(NNN) Name:_____ ← Measurer

B NON **DOM** NON	PHASE 1 BASELINE	PHASE 2 ADAPTATION		PHASE 3 TESTING
	Measure baseline accuracy. Record measurements.	Wear your prism glasses **and switch arms**!!		Remove prism glasses and **switch arms again**. Test your tossing accuracy. Record measurements,
Trial	NONDOMINANT ARM	DOMINANT ARM	Trial	NONDOMINANT ARM
1		Toss 25 times, no measurements.	1	
2			2	
3		After 25 tosses, start trying to get 4 in a row touching the vertical line (maximum of 20 additional tosses, 45 total). When the participant gets 4 in row, go to Phase 3.	3	
4				YOU'RE DONE. ENTER YOUR DATA IN MS EXCEL OR GOOGLE SHEETS.
5				
6				
7				
8		Tally number of *extra* tosses needed to get 4 in a row.		
9				
10				
	GO TO PHASE 2.	GO TO PHASE 3.		

LAB RECORD WORKSHEET FOR STUDY 5A

Name: _____ Date: _____

Research Partner's Name: _____

Purpose: *To investigate the location of perceptual aftereffects associated with perception-action coupling.*
Hypothesis: *A change in the motor neuron pathways (brain-to-muscle communication) during adaptation causes perceptual motor aftereffects. If the hypothesis is true, only muscles that were involved in the adaptation process would show evidence of the aftereffect. Arm muscles NOT involved in adaptation should behave as they did before adaptation.*

Conceptual independent variable (what did we manipulate because we hypothesized it to be the location of the aftereffects?): _____

_____

Conceptual dependent variable (what did we expect our manipulations to affect?):

_____

Operational definition of IV (how, specifically, did we define the IV? What were the two levels of our IV?):

_____

_____

Operational definition of DV (what, specifically, did we measure to look for an effect?):

_____

Prediction (if the research hypothesis we are testing is true, what, specifically, would we expect to happen with the measurements in our experiment?): _____

_____

Method

Participants: _____ *college students enrolled in introductory psychology lab participated as part of the course. Gender and age were not recorded, but gender was mixed and most participants were between 18 and 22 years old.*

Materials (list all relevant materials with brief descriptions): _____

_____

_____

_____

_____

Procedure: *Students worked in pairs and took turns as Participant (Tosser) and Experimenter (Measurer). Participants were instructed to stay at the launch line throughout their tossing trials and Experimenters were asked to retrieve and hand the bag back to the Participant and to take measurements of accuracy (horizontal displacement from a vertical line through the center of the target). To measure horizontal displacement, a straight stick was laid across the midpoint of the bean bag at its landing point, parallel to the vertical line drawn through the 20-inch mark center of the target. The number closest to where the stick crossed the horizontal number line was recorded. Data collection was a three-step process. During the first step (Baseline), tossing accuracy was measured for 10 consecutive tosses with one arm. For the second step (Adaptation), the Participant wore prism glasses while tossing the bag repeatedly with either the same arm (Group A) or the other arm (Group B) until it landed touching the vertical line a minimum of four times in a row, with no fewer than 29 tosses in all and no more than 45 tosses, regardless of whether or not this criterion was achieved. No measurements of displacement were recorded during Adaptation. For the third step (Testing), participants completed three measured tosses with the same arm they had used during Baseline. All three steps comprised one round of data collection. After the first round was completed, Participant and Experimenter switched roles. Each student completed one round of data collection as the Participant and one round as the Experimenter. Within each group (A and B), half of the participants used their dominant arm during Adaptation and the other half used their nondominant arm during adaptation.*

Data Handling: For each participant (and each arm), how did we calculate the change in accuracy?

_____

_____

_____

We used a t-test to compare _____.

Results

(see Prediction section for guidance on this) _____

_____

_____

_____

Discussion

What can we conclude about the location of perceptual aftereffects associated with perception-action coupling?_____

_____

_____

Discuss one limitation of this study _____

_____

_____

_____

_____

_____

LANGUAGE AND THOUGHT

In 1935, J. Ridley Stroop published an article based on his PhD dissertation entitled, "Studies of interference in serial verbal reactions." He went on to teach Bible studies at a small Christian college in Tennessee, leaving behind a literary battlefield strewn with published reports arguing over the best explanation for the phenomenon he had described. Almost 90 years later, the Stroop effect remains a popular topic for research in psychology.

One reason for the popularity of such research is what the Stroop effect can reveal about the complex relationship between language and thought. Try this: For just 15 s, think without words. Can you do it? For most people, whatever comes to mind is immediately translated into words, despite our best efforts.

Linguistic determinism is the idea that language dictates and limits the way we think and behave. While most psycholinguists have abandoned that extreme view, evidence remains strong for a less extreme version, called the **linguistic relativity hypothesis, or LRH**. LRH suggests that language and thought and behavior are intimately interwoven, such that language influences the way we think and act, but is not the sole determining factor. A wonderful, 14-min TED talk by a leading researcher in the study of LRH, Lera Boroditsky, provides an informative and entertaining review of the evidence for this hypothesis (search YouTube for her name and the title, "How language shapes the way we think").

For study 5B, we will use a Stroop-like test to investigate the effect of language on thinking. You

Image © iQoncept/Shutterstock

will attempt to complete a simple cognitive task with or without the presence of added language to test whether and to what extent adding language impacts the ability to complete the task.

Typically, the Stroop effect is measured using a color-naming task, where different colors of ink are printed in rows and columns. The cognitive task is to simply name the color of the ink. Due to the complexity and individuality of color perception (and color printers), the need for excellent lighting, and so forth, we will instead use a size-naming task that should work just as well, with fewer complications.

APPLYING RESEARCH TERMINOLOGY

Based on the linguistic relativity hypothesis, we can restate our research hypothesis in very general terms as "*language affects thinking*." This is a cause-and-effect hypothesis, and testing it will require the manipulation of language (the conceptual *independent variable*, or IV) and the measurement of its effect on thinking (the conceptual *dependent variable*, or DV).

We will ask participants to perform a simple cognitive task: naming the sizes of dots inside boxes.

Relative to the size of the box, there will be five dot sizes (shown below), and participants will practice using the names to make sure they can correctly identify the different sizes.

We will operationally define our conceptual IV (language) with two levels: People at one level of the IV will see words that might interfere with the task (the *experimental group*, A), and those at the other level of the IV will not see any words with the task (the *control group*, B). The operational definition of our DV (thinking) will be the time it takes to complete the task, which we can measure by observing each other in pairs and using cell phone stopwatches.

If language affects thinking, then we *predict* that people who see words should take longer to complete the simple cognitive task than people who do the same task without seeing any words.

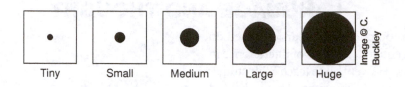

Tiny   Small   Medium   Large   Huge

Image © C. Buckley

SKILL CHECK

What is the null hypothesis in this experiment and what outcome would you predict if the null hypothesis is true? (answer in Appendix B)

_____

_____

Because this is a true experiment, we cannot allow people to choose their own group assignments. Participants must be randomly assigned to the experimental and control groups. ***Random assignment*** means that every participant has an equal chance of being placed into Group A or Group B. We will assign participants to groups with coin flips.

We will also have to control other ***extraneous variables***, such as the way in which the cognitive task is presented and timed and the amount of practice everyone gets with naming the sizes. We'll also do our best to avoid ***confounding variables***, although you might notice one or two, if you think about it afterward. If these terms are not clear, review the information on experimental research in Essay 5.1.

5B PROCEDURE

1. You will work in pairs, facing each other, at opposite sides of a desk. Flip a coin (or ask Siri or Google Assist to flip a coin) to determine which person in each pair will be in Group A and which person will be in Group B. The winner of the coin toss will be in Group A.

2. Your instructor will provide a practice sheet (stimulus card) of dots (stimuli) for each pair of students. Keep the sheet facing down on the desk between partners until you are asked to flip it over. The arrow should be pointing to the Group A person (the first participant). The experimenter should remove the answer key card that is clipped to the stimulus card and be ready to check the answers as the participant names the dot sizes.

3. When both people in the pair are ready, one person (the **participant**) will flip over the practice sheet *horizontally* (keeping the arrow pointing toward him or herself) and immediately begin reading off the sizes of the dots out loud, from left to right, one row at a time. Start with the second row; the first row is labeled, to be used as a key if you get stuck. The other person in each pair (the **experimenter**) will be looking at a list of correct answers, making sure that the correct sizes are named. If a mistake is made, the **experimenter** should immediately say "no," and the participant must try again to say the correct size.

The participant must say the correct size before going on to the next dot. Neither person should ever be pointing at the dots. It may help the participant to sit on his or her own hands while naming sizes, to avoid the temptation to point at them.

4. The participant should go through the whole sheet, left to right, row by row, correctly naming the size of every dot for practice. Once all the dot sizes have been correctly named, the experimenter should immediately flip the card over so the dots can no longer be seen.

5. Your instructor will then provide a new stimulus card, face-down so that you can't see the dots. Do not flip it over until your experimenter is ready to begin a stopwatch. If you're using your phone's stopwatch app, turn off all notifications (silence your phone) first.

6. When the experimenter is ready, he/she will start the stopwatch and say "go." The participant should immediately flip the card over and begin naming the sizes of the dots **as quickly as possible.** *Ignore any words that are included in the squares with the dots.* Instead name the **size** of each dot, just as you did during practice. The experimenter should watch the answer key carefully, as you did during practice, and say "no" if a size is incorrectly named. Immediately stop the stopwatch when the size of the *last* dot is named. **Record the number of seconds required to complete the task** on the data sheet below

7. Now go back to the practice sheet and set it face down between the two of you. This time the arrow points to the Group B person, who will become the new participant. The Group A person becomes the new experimenter. Repeat from Step 3. Make sure you wait for your instructor to provide the NEW stimulus card labeled "Group B" in Step 5.

8. All scores will be recorded on one Excel spreadsheet. The instructor will compare the mean time to complete the task for Group A versus Group B participants using a statistical analysis, and the **p-value** will be provided for the entire class.

9. Complete the lab record worksheet.

TEAR ON THE DOTTED LINE AND HAND IN ONLY THE BOTTOM OF THIS PAGE.

- -

STUDY 5B DATA SHEET

Round to nearest whole second.
Hand in only one data sheet for each pair of students

PARTICIPANT A's TIME TO COMPLETE TASK: _____ SEC

PARTICIPANT B's TIME TO COMPLETE TASK: _____ SEC

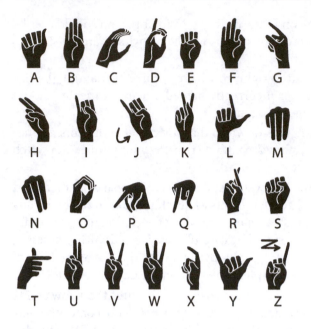

BONUS INFO:

Think with your hands: Learn to communicate in American Sign Language.

There are several good ASL apps available. Find one that suits your learning style. As of May 2020, *The ASL App* by Ink & Salt LLC is free and includes a good set of professionally made videos. *ASL American Sign Language by* 10mB also has good, free beginner videos. Both apps include advertise-ments and in-app purchases.

PLEASE   THANK YOU   FRIEND   LOVE   I LOVE YOU

YES   NO   SCHOOL   MOTHER   FATHER

This space is empty so that you can tear out
Data Sheet 5B without losing any important information.

LAB RECORD WORKSHEET FOR STUDY 5B

Name: _____ Date: _____

Group Member Names: _____

Purpose: *To use the Stroop effect to investigate the linguistic relativity hypothesis.*

Hypothesis: _____

_____

Conceptual independent variable: _____

Conceptual dependent variable: _____

Operational definition of IV (what were the two levels of the IV?):

1) _____

2) _____

Operational definition of DV (how did we measure the DV?):

_____

Prediction (if the hypothesis we are testing is true, what, specifically, would we expect to happen with the measurements in our experiment?): _____

_____

Participants: _____ *college students enrolled in introductory psychology class participated as part of the course. Age and gender were not recorded, but most participants were between 18 and 22 years old and gender was mixed.*

Method

Materials (list all relevant materials with brief descriptions): _____

_____

_____

_____

_____

_____

_____

_____

_____

_____

Procedure (Describe, in general terms, how data were collected): _____

_____

_____

_____

_____

Data Handling: How did we summarize the data for each group? _____

_____

_____

_____

_____

We used a t-test to compare _____

Results

See prediction section for guidance on this _____

_____

_____

_____

Discussion

Can we reject the null hypothesis in favor of our research hypothesis? Yes   No   Not Sure

What can we conclude about the effect of language on thinking? _____

_____

Did you notice any confounding variables? Describe at least one. _____

_____

_____

If your class observed a negative influence of language on the ability to complete a simple cognitive task, do you think it is possible that language could facilitate cognitive tasks? How would you redesign our stimuli (dot images) to test this hypothesis? _____

_____

_____

_____

STUDY 5C

MINDFULNESS AND WORKING MEMORY

There are several definitions of mindfulness, but the common thread is that it is a state of nonjudgmental awareness and attentiveness to one's immediate surroundings and internal state. Combined with meditation practice, mindfulness has become a popular way of dealing with a variety of human challenges. According to a recent CDC report (Clarke et al., 2018), meditation practice tripled between the years 2012 and 2017, from 4.1% to 14.2% of US adults. The increased interest in mindfulness and meditation has brought with it a surge in research on mindfulness as well.

The list of human endeavors that researchers have reported can benefit from mindfulness practice is so long that it would be tedious to list, but a small sample is shown in Table 5.4. If you're interested in learning more about any of these applications or would like to suggest mindfulness to a friend who might benefit, some sources are included. Each source has its own bibliography with many more sources.

Examining research on the benefits of mindfulness training can be frustrating because there are so many different definitions and training programs. Mindfulness "training" can involve anything from a five-minute exercise to 12 weeks of instruction. While it may seem like shorter training periods should be less effective, this is not always the case. It is possible that at least some of the benefits reported for longer mindfulness training can be accomplished in shorter periods of time. For example, Arch et al., (2016) found that giving brief instructions on mindfulness to students before they ate chocolate decreased the calories they consumed and positively influenced their decisions regarding healthy food choices. In this study, we will examine whether similarly brief exposure to mindfulness instruction can improve working memory.

Have you ever heard a negative voice in your head calling you an "idiot" when you made a mistake while trying to complete a task? Do you ever doubt your ability to handle a task as well as others handle it, even as you are trying your best? Have you ever changed an answer on a multiple-choice test because that negative voice said your first choice was "probably wrong?"

This kind of negative-chatter and self-judging can be destructive, particularly when your mind and body react to the negativity with more worry and stress. The purported benefit of mindfulness is that it draws one's attention to mental and sensory experiences in a completely nonjudgmental way. While a negative thought may still occur, it is not judged as such, but accepted as just one of the human thoughts you might experience, so it is less likely to add worry or stress.

Table 5.4   A Sample of Applications of Mindfulness Training to Improve Several Aspects of Life, with Resources to Begin a Literature Search to Learn More on Each Topic

Mindfulness Application	Source (See this book's reference list for complete bibliographic information)
Pain Management	Veehof et al., (2016)
Drug Abuse Rehabilitation	Tang et al., (2016)
Depression Relapse Prevention	Piet & Hougaard (2011)
Anxiety and Stress Reduction	Astin (1997); Bamber & Schneider (2016)
Sport Performance Boost	Kaufman et al., (2018)
Leadership/Management Skills	Baron et al., (2018)
First Year College Transition	Dvorakova et al., (2017)
Weight Management	Tapper (2017), Arch et al., (2016)
Working Memory/GRE Scores	Mrazek et al., (2013)

APPLYING RESEARCH TERMINOLOGY

This research will test the hypothesis that brief mindfulness exercises can improve working memory performance. We'll manipulate our **independent variable** (brief mindfulness exercises) by setting up two **levels of the IV**: One group will hear a mindfulness audio file and one will hear an audio book excerpt. Our **dependent variable**, memory performance, will be measured in both groups with a series of online games that each take only one or two minutes to play. Your average score will be used to measure your working memory performance. We'll control **extraneous variables** like gaming experience and individual differences in working memory capacity by using **random assignment** to set up the two groups. We predict that scores will be higher in the group that hears the mindfulness audio than in the group that hears the audio book excerpt.

5C PROCEDURE

In order to get the most accurate measure of your working memory performance, we'll ask you to do three (possibly four) different memory games. To minimize the stress of learning how to play the games and switching from one game to another, you'll repeat part of the mindfulness exercise just before each game. In the control group, you'll repeat a writing exercise that will take about the same amount of time.

1) Each pair of students should decide who wants heads and who wants tails, then flip a coin (if you don't have a coin handy, ask Siri or Alexa or say "Hey, Google, flip a coin."). Whoever wins the coin-toss will be in Group A, and the other student will be in Group B. Circle your own group letter on your data sheet now. (It's on the next page of this book). Each student will use his or her own data sheet.

2) Using headphones or earbuds, people in Group A should listen to the audio file A1. You'll need your data sheet and a pen or pencil before you begin. It will be a 5-min mindfulness exercise, with a practice grounding exercise. Before you begin listening, be sure to have your data sheet and pen or pencil ready, silence notifications on your phone and find a comfortable place to sit with both feet on the floor, no crossed arms or legs, and your back straight, but comfortable. People in Group B should do exactly the same thing, except that you will listen to audio file B1, which will be a 5-minute excerpt from an audio book, with a practice writing exercise.

3) After finishing the audio file, proceed to a computer or use your phone to go to the website "improve-memory.org." Click on "Memory Games," and scroll to "Pattern I." If you are on a phone, enlarge the screen image so that you can more easily see and respond to the memory task.

4) Play the game once through, until you make a mistake and it says, "Game Over." That was practice.

5) After practice, if you are in Group A, perform your grounding exercise, using your notes from audio file A1. If you are in Group B, perform your writing exercise, using your notes from audio file B1.

6) Click "play again" and do your best until the game is over. Record your score on the data sheet.

7) Click "Home" or go back to Memory Games at "improvememory.org" and scroll down to "Pattern II." Repeat steps 4, 5 & 6 (practice once, then ground yourself if you are in Group A, or write if you are in Group B, then do the "Pattern II" game a second time and record your score on the data sheet.)

8) The third game has no practice session, so do not start it until you've read these instructions. The game you will play is called "Memory III." Find it on the memory games page, and open it, but do not start it yet. First, do your grounding exercise (Group A) or writing exercise (Group B). Then start "Memory III." Remember—your first score counts, so do your best. This game will go to 9 levels, no matter how many mistakes you make, but each mistake will cost you points. It is basically a memory-card game, but it shows you where the colors are before you start. *If you are colorblind, be sure to record that on your data sheet, and just do your best.*

9) (Optional, but fun) If time allows, your instructor might assign one more memory game. This one will require two rounds of practice. Go to "Tricky Cups" on the memory games page and play the game twice through. As soon as you make a mistake, the game is over. Pay attention! As your level advances, there are more coins and sometimes the coins stay in place while the cups move, so that they are then under a new cup. You have to pay careful attention and keep track of where the coins are to get the highest score you can. After you have practiced *twice*, do your grounding exercise (Group A) or writing exercise (Group B). Then play a third round of the game and record your score on the data sheet.

10) Everyone must do the same tests, so you should *not* do the Tricky Cups Game unless instructed. You can do it for fun later, but do not record your score unless everyone in the class has been asked to do so.

11) Calculate your average memory score from all the tests you were assigned and submit this score to your instructor on your anonymous data sheet. Don't forget to circle the letter of the group you were assigned!

12) Complete the first part of the lab record worksheet while your instructor runs the statistical analysis for the experiment.

13) Discuss the results and how to interpret them, then finish the lab record worksheet.

STUDY 5C DATA SHEET

While listening to your assigned audio file, take notes as instructed inside this box.

PARTICIPANT # _____   GROUP LETTER: (CIRCLE ONE)   A   B

ARE YOU COLORBLIND?   YES   NO   NOT SURE

(If not sure, Explain: _____)

Memory Test	Score
Pattern 1	
Pattern II	
Memory III	
Tricky Cups (only if assigned)	
Average Score (Total Score/Number of Scores)	

LAB RECORD WORKSHEET FOR STUDY 5C

Name: _____ Date: _____

Group Member Names: _____

Purpose: *To examine the influence of brief mindfulness meditation on working memory performance.*

Hypothesis: _____

_____

Conceptual independent variable: _____

Conceptual dependent variable: _____

Operational definition of IV (what were the two levels of the IV?):

1) _____

2) _____

Operational definition of DV (how did we measure overall working memory performance?):

_____

Prediction (if the hypothesis we are testing is true, what, specifically, would we expect to happen with the measurements in our experiment?): _____

_____

Method

Participants: _____ *college students enrolled in introductory psychology class participated as part of the course. Age and gender were not recorded, but most participants were between 18 and 22 years old and gender was mixed.*

Materials (list all relevant materials with brief descriptions): _____

_____

_____

_____

_____

_____

_____

_____

Procedure (Describe, in general terms, how data were collected): _____

_____

_____

_____

_____

_____

_____

_____

Data Handling: How did we summarize the data for each group? _____

_____

_____

_____

_____

We used a t-test to compare _____

Results

See Prediction section for guidance on this) _____

_____

_____

_____

Discussion

What would we expect if the *null* hypothesis were true? _____

_____

Can we reject the null hypothesis in favor of our research hypothesis? Yes   No   Not Sure

What can we conclude about the effect of brief mindfulness exercises on working memory? _____

_____

Describe and explain at least one limitation of this study (a confounding variable, design flaw, or limitation on the generalizability of the results. _____

_____

MODULE 5 GLOSSARY OF TERMS AND EXAMPLES

Confounding Variable: An *uncontrolled* extraneous variable. That is, anything other than the **independent variable** that is *systematically* different for different **levels of the IV** and can affect the dependent variable. This makes it difficult or impossible to separate the effects of the IV from effects of the confounding variable. We do our best to eliminate confounding variables in the design of an experiment.

    Examples: A researcher studies the effect of mild electrical shock on self-reported happiness by asking volunteers to sign up for an electric shock study where only half of the participants will actually get a shock. To encourage those who will have to endure the shock to participate, he offers them cash, but he doesn't have enough cash to offer it to those in the no-shock group. The cash offered will be a confounding variable because it is (1) not the independent variable (shock is the independent variable), (2) it is systematically different between the experimental and control groups, and (3) it is likely to affect the scores on the dependent variable (happiness scores).

    Where to find this term: Essays 5.1, 5.2, & 5.3, Figure 5.1, Studies 5A & 5B. See also Modules 6 and 7.

Control Group: The comparison group in an experiment. This group gets treated the same way as the **experimental group** in every way possible except for the level of the independent variable, so that if we observe any differences between groups when we measure the **dependent variable**, we can conclude that those differences are due to the **independent variable**. Usually, the control group is the one where the independent variable is kept at its natural level, not purposefully increased or decreased.

    Example: In an experiment where a new creativity training method is hypothesized to increase problem solving ability, the control group would be a group that does not get any training, or a group that gets a more traditional training method.

    Where to find this term: Essay 5.2

Dark Adaptation: When exposed to the dark for an extended period of time, the eyes become better and better at detecting small amounts of light, and the ability to perceive surroundings improves. Brief exposure to light eliminates dark adaptation.

    Example: Being indoors, in a windowless room with no lights, you will slowly be able to detect more and more items in the room. If you turn on a light, then turn it back off, it will be very dark again, until dark adaptation reoccurs.

    Where to find this term: Study 5A

Dependent Variable: The "effect" in a cause-and-effect relationship. We measure this in an experiment in order to determine whether our manipulations of the **independent variable** made a difference.

    Example: For the hypothesis that caffeine increases irritability, irritability would be the dependent variable.

    Where to find this term: Essay 5.1 & 5.2 & Figure 5.1. Studies 5A, 5B, & 5C.

Experiment: The only type of research that can directly test a cause-and-effect hypothesis. Researchers tinker with the cause and measure the effect, while controlling (keeping constant) other factors that might also influence the effect.

    Example: To test the hypothesis that caffeine increases irritability, an experiment could be done where participants are randomly split into two groups; one is given caffeinated coffee while the other is given decaffeinated coffee. The irritability of all participants is then measured. Other factors that could affect irritability, such as time of day, friendliness toward participants, and the belief that the coffee is caffeinated, must be the same for all participants.

    Where to find this term: Essay 5.1 & Figure 5.1. See also Module 1 Glossary and Modules 7 & 8

Experimental Group: The group that directly experiences the manipulation of the independent variable in an experiment. This group gets treated the same as the **control group** in every way possible except for differences in the level of the **independent variable**, so that when we compare the measurements of the **dependent variable** between groups, any observed difference can be attributed to the manipulation of the IV.

Example: In an experiment where a new creativity training method is hypothesized to increase problem solving ability, the experimental group would be the group that gets the new training, whereas the other group (the *control group*) gets a traditional training method (or no training at all).
Where to find this term: Essay 5.2

Extraneous Variable: Any factor (variable) other than the *independent variable* that has the potential to affect the *dependent variable* in an *experiment*. These must be controlled (kept constant) across different levels of the independent variable. *Random assignment* is the way that we attempt to even out most extraneous variables between groups.

Example: A researcher hypothesizes that watching someone perform a heroic act increases courage. Two groups of participants watch the same video, but with two different endings. In one, a man reaches out to pull a small child from an oncoming train, but in the other, the man must stand on the tracks to get the child's shoelace untangled from the tracks. To measure courage, participants are then asked to climb a ladder as high as they can until they feel too scared to go any higher. Extraneous variables would be things like the gender of the participants, the number of people in the background of the video, and participants' knowledge of the purpose of the experiment, which should all be kept the same in both groups. Experience with ladders would be another extraneous variable that would probably be evened out between groups using *random assignment*.
Where to find this term: Essay 5.1 & 5.2 & Figure 5.1. Studies 5A, 5B & 5C. See also Modules 7 & 8

Independent Variable: The "cause" in a cause-and-effect relationship. We manipulate this in an experiment in order to determine whether those manipulations make a difference in the *dependent variable* (effect).
Example: For the hypothesis that caffeine increases irritability, caffeine would be the independent variable.
Where to find this term: Essay 5.1 & Figure 5.1. Studies 5A, 5B, & 5C.

Levels of the Independent Variable: In an experiment, the different ways in which the "cause" from the cause-and-effect hypothesis is manipulated. Levels of the IV can also be thought of as the operational definition of the independent variable.
Example: For the hypothesis that caffeine increases irritability, caffeine would be the IV, and the different levels of the IV would be caffeinated coffee and decaffeinated coffee (or caffeine versus no caffeine).
Where to find this term: Essay 5.2, Studies 5A, 5B, & 5C.

Linguistic Determinism: The somewhat outdated idea that language determines how we think and behave; hence, the words and structure of the language we use limits and dictates our capacity for reason and action.
Example: The idea that people are incapable of thinking about things for which they have no words would be linguistic determinism.
Where to find this term: Study 5B

Linguistic Relativity Hypothesis (LRH): The idea that language influences how we think and behave; hence, the words and structure of the language we use are connected to our capacity for reason and action, but are not the sole determinants.
Example: Both English and Mandarin speakers refer to time along a forward/backward axis (both refer to time as something that is "ahead" or "behind.") However, the Mandarin language also has many more phrases that refer to past events as "up" and future events as "down." Boroditsky (2001) compared how quickly native English and Mandarin speakers answer questions about time, after they were primed to think along a forward/backward (horizontal) axis, or along an up/down (vertical) axis. English speakers did better when primed to think horizontally, whereas Mandarin speakers did better when primed to think vertically, supporting the idea that one's native language has at least some influence on his or her way of reasoning.
Where to find this term: Study 5B

Measurement Error: Any source of variability in a set of measurements. This can be imprecision, ambiguity of a definition, or unknown factors. "Error" is a bit misleading, because anything that keeps us from getting the true or precise value of a measurement is considered measurement error, including unexplained individual differences, which we don't typically think of as "errors."

Examples: If two people apply an operational definition in different ways and get different measurements for the same observation, that is one type of measurement error. Even if they use the same operational definition in exactly the same way, but the observation itself, for some unknown reason, varies from one measurement to the next, that is also due to "measurement error."
Where to find this term: Essay 5.3

Null Hypothesis: See Module 4 Glossary

Operational Definition: See Module 2 Glossary

p-Value: Assuming the null hypothesis is true, p is the probability of getting whatever result we got (e.g., a particular correlation coefficient or value of t). If the p-value is very low (less than .05) that suggests the null hypothesis is probably not true, meaning our research hypothesis is supported. If the p-value is high (greater than .05) that means the odds of getting our results under the null hypothesis are too high, so we can't reject the null hypothesis, and we have no support for the alternative (or research hypothesis).

Example: In a study on driving while distracted by cell phone conversations, Strayer and Johnston (2001) asked participants to use a computerized driving simulator where they had to react to signals on the computer screen while driving. The percentage of signals that participants missed more than doubled when they used a cell phone while driving, compared to driving with no distractions. The value of t representing the difference in missed signals with versus without the cell phone was 8.8. The **p-value** for that statistic was less than 0.01, meaning that if the null hypothesis is true (i.e., cell phones do not affect driving performance), then a statistical difference of 8.8 would have had a less-than-1% chance of occurring, given the number of participants observed. Since 1% (.01) is less than 5% (.05), we can conclude that talking on the cell phone significantly affected driving performance.
Where to find this term: Essay 5.4, Table 5.3, Study 5B. See also Module 4 Glossary

Perception: The interpretation of sensory information.
Example: Whenever we look at anything, electrochemical signals passed on by ganglion cells in the retina follow the optic nerve and are integrated with other neuronal information in the brain to help us identify what we see. The brain's interpretation of those electrochemical signals creates perception.
Where to find this term: Study 5A

Perception–Action Coupling: The coordination of muscle activity with *perception.*
Example: When walking a trail with sticks and rocks, you watch where you step, and your feet seem to easily "choose" the best places to land based on your perception of the terrain.
Where to find this term: Study 5A

Perceptual Adaptation: Perception of information from the environment changes due to extended repetition of the information, thereby improving sensitivity to differences when they arise.
Example: Smell adaptation—being exposed to the same smell for a long time, we stop smelling it. But if we leave the room and come back, we can smell it again.
Where to find this term: Study 5A

Perceptual Aftereffect: When a repeating stimulus that has caused *perceptual adaptation* stops repeating, so that the adaptation is no longer appropriate for the current level of the stimulus, causing a temporary misperception of reality. This can happen with motor control (see *Perceptual Motor Aftereffect*), but it can also happen with other repeating sensory experiences.
Example: For a great example of a visual perceptual aftereffect, go to Wikipedia and search the term "Motion aftereffect." If you suffer from migraine headaches or have other visually triggered difficulties do not do this! If you have no visual issues, then watch the video for **just 10 s**, keeping your eyes focused on the center of the image, where the diamonds seem to be closing in on themselves and disappearing. Then look at something else. It's freaky. Don't panic—the effect wears off in about 30 s.
Where to find this term: Study 5A

Perceptual Motor Aftereffect: A ***perceptual aftereffect*** that is linked to perception–action coupling. A sudden change in sensory information causes a temporary misperception that affects motor coordination or the perception of what one's own muscles are doing.

   Example: As you walk on a treadmill for a while, ***perceptual adaptation*** occurs along with ***perception–action coupling***. You become accustomed to the perception that the floor is moving backward, and you adjust your center of gravity and your steps to keep your balance. You quickly adapt to the moving floor. But if you stay on for a long time, and that perceptual adaptation is strong enough, when you step off and the sensory information suddenly changes (the floor beneath you is not moving), you will experience a perceptual motor aftereffect. It will feel like the floor is moving forward under your feet, and you may even lean slightly to try to accommodate that feeling.

   Where to find this term: Study 5A

Population: See Module 3 Glossary

Random Assignment: The use of a random process for putting participants into different groups so that they will experience different ***levels of the independent variable*** in an ***experiment***. A random process means that no one in the study has a better chance of ending up in any particular group than anyone else.

   Example: People may be assigned to groups by flipping a coin, rolling a die, pulling numbers from a hat, or any other random process.

   Where to find this term: Essay 5.2, Studies 5A, 5B, & 5C.

Random Selection: The use of a random process for choosing people (or other animals) to participate in a study. A random process means that no one from the larger group (about whom we wish to draw conclusions) has a better chance of being included in the study than anyone else from that same ***population.***

   Examples: Choosing people who have a "2" in their social security number, or choosing every 10th name in the phone book.

   Where to find this term: Essay 5.2 & 5.4

Raw Data See Module 3 Glossary

Representative Sample: A subset of people or other animals that accurately represents the larger group about whom the researcher wants to draw conclusions. This is best achieved by using ***random selection.*** When random selection is used, a ***random sample*** is created, and the larger the sample, the more representative it should be of the ***population.***

   Example: A representative sample of all college students in the United States would include students from all kinds of colleges and universities, including 2-year, 4-year, and postgraduate universities, in about the same proportions as they exist in the population.

   Where to find this term: Essay 5.2

Sensation: The transduction of various forms of energy into electrochemical signals by sensory organs.

   Example: Photoreceptors (rods and cones) in the retina respond to light by releasing neurotransmitter.

   Where to find this term: Study 5A

Significant Difference: A difference between sets of numbers that would be very unlikely if the null hypothesis is true (by general consensus, it would have a less-than-5% chance of occurring when the null is true).

   Example: Ijzerman and Semin (2009) found evidence that physical warmth can increase awareness of social/emotional closeness to others. In the study, two groups of people, holding either warm or cold drinks in their hands without knowing why, were asked to describe someone and to rate their closeness to that person. Those holding warm drinks rated themselves significantly closer to the person they thought of than those holding a cold drink. Without their knowledge, the temperature of their drinks affected their thoughts of friends. These findings were replicated in 2014 by Schilder et al. Isn't psychology fascinating?

   Where to find this term: Essay 5.3, 5.4. Studies 5A, 5B, 5C, Modules 6 & 7.

Statistical Analysis: The application of mathematical formulas and probability theory to a data set in order to summarize and draw conclusions from the data.

   Examples: Testing a correlational hypothesis by calculating a correlation coefficient and determining its ***p-value*** is a statistical analysis. Testing a cause-and-effect hypothesis by calculating a number representing the difference between two sets of data from two different groups, then determining the *p*-value for getting that result is a statistical analysis. These are just two of many types of statistical analyses.

   Where to find this term: Essay 5.3

Variability: See Module 3 Glossary

*"Guess where I get my best ideas."**

*Alternate caption: "… *and according to my statistical analysis, everything came out okay.*"

Module 6 Quasi-Experimental Research

MODULE 6 LEARNING OBJECTIVES CHART

ESSAY NUMBER	MODULE 6 ESSAY LEARNING OBJECTIVES	BEFORE READING				AFTER READING			
		I don't know how **1**	I know a little about this **2**	I know enough about this to guess correctly **3**	I know how to do this and/or have already done it. **4**	I don't know how **1**	I know a little about this **2**	I know enough about this to guess correctly **3**	I know how to do this and/or have already done it. **4**
6.1	Explain why quasi-experiments are called "quasi" and how they differ from true experiments.								
6.1	Explain why two-group quasi-experiments sometimes suffer from self-selection problems.								
6.1 6.2	Discuss the similarities between correlational and quasi-experimental research.								
6.1 Box 6.1	Describe at least two types of quasi-experiments that are done with just one group, and the limitations of their findings.								
6.1 6.2 6.3	Provide an example of a study with nonequivalent groups and discuss at least one confounding variable.								
6.2	Explain two factors that can cause researchers to choose a quasi-experiment over a true experiment.								
6.2	List and define five ethical guiding APA principles for research with human subjects.								

		I don't know how **1**	I know a little about this **2**	I know enough about this to guess correctly **3**	I know how to do this and/ or have already done it. **4**	I don't know how **1**	I know a little about this **2**	I know enough about this to guess correctly **3**	I know how to do this and/ or have already done it. **4**
6.3	Describe three ways you can easily identify a quasi-experimental research design.								
6.1 **6.2** **6.3**	Explain why quasi-experimental research is valuable.								
		Read the assigned essays and actively seek answers to any questions rated less than "4." Then return to this chart and complete the white half.				Now proceed to the chart for the applications section, read the objectives for your assigned research project, and complete the gray side of the *research* learning objectives chart.			

ESSAY 6.1

QUASI-EXPERIMENTS VS TRUE EXPERIMENTS

In 2011, Daniel Shechtman won the Nobel Prize in Chemistry for his discovery of quasicrystals: *30 years after he discovered them.* True crystals are defined by their three-dimensional, repeating patterns that fit neatly together with no gaps. Quasicrystals also fit neatly together to form structures with no gaps, but they have no obvious repeating pattern in their structure. Shechtman had discovered crystals that other chemists said were "not really crystals." His discovery was so radical when he first reported it in 1982 that he was dismissed from his laboratory and accused of being an embarrassment to other chemists! After winning the Nobel, Shechtman revealed in an interview what Linus Pauling, a two-time Nobel Prize winner himself, had said years before, "There is no such thing as quasicrystals, only quasi-scientists." (Lannin, 2011).[1] Pauling was wrong. Due to their hard, yet slippery qualities, quasicrystals have found applications in nonstick frying pans and surgical tools, among other things. It took 30 years of replications and new applications before Shechtman was recognized as having radically changed our understanding of crystalline structures.

There are at least three morals to this story. First, doing science takes courage. Scientists risk ridicule when we share our evidence, especially when it disagrees with common knowledge. Second, it takes clear records, clear communication, and the work of many for scientific discoveries to find their way into everyday life. Shechtman's paper was reviewed, published, scrutinized, replicated, and expanded to arrive at our current understanding of quasicrystals and their applications. Third, the prefix "quasi" does not make something fake or useless. It just lacks some quality that defined the original.

The prefix "quasi" means "resembling, but not equivalent to." Quasicrystals have some of the same properties as other crystals, but lack the type of repeating pattern that is characteristic of true crystals. Similarly, a *quasi-experiment* has some of the characteristics of a true experiment, but lacks one very important, defining characteristic: control over *extraneous variables* that can affect the outcome.

In previous modules, we have stated the defining characteristics of correlational and experimental research: Correlational studies *measure* existing variables. There is no manipulation of those variables or control over anything that might affect them. True experiments attempt to isolate and directly manipulate one variable while keeping complete control over all other extraneous variables, keeping them the same between groups. Any that can't be directly controlled are assumed to be the same due to *random assignment* (or they are kept the same using research methods described in Module 7). An extraneous variable that ends up being different between groups is called a *confounding variable.* In general, it is a mistake or an oversight; it confuses the interpretation of the results and often leads to a dismissal of the causal conclusions. If we think of "control" on a continuum from none at all to the maximum amount, correlational research and experimental research are at opposite extremes. Quasi-experiments include a wide variety of studies that can be placed along the continuum, usually closer to the correlational end, and never sharing the same space with real evidence for a cause-and-effect relationship (Fig. 6.1).

While quasi-experimenters often claim to be testing causal hypotheses, and authors will sometimes (boldly) conclude that a cause-and-effect relationship exists, the only type of study that can provide evidence for a causal relationship is a true experiment.

But can't a well-designed quasi-experiment provide at least *some* evidence for a causal relationship? To see why the answer is no, let's examine in more detail how control differs in true experiments versus quasi-experiments. As described above, true experiments try to control everything that can affect the dependent variable, which means there is always a *control group* or control condition for comparison to the experimental condition. Some quasi-experiments don't have a control condition (see Box 6.1). Even those that include a comparison condition still lack at least some control over who ends up in the experimental or control group. In a true experiment, researchers have complete control, which allows them to use

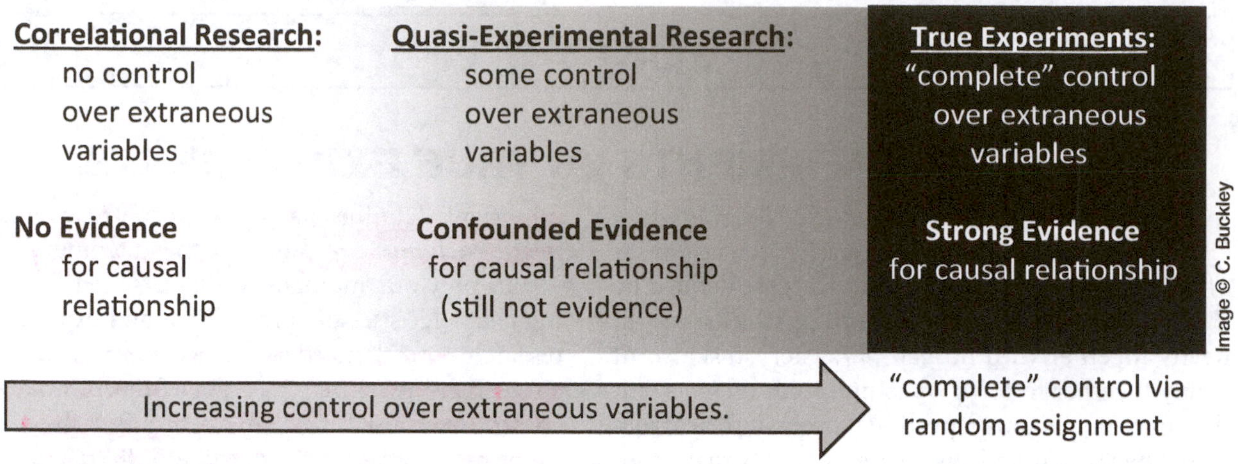

Figure 6.1   A continuum of control, showing types of hypothesis-testing research, from correlational studies, which have no control over any variables, to the opposite extreme, experimental studies that control **extraneous variables** using **random assignment** (or other research methods described in Module 7). Quasi-experiments are in a gray area between these extremes, indicating no clear evidence for causal relationships. Different types of quasi-experiments have varying amounts of control, but they all have confounding variables, which means they cannot support causal relationships. Only true experiments offer clear evidence (*not proof!*) for causal relationships.

a random process to place people in different groups. Quasi-experiments with comparison conditions must let the characteristics of the participants, or the participants themselves, determine their group assignments.

For example, to test whether a new medicine reduces headache pain, a true experiment would randomly assign people with headaches to take either the new medicine (experimental group) or a sugar pill (control group). We would then compare the number of headaches that go away in both groups. Due to random assignment of participants to the different groups, extraneous variables like the type or intensity of the headache before the medicine are assumed to be about equal in the two groups.

Extraneous variables associated with the experimental treatment, like the knowledge that one is taking a pill that should get rid of the headache, are also kept the same in both groups by the use of a placebo (inert pill that the participant believes is real medicine). Random assignment does not *guarantee* that all other extraneous variables are equally represented in different groups, but it does make differences between groups unlikely, especially for larger groups. Ideally, the consequence of such careful control is that any observed difference in the dependent variable (headache relief) between groups can be inferred to be caused by differences in the independent variable (the medicine).

BOX 6.1 Types of Single-Group Quasi-Experiments

This box presents a somewhat arbitrary selection and organization of the various types of quasi-experimental studies you might encounter as you read about research in psychology. In truth, there may be as many different iterations of quasi-experimental research as there are points along the control continuum in Fig. 6.1. Categorizing them into basic types helps organize their underlying structures, but it should also be noted that there are additional types of quasi-experimental research that do not fit neatly into any one of these categories, and that these three ways of collecting data (in bold, italicized text below) can also be applied to research with two groups (see first paragraph of Essay 6.3). Also note that these techniques and others can be combined in a wide variety of ways.

(continued on next page)

BOX 6.1, continued

1. The Single-Group, *Posttest Only* study either directly manipulates some event or takes advantage of a naturally occurring event and simply measures the dependent variable (DV) after participants are exposed to the event. This approach is often used in industry and education, as when a program for improving some aspect of production or learning is tested. For various reasons, a comparison of the DV from before to after the new program, or comparison with other businesses or schools that do not have this program is not possible, usually because data are not available. The complete lack of control over other variables that could impact the DV and lack of information about whether the DV has changed at all from before the event mean that the results of this type of quasi-experiment do not strongly support any relationship between the event and the DV. Testimonial commercials are often a good example of this.

2. We can achieve a little more control with another type of single-group quasi-experimental study called a *Pretest–Posttest* study. In this case, the DV is measured first (pretest), then some manipulation (the IV) is introduced or occurs naturally; then the DV is measured again (posttest). Also frequently used in industry and education, this is essentially the same as the posttest only design, except that measurements of the DV can be compared from before to after the treatment. Would an increase in productivity or learning from pretest to posttest provide evidence for a cause-and-effect relationship? Sadly, no. First, the IV is only presented at one level, so there is no comparison group. Only the DV is compared from before to after the IV occurred. It is possible, even likely, that when people are tested for the same thing twice, they will score higher the second time, regardless of whether or not the IV occurred between attempts. It is also quite likely that workers, teachers, or students will try harder when they know their performance is expected to improve. Therefore, although we might claim that changes in the DV were associated with the presentation of the IV, we cannot conclude that the new program *caused* any observed increase in productivity or learning.

3. Another quasi-experimental technique is the Single-Group *Time Series* study, which is very much like a pretest–posttest study, but with multiple pretests and multiple posttests. This is frequently used in marketing research. Measurements of the DV are often recorded for several weeks before the IV is introduced. This allows the researcher to establish normal, baseline behavior and avoids the problem of people just trying harder from one pretest to one post-test. After the IV is introduced or naturally occurs (e.g., a new marketing strategy starts or a competitor opens for business), continuous measurement of the DV (sales per week) allows the researcher to observe the long-term effects of the IV. There is improved control over extraneous variables, as their natural fluctuations can sometimes be identified during the course of repeated observations, and accounted for when comparing the DV before and after exposure to the IV. This approach is also often used in public policy research. For example, criminal activity is regularly monitored, and researchers examine changes in the data from before to after the introduction of new laws in order to assess the effects of those laws on crime rates. If crime rates drop after the introduction of a new law, this might be considered evidence for a cause-and-effect hypothesis, but technically, it is not. While the evidence is stronger than other single-group quasi-experimental designs, there are still confounds, particularly if the new law was introduced at the same time that some other event occurred, which may or may not have been noticed or tracked. Media attention to the crime problem at the same time the new law is passed, for example, might make potential victims more cautious, and therefore, can affect opportunities for criminal activity.

A quasi-experiment on our new headache medicine might ask volunteers to just try it and report how well it works. This would be a single-group quasi-experiment. All control over other variables that could affect headache relief is missing because there is no control group. Box 6.1 describes three types of single-group quasi-experiments (try to identify which type of study this one would be—Answer in Appendix B). While two of these approaches try to monitor other variables that can affect the results of the study, the lack of a comparison group means that the data are correlational at best, so there is still no evidence of a causal relationship.

To gain some control over extraneous variables, all three types of single-group quasi-experiments described in Box 6.1 *can* be done as two-group experiments.[2] However, in a two-group quasi-experiment, researchers usually select participants for each group based on specific characteristics. Remember that the ideal procedure for a true experiment is to consider one large population (which could be thousands of people), randomly select a large sample (perhaps 100 people) from that population, then randomly assign participants from the large sample to two smaller groups (50 people each). The random assignment to smaller groups for experimental treatment and comparison is how we control individual differences and other extraneous variables.

In a quasi-experiment, researchers might randomly *select* participants, but they do so from two *different* populations. Participants are not randomly *assigned* to experimental and control groups; they come from experimental and control populations. Another common practice in quasi-experimental research, for ethical reasons, is to give people a choice regarding which group they would prefer. For example, our headache medicine might be tested by asking

people who have a headache to decide whether they'd like to take the new medicine or aspirin, then comparing headache relief in those two groups. This poses a *self-selection* problem: participants are selected for groups based on their own decisions, not randomly assigned.

Selecting from different populations and allowing people to select their own groups produces groups that must be recognized as different to begin with, beyond their exposure to different levels of the independent variable. For this reason, quasi-experimental studies with two or more groups are often called *non-equivalent groups* research. Our self-selected groups could be different in many other ways, besides the kind of medicine they choose. They might have different expectations about headache relief, which would be a big confounding variable. They might have differences in personality or physiology. Their motivation to get pain relief, probably linked to headache intensity, might also be different. Obviously, the lack of control over these extraneous variables would cost us the ability to draw trustworthy cause-and-effect conclusions, even if those in the new medicine group report better headache relief than the aspirin group.

A practical point is worth considering here: Every time a commercial for a product claims "these people used this product, and just look at the results!" your science attitude should remind you that no evidence for a cause-and-effect relationship has been offered, even when the sad people who chose a different product are shown for comparison. Without control over extraneous variables, there are likely to be many important differences between the people who used the product and those who did not.

Are quasi-experiments "fake" or "useless?" No, not at all. They are ways of collecting data to address a question, so even single-group studies are still much better than guessing. As long as we interpret them carefully, with an awareness of their limitations, they can be useful and informative.

---

[2] Assuming participants and resources are available, and ethical principles are upheld. See Essay 6.3.

ESSAY 6.2

WHY CHOOSE QUASI-EXPERIMENTS? ETHICS AND PRACTICALITY

The lack of control in quasi-experimental research and the inability to draw cause-and-effect conclusions raises an interesting question: Why would a serious scientist ever want to do quasi-experimental research? When you have a causal hypothesis, why not do a true experiment?

Ethics are, of course, an important concern for all researchers in psychology. Whether our studies are exploratory, descriptive, correlational, experimental, or quasi-experimental, ethics will play a role in how we address our research questions.

The American Psychological Association has adopted five guiding principles for ethical conduct in research with human subjects: (1) Beneficence and Nonmaleficence, (2) Fidelity and Responsibility, (3) Integrity, (4) Justice, and (5) Respect for People's Rights and Dignity. These principles are introduced and defined below. For more information, visit apa.org/ethics/code and click on the link for "General Principles."

The principle of *Beneficence and Nonmaleficence* means that our research must produce some benefits, either by gathering information that can directly help people or other animals, or by meaningfully contributing to our understanding of the natural world. If there are risks associated with our research, the benefits must outweigh those risks, and no research should be done with the intent to harm. *Fidelity and Responsibility* means that we should be trustworthy and professionally responsible for our actions. *Integrity* requires that we provide accurate, informative accounts of our research in the service of truth, and that we are honest with our participants at all times. Where deceit is needed to test a hypothesis, any misinformation must be immediately corrected after observations are completed. *Justice* requires that we do not place unfair burdens of research participation on people who will not benefit from the information gathered, and that any benefits gained by the research are shared equitably. For instance, effective medications or treatments developed through human

subjects research must be accessible to those who participated in the research. *Respect for People's Rights and Dignity* means that we respect and value the dignity and independence of our research participants above our research goals. Among other related concerns, in cases where gathering data has any impact at all on our participants, we must make sure that they are given sufficient information to make responsible decisions regarding their participation. They must be informed and assured of their right to leave the study at any time without fear of negative consequences. Children in research must have the informed consent of a parent or guardian, and must be given the same assurances.

These principles present challenges for testing certain hypotheses. For example, given the principle of Respect for People's Rights and Dignity, we could not test the effects of public humiliation on self-esteem with a true experiment. It would be unethical (and unkind!) to publicly humiliate people on purpose. Instead, we could use a quasi-experiment and measure self-esteem in people who have already experienced severe public humiliation compared to people who have not. We would do our best to make sure the comparison group shares relevant characteristics with the first group (e.g., age, number of positive social experiences). But no matter how many relevant characteristics we control, this is not a true experiment because people are placed into groups based on their prior experiences, not randomly assigned. Embarrassment is a quasi-experimental IV; we are not directly manipulating or controlling it. Instead, we are simply measuring the what we think might be effects of a naturally occurring variable, just as we would in a correlational study. The only thing that separates this from correlational research is the purposeful selection of people for our comparison group who are matched by age and positive experiences to the experimental group. So we have some control over these extraneous variables, but not enough. Some would argue that this is just a correlational study. Because we did not randomly assign people to these two groups, we are doing *nonequivalent groups* research. We cannot suppose that the two groups are equal in any way other than the variables we purposefully matched. There are probably numerous hidden variables causing differences between our groups—we have no way of knowing. Our groups may differ in socioeconomic status, the types of friends they have, or cultural awareness, at the very least. All of these would be *confounding variables.*

While we would get more and better information from a true experiment, it would come at an unacceptable cost. Other independent variables that would be unethical to test with true experiments include smoking, certain drugs, poor air quality, unlocked firearms, child abuse… the list is not a happy one. Quasi-experiments allow us to learn from our mistakes without purposefully making more.

Practicality also plays a big role in the decision to use a quasi-experiment. It may be impossible, extremely difficult, or prohibitively expensive to experimentally test certain ideas. If we wish to test the hypothesis that optimism increases empathy, or that being elderly increases irritability (the "Hey-you-kids-get-off-my-lawn hypothesis"), or that registering with a political party increases voter participation, there is no way to randomly assign people to be optimists or pessimists, old or young, political-party affiliated or not. However, we can measure and compare empathy in samples of people who score high in optimism versus those who score low, or irritability in the elderly versus young adults, or voter participation in registered party members versus independents. In all these examples, the two groups being compared are nonequivalent groups. Any pre-existing differences between nonequivalent groups are confounding variables that undermine our ability to draw cause-and-effect conclusions, but the information gathered is still much more useful than having no information at all.

It's also important to remember that while a quasi-experimental study does not *support* a cause-and-effect hypothesis, it *can* help to rule one out. A cause-and-effect relationship between two variables cannot exist without a correlation between them. So if there is no support from a quasi-experimental study, there is no correlation, which means a causal relationship can also be ruled out.

In conclusion, when true experiments are not possible, quasi-experimental research is often our next-best alternative. While the lack of control does present some problems for interpretation, the ability to explore ideas that could not be tested with true experiments is extremely valuable.

ESSAY 6.3

THINKING CRITICALLY ABOUT QUASI-EXPERIMENTAL RESEARCH

The single-group data collection techniques described in Box 6.1 all lack the control over extraneous variables that comes with a comparison group. As noted, those same techniques can also be expanded to include comparison groups, adding some level of control. But if participants are not randomly assigned to the comparison and experimental groups, then we have a *nonequivalent groups* quasi-experiment, so we still lack control over extraneous variables which means we still can't draw cause-and-effect conclusions. However, as indicated at the end of Essay 6.2, there are still benefits to doing quasi-experimental research.

The key to getting the most out of quasi-experimental research lies in understanding the limitations and interpreting the results with caution and a persistent science attitude. Be aware of confounding variables and any other research regarding their effects on the dependent variable. Also be aware that authors sometimes use the word "experiment" when the research they are reporting is actually quasi-experimental. To easily identify quasi-experimental studies, look for one of the following characteristics:

(1) There is only a single group and no comparison group or condition, and every participant is exposed to the IV in the same way.[3] A study with no comparison group opens up the possibility that any observed "effects" might have happened without the experimental treatment. Other examples of single-group designs are listed in Box 6.1.

(2) The different levels of the independent variable are not purposefully manipulated. Instead, the levels of the IV occur naturally. It is always possible that some other event that the researcher might not know about coincides with the change in the IV, causing changes in the DV.

(3) In two-group studies, there is no control over assignment of participants to different levels of the IV (no random assignment). This results in nonequivalent groups, that is, groups that differ in ways other than the independent variable. Again, we have no way of knowing the impact of pre-existing differences between groups on the measurement of the DV.

Do these issues make it impossible to ever draw cause-and-effect conclusions in support of hypotheses that can't be tested with a true experiment? Not necessarily. While ethics and practicality may keep us from being able to do true experiments with human subjects for some hypotheses, it is still possible to compile evidence from multiple quasi-experimental, descriptive and correlational studies, as well as true experiments with other species and/or related variables, and arrive at a strong cause-and-effect conclusion.

One example would be the hypothesis that smoking causes cancer in humans. Obviously, for ethical reasons, we cannot manipulate the number of cigarettes smoked, or randomly assign humans to smoking and nonsmoking groups. Instead, the Surgeon General's warning that smoking causes cancer is based on thousands of studies, some of them true experiments showing that exposure to cigarette smoke causes cancer in laboratory animals, many molecular studies of the biological activity of carcinogens contained in cigarette smoke, plus correlational and quasi-experimental studies in humans that statistically control for other known factors that could affect cancer rates, plus other research. The fact that all these various lines of evidence have repeatedly come to the same conclusion is very strong evidence for a cause-and-effect relationship between smoking and cancer in humans, even though no true experiments could be done to test that hypothesis.

In conclusion, quasi-experimental research attempts to study cause-and-effect relationships

Credit:Douglas Kirkland / Getty Images 644194384

"The true delight is in the finding out rather than in the knowing."

—IsaacAs imov
(Biochemist and prolific author)

---

[3] Module 7 will describe "within-participants" research, where there is only one group of participants, but they undergo multiple levels of the independent variable. This is different from the single-group quasi-experiment because (1) multiple levels of the IV are tested, and (2) the order of exposure to the different levels will be counterbalanced to control for order effects. For more information, see Module 7.

but lacks proper experimental control. There are many different types of studies that would fall into this category, and one should keep in mind that any quasi-experimental study can be modified in ways that increase control or relinquish it. In other words, quasi-experimental research falls to the right or left on our control continuum (Fig. 6.1) based on how much consideration is given to controlling or statistically correcting for extraneous variables. As we increase control, we get closer to a true test of a causal hypothesis, but we don't reach without true experimentation. The ways in which control can be increased will be discussed in more advanced research design courses.

MODULE 6 RESEARCH LEARNING OBJECTIVES CHART

STUDY NUMBER	MODULE 6 RESEARCH LEARNING OBJECTIVES	BEFORE READING				AFTER DOING PROJECT			
		I don't know how 1	I know a little about this 2	I know enough about this to guess correctly 3	I know how to do this and/ or have already done it. 4	I don't know how 1	I know a little about this 2	I know enough about this to guess correctly 3	I know how to do this and/ or have already done it. 4
6A	Use sleep deprivation research as an example to explain two reasons why some questions must be addressed with quasi-experimental research rather than true experiments.								
6A	Explain how a median split can be used to set up groups in a quasi-experiment.								
6A	Explain how self-selection factors can influence the conclusions of a quasi-experiment.								
6A 6B 6C	Gain experience with quasi-experimental research design and discuss one specific type of design and how to interpret the results.								
6A 6B 6C	Identify confounding variables in quasi-experimental research.								
6B 6C	Gain experience with assessment tests for psychological constructs like humor style, self-esteem, and social support network strength.								

		I don't know how 1	I know a little about this 2	I know enough about this to guess correctly 3	I know how to do this and/ or have already done it. 4		I don't know how 1	I know a little about this 2	I know enough about this to guess correctly 3	I know how to do this and/ or have already done it. 4
6B 6C Box 6.2	Appreciate and explain the importance of keeping assessment results confidential, and know how to help someone who is bothered by his or her assessment results.									
6C	Define a social support network and discuss its relationship to mental health.									

Now read about the project to prepare for lab. For any scores less than "4," keep those questions in mind as you complete the research project(s). Do not do the white half of this chart until after you've completed the assigned research project(s).

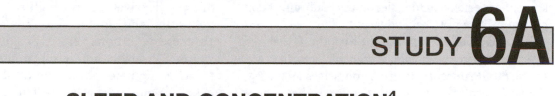

SLEEP AND CONCENTRATION[4]

"Work eight hours and sleep eight hours, and make sure they're not the same eight hours."
—T. Boone Pickens,
American Capitalist

We've all been told that 7 or 8 hours of sleep every night is generally required for a healthy mind and body. But the demands of modern life, the stress of college exams and assignments, and the glare of an irresistible phone screen seem to conspire to rob us of a good night's sleep, night after night. Your lecture textbook probably devotes considerable space to the negative effects of sleep deprivation on cognition, behavior, and health, so we don't need to review them here. If you'd like more information than your textbook provides on the effects of sleep deprivation, try searching "WebMD, 10 things to hate about sleep loss." Some of them may surprise you.

One of the most common claims about the cognitive effects of sleep loss is an inability to concentrate or stay focused on a task. If true, that's a big problem for the average college student: Of the many things you need to be able to do, concentration and focus are probably near the top of the list. And yet, out of all studied populations, high school and college students are at the highest risk for severe sleep deprivation (Lund et al., 2010).

When it comes to negative consequences of sleep deprivation, the majority of college students readily admit that they are functioning "below their peak" (Kiefer, 2003, 2005; Carskadon, 2002). However, the evidence from these studies is descriptive in nature, based on Gallup survey results. It merely describes the desire to "get more sleep on weekdays," and reports on students' perceptions of their own low level of functioning when they are tired. It is possible that these perceptions are influenced by popular culture and the often-repeated mantra that sleep deprivation "makes you stupid" (Carskadon, 2002).

It might be an uncomfortable thing to admit, and it might not even be true for some people, but there is a natural human tendency to complain about one's difficulties, and sharing stories about "how little sleep" one got the night before can be a good way of either garnering attention or just commiserating with others, since lack of sleep is such a common college

---

[4] This study derives from an Introductory Psychology research project idea proposed by Ralph Barnes (Montana State University).

student experience. Does sleepiness really affect concentration to a noticeable degree?

In this study, we will test the hypothesis that *sleep deprivation decreases college students' ability to stay focused and concentrate*, using ourselves as the participants. Ethically, we cannot assign some students to get 8 hours of sleep while others are only allowed 2 hours. Even if it were ethical to ask you to lose sleep for science, it would be practically impossible to control without a sleep laboratory.

Due to these ethical and practical concerns, this hypothesis is a good candidate for a quasi-experiment. The design of this study is a two-group comparison with participants assigned **to nonequivalent groups** based on a common quasi-experimental procedure called a **median split**. That is, we will measure sleepiness on a continuous scale, calculate the median score for the whole class (our research sample), then divide participants into those who scored above the median and those who scored below. These two groups will be our experimental, high-sleepiness group and our control, low-sleepiness group.

Notice the conceptual variables from our hypothesis: *sleep deprivation*, and *ability to focused and concentrate*, and how these concepts differ slightly from our operational definitions. The levels of sleep deprivation are "high score on the sleepiness scale" and "low score on the sleepiness scale." Do these definitions perfectly capture "sleep deprivation?" Probably not, but it would be unethical to try to manipulate the amount of sleep that students get. Also notice that these two groups are nonequivalent to start, and their differences might be made worse by **self-selection** factors—participants are selecting their own type of participation, either by being sleep-deprived or by the way we are doing our median split (see step 5 of the procedure). The choices participants make often come with associated behaviors or personality traits. For instance, the high sleepiness group might include students who are perhaps lacking in nutrition (no time to eat breakfast?), experiencing more stress, or feeling more hopeless, all of which could affect their concentration, regardless of how much sleep they got.

We will operationally define the ability to stay focused and concentrate with the average score on various 2-minute reaction time tasks, two of which require some decision-making. Is a 2-minute task long enough to lose focus? You'll have a better sense of this after you've played the games, but this is worth considering as you interpret your results with a science attitude.

6A PROCEDURE

The procedure described below can easily be adapted to test other hypotheses regarding the effects of sleep deprivation, for example on memory, problem-solving, reading comprehension, or any other cognitive or behavioral task. This study uses online resources to test extended concentration and focus. The Epworth Sleepiness Scale may be presented on paper or online.

1. Answer a few survey questions about how tired you feel (the Epworth Sleepiness Scale, or ESS). Total your responses and write your score on the data sheet AND on a small scrap of paper. Fold up the small scrap of paper with your score, and drop it in the bag that will be provided to assure anonymity. It is important that you answer the questions on the ESS based on your current understanding of how sleepy you have felt *over the past two days*. Don't forget to record your score on your data sheet!

Based on time and technology availability, any or all of the next three steps may be used. They are all online measurements of concentration. Completing all three should take less than 10 minutes, including instructions, and will result in the most reliable measurement (an average score).

2. Visit the website sleepdisordersflorida.com/pvt1.html to take the Psychomotor Vigilance Test. It is a 2-minute vigilance and reaction time test and must be done on a computer (laptop or desktop). Phones

create too much lag and drag down scores. When you find the page, look for a white square. Keep your eyes focused on the center of the white square and your hand on a computer mouse with the cursor inside the square, but not blocking your view of the center. After you click "Start Test," a counter with red numbers will appear at random intervals in the center of the square. Your goal is to click or tap inside the square as quickly as possible to make the counter disappear. Please do your best to stay focused on the white square, minimize blinking, and react as quickly as possible for the full 2 minutes. Record your reaction time (in ms) on the data sheet, and do the calculations on the data sheet to bring this score into the same scale as the other two measures. Start whenever you are ready, as this test is self-timed.

3. Go to improvememory.org/reflex-reaction-games and scroll down to "Two Dots." Click on "View" and then select "Play in Fullscreen." Click the sound icon to turn off background sound and music, BUT DO NOT START. Since there is no timer, your instructor will set a timer for two minutes. *Everyone must start and stop at the same time.* Your goal is to get the highest score you can within this 2-minute period, so each time you fail, immediately try again. The game will keep track of your high score. Make sure you understand the instructions before you start. Watch an instructor demo, if possible. When you click "start," the game will display a 3-second countdown. Beneath the countdown, there will be two vertical dots, one brown, one white. Note the color of the top dot. When the countdown hits zero, new brown or white dots will begin falling from the top of the screen rather quickly. If the color of the falling dot matches the top dot, let it fall to earn a point. If it does not match the top dot, click or tap your screen to flip the positions of the vertical dots. If the falling dot hits a non-matching top dot, it's "game over." Immediately begin again and try to get the highest score you can within the two minutes. This can be frustrating, and students sometimes feel tempted to describe how they feel about the game, but remember that taking time to do that will decrease your high score. If you are mid-game when the 2-minute timer ends, just stop clicking and record your high score. Do not include dots that happen to fall correctly after the timer ends.

4. Return to improvememory.org/reflex-reaction-games. This time scroll to "Two Sides." Click "View" and "Play in Fullscreen" BUT DO NOT START. Since there is no timer, your instructor will set a timer for two minutes. *Everyone must start and stop at the same time.* Your goal is to get the highest score you can within this 2-minute period, so each time you fail, immediately try again. The game will keep track of your high score. When you click start, your screen will be divided into a blue side and a yellow side. A small blue or yellow box will appear on the vertical line separating the two sides. The box requires one of three responses: (1) If it's a plain blue or yellow box with nothing in it, click on the side that is the same color as the box. (2) If the box contains arrows pointing in the *same* direction, ignore the color and instead click on the side that the arrows are pointing to. (3) If the box contains arrows pointing *at each other*, click on the side that is *opposite* the color of the box. Repeat those rules aloud from memory to make sure you know what the rules are before we start. You will have about 2 seconds to react for each box. If you don't respond on time or you respond incorrectly, it's "game over." Immediately begin again and try to get the highest score you can within the two minutes. This can be frustrating, and students sometimes feel tempted to describe how they feel about the game, but remember that taking time to do that will decrease your high score. If you are mid-game when the 2-minute timer ends, just stop clicking and record your high score.

5. While you are completing the concentration tasks, anonymous ESS scores you put in the bag (from Step 1) will be ranked from high to low and the results of a **median split** will be announced in lab. Check the score you recorded from your ESS on your data sheet (also from Step 1). If you scored below the median, circle "Low Sleepiness," and if you scored above it, circle "High Sleepiness." Normally, people who score exactly at the median in a median split are dropped from the analysis, but in this case, we will defer to your subjective opinion: *if you scored <u>exactly</u> at the median,* put yourself in the group you feel best describes your sleepiness level.

6. Because higher scores reflect *poorer* performance on the PVT, which is the opposite of the other tasks, we will modify these scores to be more intuitive and to better match the scales on the other concentration

tasks. Subtracting your score on the PVT from 1,000 will reverse it so that a higher result means you performed better. If your score was above 1,000, first wake up, then give yourself a zero (no negative scores). Or do the test again if you used your phone, because it should be done on a computer for an accurate score (see step 2). If you did either step 3 or 4, then divide your reversed PVT score by 10 to bring it to scale with the other test(s) of concentration. Calculate your average on all the concentration tasks you completed, then fold over your data sheet so that your scores do not show and hand it in anonymously.

7. A *t*-test will be used to compare average concentration scores for high sleepiness vs low sleepiness groups. Complete the Lab Record Worksheet for Studies 6A/B/C, located at the end of Study 6C.

- -

STUDY 6A DATA SHEET

Participant # _____

ESS SCORE: _____ Circle your group: High Sleepiness   Low Sleepiness

PVT Score _____ 1000 minus PVT Score = _____ ÷ 10 = [   ]

Two Dots High Score → [   ]

Two Sides High Score → [   ]   Average of boxed scores: _____

STUDY 6B

HUMOR STYLES AND SELF ESTEEM

What do you call a group of rabbits hopping backwards? A receding hare line.

To whoever stole my Prozac: I hope you're happy now.

(They also stole my mood ring. I don't know how I feel about that.)

Although some jokes seem (to me) like they should be universally funny, the truth is that different people have different ideas about what is funny and what is not. Martin et al., (2003) designed and validated a scale for measuring different styles of humor, and in less than 20 years, their work has been applied in several hundred other research papers. Their 32-item questionnaire has been translated into multiple languages, a work-related short version, and versions for children. To read research using this questionnaire, search "humor styles questionnaire" on google scholar. Apparently, humor is a subject of great interest to psychologists.

The purpose of this study is to examine the relationship between styles of humor and self-esteem. More on that later, but first, please read the very important warnings and notices in Box 6.2.

Box 6.2 Read Before Doing Studies 6B or 6C!!

WARNINGS!!

For this research you will complete surveys that produce PERSONAL scores. You may, at any point during this research, decide NOT to contribute, and your decision will not affect your grade in this class. If you do participate, it is morally imperative that you keep your scores and all results CONFIDENTIAL and that you hand in your scores for analysis ANONYMOUSLY (fold over papers so that no one can see your scores as they are handed in). What if you are among the few who score high and want to tell all your friends what a great sense of humor you have, and how your self-esteem and/or social support are through the roof? Even then, speaking with your classmates about these scores is absolutely morally and ethically WRONG.

WHY IS SHARING MY RESULTS SO WRONG? Imagine your feelings if you had not scored so high on self-esteem or social support, or perhaps you discovered something about your sense of humor that you didn't realize and don't like. By the law of averages, this will be true for you or some of your classmates. Please don't even try to figure out who: You might be surprised by the people who would be most affected. Hearing other people brag about their scores puts social pressure on a person to share their own, and may exacerbate very real social anxiety, painful loneliness, or a lack of self-esteem. DO NOT DISCUSS OR SHARE YOUR RESULTS WITH ANYONE IN THIS CLASS.

If you are concerned about your own or someone else's feelings regarding these scores, please read the information below on counseling services and seek help or encourage others, as needed.

(continued on next page)

BOX 6.2, continued

Counseling Services

If you don't understand why this is so important, please read Essay 6.2 again. As a researcher in psychology, you have a moral obligation to uphold the principles of beneficence and nonmaleficence, and to treat others, including the data representing their feelings and points of view, with respect and dignity.

If you are suffering or struggling with the issues explored in this research, please contact your campus counseling services. The easiest way to do this is to simply search "counseling services" on your school's webpage, or speak to your professor, instructor, or a friend about your concerns and how to get free or low-cost professional help. You might also consider calling or texting the national helplines in the white box. No one should have to go through life thinking bad thoughts about themselves or being unhappy with the way they see themselves, and counseling can definitely help.[5]

Free helplines offered by The Crisis Text Line and
The National Alliance on Mental Health (nami.org/help)
(accurate as of May 2020)

Crisis Text Line – Text HOME to 741741
Connect with a trained crisis counselor to receive free, 24/7 crisis support via text message.

National Suicide Prevention Lifeline – Call 800-273-TALK (8255)
If you or someone you know is in crisis—whether they are considering suicide or not—please call the toll-free Lifeline at 800-273-TALK (8255) to speak with a trained crisis counselor 24/7.

At this point, you would normally start reading about the rationale for our hypothesis, how we plan to test it, and our predictions. But because reading about these things might impact your responses on the HSQ, we're going to ask you to complete the HSQ first. So, **before you read any further**, you should take the HSQ online at https://www.psytoolkit.org/survey-library/ humor-hsq.html. PsyToolKit is a nonprofit website devoted to making data collection easier for students and other researchers (Stoet, 2010, 2017). Please note the "data protection information" as stated on the website. While PsyToolKit does not sell or use data for commercial purposes, it is a data collection site for research in psychology. However, the survey you'll be taking is a demo for their website, so your data will not be saved.

---

[5]On a personal note, I am speaking from experience. As an undergraduate, struggling with self-esteem and self-sabotage, I sought counseling on my own college campus, and it strongly influenced my attitude, decision-making, and happiness from that point forward. It was one of the reasons I decided to major in psychology.

HAVE YOU COMPLETED THE HSQ ONLINE AND RECORDED YOUR SCORES? If not, STOP HERE UNTIL YOU DO.

Reading the information beyond this point could change your natural answers
to the questionnaire, either consciously or subconsciously.

Again (one more time!) do not read the information below until you have finished taking the HSQ online and recorded your scores someplace confidential. A screen capture or a picture with your phone would work well, as long as you can keep the image private and access it in lab.

The HSQ identifies and measures four humor styles (Martin et al., 2003). Two of them are positive ways of using humor, and two of them are common, but not positive. Please realize that your scores are NOT a reflection of your value as a person, nor should they be considered evidence that there is anything "wrong with you." A negative style of humor is not equivalent to a negative person. If your results bother you or make you unhappy, please consider speaking with a counselor (see "counseling services" in the white box within Box 6.2).

An *affiliative* style uses humor to strengthen relationships. Nonaggressive and accepting of differences, a person with an affiliative style shares spontaneous jokes and witty comments to please others and reduce tension in social situations. Occasionally, mildly self-deprecating jokes may be used to smooth social relationships and demonstrate a casual acceptance of one's own flaws.

A *self-enhancing* humor style shows an appreciation for the funny things in life and an ability to see the funny side of stressful or difficult situations. People with a self-enhancing humor style use humor as a positive coping mechanism.

While affiliative humor is focused on interpersonal relationships, and self-enhancing humor is more focused on an individual's view of the world, both styles are positive ways of using humor. Two other styles of humor are common, but less positive: Those with an *aggressive* humor style tend to ridicule others, often without knowledge of, nor concern for, negative effects on the well-being of others. Racist and sexist humor are good examples, as are blonde jokes. People with an aggressive humor style sometimes tell jokes in situations where they are not appropriate. While the superficial intent may be to elicit laughter, the underlying intent may be to boost one's own social standing, often by lowering others relative to oneself. People with a *self-defeating* style of humor frequently put themselves down to amuse others, or allow others to repeatedly ridicule them in order to fit in or gain acceptance. This may be influenced by the social groups one chooses to spend time with.

In this study, we will test the hypothesis that a positive humor style affects self-esteem; specifically, that using humor in a socially and individually positive way leads to higher self-esteem than using humor in a negative way.

We are testing this because a recent review and statistical synthesis of existing research on humor styles and mental health (Schneider et al., 2018) found that while affiliative and self-enhancing humor styles were each associated with better mental health (higher optimism and life satisfaction scores), aggressive and self-defeating styles were each negatively correlated with self-esteem measures. In their research, Schneider et al. separated the four humor styles to examine their relationships to mental health measurements, and their findings suggest that a simpler relationship may exist. The purpose of our research is to clarify that simple relationship, as described in our hypothesis.

PROCEDURE

1. If you have not taken the HSQ, do so now. As a further protection of your personal data, do not record any scores <u>on the data sheet</u>. Instead, privately total your affiliative and self-enhancing scores (Total "A"). Then total your aggressive and self-defeating scores (Total "B"). Write the letter (A or B) that has the HIGHER total on your data sheet. If A and B were the same, write "same" instead of "A" or "B."

2. Be sure to indicate on your data sheet whether you read about the meaning of the HSQ before or after completing it (or did not read it at all). Answering honestly will not affect your grade, and is important to preserve the accuracy of the data. Remember, your answers are anonymous.

3. The RSE is only 10 questions and should not take long to complete. It can be found at https://openpsychometrics.org/tests/RSE.php. When you get your score, record it confidentially, tear out this whole page, including the data sheet, fold it to hide your data, and hand it in. Use blue or black ink or pencil, and do not put your name or any identifying information on this page.

4. Data will be collected and entered into an MS Excel file. If your class has fewer than 20 students, it is possible that data will be combined across multiple classes to protect anonymity. Follow your instructor's guidelines on completing the Lab Record Worksheet, located after Study 6C.

After you have answered the questions on the data sheet below, tear out
this whole page, fold it over to hide your answers, and hand it in.

- -

STUDY 6B DATA SHEET

When did you read the information regarding the meaning of the HSQ data and styles of humor? (circle the honest answer)

Before doing the HSQ   After doing the HSQ   I have not read it

A. Total your HSQ Scores for Affiliative and Self-Enhancing Humor, but do not write the total on this data sheet. This is TOTAL "A."

B. Total your HSQ Scores for Aggressive and Self-Defeating Humor, but do not write the total on this data sheet. This is TOTAL "B."

Write the letter of the total that was higher on this line (A or B or SAME): _____

RSE Score: _____ **NOTE: These surveys are meant to be informative, not diagnostic.**

STUDY 6C

SELF-HELP AND SOCIAL SUPPORT NETWORKS

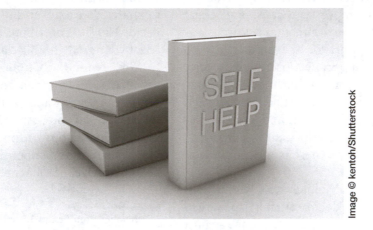

Image © kentoh/Shutterstock

"I went to a bookstore and asked the saleswoman, "Where's the self-help section?"

She said if she told me, it would defeat the purpose.

—George Carlin

Placing a monetary value on the self-help industry in the United States would be difficult, and by most accounts, would probably result in an underestimate. As of July 2017, typing "self-help" into the search bar of one leading online bookstore produced 700,011 hits.[6] These books promise to improve readers' self-esteem, organizational skills, love-life, friendships, financial status, brain power, and a whole host of other things people might not have even thought needed improving. Add the overwhelming number of websites with self-help content, and it becomes clear that there is no shortage of opinions on what is wrong with us and how to fix it.

What is unclear is the extent to which any of this information actually helps people. A handful of studies have shown some empirical support for the effectiveness of specific self-help books and information (e.g., Bjorvatn et al., 2011; Cunningham et al., 2005),

but given the number of self-help books in existence and their growing impact on the US economy, one would expect more attention to this question.

In this research, we will investigate a possible role for self-help advice in improving social support networks. A ***social support network*** consists of the people you turn to for help when you are dealing with something difficult or stressful. Friends, family, special acquaintances, groups, and communities to which we belong can all be part of a social support network. Whether you're in need of a loan, advice, or just someone to talk to, the feeling that you know someone who will try to help you is an important source of good mental health.

Compared to people with strong networks of friends and family, people with less social support tend to have more difficulty dealing with stress. There are ways to build social support networks, and plenty of self-help advice is available in both hard copy and electronic resources. In this study, we will first *anonymously* measure the strength of the

---

[6] Apparently, even the computers have given up counting – as of May 2020, the same site simply reports a "greater than" estimate.

social support networks in your class, then expose the class to self-help information on how to build and extend social support networks. You'll have two or 3 weeks to try out any parts of the advice you care to try, after which we will again measure the whole class's social support to see whether there have been any changes.

The idea that exposure to self-help information improves social support is a cause-and-effect hypothesis, so our quasi-experimental research cannot provide strong support for it, even if we do see the strength of social support networks increase after exposure to self-help information. In that case, our main conclusion would be a possible link between exposure to self-help information and an improvement in social support, but the cause of that link would not be clear because there is no comparison group.

On the other hand, if absolutely no relationship is found, or if social support decreases after exposure to self-help information, that could be evidence against the idea that exposure to self-help advice improves social support networks, because a cause-and-effect relationship, if it exists, would naturally produce a correlation.[7] Of course, whether our results agree or disagree with our hypothesis, all possible explanations for whatever we observe should be considered, including, but not limited to the accuracy of the hypothesis.

Another important point is that your data must be gathered anonymously. Data will be based on a short survey of social support strength, which is personal information that you should not feel obligated to share. You may, at any point during this study, decide NOT to contribute, and your decision will not affect your grade in this class.

Scores for the whole class will be grouped to arrive at a class average, so only your instructor will see all the scores, and will not have any identifying information. If you wish to know your own score, you may request a copy of the scoring rubric from your instructor, but remember that this survey is meant to be informative, not diagnostic.

---

[7] Remember from Essays 3.5 and 4.3 that the existence of a correlation does not mean there is necessarily a cause-and-effect relationship, but the existence of a cause-and-effect relationship DOES mean that there must be a correlation, because every time the cause changes, so must the effect.

And then it occurred to him:
the world needed yet another book on leadership.

PROCEDURE **6C**

READ BOX 6.2 BEFORE YOU DO ANY SURVEYS. (IT'S WITH THE DESCRIPTION FOR STUDY 6B)

1. Make sure you have read Box 6.2 before you do this survey.

2. You will be given a social support survey called the Interpersonal Support Evaluation List (ISEL) (Cohen and Hoberman, 1983). It has 40 statements that you should rate based on how well they apply to you, using a 4-point Likert-type scale, where 0 = definitely false, 1 = probably false, 2 = probably true, and 3 = definitely true. Read the statements carefully, as they are not all in agreement that 0 is bad and 4 is good. Sometimes, a 0 will mean that you have good support, and sometimes, it will mean that you have poor support. This makes it difficult for participants to fake having a good (or poor) score, and makes it difficult for anyone to determine your total score just by glancing at your individual answers. It also means you should not try to get the highest or lowest total; just rate the truth of the statements honestly and to the best of your ability. The entire survey will take about 10 minutes to complete.

3. Submit your answers **anonymously**, according to the instructions provided by your lab instructor. Your lab instructor will electronically capture your answers only, with no identifying information, and paste them into a spreadsheet, so that all scores will be combined for the whole class BEFORE any individual scores are calculated. This will assure anonymity of your ISEL score.

4. Once all scores have been recorded, you will be given a handout or webpage to go to for self-help advice on how to build social support networks, and told how and when and for how long you should attempt to follow some of the advice.

5. At the end of the study, you will again complete the ISEL survey, which will again be anonymous and scored in the same way.

6. Your instructor will provide the results of a statistical comparison between pretest and posttest ISEL scores for the class.

STUDY 6C DATA SHEET

YOUR SURVEY ANSWERS: PRETEST

USE ONLY THIS SHEET TO SUBMIT YOUR DATA WITH NO NAME.
UNIFORMITY HELPS MAINTAIN ANONYMITY.

1. _____	11. _____	21. _____	31. _____
2. _____	12. _____	22. _____	32. _____
3. _____	13. _____	23. _____	33. _____
4. _____	14. _____	24. _____	34. _____
5. _____	15. _____	25. _____	35. _____
6. _____	16. _____	26. _____	36. _____
7. _____	17. _____	27. _____	37. _____
8. _____	18. _____	28. _____	38. _____
9. _____	19. _____	29. _____	39. _____
10. _____	20. _____	30. _____	40. _____

- -

After your pretest, tear out this page, cut or carefully tear on the dotted line, and put the bottom half back into your book in the same place. You will need it in 2 or 3 weeks.

YOUR SURVEY ANSWERS: POSTTEST

USE ONLY THIS SHEET TO SUBMIT YOUR DATA WITH NO NAME.
UNIFORMITY HELPS MAINTAIN ANONYMITY.

1. _____	11. _____	21. _____	31. _____
2. _____	12. _____	22. _____	32. _____
3. _____	13. _____	23. _____	33. _____
4. _____	14. _____	24. _____	34. _____
5. _____	15. _____	25. _____	35. _____
6. _____	16. _____	26. _____	36. _____
7. _____	17. _____	27. _____	37. _____
8. _____	18. _____	28. _____	38. _____
9. _____	19. _____	29. _____	39. _____
10. _____	20. _____	30. _____	40. _____

LAB RECORD WORKSHEET FOR STUDY 6A, 6B, OR 6C

Name(s): _____

Purpose _____

_____

Hypothesis _____

_____

What was the conceptual independent variable? _____

How was it operationally defined? _____

What was the conceptual dependent variable? _____

How was it operationally defined? _____

Prediction _____

_____

_____

Method

Other modules provide practice with recording **Participants**, **Materials**, and **Procedure** (the standard components of a Method section). To give you some practice identifying quasi-experimental methods, we'll just practice applying the terminology of the research techniques you used.

What type of study is this? (circle all correct answers)

Single-Group	Quasi-Experimental	Experimental	Correlational
Time Series	Pretest–Posttest	Nonequivalent Groups	Posttest Only

Define the types of research you circled and tell why each term applies to this research.

_____

_____

_____

_____

_____

_____

_____

Results

Results will be provided and discussed in lab. Take notes on the relevant results here:

_____

_____

Discussion

Was the research hypothesis supported?   Yes   No

Evidence? (describe the logic behind your conclusion) _____

_____

Answer only one of the next two questions (Based on results)

If the hypothesis was supported, how strong is the evidence FOR a cause-and-effect relationship?

No Evidence	Very Weak	Weak	Average	Strong	Very Strong	Perfect

If the hypothesis was NOT supported, how strong is the evidence AGAINST a cause-and-effect relationship?

No Evidence	Very Weak	Weak	Average	Strong	Very Strong	Perfect

Answer all remaining questions

Explain why you circled that strength of evidence for or against the hypothesis _____

_____

_____

Name ONE confounding variable in this study and explain what impact it might have had. Remember: Anything that would be the same for both groups is not a confounding variable.

_____

_____

_____

Choose ONE of the other types of research THAT YOU DID NOT CIRCLE on the previous page, and briefly suggest how this study could be done using that type of research.

_____

_____

_____

MODULE 6 GLOSSARY OF TERMS AND EXAMPLES

Control Group: See Module 5 Glossary

Confounding Variables: See Module 5 Glossary

Extraneous Variables: See Module 5 Glossary

Median Split: A technique for creating categorical data out of interval data, so that groups may be formed to test a hypothesis. Participants are measured on some scale, then ranked from highest to lowest scores to determine the median score. Participants are then split into two groups: those who scored above or below the median. To maximize the signal (difference between means for the DV, those who score at the median are often dropped from the data analysis. Note that the groups formed by a median split are **nonequivalent groups.**

>   **Example:** To separate participants for a study into optimists and pessimists, all participants might be given a test to assess their level of optimism. Researchers would then rank the participants from highest to lowest optimism scores, calculate the median score, and assign participants who scored above the median to the "Optimistic Group" and those who scored below the median to the "Pessimistic Group."
>   **Where to find this term:** Study 6A

Nonequivalent Groups: A study design that compares two or more groups that differ in important ways other than the levels of the IV. This is usually because participants were selected for the groups based on pre-existing differences with respect to the IV, in order to measure the "effects" of those differences. Since the participants in these groups differ in multiple ways other than the levels of the IV, one cannot conclude that any observed difference in the DV was caused by differences in the IV.

>   **Example:** A researcher is testing the idea that attending plays at the theatre makes people happier than going to the movies, so she takes surveys of happiness levels from people leaving live performances at a theatre and people leaving the movies. She compares them and finds that people leaving the theatre reported being happier than those leaving the movies. The groups she compared are nonequivalent. The stories they just watched were probably different, and there may be personality differences between theatre-goers and movie-goers, including a general disposition toward more or less happiness, regardless of whether one has just seen a play or a movie.
>   **Where to find this term:** Essay 6.1, 6.2, 6.3, and Studies 6A & 6B.

Posttest Only (single group): A quasi-experimental study where the dependent variable is measured only once, after the independent variable is either introduced or occurs naturally. If predicted scores are observed for the DV, this might be incorrectly presented as evidence that the IV affected the DV. Because there is nothing to which the scores may be compared, the evidence for a cause-and-effect relationship is nonexistent.

>   **Example:** Acne medication commercials where people show off how great their skin looks after using a certain product are attempting to convince viewers of a cause-and-effect relationship with a single-group, posttest only report. Sadly, some viewers do not recognize the complete lack of evidence for a cause-and-effect relationship. The actors may have had great skin *before* using that product, or other factors may be responsible for the lack of acne (More frequent face-washing? Professional makeup artists? CGI?).
>   **Where to find this term:** Box 6.1

Pretest–Posttest: A study where the dependent variable (DV) is measured first (pretest), then the independent variable (IV) is either introduced or occurs naturally, then the DV is measured again (posttest). Changes in the DV from before to after the IV are used as evidence of a relationship between the IV and the DV. This research technique can be used with no comparison group (a single-group, pretest-posttest study), but is also often used with a nonequivalent comparison group that did not experience the IV, but does take the Pretest and Posttest. (This can also be used in true experiments, where participants are all given the pretest, randomly assigned to different levels of the IV, then given the Posttest.)

Example: A researcher wants to know whether having a pet decreases stress levels, so he asks a pet adoption agency to administer a survey of stress levels to first-time pet adopters before they take their new pet's home (pretest). After one month of pet ownership (IV), each pet adopter completes the stress survey again (posttest). If stress levels have decreased, one might conclude that there is a relationship between pet ownership and stress levels, but cannot conclude that owning the pets *caused* the decrease, because there was no randomly assigned comparison group who did not get pets. Another explanation is that the mere process of looking for a pet increased stress levels, rather than the pet ownership decreasing stress.
Where to find this term: Box 6.1

Quasi-Experiment: A study that attempts to examine a cause-and-effect hypothesis, but lacks control over important extraneous variables. The reasons for lack of control are varied and can include the lack of any control group or comparison group or condition, a naturally occurring (not manipulated) independent variable, comparison of groups that are not equal in terms of important extraneous variables, or a combination of the above.
Example: In a *nonequivalent groups* study, a quasi-experiment on the relationship between funding for field trips and student enthusiasm for school uses two different schools: one with funds for field trips, one without, and measures student enthusiasm by giving a survey to all the students in both schools. Note that students are not randomly assigned to a group that gets funding and a group that does not, so there is no control over other things that could affect student enthusiasm for school, like parents' and teachers' enthusiasm, school culture, and so on (these extraneous variables are confounding variables). Thus, if differences in the DV (student enthusiasm) are found, that is not evidence that funding for field trips *caused* those differences. On the other hand, it does make that conclusion more likely than if there had been no relationship.
Where to find this term: Essays 6.1, 6.2, 6.3, Box 6.1

Random Assignment: See Module 5 Glossary

Self-Selection: When participants are assigned to groups or selected for study based on their own choice of group, or their choice of a behavior or characteristic that places them into a particular group. This is a problem because they bring along with them all the traits that are associated with the conceptual variable (the trait that was selected). Researchers cannot tell which trait is responsible for any observed differences between groups, the trait that was selected, or those than were selected accidentally along with it.
Example: A researcher hypothesized that playing online video games more than five hours in one day causes sadness the following day. After obtaining permission from her local Institutional Review Board, she posts a flyer at a video store, and when people contact her, she asks if they would be willing to play video games for at least 5 hours in one day, then do a survey on their emotional state the next day. If they say no, she asks if they would be willing to play NO video games for a day, then do the survey the next day. In this way, she finds 15 people for each group. These participants were self selected for inclusion in the study, and self-selected their groups. So the participants may not accurately represent the population of all potential video game players, and the two groups may differ in many ways in addition to the 5 hours of video games they play in one day.
Where to find this term: Essay 6.1 and Study 6A.

Social Support Network: The people to whom one turns for help when problems arise, such as when there is a need for advice, money, or just someone to talk to.
Examples: Anyone you feel you could trust to help you when you need it could be considered part of your social support network. This includes friends, family, neighbors, team members, coaches, fraternity or sorority members, church members or leaders, and any others to whom you can turn for support.
Where to find this term: Study 6C

Time Series (single group): A quasi-experimental study where the dependent variable is measured repeatedly over time, and at some point during that time, the independent variable is either purposefully introduced or occurs naturally. Measurements of the DV continue, and if a change in the DV coincides with the introduction of the IV, this is interpreted as evidence of a relationship between the IV and DV. However, caution must be used, as it is possible that some other variable is causing changes in the DV.

Example: A bathroom tissue company believes that an ecofriendly stamp on their packaging will improve sales. Biweekly sales data are collected over the course of the whole year (time series data on the DV), and during that year, the new packaging is introduced (IV). A spike in sales is seen shortly after the eco-stamp packaging is introduced, and a few months later, sales remain higher than before the change. However, a pandemic also began the same month as the eco-stamped packaging, and spurred a social media panic over a toilet paper shortage. This does not mean that the eco-packaging was ineffective, only that one should exercise caution in assuming a cause-and-effect relationship between the new packaging and the increased sales. The time-series technique alone cannot provide sufficient evidence for a cause-and-effect relationship.
Where to find this term: Box 6.1

"The Self Esteem Seminar seems to have helped you."

7B
Effect of Conversation on Reaction Time

MODULE 7 LEARNING OBJECTIVES CHART

ESSAY NUMBER	MODULE 7 ESSAY LEARNING OBJECTIVES	BEFORE READING					AFTER READING			
		I don't know how **1**	I know a little about this **2**	I know enough about this to guess correctly **3**	I know how to do this and/or have already done it. **4**		I don't know how **1**	I know a little about this **2**	I know enough about this to guess correctly **3**	I know how to do this and/or have already done it. **4**
Review	"Pass" a "quiz" on experimental terminology and the logic of hypothesis testing.									
7.1	Explain the goals of experimentation with respect to proof, verification, falsification, and evidence.									
7.1	Ignoring practical limitations, what is the easiest way to increase the power to detect differences between groups?									
7.2	Using a signal-to-noise analogy, describe two ways to improve the power of an experiment to statistically detect differences between levels of the IV.									
7.2 7.3 7.4	Compare a "between-groups" experiment to a "within-participants" experiment, in terms of how data would be collected and what would be compared.									

		I don't know how **1**	I know a little about this **2**	I know enough about this to guess correctly **3**	I know how to do this and/ or have already done it. **4**		I don't know how **1**	I know a little about this **2**	I know enough about this to guess correctly **3**	I know how to do this and/ or have already done it. **4**
7.3	Describe the purpose of matching samples in an experiment and how you would do this with random assignment.									
7.4	Describe two advantages of a within-participants experiment compared to a between-participants experiment.									
7.4	Explain what "order effects" are, when (and why) they are a problem, and how they can be avoided.									
		Read the assigned essays and actively seek answers to any questions rated less than "4." Then return to this chart and complete the white half.					Now proceed to the chart for the applications section, read the objectives for your assigned research project, and complete the gray side of that chart.			

A REVIEW OF EXPERIMENTAL TERMS AND LOGIC

This module will use experimental terminology. A lot. Take this quiz to make sure you can correctly apply the terms and understand the logic of hypothesis testing. The answer key is in Appendix B. If you get 100%, great! You're ready to read on. If not, refer to the essays and glossaries after each question to review the necessary information before proceeding.

Professor Jackson tested the hypothesis that relaxing for 15 minutes immediately before exams leads to better exam performance. Forty students who volunteered to participate were randomly assigned to two groups when they arrived for their 3-hour exam period. In the first 75 minutes, all students were given 1 hour to study and 15 minutes to relax. Group R studied first, then relaxed, then took the exam, while group NR relaxed first, then studied, then immediately took the exam. The research design and results are shown below. The p-value for the comparison was .049.

Average Score

Group R ⟶	Study for 1 hour	Rest for 15 min	Take Exam	86% ($SD = 11.1$)
Group NR ⟶	Rest for 15 min	Study for 1 hour	Take Exam	79% ($SD = 11.3$)

The Question	Your answer	Essays and Glossaries to Review
What is the null hypothesis?		5.3, 5.4, Glos. 5
What is the conceptual independent variable (IV)?		5.1, 5.2, Glos. 5
What is the conceptual dependent variable (DV)?		5.1, 5.2, Glos. 5
How is the IV operationally defined (what are the levels of the IV?)		2.2, 5.2, Glos. 5
How is the DV operationally defined?		2.2, 5.2, Glos. 2
State the prediction in terms of operational definitions.		4.1, 4.4 Fig.4.5
What do the SD's tell you?		3.3 Glos. 3
If the *p*-value is 0.049, what can Prof. Jackson conclude?		5.4, Glos. 5
Name one extraneous variable that is effectively controlled and explain how it is controlled.		5.1, 5.2, Glos. 5
Name a confounding variable and explain why it is confounding		5.1, 5.2, 5.3, Glos. 5

This page is blank so that you can tear out the review page, which should make it easier to flip through the book for information while working on the review page.

ESSAY 7.1

DESIGNING EXPERIMENTS TO *TEST* HYPOTHESES

Testing a cause-and-effect hypothesis with a true experiment usually requires participants, time, approval from an Institutional Review Board, facilities, and supplies. All of these can be hard to get. Because of this, and for ethical reasons, we do not take experimentation with human participants lightly. Experiments must be designed carefully to have every chance of finding evidence for our hypothesis *if it is true.*

Those words, "if it is true," are important to remember. As discussed in Module 1, our goal in the design of an experiment is to *test* our hypothesis, *not to verify it.* Researchers do *not* set out to "prove" a hypothesis is "true," nor to "show that it is correct," nor to do anything of the sort. Instead, we strive to put the hypothesis to the test; *we try to falsify it.* If the hypothesis stands up to this test, then we can say we have evidence to support it. It is *evidence* we seek, *not* proof, and *not* verification. Even if evidence is found, our single study will not allow us to claim we have "proof" for our hypothesis, nor that it is "correct." To a scientist, "proof" has a different meaning than "evidence." Proof is usually thought of as established truth, whereas evidence is understood to be dynamic and open to further study.

Attempting to falsify our hypothesis does not mean we believe it is false, or that we don't want to find support for it. Certainly, if our research hypothesis is true, we want to be able to reject the null hypothesis. We must therefore design experiments that maximize our chances of finding evidence, if it can be found. At the same time, we must avoid stacking the cards in favor of supporting our research hypothesis with an experiment that does not rigorously test it.

For example, consider the experiment described in the review question that started this module. It was designed to compare two groups of students: those who relaxed for 15 minutes just before an exam and those who did not. If there had been no difference in their scores, that would have falsified Professor Jackson's research hypothesis that relaxing before a test improves performance. To improve his chances

of seeing the difference he predicted between groups, he could have assigned his best students to the relaxation group. While that would probably lead to significantly higher scores in the relaxation group, it would not be a real test of the hypothesis and would not produce any useful information. Using random assignment helped assure that the students in each group came into the exam with about the same chances of success.

You might be bothered by the notion that true experiments, though they claim to have the best control over extraneous variables, rely mostly on random assignment to obtain that control. Can random assignment be trusted to perfectly distribute the students into groups with equal chances of success on the exam? Study 3B revealed that the larger the number of observations we make, and the smaller the variability in those observations, the more we can trust random assignment to do its job. If Professor Jackson had been able to test 100 students in each group, with about the same variability in their scores, that would have made his 7-point difference in means much (much!) less likely under the null hypothesis. Two groups of 20 people can differ by 7 points relatively easily, just by chance. But if 200 people are randomly assigned to groups with 100 people in each group, their means are extremely unlikely to differ that much, just by chance. (The p-value would be less than .0001.)

Given enough willing people, increasing the number of participants in an experiment is the easiest way to increase your power to detect differences due to IV manipulation.

With only 20 participants in each group and so much variability in scores (SDs were about 11 points in each group), should Professor Jackson really place that much trust in random assignment? What if, just by chance, *even without manipulation of relaxation times*, these two groups happened to differ this much on their exam scores? The p-value tells us that the probability of that happening, (with SDs of 11.1 and 11.3) is less than 5%, but only barely (it was .049).

A few students scoring a little higher or lower could have wiped out his chances of detecting any effect of relaxation. Thankfully, random assignment is not the only tool scientists have to improve control over extraneous variables and increase the power to see differences between the levels of the IV.

ESSAY 7.2

INCREASE THE SIGNAL, DECREASE THE NOISE

What are we looking for when we design an experiment? The question becomes almost too easy when you consider that the purpose of an experiment is to test a cause-and-effect hypothesis. We manipulate the cause, and we look for the… ???

Effects come in the form of *significant differences* between groups. Detecting differences due to our manipulation is difficult; sometimes it feels like the cards are stacked against us. Random assignment can be cruel, and accidentally put low scorers in a group that would otherwise score high if our hypothesis is true. It can also be kind and do the opposite. Thanks to variability, probabilistic reasoning is like bobbing for apples … sometimes you can pin one against the wall of the bucket, and sometimes you can't.

But there are ways to optimize our ability to detect differences—to see the effects of our manipulations—without compromising the integrity of the test of our hypothesis.

Module 3 explained why the more variability there is, the less you can trust the mean to tell you the truth about the group it is representing. Variability makes it harder to tell whether or not there is a real difference between the sets of scores, even when the means appear to differ a lot. If Professor Jackson's students had more variability in their exam scores, with SDs closer to 20 points instead of about 11, the 7-point difference in means would not have been enough to overcome all that variability. It would have been like trying to hear the difference between a tap and a stomp in a room full of drummers.

The **estimated difference** between groups can be thought of as a signal-to-noise ratio $=$ $\dfrac{\text{The } \textbf{difference between the means} \text{ of the two groups} \ \leftarrow \text{SIGNAL}}{\text{The } \textbf{variability} \text{ among the scores in each set} \qquad \leftarrow \text{NOISE}}$

That analogy is a good one—it helps to think of our measurement of the difference between groups as a "signal-to-noise" ratio, where the difference between means is the signal, and variability within the groups is the noise.[1]

Imagine you really wanted to detect the difference between a tap and a stomp in a room full of drummers. How could you improve your chances of detecting that difference? There are two obvious ways: Ask the stomper to stomp harder or ask the drummers to quiet down. By analogy, to maximize the chances of detecting a difference between two groups in an experiment, we must design effective manipulations

---

[1] This is the same "signal-to-noise ratio" described in Box 5.1 as a *t-ratio*.

that strengthen the signal by creating real differences between different levels of the IV (stomp harder), or minimize the noise by decreasing the variability in our measurements (quiet the drummers). Ideally, we should do both.

If Professor Jackson had "stomped harder" and chosen 30 minutes of relaxation for the experimental group instead of 15 minutes, he might have seen a bigger difference in students' scores. But sometimes this can backfire. In this case, too much relaxation before the exam could lead to more forgetting. To maximize the difference between different levels of the IV (increase the signal) without erasing it, we must know as much as possible about the conditions under which the hypothesis should hold true. It helps to read research articles on related topics before making decisions about how to manipulate the levels of the IV.

In contrast, variability can be decreased with generalizable research methods, introduced in Essays 7.3 and 7.4. To understand why these methods help, let's first clarify where the noise is coming from in the true experiments we've discussed so far.

Much (though not all) of the variability that makes it difficult to detect a difference between groups comes from *individual differences between participants*—everyone beating their own drum, so to speak. In the true experiments of Module 5, comparisons were made between different individuals *in different groups*. We call these studies **between-groups experiments** (also called **between-subjects** or **between-participants.**

A between-groups experiment is one where two or more groups are formed by random assignment; each group experiences one level of the IV, and comparisons are then made between those groups. It's a simple and common form of experimentation that is generally capable of detecting effects. But let's face it; different people differ in a lot of ways, and if the specific difference you're looking for is small and your manipulation/signal can't be increased without erasing it, you're not likely to detect the difference it causes with all that noise going on. So what can we do to minimize the impact of individual differences on our comparisons?

ESSAY 7.3

MATCHING SAMPLES REDUCE NOISE

When a between-groups experiment is the best option (for reasons that will be discussed in Essay 7.4), and the researcher wants better control over extraneous variables than random assignment can achieve, using *matched samples* can be a useful strategy. In the simplest form of this between-groups research design, participants are matched as closely as possible in pairs on some important trait; then each pair is split up, with one participant randomly assigned to each of the two different groups.

For example, if Professor Jackson (our review-quiz friend) had wanted more control over individual differences in test-taking ability between his two groups of students, he could have matched his

samples (groups of students) based on their grades on the previous exam. To do so, he would first list all the students in order, from highest to lowest scores on the previous exam. Then he would use some random process, such as the flip of a coin, to place the top student in one of the groups. The next student would be placed in the other group. Another coin toss would determine the placement of the next two students on the list, and so on. Using this modified system of random assignment, each participant would still have an equal chance of being assigned to either group, but both groups should end up about the same in terms of variables related to their scores on the previous exam. In other words, they would be "matched samples."

One caveat when matching samples: It works best when there is good *validity* to the measure used for matching. In the example above, the measure used for matching is performance on the previous exam. Many things can affect how students perform on one exam, including the type of content, the style of questions, and individual differences in stress the students are experiencing at the time. It might be more valid, if the information is available, to match the groups based on their current overall grade in the course. Whatever measure is used, one should never assume it is a perfectly valid measure (these rarely exist in nature). Although matching samples can be a useful technique for decreasing the variability between groups, careful consideration must be given to the measurement used to match the samples, in both the design of the study and the interpretation of the results.

Fred and Bill begin their long day setting up matched research samples.

ESSAY 7.4

WITHIN-PARTICIPANTS DESIGNS: LESS NOISE, MORE DATA

The matched-samples technique described in Essay 7.3 is not always the best way to decrease unnecessary variability in an experiment. Even if Professor Jackson (of review quiz fame) matches his samples based on the previous exam grade, there are bound to be some between-group differences in test-taking and study habits. The only way to get rid of all individual differences between groups would be to have the same students in both groups. That might sound impossible, but it's not. We can expose all participants to both levels of the IV, one level at a time. Rather than having an R group and an NR group, we would have an R *condition* and an NR *condition*. We'd ask all participants to take exams in both conditions, and then we'd compare each participant's R score to his or her *own* NR score. This means there are no more individual differences between the R and NR conditions because the individuals are the same at both levels of the IV. By decreasing variability, this research design gives us more power to detect differences that are due to the different levels of the IV.

Studies designed in this way are called *within-participants experiments* because the final comparisons are made, literally, within the same participants. They are also called *repeated measures* experiments because measurements of the DV are repeated for the same participants under different conditions.

We can set up a within-participants experiment to test Professor Jackson's hypothesis that relaxing immediately before an exam improves exam scores. Figure 7.1 shows what that experiment *might* look like.

For the midterm exam, *all participants* might be instructed just as they were for Group R in the between-groups experiment: Study 1 hour, relax 15 minutes, then take the exam. For the final exam, they might all be instructed as they were for Group NR: Relax 15 minutes, study for 1 hour, then immediately take the exam. Exam scores could then be compared

All Participants

For the Midterm Exam (Condition R)

Study for 1 hour

Rest for 15 min
Take Exam
Average Schore 96% (SD = 10.8)

THEN
For the Final Exam (Condition NR)

Rest for 15 min

Study for 1 hour
Take Exam
Average Schore 75% (SD = 11.2)

C. Buckley, using artwork from Leremy

Figure 7.1 A *possible* within-participants experiment to test the hypothesis that relaxation just before an exam improves scores. Although it deceases variability due to individual differences, **this experiment has at least one major *confounding variable*.**

within each participant for Conditions R versus NR. Note that in this within-participants experiment, we would no longer call them "Group R" and "Group NR." That would imply that they are different groups of people, which they are not.

If the average scores in Figure 7.1 were real, we *might* conclude that Professor Jackson had support for his hypothesis in the form of a significant difference in exam scores for the relaxation condition versus the no-relaxation condition. However, as noted in the caption to Figure 7.1, there is at least one major *confounding variable* in this experiment. Do you see it?

In a between-groups experiment, a confounding variable is a systematic difference *between groups*,

other than the IV. In a within-participants experiment, it's a difference *between conditions*, other than the IV. In both cases, it confuses the results because the intentional manipulations are not the *only* thing that differs at different levels of the IV. In Figure 7.1, exam performance is measured in the R condition with a midterm exam, but in the NR condition, it's the final exam. Not only do final exams often cover more material than midterms, but final exam week also tends to be a time of more stress, with major term papers and projects due the same week. It would not be surprising if people scored much lower on the final exam, regardless of the IV manipulations.

The problem gets bigger: Between taking the midterm and taking the final, students might get better at taking exams (*practice effect*) or worse at taking exams (*fatigue effect*). Thus, even if the exams and the levels of stress were the same, a significant difference in exam performance could not be exclusively attributed to the relaxation, because it could also be due to the effects of practice or fatigue when taking the second exam.

In every within-participants experiment, variables related to the order in which the levels of the IV are presented can cause *order effects* (like practice or fatigue), making it impossible to determine what, exactly, caused any differences between different levels of the IV. Order effects are also called *carryover effects* because they suggest that experience with one level of the IV can be *carried over* to another level, and can affect the DV measurements in the second condition. By either name, that is bad, because it is a systematic difference between levels of the IV other than the IV itself. In other words, order effects are another confounding variable.

Thankfully, these problems can easily be avoided using a technique called *counterbalancing*, in which we vary the order of conditions for different participants. Figure 7.2 shows a counterbalanced, within-participants test of Professor Jackson's hypothesis.

This experiment will take half of the participants in the experiment described in Figure 7.1 and reverse the order of the conditions for them, as shown in Figure 7.2. While half the class will be in condition R for the midterm, the other half will be in condition NR for the midterm. Then, during finals week, participants who relaxed just before the midterm will

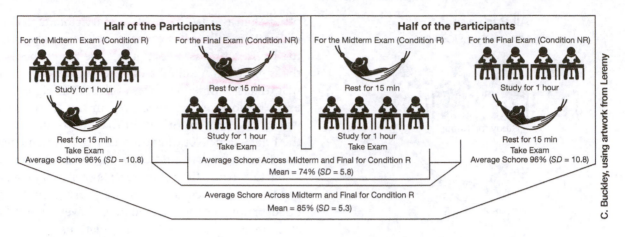

Figure 7.2 A better within-participants experiment to test the hypothesis that relaxation just before an exam improves scores. This research design uses **counterbalancing** to minimize order effects.

not relax just before the final, and those who did *not* relax before the midterm *will* relax before the final. In this way, all participants will be exposed to both levels of relaxation (Conditions R and NR), but the order of exposure to R and NR will be balanced across the two types of exams.

Since the mean for Condition R is composed of both midterm and final exam scores, and so is the mean for condition NR, Professor Jackson can now compare means between conditions and not worry about differences in the exam, or the timing of it. There is nothing systematically different about Conditions R and NR, other than the IV.

With proper counterbalancing, a within-participants design is a powerful way to decrease noise in order to see the effects of our manipulations. In other words, it's a powerful way to test a hypothesis.

There is another huge benefit to the within-participants research design. By exposing every participant to two levels of the IV rather than just one, we obtain twice as much data with the same number of participants. Study 3B demonstrated that having more data means we can place more trust in the means, which makes it easier to find evidence for our hypothesis, if it is true. When Professor Jackson designed his study as a between-groups experiment, he was able to compare 20 scores from Group R to 20 scores from Group NR. Each of his 40 students only contributed to one

level of the IV. But in a within-participants experiment, he can compare 40 scores in Condition R (20 midterms and 20 final exams) to 40 scores in Condition NR. This, too, makes the within-participants design a much more powerful technique for testing hypotheses.

So why would we ever want to use a between-groups experiment?

Sometimes, a within-participants experiment is not practical. What if Professor Jackson only has one 3-hour exam period available for his experiment?

Another problem is that counterbalancing is not always enough to keep knowledge of one level from affecting another. For example, in an experiment to test the hypothesis that training in kick-boxing improves Zumba workout intensity, one cannot train participants in kickboxing before their first Zumba workout, and then expect them to forget that training before their second workout. In any study with carry-over effects that can't be fixed by counterbalancing (i.e., where knowledge or experience with one level of the IV must affect the way participants respond to the other level of the IV) it is best to use a between-groups research design, rather than within participants.

The advantages, disadvantages, and caveats of the true experimental research designs discussed in this module are compared in Table 7.1.

Table 7.1 Summary of the Types of **True Experimental Research Designs** Discussed in This Module, Their Advantages, Disadvantages, and Caveats

Research Design	Is Random Assignment Needed?	Advantages	Disadvantages	Caveats
Between-Groups	Random assignment is required.	No order effects; less chance of participants figuring out the hypothesis	Relatively few observations per level of IV (given the same number of participants)	Individual differences increase variability
Between-groups with Matched Samples	Random assignment should be used with each matched pair of participants (based on pairing technique)	Same as above, but also has better control over one (or a few) related extraneous variables (decreased individual differences)	Relatively few observations per level of IV (given the same number of participants)	Measurement of the variable(s) used for matching must have good validity
Within-Participants (Repeated Measures)	Random assignment is not critical, but should be applied to the order of conditions when counterbalancing (see text)	A lot more data from the same number of participants; minimizes individual differences, which minimizes noise	Not always practical, especially when knowledge of one level of the IV could affect performance or responses at other level(s)	Counterbalancing is needed to avoid order effects (see text)

MODULE 7 RESEARCH LEARNING OBJECTIVES CHART

STUDY NUMBER	MODULE 7 RESEARCH LEARNING OBJECTIVES	BEFORE READING					AFTER DOING PROJECT			
		I don't know how 1	I know a little about this 2	I know enough about this to guess correctly 3	I know how to do this and/ or have already done it. 4		I don't know how 1	I know a little about this 2	I know enough about this to guess correctly 3	I know how to do this and/ or have already done it. 4
7A	Define "hysterical strength" and explain why there has been no experimental research on its cause.									
7A	Describe in general what social psychologists study.									
7A	Describe the conditions under which a between-groups experiment should be done with matched-samples, and how that differs from normal random assignment.									
7A	Gain experience with the use of an Informed Consent Form for experimentation with human participants.									
7B	Discuss correlational evidence that phone conversations while driving are related to accident rates.									
7B	Correctly use the terms bidirectionality, third variable, and self-selection to generate at least three hypotheses to explain the correlational evidence that phone conversations while driving are related to accident rates.									

		I don't know how 1	I know a little about this 2	I know enough about this to guess correctly 3	I know how to do this and/ or have already done it. 4		I don't know how 1	I know a little about this 2	I know enough about this to guess correctly 3	I know how to do this and/ or have already done it. 4
7B	Discuss experimental evidence that phone conversations impair driving performance.									
7B	Gain experience using a within-participants experiment to test a hypothesis.									
7C	Discuss what it means to be a skeptical thinker and contrast that with cynical thinking.									
7C	Discuss logical reasons why most scientists are reluctant to study parapsychology.									
7C	Conduct a scientific study to examine the evidence for or against psi abilities.									
7C	Given a research design that uses multiple strategies, correctly identify and explain the design strategies being used.									

Now read about the project to prepare for lab. For any scores less than "4," keep those questions in mind as you complete the research project(s). Do not do the white half of this chart until after you've completed the assigned research project(s).

EFFECT OF ENCOURAGEMENT ON GRIP STRENGTH

In July of 2006, Ken Boyle lifted a car off a cyclist who had been hit, dragged, and pinned under the car. Granted, Ken Boyle was a 300-pound power weightlifter, but his maximum dead-lift prior to that experience had been 700 lb. The car weighed 3,000 lb.

Even if we concede that only one side of the car was lifted, and we're not sure how that weight was distributed, it is quite likely that this was a new record for Ken. The technical term for his experience is "hysterical strength." It is commonly explained as an adrenaline rush—an autonomic nervous system (neuroendocrine) response to an extreme situation, based on what Walter Cannon called the "fight or flight" response.

Unfortunately, there is no scientific research that can directly test or fully explain anecdotes like this. A surge of adrenaline can temporarily increase muscle strength, but to what extent this happens in hysterical strength situations remains a mystery. To study these events, we would have to reproduce them, and we can't go around pinning cyclists under cars in front of weightlifters. Biomechanical researchers have examined the physical limits of muscular and skeletal forces, and determined that indeed, our bodies are theoretically capable of strength beyond that which we would each consider our own maximum, though not to the extent reported in Ken's story. Nevertheless, on a much smaller scale, it is possible that we can be stronger than we believe ourselves to be. This research application asks: Can encouragement from others make us stronger?

We ask this question because humans are social creatures, capable of both nurturing one another and of manipulating others to our own advantage. The flip side of that coin is that we can easily be influenced by others. Social psychologists study how the behavior of individuals is shaped by social situations. This is evident in the seminal studies of Solomon Asch and Stanley Milgram, as well as Barbara Fredrickson's work on positive psychology and where happiness comes from. Fredrickson, a prolific researcher in social psychology, was also an influential writer on Objectification Theory, which examines sociocultural

Image © Greg Epperson/Shutterstock

influences on female mental health (see her 1997 review, listed in the References section of this book). Social psychologists have contributed much to our understanding of human behavior. In this study, you will examine whether social influence can affect physical strength.

Yours will not be the first study to ask this question. Jung and Hallbeck (2004) used a small sample of 21 male students and found that encouragement significantly increased peak grip strength measurements. However, 21 participants, as you know, is not a large sample, and no information is available on whether females would respond in the same way. You will use a dynamometer to measure your own peak grip strength, both alone and with encouragement. Grip dynamometers are commonly used by many athletes and their trainers, from gymnasts to weightlifters, and scores vary considerably. Some research suggests that norms can even differ between very large samples of people in different countries (Massy-Westropp et al., 2011), so we can expect considerable variation in our small classroom groups of participants.

In cases where we have a relatively low number of participants ("low N"), and a lot of variability in the dependent measure (in this case, grip strength), random assignment is less likely to balance individual differences between groups. It therefore makes sense to use a matching samples technique to reduce the between-groups variability. To minimize the impact of your own expectations on the results, you will see that the procedures outlined below are brief. You will receive more detailed instructions in lab.

In the meantime, note that although published norms exist for different age groups and genders, they are based on professional therapeutic and training techniques and equipment, and will not be comparable to the measurements we take. Furthermore, no

one should be embarrassed by his or her grip strength, as it is primarily a measure of forearm strength, not overall strength. It's not even what we usually think of as arm strength, which is in the upper arm. Those who have worked hard to develop forearm strength will generally have higher scores, just as those who work hard at any skill will generally perform better on that skill than the norm. Nevertheless, your scores will remain confidential (no one other than your partner will know them), so you will not have to publicly share your own grip strength. Also know that you do have the option of not participating, without negative consequences.

Lastly, if you have read Essay 6.2, you know about the APA's principles for ethical research with human participants. In this research, we will again take deliberate measures to demonstrate how researchers in psychology assure the safety and respect the dignity and autonomy of research subjects, as you read and consider signing a standard "ICD" (Informed Consent Document), specific to this research project.

© Cartoon Resource /Shutterstock.com
(Image modified and captioned by C. Buckley)

"Come on, Tabby!"
"You know, you're right! With enough encouragement, Tabby has great grip strength!"

PROCEDURAL NOTES 7A

Describing the entire procedure before you participate in this study is likely to impact your data. Risks are minimal and are outlined in the Informed Consent Document you will be given. Rather than a complete procedure section (which you will get in lab), here are three very important notes that you MUST read before participating in this study:

1. If you have either high blood pressure or any reason at all for concern regarding past or future injury to your wrists, arms, or fingers, that has been or could be caused by squeezing a dynamometer as hard as you can, DO NOT PARTICIPATE. Everyone who does participate will be asked to sign an informed consent form, confirming that you have no such concerns, and agreeing to stop squeezing if you feel any pain or discomfort.

2. Research on grip strength is typically performed with very expensive ($500--$1,000 ea.), carefully calibrated dynamometers that are recalibrated between each use or every time they are bumped. The dynamometers we will use are very inexpensive, by comparison, not carefully calibrated, and therefore, will undoubtedly be less accurate. Accepting that variability is a natural part of research, we are hopeful that they will at least be consistent enough to detect an effect, if it exists. Regardless, you should NOT use your readings for diagnostic or competition-related information. As in all psychological research, with the notable exception of research on gambling, no wagering is allowed.

3. Body position affects grip strength readings, so it is important that you follow the directions you are given precisely. Do not change your body or arm position to try to get more comfortable before your measurement.

LAB RECORD WORKSHEET FOR STUDY 7A
GRIP STRENGTH

Name: _____ Date: _____

Group Member Names: _____

Purpose *To examine the influence of positive social interaction (encouragement) on physical strength.*

Hypothesis _____

_____

Conceptual independent variable _____

Conceptual dependent variable _____

Operational definition of IV

1. _____

2. _____

Operational definition of DV _____

Prediction _____

_____

_____

_____

Method

Participants _____ *male,* _____ *female, and* _____ *non-binary college students enrolled in introductory psychology lab participated as part of the course. Age was not recorded, but most participants were between 18 and 22 years old.*

Materials _____

_____

_____

_____

_____

_____

_____

_____

_____

_____

_____

Procedure _____

_____

_____

_____

_____

_____

_____

Data Handling _____

_____

_____

We used a t-test to compare _____.

Results

_____

_____

_____

_____

_____

Discussion

What would we expect if the *null* hypothesis were true? _____

_____

_____

Can we reject the null hypothesis in favor of our research hypothesis?   Yes   No   Not Sure

What can we conclude about the effect of encouragement on strength? _____

_____

_____

_____

We kept natural grip strength approximately constant across groups in this study using a matched samples technique. Describe another way to control the same variable using a within-participants experiment. Make sure you include a way to control for order effects, if needed.

_____

_____

_____

STUDY 7B

EFFECT OF CONVERSATION ON REACTION TIME

We have all heard the horror stories and been warned a thousand times not to text while driving. Bumper stickers and laws agree; texting while driving is the wrong thing to do. There is relatively little public agreement about placing a call or having a phone conversation while driving, though most people seem to feel that as long as a hands-free device is used, phone conversations do not impair driving safety.

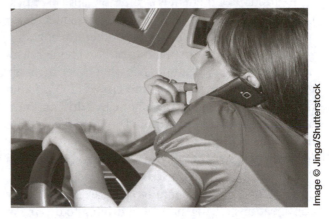

Empirically speaking, however, that conclusion is not well-founded. First, there is no shortage of correlational research showing a relationship between cell phone conversations while driving and accident rates. In a study of nearly 700 people who had been in car accidents, Redelmeier and Tibshirani (1997) examined phone records and found that nearly a quarter of the drivers had been conversing (not texting) on their phones within a 10-minute period approximating the time of their accidents. Comparing this to normative data on accident rates, they concluded that there was a four-fold increase in accident rates among people who converse on phones while driving. Furthermore, they found no difference in this relationship for hands-free (compared to handheld) phones. In other words, their correlational research suggested that the increased accident risk was associated with conversation itself, not dialing or holding a phone.

Cramer et al. (2007) reported descriptive data indicating that college students are a particularly high-risk group for cell phone use while driving. This correlates strongly with a very high accident rate among young adults. A science attitude requires that we consider all possible explanations for these observed correlations and don't jump to causal conclusions without an experiment.

Third variable explanations for these correlations are not hard to find. Age might be a factor. Maybe college students talk on the phone while driving because they represent the greatest proportion of cell phone users, in general, and this is no different whether they are driving or not. Younger drivers also have less experience dealing with road hazards,

etc., and might have more accidents for that reason. Another third variable explanation: The relationship between talking on the phone and accident rates might be partially explained by heavier-than-normal traffic, which could cause increases in cell phone use *and* higher accident rates, rather than phone use causing the accidents.

Bidirectionality is also worth considering. Depending on how data are collected, some of these calls might be immediately *after* an accident to report that they need help or that they will be late for appointments.

There is also a *self-selection* problem at work in these studies because those who admit to using a cell phone while driving carry with them a whole set of other behaviors that could put them at risk for more accidents. Beck et al. (2007) published a correlational study that documents an association between the use of a phone while driving and other risky driving behaviors (e.g., speeding, ignoring traffic signals). It might be the tendency to engage in those behaviors, and not the phone conversations, per se, that increases the risk of accidents.

If you think these explanations suggest that it's probably okay to have a phone conversation while driving, keep reading.

If the arguments above suggest to you that these correlations are not due to a cause-and-effect relationship between cell phone use while driving and accidents, think more about your science attitude.

Remember that third variables, bidirectionality, and any other *potential* explanations for correlations, no matter how reasonable they sound, are *not* evidence against a causal relationship, and should never be used as such. They are empirical questions, not answers. They must be tested with experiments to gather evidence to support them. It is a common lapse in critical thinking to assume that a reasonable explanation for an observation is evidence against other explanations.

The hypothesis that talking on the phone causes an increase in accident rates has been experimentally tested several times. Strayer and Drews (2004) found that talking on a hands-free phone in a driving simulator increased reaction time and doubled the number of rear-end collisions compared to driving the simulator without distractions. Alm and Nilsson (1995) and Strayer et al. (2003) reported similar findings. Strayer et al. (2006) experimentally compared cell phone conversations during simulated driving to driving at the legal blood-alcohol limit of 0.08%. Participants consented to drink vodka and orange juice until their blood alcohol reached this level. Significantly more accidents and slower braking time occurred in the cell phone conversation condition than in the drunk driving condition. The fact that these studies have been completed with simulators, rather than actual cars, should not detract too much from their importance. In combination with all the naturalistic and correlational research on this topic, the evidence strongly suggests a very real cause-and-effect relationship between drivers' cell phone conversations and car accidents.

Just et al. (2008) used functional MRI (images of activity in the brain) to test the idea that speech comprehension affects brain areas that are needed for (simulated) driving. They found that just listening to sentences decreased activity in areas used during the simulation, and being asked to judge the truth of those sentences decreased activity in those areas even more. Decreased activity might affect reaction times for driving-related tasks.

This research project will address *how* conversation might impair driving: by slowing reaction times. Previous research suggests that talking at all (just producing speech) can slow reaction times, but we want to know how much more reaction time is affected when the talking requires listening and processing language. Therefore, we are going to compare the effects of normal conversation to a control condition of simply repeating words.

Because reaction times differ greatly from one person to the next, and to get more data from the limited number of participants, we will use a within-participants design for this experiment.

7B-1 PROCEDURE

For use with Humanbenchmark.com/tests/reactiontime/

1. Each pair of students will be given a set of four wordlists, labeled A, B, C, and D. The pair will use all four wordlists, with each participant using either A & B or C & D. Every list is on a two-sided card or paper and is composed of a set of about 55 words in red ink. For the first half of the list, each word has a question associated with it, such as "How many vowels are in the word "bike?" An answer is provided in parenthesis after the question. During the conversation condition (C), the Experimenter (E) will read the questions to the Participant (P), who will be expected to answer them while completing the reaction time task. If their answer is wrong, E should say "try again" until a correct answer is given, up to three times. If the third answer is still wrong, proceed to the next question. During the word repetition (WR) condition, E will simply read the words in red, ignoring the questions. P will just repeat the word; then E will say the next word. If you run out of words before the 2 minutes are up, there are more red words on the back of the page.

2. Each pair of students should use one computer. Do not use phones or tablets as they are slower and will lengthen your reaction time. Go to humanbenchmark.com/tests/reactiontime/ and x-out any

advertisements so that your browser window is completely blue, and you can see "average time" and "tries."

3. Assign one person in your group as the experimenter (E) and one as the participant (P). After the first P completes BOTH conditions (WR *and* C), you will switch roles. To decide which condition to start with, flip a coin. If it's heads, start with WR and Wordlist A. If it's tails, start with the Conversation condition and Wordlist A. **On the data sheet for procedure 7B-1, circle the appropriate letters to indicate the order of conditions BEFORE you go on to Step 4 below.**

4. The P should attempt one set of five measurements of reaction time without recording scores, just to get used to how reaction time is measured. Keep track of your number of tries and stop after you complete 5 tries. (The counter will say "Tries 5 of 5.")

5. When five measurements have been completed, **reload the page** before starting the first experimental trial. This will reset the trial number and the average reaction time on the screen to zero. If you do not reload the page, your reaction time will include your practice trials. That's not a good thing. Reload the page.

6. Before you start data collection, make sure everything is ready: The page has been reloaded and says "Tries 0 of 5; the experimenter has a phone timer set to ring or buzz in 2 minutes; and Wordlist A is in-hand, ready to read (Question side! If you're doing WR first, just ignore the questions and read the words in red). When both people are ready, P begins the reaction-time task. At the same time, E begins the timer and starts either asking questions from the script, which P must immediately answer (condition C); or reading the words in red from the word list, which P must immediately repeat (condition WR). The condition that is completed first is based on P's assignment from Step 1 above. The participant will keep doing the reaction time task for the entire 2 minutes. By the end, the counter on the screen might say "Tries 34 of 5" which makes no sense, but that's okay—you only need the reaction time data, not the number of tries. When the timer ends, record your average reaction time and **reload the page**.

7. *The same participant* will repeat Step 6 for the other condition (word repetition or conversation). The Experimenter will switch to Wordlist B and either read just the red words (word repetition task) or the whole questions (conversation task), whatever they did NOT do with Wordlist A. When complete, record reaction time and reload the page.

8. Switch roles and repeat Steps 4 through 7. After the new participant completes 5 of 5 tries, reload the page again. The new Experimenter will start with Wordlist C. Remember to counterbalance the order! If the first participants started with word repetition, the second participant should start with conversation. Data collection is complete when both people in the pair have completed steps 4 through 7 as participants.

9. Either hand in your data or enter them on a Google Sheet (a template might be provided).

10. Begin work on the Lab Record Worksheet while your instructor runs the data analysis. Discuss results as a class and finish the worksheet.

DATA SHEET FOR USE WITH PROCEDURE 7B-1

Before you start data collection (Step 4), flip a coin to determine the order of conditions.

Important: BASED ON THE COIN TOSS, Circle "WR" for Word Repetition, or circle "C" for Conversation to indicate the order of data collection for each participant.

IF IT WAS HEADS:
Participant 1's 1st condition is WR and 2nd condition is C.
Participant 2's 1st condition is C and 2nd condition is WR.

IF IT WAS TAILS:
Participant 1's 1st condition is C and 2nd condition is WR.
Participant 2's 1st condition is WR and 2nd condition is C.

Participant 1 1st condition, Wordlist A →   WR   C   Reaction time was: _____ ms

                          2nd condition, Wordlist B →   WR   C   Reaction time was: _____ ms

Participant 2 1st condition, Wordlist C →   WR   C   Reaction time was: _____ ms

                          2nd condition, Wordlist D →   WR   C   Reaction time was: _____ ms

PROCEDURE **7B-2**

For use with railroadersleep.fra.dot.gov or PsyToolKit

1. Read Step 1 of procedure 7B-1, which explains the Wordlists and how to use them.

2. Flip coins and fill in the boxes on the data sheet for procedure 7B-2, indicating the order of the conditions BEFORE YOU BEGIN ANY DATA COLLECTION.

3. On one computer (not phone or tablet), with your partner, go to the reaction-time website "https://railroadersleep.fra.dot.gov/". Use either Safari or Edge as your browser, and select "allow Flash" to play. Chrome does not support Adobe Flash Player. As of Dec 2020, other browsers will also drop Flash Player. This link *might* still work. If it does not, use procedure 7B-1 or check with your instructor to see if this app has been moved to PsyToolKits. Assuming the program works when you are reading this…

4. On the railroadersleep webpage, click on the wonderfully inviting tab that says "Explore Sleep." Then click "Your Sleep Toolkit," then "Test your Reaction Time." Click "Ramp up." Ignore the sleep questions, and click "You're all set to go." Read the rest of these instructions BEFORE you press the spacebar to start.

5. In the following steps, P stands for the participant and E for the experimenter. After P has completed both Word Repetition (WR) and Conversation (C), you will switch roles. E always sits to the right of P, like a passenger in a car (in the US). This is so that E can reach the "bail out" button when the trial ends.

6. The driving task will show a two-lane highway on which P is "driving." Objects will randomly appear in the driver's lane. P must avoid hitting the objects by tapping the spacebar as quickly as possible to change lanes. Aim for fast, accurate responses. Tapping the spacebar when there is no object in your lane is a "false start" and waiting too long to tap the spacebar causes a "crash" (accident). There are scoring penalties for both.

7. Before you start data collection, make sure everything is ready: The website should say, "Hit the spacebar to begin; E has a phone timer set to ring or buzz in 2 minutes; and Wordlist A is in-hand, ready to read (Question side! If you're doing WR first, just ignore the questions and read the words in red). When both people are ready, P hits the spacebar. At the same time, E begins the timer and starts either asking questions from the word list that P must immediately answer (conversation condition), or reading red words from the word list that P must immediately repeat (word repetition condition), based on Step 2 above and the instructions on data sheet 7B-2. P should keep doing the driving task while repeating words or answering questions, for the entire 2 minutes.

8. **When the timer rings at 2 min**, the EXPERIMENTER should use the computer mouse to click on "Bail Out." (E should do this, not P, because P needs to keep paying attention to avoid a last-second crash). Click on "See Results" and record your reaction time, plus the number of false starts and accidents. Calculate your score.

9. Repeat Step 7 with the same Participant, but use Word List B and switch conditions (from WR to C or C to WR, as indicated on your data sheet).

10. Switch roles and repeat Steps 7, 8, and 9, but use Word Lists C and D. Make sure you switch the order of conditions!

11. Report all four scores to your lab instructor and begin work on your lab record.

DATA SHEET FOR USE WITH PROCEDURE 7B-2

For use with railroadersleep.fra.dot.gov or PsyToolKit

Important: Do TWO coin tosses: WINNER of the 1st COIN TOSS is PARTICIPANT 1.

2nd COIN TOSS – If HEADS, Wordlist A is the Word Repetition condition (WR). Fill in the Wordlist boxes on the data sheet as follows:

Wordlist →	A	B	C	D
Condition →	WR	C	C	WR

2nd COIN TOSS – If TAILS, Wordlist A is the conversation condition (C). Fill in the Wordlist boxes on the data sheet as follows:

Wordlist →	A	B	C	D
Condition →	C	WR	WR	C

Participant 1: Is English your first language? **Yes** **No**					
Word List A: First Condition →		**Word List B:** Second Condition →			
Average Reaction Time →			Average Reaction Time →		
Number of False Starts		×.02 =	Number of False Starts		×.02 =
Number of Accidents		×.05 =	Number of Accidents		×.05 =
SCORE (total) →			SCORE (total) →		

Participant 2: Is English your first language? **Yes** **No**					
Word List C: First Condition →		**Word List D:** Second Condition →			
Average Reaction Time →			Average Reaction Time →		
Number of False Starts		×.02 =	Number of False Starts		×.02 =
Number of Accidents		×.05 =	Number of Accidents		×.05 =
SCORE (total) →			SCORE (total) →		

Score = Average + (Fasle Starts × 0.02) + (Accidents × 0.05)

Each false start adds 2% of a second to your average reaction time.
Each accident adds 5% of a second to your average reaction time.

LAB RECORD WORKSHEET FOR STUDY 7B
CONVERSATION AND REACTION TIME

Name(s): _____

Purpose: *To compare the influence of simple speech versus conversation on reaction times.*

Hypothesis _____

_____

Conceptual independent variable _____

Conceptual dependent variable _____

Operational definition of IV

1. _____

2. _____

Operational definition of DV _____

_____

Prediction _____

_____

_____

Method

Participants _____ *college students enrolled in introductory psychology lab participated as part of the course. Age and gender were not recorded, but most participants were between 18 and 22 years old and gender was mixed.*

Materials _____

_____

_____

_____

_____

_____

Procedure _____

_____

_____

_____

_____

_____

_____

_____

Data Handling _____

_____

We used a t-test to compare _____.

Results

The mean driving impairment score in the Conversation Condition was _____ *(SD =* _____*), and the mean score in the Word Repetition Condition was* _____*(SD =* _____. *The difference (was/was not)* significant, t(____) = _____, p _{<, >, or =} , _____.

circle one

Discussion

What can we conclude about the effect of conversation on reaction time?

_____

_____

Natural reaction times vary from one individual to another and can affect driving impairment scores. Circle the term that most accurately describes natural reaction times in our experiment:

Extraneous Variable   Confounding Variable   Independent Variable   Dependent Variable

Explain why you circled that term: _____

_____

ANSWER QUESTION ONE OR QUESTION TWO, DEPENDING ON THE RESULTS:

1. If we observed a significant increase in impairment scores during conversation compared to word repetition, explain what caused this difference, whether this finding can be generalized to actual driving, and why or why not.

    _____

    _____

    _____

2. If we did not observe a difference in impairment scores between conditions, this could mean that both levels of speech are distracting, or that neither simple speech nor conversation is distracting. What level of the IV (what condition) would you add to our experiment to test the hypothesis that both levels of speech increase driving impairment scores?

    _____

    _____

STUDY 7C

SKEPTICISM AND PARAPSYCHOLOGY[2]

Image © Fabio Berti, 2014. Used under license from Shutterstock, Inc.

In Module 1 of this book, skepticism was presented as a willingness to examine the evidence for or against an idea, regardless of one's own personal views. The paragraph on skepticism concluded with the idea that true skeptics are as willing to challenge their own ideas as they are to challenge ideas with which they disagree. This is a high standard that even many scientists are not quite willing to fully embrace.

For example, the majority of psychologists and other scientists have concluded that paranormal phenomena (telepathy, clairvoyance, psychokinesis, ESP, and other psychic claims), often called psi phenomena, are not real. It is a fair bet that many have done so without doing any research in the field or even reading the scientific literature. Everyone has a natural tendency to doubt ideas that are uncomfortable, even the best scientists. Einstein doubted the probabilistic nature of the universe described by quantum mechanics, famously saying

that "God does not play dice with the universe." And today, quantum mechanics is responsible for so much of our current technology that physicist James Kakalios (2011) introduced his book on the subject with the quote: "Quantum physics? You're soaking in it!"[3]

For those who have read the literature, there is a conspicuous absence of empirical evidence for paranormal phenomena, not to mention a very strong logical case against them. From 1996 to 2015, James Randi, noted magician and skeptic, offered a $1,000,000 reward to anyone who could show, with a properly controlled scientific experiment, that he or she has a psi ability. According to the James Randi Education Foundation, several hundred people applied to be tested, and not one successfully demonstrated such ability.

One would think that the first people in line for the prize money would have been professional

---

[2] The research design for this application was created by Ralph Barnes (Montana State University).

[3] In an interesting coincidence, the wave function, the central theoretical construct of quantum mechanics, is represented by Ψ, the Greek letter *psi*. Ψ is also the first letter of the Greek word 'psuche,' which means mind, and it is the symbol of psychology.

psychics. Strangely, most high-profile professional psychics ignored invitations to the JREF Challenge, and those who tried it failed. Nevertheless, IBISWorld reported in 2019[4] that psychic services in the United States are a $2 billion/year industry. Based on average cost, we can estimate the number of psychic services sold at no less than 30 million each year, allowing for some pricey outliers. Are that many people being so easily misled? Or are scientists missing something?

If we are, it is not from lack of trying. Even William James, often called the father of American psychology, tried to convince colleagues that parapsychology should be scientifically investigated. A handful of parapsychology laboratories have been set up around the world, most of them at least temporarily affiliated with major research universities. And yet, peer-reviewed publications of paranormal findings in reputable journals remain extremely rare.

Some scientific reports of psychic phenomena have been published. Regarding those studies, one might ask, as a visitor to the JREF website did, "How can you deny them?" To which James Randi replied,[5]

> *Scientists can be wrong . . . The history of science is replete with serious errors of judgment, bad research, faked results, and simple mistakes, made by scientists in every field. The beauty of science is that it corrects itself by its own nature and design. By this means, science provides us with increasingly clearer views of how the world works.*

One highly active center for parapsychology research, the Rhine Research Center, was founded at Duke University in 1935 by Joseph Banks Rhine, with his wife, Louisa Rhine. While at Duke, the Parapsychology Laboratory studied clairvoyance (knowledge gained through unknown senses), using sets of cards with five symbols developed by Karl Zener, a colleague at Duke. The Zener symbols, shown in the illustration accompanying the heading for Study 7C, were designed to be vivid and easily recognizable. The Rhines were quite successful in using these cards to demonstrate the existence of what they thought were psychic abilities, and even established the *Journal of*

Parapsychology for publication of these results and other reports of psi phenomena from around the world.[6]

However, true to James Randi's description of science, it is self-correcting, and eventually, methodological flaws in the Rhine research were brought to light. Attempts to replicate the studies under more scientifically rigorous conditions produced no evidence of psi ability, and in 1969, Duke University cut its ties with the Rhine Research Center. Undeterred, the Center remains active today. They have exchanged Zener cards for much more sophisticated measurement techniques, and they continue to publish the *Journal of Parapsychology*, though only twice a year.

Whether you believe psi abilities are real or not, the main point of this research will be our scientifically rigorous (skeptical) approach to studying them. Remember that a skeptical approach is not a cynical approach. We will give full consideration to the research hypothesis which states that psi abilities can influence knowledge acquisition. We'll test it against the null hypothesis which states they cannot (knowledge only travels via conventional means). We will test this hypothesis indirectly, using the well-established understanding that knowledge acquisition improves with accurate feedback.

To test whether psi abilities can influence knowledge acquisition, we will use a within-participants **experiment**. All participants will be given a clairvoyance test, measuring their ability to detect the symbols on a series of cards. We'll give participants the test twice: In the Feedback condition, participants will be told whether they were correct each time they guess. In the No Feedback condition, participants will make all their guesses without knowing whether any guesses are correct. In this way, undetected psychic abilities, if they exist, will have a better chance of showing themselves, assuming they follow the general rule of learning: Feedback improves knowledge acquisition. The feedback rule is particularly strong when people are learning something new, so if clairvoyant ability exists and follows that rule, we would predict that scores would be significantly higher in the Feedback condition, compared to the No Feedback condition (Fig. 7.3). But what if psi abilities are real and unaffected by feedback?

---

[4] https://www.ibisworld.com/united-states/market-research-reports/psychic-services-industry/
[5] From JREF website: http://www.randi.org/site/index.php/1m-challenge/challenge-faq.html

---

[6] http://www.rhine.org/who-we-are/history.html

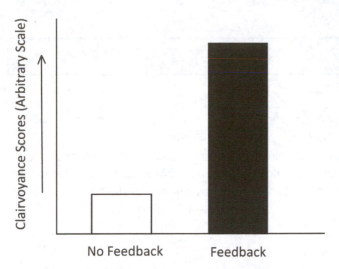

Figure 7.3 Expected outcome of Feedback vs No Feedback **experiment** if psi abilities are real and are affected by feedback. Note that the difference between F and NF conditions would have to be a **statistically significant** difference, not just a similar pattern in bar shapes, which is quite likely to occur just by chance when the null hypothesis is true.

The data we collect can also be used to test a **correlational** hypothesis that will address that question. If psi abilities are real but do not follow the feedback rule, then people who demonstrate psi ability by guessing correctly more often than expected should score high in both the Feedback and No Feedback conditions. Anti-psi people who guess incorrectly more often than expected should score low in both conditions. Therefore, if psi ability is real and feedback has no effect on it, we would predict a positive correlation between Feedback and No Feedback conditions, similar to the results shown in Figure 7.4A. But if psi is not real, most people will perform at chance levels, regardless of feedback. Performance in the Feedback condition will be unrelated to performance in the No Feedback condition. If this is the case, our results would look more like Figure 7.4B.

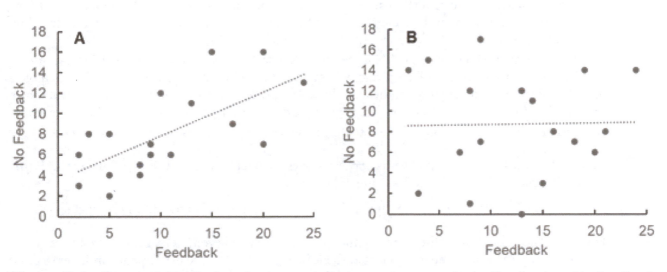

Figure 7.4 Expected *correlations* for the number of correct guesses in the Feedback vs No Feedback conditions. (A) If feedback has no effect, but psi abilities are real, and (B) If feedback has no effect and psi abilities are a result of chance occurrences (B). Note that both scatterplots show the predicted scores when feedback has NO effect on performance. The only difference between these scatterplots is that results like panel A would suggest psi abilities are real, and results like B would suggest they are not. If psi abilities are real *and* are improved by feedback, we would expect to see a significant difference between the Feedback and No Feedback conditions in our *experiment*, as explained in the caption of Figure 7.4

PROCEDURE

1. Work in pairs. One person will be the Participant (P) and the other will be the Experimenter (E) for each set of trials. After each set of 30 trials is completed, you will switch roles.

2. To counterbalance the order of the two conditions, one person in your pair will do the Feedback condition first, then the No Feedback condition, and the other person will do the No Feedback condition first, then Feedback. Flip a coin once to set up the order of these conditions before you start:

   HEADS: The order of conditions will be F → NF → NF → F.

   TAILS: The order of conditions will be NF → F → F → NF.

   BEFORE YOU BEGIN ANY DATA COLLECTION, write the conditions on the data sheet (in the gray boxes at the top of each column. The pattern should match one of the above patterns, going from left to right in the gray boxes across the top of the data sheet. You will switch roles between each set of 30 trials. Each P will end up doing one F and one NF set of trials, in randomized, opposite orders.

3. To prepare for data collection, E and P must sit facing each other, with a deck of cards on the table between them, face down. *E should keep the data sheet where it cannot be seen by P.* Remove all cards from the deck *except* aces through tens, leaving 40 cards (10 of each suit). Shuffle thoroughly without letting E or P see the numbers on the cards. Use one set of the "face cards" (the Jacks or Queens or Kings) and spread them face-up on the table in front of the participant. This will serve as a reminder of the choices available while guessing (hearts, spades, diamonds, or clubs).

4. When P is ready, E will take one card off the top of the deck and set it down on the table, face-down. NO ONE should see the face of the card. P will guess at the suit of the card (hearts, spades, diamonds, or clubs). E will record the guess on the data sheet (H, S, D or C, respectively), then only E will look at the card and record the actual suit. Be sure to keep the data sheet hidden at all times, in both conditions.

5. After recording *both* the guess and the actual suit, the next step depends on the condition:

   Feedback Condition: If the guess was correct, E says "correct," and if not, E says "incorrect." E then moves the trial card off to the side, keeping it face-down.

   No Feedback Condition: E says nothing and moves the trial card off to the side, keeping it face-down.

   Note that P never sees any of the cards, nor the data sheet itself, not even after a guess. E should be careful not to show any emotion—no excitement, disbelief, or cynicism—as the participant continues to guess. There should be no side discussion to distract from the task. Continue with the same condition for 30 consecutive guesses. Then shuffle the used cards, mixing them thoroughly with the unused cards.

6. Switch roles so that E becomes P, and P becomes E. Repeat step 4, using the opposite condition, then switch roles two more times, making sure you follow the correct order for participants and pattern for Feedback versus No Feedback, indicated at the top of each set of 30 trials.

7. *After all trials are complete*, carefully check every row of data and circle the rows where guesses matched actual suits. Do not do this while collecting data, as P might hear the sound your pen makes as you circle the row. Write the total number of hits (circled rows) at the bottom of the columns.

8. Double-check that you have written in the conditions that were used to collect data in the gray boxes at the top of each column, and either hand in your data sheet or enter your data on a Google Sheets or Excel file provided by your instructor. Begin work on the Lab Record Worksheet.

STUDY 7C DATA SHEET

Order →	**1st**	**3rd**			**2nd**	**4th**
	First Participant				Second Participant	
Condition →						
Trial	Guess	Actual		Trial	Guess	Actual
1				1		
2				2		
3				3		
4				4		
5				5		
6				6		
7				7		
8				8		
9				9		
10				10		
11				11		
12				12		
13				13		
14				14		
15				15		
16				16		
17				17		
18				18		
19				19		
20				20		
21				21		
22				22		
23				23		
24				24		
25				25		
26				26		
27				27		
28				28		
29				29		
30				30		
Total Hits (Circled Rows) =				Total Hits (Circled Rows) =		

LAB RECORD WORKSHEET FOR STUDY 7C
SKEPTICISM AND PARAPSYCHOLOGY

Name: _____ Date: _____

Partner's Name: _____

Purpose *To critically evaluate the possibility of psi phenomena by 1) asking whether receiving feedback impacts psi abilities, and 2) asking whether psi ability exists at the same levels in each person regardless of feedback. If it does, there should be a correlation between psi abilities with feedback and those without.*

Hypothesis 1 (experimental) _____

Conceptual IV _____

Operational definition of IV (what were the two levels of the IV)?

1. _____ 2. _____

Conceptual DV _____

Operational definition of DV _____

Prediction (if research Hypothesis 1 is true, what, specifically, would we expect to happen with the measurements in our experiment?): _____

_____

Hypothesis 2 (correlational) _____

Conceptual Variables 1. _____ 2. _____

Operational definitions the CVs 1. _____

2. _____

Prediction (if research Hypothesis 2 is true, what, specifically, would we expect to happen with the measurements in our experiment?) _____

_____

Method

Participants _____ *college students enrolled in introductory psychology lab participated as part of the course. Age and gender were not recorded, but most participants were between 18 and 22 years old and gender was mixed.*

Materials (list all relevant materials with brief descriptions): _____

_____

_____

_____

_____

Procedure _____

_____

_____

_____

_____

_____

Data Handling How did we summarize the data for each condition? _____

_____

What type of statistical test did we use to test Hypothesis 1? _____

What type of statistical test did we use to test Hypothesis 2? _____

Results

Hypothesis 1 _____

_____

Hypothesis 2 _____

_____

Discussion

What can we conclude from the results of our *experiment*? _____

_____

Explain the evidence for that conclusion _____

_____

If feedback does not influence psi abilities, do we have any evidence that psi abilities exist from our correlational data (circle one)?   Yes   No

Explain the evidence for your choice _____

_____   _____

_____

Circle **two** terms that best describe this research

Exploratory Research   Descriptive Research   Correlational Research

Within-Participants Experiment   Quasi-Experiment   Matching Samples Experiment

For each term you circled, explain the characteristics of our research that fit that term

1. _____

_____

2. _____

_____

MODULE 7 GLOSSARY OF TERMS AND EXAMPLES

Between-Groups Experiment: Describes an experiment that uses different participants at each **level of the independent variable.** Also called "**between-participants**" or "**between-subjects.**"

Example: Research by Albert Bandura allowed a group of children to witness an adult model beating up on an inflatable clown-doll in the room where they were playing. A different group of children played in the same room with the same toys at another time, and did not witness the adult's violent behavior. Both groups of children were later observed in a room with a variety of toys, including the inflatable clown. Those who witnessed the adult beating up on the doll displayed significantly more aggressive behavior. The **two levels of the independent variable** were exposure to the violent adult model versus no exposure to that model, and they were experienced by two different groups of children. The children were randomly assigned to one group *or* the other, so this is a between-groups, true experiment. The aggressive behavior that the children displayed (the DV) was compared *between groups* of participants.

Where to find this term: Essay 7.2, Table 7.1

Between-Participants Experiment: See **Between-Groups Experiment**

Between-Subjects Experiment: See **Between-Groups Experiment**

Bidirectionality: See Essay 4.3, Module 4 Glossary

Carryover Effects: See **order effects**.

Confounding Variable: See Essays 5.1, 5.2, 5.3, 6.1, 6.2, 6.3, Module 5 Glossary

Counterbalancing: In a **within-participants experiment**, the order in which the levels of the IV are presented must be different for different participants. For proper counterbalancing, whenever conditions of the experiment permit, all possible orders should be systematically represented across all participants and participants should be randomly assigned to complete the conditions in each possible order.

Example: Imagine a within-participants experiment to test the hypothesis that room temperature affects reaction time, with three levels of room temperature, 50°F, 70°F, and 90°F. All participants would take the same reaction time test three times, once at 50°F, once at 70°F, and once at 90°F. Since they could get better at the test each time they take it (**practice effect**) or they could get more bored/tired each time they take the test (**fatigue effect**), the order in which they are exposed to the three temperatures must be counterbalanced. There are six possible orders for three different temperatures, so one sixth of the participants should be randomly assigned to each of those six orders (50-70-90, 50-90-70, 70-50-90, 70-90-50, 90-50-70, and 90-70-50)

Where to find this term: Essay 7.4, Figure 7.2

Fatigue Effect: In **within-participants experiments**, because participants are exposed to the measurement of the DV more than once, they can get tired and get worse at it each time. If a worse score is observed the second time the DV is measured, that could be due to the fatigue, rather than the manipulation of the IV.

Example: See example given for **order effects**.

Where to find this term: Essay 7.4

Levels of the Independent Variable: See Essay 5.2, Module 5 Glossary

Mod 7 Glossary

Matched Samples: In a between-groups experiment, a technique that is designed to minimize between-group differences in the DV or some extraneous variable related to the DV. We purposefully set up the groups so that they are matched using some measure of that variable. Participants are first measured for that variable, then ranked according to their score. Starting with the top ranking, pairs of participants are split and randomly assigned to groups that then experience different levels of the IV.

> ***Example:*** To test the hypothesis that fear of flying can be decreased with her therapy technique, a researcher recruits 50 volunteers. Because they vary a lot in terms of how afraid they are of flying before the experiment, she gives them all a survey to measure their fear of flying. To match her samples (groups), she lists participants in order from the highest to the lowest fear score, and breaks this list up from top to bottom in pairs. She randomly assigns one person from each pair to be in the therapy group and the other in a no-therapy group. In this way, the groups will be closely matched in terms of their baseline fear of flying, but still randomly assigned to different groups.
>
> ***Where to find this term:*** Essay 7.3, Table 7.1

Order Effects: In a ***within-participants experiment***, the order of exposure to different levels of the IV can become a ***confounding variable***. Order effects can improve performance each time the participant is exposed to a new level of the independent variable (***practice effect***), or they can impair performance each time (***fatigue effect***).

> ***Example:*** In an experiment designed to test the hypothesis that the presence of a female observer improves men's free-throw basketball performance, a female is counting the number of baskets made as each participant throws 20 times. That experimenter is then called away under pretense of an important phone call and a male experimenter takes her place. Researchers predict males will make more baskets for the female experimenter than for the male. Because every participant did free throws with the female first, and then the male, the researchers should be concerned about order effects. If the hypothesis appears to be supported, it could be due to a fatigue effect (arms got tired after the first 20 throws). To avoid this confounding variable, one half of the participants should see the female experimenter first, and one half should see the male experimenter first (see ***counterbalancing***).
>
> ***Where to find this term:*** Essay 7.4

Practice Effect: In ***within-participants experiments***, because participants are exposed to the measurement of the DV more than once, they can get better at it. Thus, if a better score is observed the second time the DV is measured, the effect of the purposeful manipulation of the conditions is confounded with the effect of practice.

> ***Example:*** See example given for ***order effects***.
>
> ***Where to find this term:*** Essay 7.4

Repeated Measures: See ***within-participants experiment***

Self-Selection: See Essay 6.1, Module 6 Glossary

Significant Difference: See Essays 5.3, 5.4, Module 5 Glossary

Third Variable: See Essay 4.3, Module 4 Glossary

Validity: See Essay 2.2, Module 2 Glossary

Within-Participants Experiment: Describes an experiment that uses the same participants at each level of the independent variable. Also called "repeated measures."

Example: An experiment by Vliek and Rotteveel (2012) tested the hypothesis that "when time flies, people are more likely to assess the experience positively than when time drags." All participants were asked to assess the emotion expressed on individually presented faces, and were told that the faces would be presented on a computer screen for 8 sec each. In truth, sometimes the faces were shown for only 6 sec (the "time flies" condition), and sometimes they were shown for 10 sec (the "time drags" condition). People rated the same faces more positively when they were only viewed for 6 sec, compared to when they were viewed for 10 sec. Because each participant experienced both the "time flies" and the "time drags" conditions, this was a within-participants experiment. Ratings of faces were compared for each time condition *within* participants. In other words, there were *repeated measures* of face ratings.

Where to find this term: Essay 7.4, Table 7.1

Frankenphobia: the inability to focus on today's experiment because last week's is sneaking up on you.

Image © Cartoonresource/Shutterstock

Module 8
The Next Steps: Designing, Interpreting, and Reporting Research

MODULE 8 LEARNING OBJECTIVES CHART

ESSAY NUMBER	MODULE 8 ESSAY LEARNING OBJECTIVES	BEFORE READING				AFTER READING			
		I don't know how 1	I know a little about this 2	I know enough about this to guess correctly 3	I know how to do this and/ or have already done it. 4	I don't know how 1	I know a little about this 2	I know enough about this to guess correctly 3	I know how to do this and/ or have already done it. 4
8.1 8.3	Give two examples of complex research designs that can be built from the simple designs you have learned previously.								
8.2	Explain how adding predictions to a study affects the probability of accidentally supporting a research hypothesis that is not true.								
8.2	Explain how an overall comparison helps reduce inflated error rate.								
8.3	Distinguish between a one-way experiment and a two-way experiment.								
8.3	Explain the difference between a main effect and an interaction effect.								
8.4	Debunk the "common sense problem" in psychology.								
8.4	Debunk the "artificiality problem" in psychology.								
8.4	Debunk the "I am not a rat" problem" in psychology.								

		I don't know how 1	I know a little about this 2	I know enough about this to guess correctly 3	I know how to do this and/ or have already done it. 4	I don't know how 1	I know a little about this 2	I know enough about this to guess correctly 3	I know how to do this and/ or have already done it. 4
8.5	Explain how connectivity, replicability, integrity, and convergence guide science.								
8.5	Explain how connectivity, replicability, integrity, and convergence should be expressed in the four content sections of a formal scientific report.								
		Read the assigned essays and actively seek answers to any questions rated less than "4." Then return to this chart and complete the white half.				Now proceed to the chart for the applications section, read the objectives for your assigned research project, and complete the gray side.			

ESSAY 8.1

BUILDING MORE COMPLEX EXPERIMENTS

In Modules 5, 6, and 7, we tested cause-and-effect hypotheses with true experiments and quasi-experiments in which a single independent variable was manipulated at two levels (experimental and control) and the effect of that manipulation was measured in only one way. Browsing the published research literature in psychology, you'll quickly discover that this type of simple, two-group comparison with just one measurement of the effect is rare. The vast majority of experiments in psychology are more complex. Most have more than two levels of the IV, more than one DV or operational definition of the DV, or some combination of these. Many published experiments have two

or more independent variables. Essay 8.3 describes why that is sometimes necessary to test a hypothesis, and how it can be done without confounding variables. Sometimes, in the same experiment, one IV is tested with a *between-groups* design, while another is simultaneously tested *within-participants.* Sometimes, one IV is experimental and another is quasi-experimental. The number of possible combinations of the tools presented in Modules 1 through 7 is limited only by human imagination.

Table 8.1 shows some examples of more complex research designs, all of which lead to multiple comparisons testing the same hypothesis: that eating

Table 8.1 Examples of Ways that One Could Test the Hypothesis that Eating Chocolate Makes Children Hyperactive, with Research Designs Leading to Multiple Comparisons

Design Possibilities	Examples				Possible Multiple Comparisons
More than two levels of the IV	**Amount of Chocolate**				Kids in the no-chocolate group will show less hyperactivity than the 24-ounce group and the 12-ounce group, but not compared to the 48-ounce group, since they could be feeling sick.
	No chocolate	12 ounces	24 ounces	48 ounces	
	40 kids	40 kids	40 kids	40 kids	
More than one operational definition of the DV	Hyperactivity could be measured by: 1. the number of times a child's buttocks leaves his/her chair. 2. the number of times a child's head moves. 3. the number of times a child speaks out of turn.				Chocolate will affect the ability to sit still and the number of times a child's head moves, but will not affect speaking out of turn.
More than one conceptual IV		No Chocolate		24 ounces	Chocolate will affect younger kids, but not older kids. Or, it will affect young kids more than it affects older kids (age of students is a quasi-experimental variable—see Module 6)
	Second Graders	40 kids		40 kids	
	Eighth Graders	40 kids		40 kids	
More than one conceptual DV	The hypothesis could be that chocolate affects both hyperactivity and mood.				Chocolate will make kids generally happier, but also more active.

chocolate makes children hyperactive. Rather than just compare chocolate to no chocolate, a researcher could ask how much chocolate is needed to see an effect on hyperactivity by doing a true between-groups experiment with four groups (no chocolate, 12 oz, 24 oz, or 48 oz). The same experiment could use multiple measures of hyperactivity. An experiment with two IVs could ask whether chocolate affects 2nd graders and 8th graders differently. Or, a researcher could expand the hypothesis to include effects of chocolate on moods, in addition to testing effects on hyperactivity. These are just a few possibilities...

Designing research is like building with Lego ® bricks. The techniques and terms you have learned in this course are a good starter set, and there are countless ways to combine them into new ideas and projects. You now have enough bricks to allow you to design a scientific test of your own idea about human behavior, and you might have the chance to do so in this Module (Study 8D), or in future psychology coursework. If you have the curiosity and the drive to learn more, you will find more blocks in a variety of shapes and colors as you explore psychology. Of course, you must follow the ethical guidelines presented in Essay 6.2 by getting IRB approval for your research before you begin. But even if you never collect behavioral data again, the skills you have learned here will be helpful in critically evaluating at least some of the scientific research that crosses your path, wherever that path leads.

Since more complicated experimental designs are the norm, this module provides more information to help you think critically about the next level of research design and interpretation. Applications in this module are all experiments with more than one specific prediction. To properly interpret that research, we must first understand how adding predictions affects the objective decision-making process.

ESSAY 8.2

ADDING PREDICTIONS ALTERS OBJECTIVE DECISION MAKING

Back in Essay 5.2, you may have read about an experiment testing the hypothesis that *classical music improves math performance*. It was a simple, between-groups study where one group of children was exposed to classical music for 3 hours per day, while the other group was not, and all the children were given a math test. Questions were raised about whether this was the best way to test the hypothesis. If the classical music group did better on the math test than the no-music (control) group, could we conclude that it was the classical nature of the music, or might any music at all improve math performance? A suggested improvement was to expose several groups of children to different kinds of music, and compare math test scores among all those groups, rather than just compare classical music to no music. At the time, we said that this would add complications to the interpretation of our results and left it at that. Now it's time to deal with those complications.

Each experimental outcome we've observed so far has been *statistically tested* based on the odds of seeing it happen when the null hypothesis is true. In every case, we predicted a difference between two groups or conditions and then calculated the magnitude of the observed difference. We asked, assuming the null hypothesis was true, what were the odds that we would see that much of a difference? If the odds were low (less than 5% chance), we rejected the null and claimed support for our research hypothesis. There was one hypothesis, one prediction, and one odds-based test of the outcome.

But if we revised the classical music experiment to better test the hypothesis that it is the classical nature of the music that improves math performance, not just any music, then our single hypothesis would lead to several predictions: Children in the classical music group would be expected to perform better than children in the control group (that's 1). The classical music group would also be expected to perform better than a rock music group (2), a country music group (3), a rap music group (4), or a jazz group (5). We could add more different types of music, but we already have five predictions from one hypothesis!

So what? Isn't information like friendship? The more, the merrier? Unfortunately, multiple predictions in the same study can pose a problem for our objective decision-making process, because *probability* is the basis on which we decide whether each prediction is supported.

Although it is an oversimplification, the problem can best be understood with an example from dice-tossing. Suppose you predict, before tossing one die, "I'm going to roll a 1." You have a 1 in 6 chance of being correct (about 0.17). But if you make three predictions, saying, "I'm going to roll a 1 or a 2 or a 3," there is now a 3 in 6 chance that at least one prediction will be correct. You have just increased the chances that the outcome will support your prediction, from a 17% chance to a 50% chance! (notice how the odds of each prediction separately add up to the odds for any one of them happening: 0.17 for a "1," plus 0.17 for a "2," plus 0.17 for a "3" ≈ 0.50). Instinctively, you can see how each prediction you make increases the chances that at least one of your predictions will happen, just by chance. Of course, if you predict that you will roll a 1, 2, 3, 4, 5, or 6, you have a 100% chance of being right

As noted, the example above is an oversimplification, but like the roll of a die, each time we test the null hypothesis, we are trying to determine the likelihood of seeing a truly random event turn out in a particular, predicted way (under the null hypothesis, observations should be truly random, not predictable). We must remember that every "statistically significant" outcome (prediction) has up to a 5% chance of happening just by chance when the null hypothesis is true, meaning we have a 5% chance of being *wrong* to reject the null hypothesis. We accept that risk when we apply our decision rule. But if we make *multiple* predictions, and *each one* has a 5% chance of being wrong, those chances of being wrong increase quickly! They don't exactly add up like the dice example because they are independent decisions, but the basic idea is similar (see Appendix A for an explanation of the difference).

Consider again our experiment on classical music. Suppose we compared classical music to no music, jazz, rock, rap, and country. In this case, we have six groups and five predicted differences, comparing each other type of music to classical. For *each prediction*, our chances of wrongly rejecting the null hypothesis are 5%. Assuming the null hypothesis is true, and the children in different groups have absolutely no reason to perform differently on their math test, we would still have a 23% chance of finding a significant difference supporting at least one prediction! Using the "adding rule" described for the dice, 5% for each of five predictions would be 25%, but the adding rule doesn't exactly apply to hypothesis testing, so the actual risk of being wrong would be about 23%.[1]

In summary, when designing experiments, we have to remember that *the more predictions we make about how a random data set will turn out, the more likely it is that one of those predictions will be observed, not because it reflects the truth about the research hypothesis, but just by chance alone.* This increases our chance of concluding that there is a real difference when in fact, there is not. In making just five simple comparisons, we went from having a 5% (1 in 20) chance of being wrong to having a 23% (nearly 1 in 4) chance of being wrong! This **inflated error rate** is not an acceptable standard for falsification.

Thankfully, there are several ways around this problem. One approach is to use an **overall comparison**. Rather than test each difference between any two groups with one comparison at a time, it tests whether there are any differences at all among multiple groups, simultaneously.

The reason this works is because it substitutes one single odds-based decision in place of several. In an experiment with three conditions, labeled A, B, and C, you could ask, under the assumption that the null hypothesis is true, "What are the odds I'd see this much of a difference between A and B?" Or "...between B and C?" Or, "...between A and C?" Or you could ask just one question: "What are the odds that any of these three conditions would differ this much from any of

---

[1] Statistically, the probability of wrongly rejecting the null hypothesis for multiple comparisons is not as simple as adding the individual probabilities, because we are no longer dealing with just one decision. Instead, we are now dealing with multiple, independent decisions. It's more like asking, what are the chances of getting at least one "3" on two rolls of the die? Each roll is an independent event, so we can't just add the probabilities; we have to take a different approach. Appendix A has more information on how to calculate the probability of one thing happening in multiple independent events, including rolls of the die and accidental rejections of the null hypothesis.

the others?" That's what the overall comparison does. If the overall comparison is significant, then there is almost always at least one difference among the conditions. We still won't know where that difference is, but the significant overall comparison has revealed that a difference exists somewhere among our groups. And because it is just one decision, it only has a 5% chance of being wrong, no matter how many specific predictions it is combining.

It's a clever little bit of statistical reasoning, to say the least. But we have to follow the rules of probability. If the overall comparison is not significant, we're not allowed to keep hunting for differences! *Only if the overall comparison is significant* can we make further comparisons to see which specific groups differ from one another. Comparisons made after a significant overall statistical test are often called *pairwise comparisons,* because we are pairing off each of our conditions and testing to see which differences are significant. We still have to be concerned about the inflated error rate problem (there is a limit to the number of further comparisons we

can make) but the problem is less drastic, since we're now reasonably sure that at least one significant difference exists.

Another popular way of correcting for inflated error rate is called the Bonferroni correction. It's quite simple: We divide our required p-value for significance (.05) by the number of comparisons we want to make. For example, if we want to make five comparisons in the same study, we would decide ahead of time that we're only going to reject the null hypothesis for any one decision if the probability of getting that result is less than .01, rather than .05 (.05 ÷ 5 decisions = .01). In some types of research, the Bonferroni correction works well, but in others, it can be overly cautious and makes us too likely to dismiss our research hypothesis when it is, in fact, true.

The important point to remember from this essay is that when we design more complex research, we have to be aware of the inflated error rate that comes with multiple predictions, and do our best to correct it, or we risk accidentally reporting misinformation about support for our research hypothesis.

ESSAY 8.3

EXPERIMENTS WITH TWO IVs[2]

In our previous experiments, we have investigated cause-and-effect relationships by manipulating an IV and measuring the effects on the DV. But life is complicated, and relationships often interact. That is, whether or not a cause (variable A) has an effect (on variable B) can depend on the presence of some other variable (C). If C is treated as an extraneous variable, we do our best to hold it constant while we manipulate A and measure B. However, if we want to test the idea that variable C influences the effect of A on B, we can do that with one experiment. Rather than keeping variable C constant, we can systematically manipulate it, so that we manipulate both A and C and measure B. In other words, we can design an experiment with more than one IV. Experiments with two IVs are called *two-way*

experiments; if there are three IVs, it is a *three-way* experiment. Studies 8A and 8B are *one-way experiments*; each has three levels of one IV. Study 8C is a *two-way experiment* with two levels of each IV.

Doing a two-way experiment is a lot like doing two "mini-experiments" at the same time, with the same DV. We can still statistically test differences in a way that will tell us the effect of each IV alone, as though we did two separate experiments. But the advantage of combining them into a single experiment is that we can gain valuable insight into how these two IVs might interact. Does the effect of one variable depend on the presence or absence of the other variable? The ability to answer this question is the main reason we design experiments with more than one IV.

---

[2] Please pardon the pun in the banner image. This essay is about independent variables, not intravenous medications. See Study 6B for research on humor styles.

This is best explained with an example. Suppose we have a new drug, "X," which is hypothesized to decrease cholesterol. We've also been told that regular exercise decreases cholesterol. As you know, to test both claims, we could do two separate experiments.

SKILL CHECK

Review the terminology (answers are in Appendix B):

1. To test the hypothesis that Drug X decreases cholesterol…
   a. What would be our IV? _____
   b. What might be two levels of the IV? _____
   c. What would be our DV? _____
2. To test the hypothesis that exercise decreases cholesterol…
   a. What would be our IV? _____
   b. What might be two levels of the IV? _____
   c. What would be our DV? _____

But suppose we hypothesize that Drug X will *only* decrease cholesterol *if* the patients exercise regularly. Those two experiments alone would tell us nothing about whether *combining* Drug X and exercise decreases cholesterol more than either one alone. We might be tempted to try four experiments:

1. Test Drug X versus placebo in exercising patients (the placebo looks like Drug X but is inert)
2. Test Drug X versus placebo in nonexercising patients
3. Test exercise versus no exercise in patients who are all on Drug X
4. Test exercise versus no exercise in patients who are all on a placebo

Let's assume this would require 100 participants per group (diet and lifestyle vary a lot in humans; all this variability requires many more participants in order to detect differences due to the drug or the exercise, if differences exist). That's 200 participants per study, times 4 studies, which is 800 participants. If you've ever tried to collect signatures for a petition, you know how difficult it can be just to get people to sign their name to a cause; imagine trying to find 800 people who are willing to participate in your research by taking an untested drug and/or exercising daily!

But there is another fundamental problem with performing four separate experiments: We could not test the hypothesis that the effects of Drug X *depend on whether or not the patient is exercising.* Here's why: Suppose the outcome of experiment 1 shows a *p*-value of .04, and the outcome of experiment 2 has a *p*-value of .11. We would conclude that Drug X decreased cholesterol in exercising patients, and that it did not decrease cholesterol in patients who were *not* exercising. But is there a real difference in the way the drug worked for exercising versus nonexercising participants?

Remember, we based our decision about whether the drug works on probability. Notice that the only

difference between concluding that the drug worked and that it did *not* is on which side of 0.05 our *p*-value falls. Is there a real difference between probabilities of .04 and .11? Unless those differences are part of the same experiment, we can't statistically compare them. Even doing experiments 3 and 4 would not allow us to ask whether Drug X makes *more* of a difference in exercisers than it does in nonexercisers. We cannot statistically test this question with separate experiments.

In cases where we want to hypothesize that two IVs interact (the effect of one IV is different for different levels of the other IV) we need a ***two-way design***, where we can *systematically* manipulate the two IVs in the same experiment. In this case, we would manipulate *both* the level of Drug X and the level of exercise. The design of this two-way experiment is shown in Figure 8.1.

This solves both of the problems we faced when doing four separate experiments. First, we no longer need 800 participants. In a single experiment with only 400 participants, we now have 200 people who get Drug X and 200 who do not. We also have 200 people who exercise and 200 who do not. Since the proportion of exercisers to nonexercisers is the same

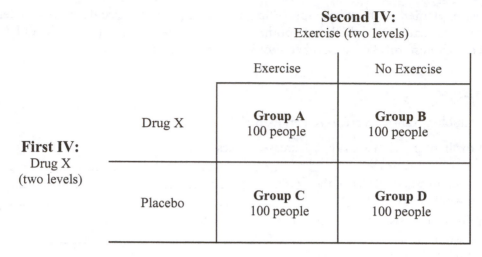

Figure 8.1   Research design for a two-way experiment testing the hypothesis that Drug X decreases cholesterol more for people who exercise than for those who do not.

for those taking Drug X as it is for those not taking it, we can think of exercise as an extraneous variable that is balanced across drug treatment groups and ignore it when we test for the effect of Drug X alone on cholesterol. That is, we can statistically compare the 200 participants who got Drug X (all those in Groups A and B together) to the 200 participants who did not (all those in Groups C and D together). When we test for the effect of either IV alone, ignoring the manipulation of the other IV, we're looking for a *main effect*. In this case, we would be testing for the main effect of the

drug. Likewise, we can statistically test the main effect of exercise on cholesterol by comparing the average cholesterol levels of all 200 participants who exercised (Groups A and C combined) to the 200 participants who did not exercise (Groups B and D combined).

We have not lost our ability to answer the questions posed by Experiments 1 through 4 on the previous page, either. For example, Experiment 1, which tests Drug X versus placebo in exercising participants, can be statistically tested by comparing group A to group C.

SKILL CHECK

What groups would you compare to perform Experiments 2 through 4? (Answers in Appendix B)

Compare Groups

2. Test Drug X versus placebo in nonexercising patients _____ to _____
3. Test exercise versus no exercise in patients who are all on Drug X _____ to _____
4. Test exercise versus no exercise in patients who are all on a placebo _____ to _____

These comparisons between the individual groups in Figure 8.1 are called "simple effects." So in a single two-way design with two levels of each IV, we can do four experiments on simple effects, plus two experiments on main effects, all in *one* experiment with *half as many* participants! But wait! It gets even better...

This approach will also allow us to test the *interaction hypothesis*: the idea that the effect of Drug X is significantly stronger in people who exercise than in people who don't (recall the question of whether a *p*-value of .04 is different from a *p*-value of .11). It's like a simple, two-group experiment that is tested in two different conditions so that we can compare how it works in one condition with how it works in another. We're testing the same hypothesis (that Drug X decreases cholesterol) under two different conditions (one with exercising patients and one with nonexercising patients). If the results with exercising patients significantly differ from the results with non-exercising patients, that's called an *interaction effect*. In a significant interaction, the results from the test of one IV are significantly different when tested at different levels of a second IV.

As you can see, there are some new terms and new ways of thinking associated with the two-way design, but they all stem from what we already know about experiments with only one IV. These concepts will become clearer if you go on in psychology or another science, but for now, it is sufficient to realize that we are not limited to experiments with one IV, and that more complicated relationships among variables can be studied in a single experiment.

This brief introduction to more complex designs leaves out many other statistical considerations, but that will be true of any introduction. At this point, you have what you need to understand the basics of how psychological science is done. Our last two goals for this module, and for this course, are to address three common complaints about research in psychology and to provide information that will help you find, interpret and critically evaluate published research.

ESSAY 8.4

"THE PROBLEM WITH RESEARCH IN PSYCHOLOGY IS . . ."

When people meet for the first time at social gatherings, they often turn to the standard conversation-starter, "What do you do?" meaning, "What is your profession?" For almost 20 years, I have been pleased to reply with, "I teach psychology." But I am not always pleased at the conversations that follow. People have said things like, "I find so much of psychology to be common sense." And, if we get into the subject of research in psychology, they say, "But what happens in the lab can't be applied to real life." And my personal favorite, as an animal behaviorist, is when people say, "It's funny that psychology studies rats… Humans are nothing like rats!"

What's "funny" is that people share these opinions with complete confidence that anyone who studies psychology *must* feel the same way, and they are generally surprised when I disagree. I don't take offense or get angry—they're not intentionally being disrespectful—their only experience with psychology might be the way the media present it, which (sadly) lacks perspective and is full of misconceptions.

Because psychology is largely about humans and how they think and act, and everyone, being human, is at least a little qualified to speak and write on these subjects, the public is often misled by untested claims presented as fact. These misconceptions are compounded by a general lack of knowledge about how science is done, which easily morphs into the belief that psychology is either not a science or is somehow different from other sciences.

In Essay 1.1, we encouraged you to continue thinking about the extent to which psychology belongs among the sciences. By now, we hope you have realized that it is as much a science as biology or chemistry. The content is more personal, more nuanced, and perhaps less amenable to our attempts to pin it down for study, but these challenges should not stop us from trying. Indeed, they might be a temptation to ambitious scientists. Whether or not you will study more psychology yourself, we hope that you will leave this course with the knowledge and conviction to dispel common misconceptions if ever and whenever you hear them in casual conversation. Toward that end, the three misconceptions mentioned above are addressed here:

THE "COMMON SENSE" PROBLEM

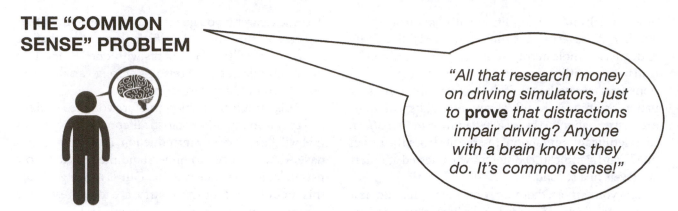

*"All that research money on driving simulators, just to **prove** that distractions impair driving? Anyone with a brain knows they do. It's common sense!"*

First, as you, the student of psychology, are now well-aware, we aren't trying to "prove" anything. In the example of research being criticized here, we seek evidence to test the idea that distractions impair driving performance.

It is true that a distraction, by definition, diverts attention away from another task. But many drivers claim they can do other things while driving because they are on "autopilot." They say it's common sense: they've been driving for so long, they can do it without thinking. Is that even possible? Our so-called "common sense" research has determined that for the vast majority of people, it is not. Without this research, it would be more difficult to pass laws that save lives.

Furthermore, while some might think it is "common sense" that hands-free phones are less distracting than hand-held phones, research in psychology has shown that this is not the case. Perhaps your own research in Study 7B found that conversation, even without holding a phone, impacted reaction times. These are testable questions, and basing our answers on actual observations rather than "common sense" might save lives.

Before one suggests that scientists are wasting time and money testing common sense ideas, one should first ask, "What defines common sense?" Although the term implies otherwise, "common sense" is not common to every situation or person. It is most often whatever sense best fits the situation in hindsight, and is rarely able to predict what will happen in a new situation.

Assume, for example, Jack and Jill started dating during their senior year in high school, but Jill's parents disapproved and decided to keep them apart by moving to a different city. You might think it's common sense, "absence makes the heart grow fonder," and predict that they will find a way to stay in touch, maybe run away together, or maybe even elope in Vegas. But common sense also says, "Out of sight, out of mind." So maybe they will eventually meet new friends and start dating other people. The common sense explanation we call to mind will depend on whether Jack and Jill eventually eloped or fell out of touch. Waiting until after an event happens to explain what caused it is not a practical way to make "predictions." It is generally not useful, and it is not science.

THE "ARTIFICIALITY" PROBLEM

"You can't study human behavior in a lab. It's so contrived and artificial! People in a lab don't behave the way they would in the real world."

Admittedly, there are some questions in psychology that are better answered with "field research" (i.e., research conducted in natural settings). And there are many (many!) field studies in psychology. But the fact that one cannot perfectly recreate an exact replica of a real airplane full of passengers in a laboratory should not preclude a laboratory study of how pilots handle stressful situations. Critics point to the lack of real-life complications in these laboratory studies and say, "that won't apply in real life—it's a contrived situation." This criticism stems from a lack of understanding that the goal of all true experiments is to test the existence of real cause-and-effect relationships, and this requires manipulation and control. We cannot manipulate the IV and control extraneous variables without creating a situation that is at least partially contrived.

This "problem" is not unique to psychology; experiments in all areas of science create artificial situations to test ideas. Chemists, for example, typically use purified chemicals that do not exist in pure form in nature. Most would not dismiss the chemist's conclusions on the basis that the research was artificial, or that it doesn't apply to chemical reactions in the real world. Yet, psychological research is often dismissed for being artificial or contrived. Maybe this is due to the normal human tendency to reject or ignore evidence that challenges our previously held beliefs, or maybe people hold more deep-rooted beliefs about human behavior than they do about chemistry. Regardless, in psychology, just as in other sciences, what is exposed by artificial manipulation is not necessarily artificial, particularly if it can also be seen to apply in naturally occurring situations. Evidence from each experiment is just one piece of the puzzle that scientists use to collaboratively assemble an understanding of reality.

THE "I AM NOT A RAT" PROBLEM

Ahhhhh...

SQUEAK?

"Humans are so much more sophisticated than other animals! You can't learn anything about human behavior by studying rats!"

Many books have been devoted to what we can learn about ourselves by studying rats and other animals. Most colleges have courses devoted to the study of animal behavior. In my own view (as an animal behaviorist), taking other animals out of the study of human behavior and cognition would be like trying to understand international government and law without any research on history or cultures. It is perhaps possible, but would be missing a great deal of coherence and context.

Many psychologists study nonhuman animals. Some are simply interested in why animals do the things they do and/or how certain behaviors evolve (animal behaviorists and evolutionary psychologists). This type of research, with the goal of understanding more about a particular subject, is often called *basic research*. Others seek to improve the care and conservation of nonhuman animals, to find better ways to train them, or to improve agricultural practices. This is called *applied research* because it is designed to provide information that can be directly applied to specific problems.

Though they have different goals, basic and applied research are not mutually exclusive because information obtained with either goal in mind can simultaneously achieve the other goal. That is, basic research often ends up finding applications that were not foreseen by the researchers, and applied research often leads to better basic understanding of the natural world. Whether basic or applied, many psychologists study nonhuman animals when their research questions cannot practically or ethically be answered with human participants. Like medical science, behavioral science is helped tremendously by a better understanding through the study of simpler systems.

Rats, in particular, are an excellent animal model for behavioral research because like humans, they are social and intelligent—they can solve problems and respond quickly to training—and their physiology is quite similar to human physiology. They enjoy interactions with humans and other species, and even laugh when tickled (though you need special equipment to hear the laughter). For all these reasons, we can learn so much from studying their behavior.[3]

---

[3] For the same reasons, they also make wonderful pets. I currently have four. Their names are Quirky, Dumbo, Oreo, and Steve. Unfortunately, they only live about 3-4 years. R.I.P: Ubu, Eliza, Schnookie, Hokio, Remy, Doof, & Schmirtz.

As with human studies, before we do any type of animal research, it is important to consider the ethical implications. This is perhaps even more important in animal studies because they cannot speak up for their own interests or give us their informed consent to participate. You will find the APA's guidelines for ethical research on nonhuman animals at the following link:

apa.org/science/leadership/care/guidelines.aspx

ESSAY 8.5

READING AND WRITING SCIENTIFIC REPORTS: CONNECTIVITY, REPLICABILITY, INTEGRITY, AND CONVERGENCE

We end as we began, with an emphasis on science as a collective endeavor. None of what we do as scientists actually contributes to science until it is publicly communicated and scrutinized. It is through this process that we gain a better understanding of the natural world, and it all depends on our ability to clearly and accurately report our work.

The introduction to Study1B explains how to use a psychology research database called PsycInfo to find examples of published research in psychology on any topic of interest to you. Here, we will focus on what you should be looking for as you read published research and how to write about your own research.

As in any profession, there are standards and expectations for reporting in science. The types of required content and formats for presenting them have evolved over many years of public scientific discourse, and while the formats continue to evolve, the required content remains essentially the same: **Introduction, Method, Results,** and **Discussion**. The centered, bold headings that you have seen repeated on most of your Lab Record Worksheets should have already given you a basic sense of the types of content that are appropriate to each of these sections of a formal lab report: An introduction includes a brief description of the purpose, hypothesis, and predictions. The Method section includes detailed descriptions of participants, materials, and procedures. Results are a

statistical description of what was observed, and Discussions include comments on how the results can be interpreted. While many of the details in a Lab Record necessary in a scientific report, they are not sufficient.

The main reason for completing Lab Record Worksheets was to practice articulating the relevant aspects of your research. But a formal scientific report is so much more than the content of a lab record. It is a tribute to a long tradition of acknowledging the work of others in the formation of our ideas, clearly expressing the procedures we followed in testing our ideas, reporting our observations with precision, and encouraging continued study and dialogue.

The four content sections are intimately linked to four guiding principles of scientific inquiry: *connectivity, replicability, integrity, and convergence*. Familiarity with the meaning of these principles and how they should be followed will help you critically evaluate published research and improve your own scientific reporting.

So let's assume you've done some impressive research and you want to publish it. Or, you need to write about a research project in APA style to meet the requirements for a course. It might help to think of the four parts of a report with this simple rhyme: "Why, how, what, and wow!" The Introduction tells *why* the work was important; the Method tells *how* you collected data, the Results tell *what* you observed, and the Discussion (wow) impresses your reader with the meaning and importance of it all. Your goal is to follow the guiding principles as you fill in the details of that little rhyme.

As a whole, the introduction should provide a strong answer to the question of "why:" a *rationale* that convinces the reader the author of the report had *good reasons* for doing the research that is being reported, and those reasons must recognize and credit the work of other scientists. The guiding principle is to establish the **connectivity** of your research to previous knowledge on the topic and to the broader context from which the hypothesis was derived. Often, the author's own previous work will be cited, but it is never the only work mentioned.

The principle of connectivity does not mean that all new science must *agree* with other scientists to be accepted. It simply states that good science does not come from an empty space—it emerges from a culture of previous knowledge. It doesn't have to agree with that culture, but it does have to know about it. Often, the work of other scientists sparks disagreement, and this is the point of connection. A lack of connectivity in the introduction should be a warning to the skeptical reader that the research might be based more on assumptions than on previous knowledge. The introduction ends with a paragraph or two about the hypothesis, how it was tested, and the predictions, all of which should logically flow from the rationale and connections to previous research.

The **Method** section of a scientific report answers the question of "how" by providing the *relevant* details of data collection. Figuring out what is relevant is not as easy as it might seem, especially when you're just starting out as a researcher. Following the principle of **replicability,** your goal is to include details that were unique to your research and may have influenced your results, so that any interested reader could follow your procedure and expect to replicate your results.

The Method section is often (though not always) broken down into the same three subsections you've seen so many times on your Lab Record Worksheets: *Participants*, *Materials*, and *Procedure*. The *Participants* subsection describes their relevant characteristics, including how many there were, how they were selected or recruited and whether they were compensated for their participation. The *Materials* subsection describes what was used to collect data, particularly anything unique to the study, like surveys, inventories, equipment or software. The *Procedure* subsection should focus on how data were collected, including what participants experienced, what they were asked to do, and in what order. Some researchers include information on how data were summarized and statistically analyzed as part of the procedure, while others include this as part of the Results section, and still others insert it as a separate "Data Analysis" subsection, within the Method section.

A thorough critique of a published Method section requires a fairly advanced level of experience with research designs and statistical techniques, but at a basic level, consumers of science should be able to tell when a research article is missing important information, such as the number, age and gender identity of the participants, how they were recruited, and whether they were compensated, particularly in research where compensation might affect how participants behaved in the study.

The **Results** section answers the what-questions. What happened in your study? What was observed? What was statistically significant and what was not? Although **integrity** is a guiding principle for all aspects of scientific research—the purpose of science is, after all, to collectively figure out the truth—it is particularly useful to think about this principle as we write or read a **Results** section. Results must provide an accurate account of precisely what was observed in the data, and the outcome of the statistical analysis that was the true test of the hypothesis. Due to the probabilistic nature of the evidence, honesty is critical in analyzing and reporting the results. A "significant" p-value ($< .05$) that was discovered by surfing through the data with no specific predictions must not be reported as evidence for a hypothesis.

Back in Module 4, we said that looking at the data *before* stating the predictions would be tantamount to flipping a coin first, then claiming that because it landed on heads, you have evidence that you knew it was going to be heads all along. The *evidence* relies on making the prediction *before* seeing the data. "Predictions" that come after we see the data are not predictions at all, nor are they evidence; they are merely descriptions of observed patterns, and must be reported as such. Without the integrity to report these things honestly, researchers may find that their results are not replicable.

Skeptical readers will therefore pay close attention to the description of how the data were analyzed. If the author says that a statistical test was performed *because of an observed pattern in the data*, then the results of that statistical test should not be taken as evidence for or against the hypothesis, no matter how the researcher interprets them in the Discussion. Statistical analyses performed after the data were seen *can* be used to suggest further examination of an idea, but not as evidence for that idea.

Another definition of the word integrity is the quality of being whole and uncompromised. A container with no leaks has integrity. A well-written Results section should include all relevant observations (even those that might not support the hypothesis) and not let interpretations leak in and contaminate the objectivity of those observations. Scientists are independent thinkers, and may want to decide for themselves whether your observations support your hypothesis. If they want to know the author's interpretation of the results, they'll turn to the Discussion section. Although some scientific reports will combine the Results and Discussion sections, this is not the norm. In general, there should be no interpretations of the *meaning* of the results in a Results section.

In the **Discussion**, the author shares that "wow" feeling that was experienced when the results were first discovered. Imagine that moment as a scientist: You've poured all your time and energy into testing an idea, and now you know something that no one else knows. Wow, right? You are called by your profession to share the new knowledge you've created and to explain what you think it means. Although the Discussion section must describe the observations, it should do so within the context of interpreting their meaning. It should *not* simply repeat the results; instead, the focus is on the new knowledge that is gained, while backing up that new knowledge with specific observations from the results that support the claims.

The goal, in accordance with the principle of **convergence,** is to pull together your (new) evidence with the existing body of evidence for or against the hypothesis, and explain where the new information from your research fits into the current knowledge on the topic. The hypothesis itself should be a clear and central theme.

Often, readers of scientific reports skip right to the Discussion to see what the authors are thinking and why, then go back to other parts of the paper for more details to decide whether they agree. It is therefore important, in the first paragraph of a Discussion, to make the hypothesis clear, and to use plain language in describing the observations that support or refute it, not technical lingo that is only meaningful to people who've read the whole paper or have experience in the field.

Beyond that, if results differed from specific predictions or did not support the hypothesis, testable explanations for the differences should be presented. Limitations of the current study, in terms of research design, potential confounding variables, and/or generalizability of the findings, should also be discussed. Where possible, other published research that provides insight into these concerns should be referenced.

As scientists, we are attempting, through our Discussion sections, to collaborate with other scientists, to open a dialogue of coactive and competing explanations that will converge on the best hypotheses. Taken together, what does the body of research, including this study, suggest about the hypothesis and related ideas, and the bigger context to which the hypothesis contributes? How do other hypotheses on this subject compare? Do the current observations agree or disagree with other hypotheses? If there are disagreements, the discussion should attempt to explain them. Do the differences suggest that a change in thinking might be warranted? The answers to these questions may become the basis for future research, which is usually the closing topic of a good Discussion section.

Future research is also the perfect segue to one final note from me to you...

Long after you leave this course, and whether or not you major in psychology, you will continue to see reports of research in this field, if not in scientific journals, then certainly in the popular media. I hope your experiences in this lab course will leave you with the skills and knowledge needed to critically evaluate those reports, to understand the basics of the science behind them, and to appreciate the "wow" moments behind each new discovery.

MODULE 8 RESEARCH LEARNING OBJECTIVES CHART

STUDY NUMBER	MODULE 8 RESEARCH LEARNING OBJECTIVES	BEFORE READING					AFTER DOING PROJECT			
		I don't know how 1	I know a little about this 2	I know enough about this to guess correctly 3	I know how to do this and/ or have already done it. 4		I don't know how 1	I know a little about this 2	I know enough about this to guess correctly 3	I know how to do this and/ or have already done it. 4
8A	Describe Craik and Lockhart's Levels of Processing Theory.									
8A 8B 8C	Gain experience doing an experiment with multiple predictions and interpreting the results.									
8A 8B	Explain how to counterbalance the order of multiple levels of an independent variable.									
8C	Gain experience conducting and interpreting an experiment with more than one IV.									
8C	Give an example of an interaction hypothesis.									
8C	Recognize and distinguish between main effects and interaction effects.									
8D	Formulate a cause-and-effect hypothesis about human behavior and design a way of testing it.									
8D	Use PsycINFO® or another database to find original research on a topic of interest and be able to summarize the important findings.									

		I don't know how 1	I know a little about this 2	I know enough about this to guess correctly 3	I know how to do this and/ or have already done it. 4		I don't know how 1	I know a little about this 2	I know enough about this to guess correctly 3	I know how to do this and/ or have already done it. 4
8D	Explain the role of the Institutional Review Board in assuring ethical conduct in psychology research.									
8D	Communicate your research findings using a poster, PowerPoint and/ or standard scientific reporting guidelines.									

Now read about your assigned project(s) to prepare for lab. For any scores less than "4," keep those questions in mind as you complete the research project(s). Do not do the white half of this chart until after you've completed the assigned research project(s).

STUDY 8A

LEVELS OF PROCESSING AND MEMORY PERFORMANCE

As you've studied psychology, among the many useful pieces of information you may have committed to memory is Craik and Lockhart's Levels of Processing theory, which explains how new information is most effectively memorized. We can call it a ***theory***, not a hypothesis, because there has been so much evidence for this idea that it has become a useful framework for thinking about how memory works, and applying that framework has led to new hypotheses and predictions that contribute to our understanding of how the theory (and human memory) works. If you don't remember the Levels of Processing theory, then it's possible you didn't process that information at a deep enough level.

As a refresher (or a basic introduction), the theory states that there are different levels of thinking about information, and how well we remember new information depends on the level at which we think about it. The *structural* level of processing pays attention to the way things look on the surface. For example, the word "book" has four letters—two vowels and two consonants. *Phonemic* processing goes deeper and pays attention to the sound of the information: "Book" sounds like "look" and "cook." *Semantic* processing is the deepest level and pays attention to the meaning of the information: A "book" is a written collection of words that have some coherent meaning to the reader.

Craik and Tulving (1975) found that information processed at the structural (appearance) level was poorly remembered, whereas phonemic (sound) processing led to better retention, and semantic processing (thinking about meaning) led to the best memory performance.

One of the criticisms of the Levels of Processing theory is that structural processing requires less time than semantic processing, so the longer time spent engaging with the new material may at least partially explain improved retention with semantic processing.

In other words, time spent processing at each level was a confounding variable. Craik and Tulving addressed this issue with another experiment published in the same paper. By comparing a structural task that was time-consuming to a semantic task that took less time, they were able to show that semantic processing still led to better memory, even when the structural task took more time. However, it could be argued that their structural task was not only time-consuming, but also distracting. In this research project, you will use a different approach to further test their claim that it is the type of processing that is important, not the duration.

You will do this by controlling the time participants spend at each level of processing, making sure it is the same across conditions. You'll use a within-participants design with three levels of the IV (level of processing), and make three comparisons: structural versus phonemic, structural versus semantic, and phonemic versus semantic. If the Levels of Processing Theory holds up, we predict more words will be remembered in the semantic condition, fewer in the phonemic condition, and still fewer in the structural condition. To control for ***inflated error rate***, an overall comparison will be done first to determine whether there are any differences among the three conditions, and ***pairwise comparisons*** will only be done if the overall comparison is significant.

8A PROCEDURE

Since this is a *within-participants* experiment, each person in the study will be exposed to all three levels of processing, with three different lists of words to remember. At your instructor's discretion, the participants in your study might be you and your classmates, or could be volunteers (friends whom you recruit). Be sure to follow the correct set of procedures, as assigned by your instructor.

If you and your classmates are participants:

1. You will be given a set of instructions to read and asked to summarize the instructions in writing at the bottom of the page as a way of ensuring that you are fully aware of and agree to commit to those instructions as you study a word list.

2. You will then receive a folded paper with a hidden list of words. Do not open the paper until instructed to do so. To keep the extraneous variable of time spent studying constant, everyone must start and end at the same time. The word lists will be identical for everyone, but this will not affect the results because the order of conditions will be *counterbalanced* across participants, and therefore, balanced across word lists.

3. When instructed to open the paper, immediately begin studying it in exactly the way you were instructed. Different participants will be following different instructions at the same time. Ignore them and follow your own instructions. If you reach the end of the list before time is up, start again at the beginning and perform the same task a second time for each word, until time is called. Close the paper.

4. Turn to your partner and play tic-tac-toe until time is called again (30 seconds).

5. Immediately begin writing down as many words as you can recall from your list. DO NOT look at anyone else's list. If you need to look away from your own paper, look straight UP, not to either side. Keep your list covered as you work. You will have as much time as you need to recall as many words as you can. When you can't remember any more words, fold the paper over and leave it closed until the end of this experiment.

6. Steps 1 through 6 will be repeated twice with new instructions for your study technique each time. Although it will be tempting to use other methods, try very hard to use ONLY the study method assigned to each word list. If you accidentally find yourself using a method from a previous list, immediately refocus your efforts to use the correct study method. Concentrate and stay focused on using only that technique.

7. When all three conditions are completed, record the Wordlist you used for each condition and the number of words correctly recalled on the data sheet for use with classmates. Complete the Lab Record Worksheet, located after Study 8B.

If you are recruiting participants:

1. You will recruit six participants so that you can collect data in all six versions of the counterbalanced order. *Make sure each participant signs the informed consent document (ICD).* You should also sign it in front of each participant. This gives the participant greater confidence that you are aware of what the ICD says.

2. Cut all instruction sheets and tic-tac-toe sheets in half on the dotted line.

3. Your first participant will be Participant #1, second will be #2, and so on. Each time you start with a new participant, write the PARTICIPANT ID NUMBER at the top of all three pages of the set of tic-tac-toe sheets.

4. In the space for Wordlist Number on the tic-tac-toe sheets, write the list number to be used with each set of instructions. Carefully follow the pattern on the "recruited participants" version of the data sheet, using the correct combinations of Instructions (A, B, and C) and Wordlists (1, 2 & 3). The letters will be counterbalanced, but the numbers will always be in the same order. For example, if Participant # 5 gets the instructions in the order C, A, B, then C will be numbered 1 (for Wordlist 1), A will be numbered 2 (Wordlist 2), and B will be numbered 3 (Wordlist 3).

5. Give the participant the first set of instructions, A, B, or C, depending on the participant number. Make sure you give the CORRECT set of instructions! Counterbalancing of order is IMPORTANT! Ask them to read the instructions and then explain to you, in their own words, what they will do with the word list. It should be clear from their explanation that they will follow the instructions given. If it is not clear, ask them to read the instructions again and repeat the explanation. Continue this until they have got it right.

6. Then say, "This paper has a list of words. Do not open it yet." Hand them Wordlist 1 and get your timer ready (set to 90 seconds). When you're ready, say "Open it now, and follow those instructions as you look at the list." Start the timer precisely when they look at the list.

7. When 90 seconds is up, say "Close the paper."

8. Take the word list away and set down the paper labeled for Wordlist 1 with the tic-tac-toe designs at the top. It should have a letter on it that matches the condition they used for Wordlist 1. Put a circle in any position to start playing tic-tac-toe and continue until you've played three rounds.

9. Then say, "Now please try to recall as many words as you can from the list. You will have as much time as you need. When you can't remember any more words, fold the paper over."

10. Take the folded paper. Repeat Steps 3 through 6 with the other two sets of instructions, in the order indicated on your data collection sheet for that participant number. EXCEPTIONS: The second time through, before Step 5, say: "Although it will be tempting to use other methods, try very hard to use ONLY the method you were just given. If you accidentally find yourself using a method from a previous list, immediately refocus your efforts to use the correct method. Concentrate and stay focused on using only that technique. Will you try to do that?" Wait until the participant confirms, then proceed to Step 5. The third time through, before Step 5, say, "Remember to concentrate and use ONLY the method you're supposed to use with this list. Agreed?" Wait until the participant agrees, then proceed to Step 5. ALSO: In Step 5, be sure to give them Wordlist 2 the second time, and Wordlist 3 the third time.

11. To summarize your data, count the number of words correctly recalled from each list and write the score at the bottom of each tic-tac-toe sheet. Follow instructions provided by your professor to summarize and hand in your data, and complete the Lab Record Worksheet.

DATA SHEET FOR STUDY 8A (CLASSMATE VERSION)

Note that only 1/6 of the class will complete the data collection in ABC order. Make sure you record the Wordlist number you used (1, 2, or 3) and the number of words correctly recalled in the proper rows, corresponding to the instructions you followed.

Condition (Instructions)	Wordlist Number	Number of Words Recalled
A		
B		
C		

DATA SHEET FOR STUDY 8A (RECRUITED PARTICIPANTS VERSION)

Proceed across each row, in order, for each of six participants. Label all materials with the participant ID number (not name!), instruction letter, and Wordlist number for all three conditions, and for every participant. Score = the number of words recalled correctly in each condition. Do not check for correct words until all three conditions have been tested.

Don't forget to debrief your participants! Read the debriefing statement to each participant as soon as they finish their third condition.

Participant #	Instr.	WL#	Score	Instr.	WL#	Score	Instr.	WL#	Score
1 →	A	1		B	2		C	3	
2 →	A	1		C	2		B	3	
3 →	B	1		A	2		C	3	
4 →	B	1		C	2		A	3	
5 →	C	1		A	2		B	3	
6 →	C	1		B	2		A	3	

Debriefing Statement

Thank you for participating in our study. The purpose of this study was to test the Levels of Processing Theory of Memory. This theory says that concentrating on the meaning rather than structure of new information improves the ability to recall that information. Previous reports of this finding do not always correct for the fact that it takes more time to process meaning. It might be the increased time with content that improves memory, rather than the level of processing. We are giving all participants the same amount of time to process new information at each level of processing. Your participation will help us better understand how the way we study influences what we can recall. If you have any questions, please contact me at _____ (email). Do you have any questions right now? [If questions are asked do your best to answer them or promise to try to find out, then follow through. If there are no questions, thank the participant again.]

STUDY 8B

MUSIC AND READING COMPREHENSION[4]

To see whether this research project is relevant to your campus, try an informal descriptive field study: Create a data sheet with three columns. Number the rows, 1 through 25, down the first column. These are your participant numbers for the first 25 people you see studying in the library. The second and third columns should be labeled "yes" and "no." Walk through the campus library during a popular studying time and for each person you see studying, check the "yes" column if they are wearing earbuds while studying, and check the "no" column if they are not. Then count up the yes's and calculate the percent of students who appeared to be listening to music out of all those you saw studying. Granted, this might not be the most valid definition of music-listening—some might have been studying a language or listening to audio lectures—but the chances are good that most students wearing earbuds are listening to music. Students often report that music helps them focus and drowns out other distractions. But is that true? Or is the music itself a potential distraction?

This will be a *within-participants* study to test the hypothesis that listening to music impairs reading comprehension, particularly if the music has lyrics. The experiment will have three levels of listening to music: (1) a control (no music) condition, (2) an instrumental music condition, and (3) the same song with lyrics. Reading performance will be measured with an online speed reading test that measures how long it takes you to read a few paragraphs well enough to be able to get 3 out of 4 questions about the passage correct. The music you play will be decided upon by you and your classmates.

Other variables might influence the effect of music on reading comprehension, such as familiarity with the song or the genre and/or tempo of the music. You might decide to select music for this study that holds the genre and tempo variables constant by using the same music selections for everyone. You might decide to control for familiarity by allowing people to select their own "favorite" songs, as long as they can find both instrumental and lyrics versions, or by selecting music that very few people have ever heard. Your class should discuss how these decisions might influence the generalizability of the results, as well. You will want to design the study to control the extraneous variables you believe are most important to control, while keeping in mind whether the results will be generalizable to the kind of music students most often listen to while studying.

Because there are three levels of music, you will have more than one prediction for this study. You will compare no music to instrumental, no music to music with lyrics, and instrumental to music with lyrics. To control for *inflated error rate*, an overall comparison will be done first to determine whether there are any differences among the three conditions, and *pairwise comparisons* will only be done if the overall comparison is significant.

[4] Between 2007 and 2020, many groups of students in Intro Psych Lab at Lafayette College independently tested this hypothesis in similar ways, and thereby contributed to the design of this application. I am grateful to all those students (too many to name) for their enthusiasm and for convincing me of the relevance of this research to so many college students.

8B PROCEDURE

IMPORTANT: This experiment requires that each student in the class have a mobile device with earbuds or headphones and access to both forms of the music (with and without lyrics). In addition, each student must either (1) be able to access music while browsing a website on their phone OR (2) have access to their phone AND a computer for approximately 5 to 10 minutes during lab.

1. Before lab, make sure your phone battery is charged and that you have access to the correct music selections before you arrive, if that information is available. Also, don't forget to bring earbuds or some other way of privately listening to music on your phone, unless your lab can provide computers with headphones.

2. The order of conditions will be ***counterbalanced*** across all students in the lab, with 1/6 of the class following each possible order (see data sheet). These will be randomly assigned. When you find out your personal order of conditions, circle that row on the data sheet.

3. Set up your first listening condition on your phone, either by putting in your earbuds and finding the correct music selection (but not playing it yet), or by just putting in your earbuds (you should wear them even in the control condition, just in case the wearing of earbuds, with our without music, somehow affects the ability to concentrate).

4. On your phone's browser or on a computer, go to **freereadingtest.com**. Select any theme you like (except Famous People, which presents longer passages). Select Text Complexity level 10 and Story 01 for your first condition.

5. When you're ready, if you are in a music condition, start the music first, then click "Begin" in the lower right corner of the reading test. Immediately and carefully read and study the short passage with the intent to remember the details of what you are reading, but also try to go as quickly as you can. As soon as you finish reading, click on "Done Reading." Read carefully, but quickly. Your score depends on how fast you can absorb the material in the passage. You must score at least 75% (3 out of 4) on the quiz in order to count the trial. After you click on "Done Reading," take your time and do your best to select the correct answers on the quiz. Then click "Done" to see how many you got right. Then click "View Results" to see your speed score and your comprehension score.

6. If your comprehension score is less than 75%, go back to the same subject (theme), go down one Text Complexity level (to 9) and select Story 01 again (always stay on Story 01 for Listening Condition 1). If this is a music condition, restart the same music selection and then click "Begin." Repeat the procedures outlined in Step 5. If you still score less than 75%, go down to Complexity Level 8 and repeat. Each time you score less than 75%, go down one more level and try again with the same music and Story 01. When you score 75% or better, record the Complexity Level and your speed score on the data sheet.

7. Now set up your second Listening Condition on your phone, but don't hit play yet. Change the theme of your reading passage (choose anything except the one you just used or the Famous People (long passages) and set it to Complexity Level 10 again, but use Story 02 (always stay on Story 02 for Listening Condition 2). When you're ready, start the Listening Condition and click "Begin." Follow the same procedure to get a speed score where you scored at least 75% on the quiz. Record your Complexity Level and speed score.

8. Set up your third Listening Condition on your phone and repeat, by selecting a third new theme, beginning at Complexity Level 10, and always using Story 03 at each new Complexity Level (if you score less than 75% at the previous level).

9. When all three conditions have been completed, make sure your entire data sheet is filled out and hand it in or enter your data on an Excel or Google Sheets page, as instructed in lab.

10. Begin work on your Lab Record Worksheet.

DATA SHEET FOR STUDY 8B

There are six possible orders to complete the three conditions. Circle all three conditions across one row representing your assigned order. For example, if you were assigned order # 4 below, you would circle "Instrumental Music, Music with Lyrics, Control" in one big circle across that row.

Order	1st Listening Condition	2nd Listening Condition	3rd Listening Condition
1	Control	Instrumental Music	Music with Lyrics
2	Control	Music with Lyrics	Instrumental Music
3	Instrumental Music	Control	Music with Lyrics
4	Instrumental Music	Music with Lyrics	Control
5	Music with Lyrics	Control	Instrumental Music
6	Music with Lyrics	Instrumental Music	Control

Complete the first column of the data table before you begin collecting data. Fill in the other columns as you complete each Listening Condition.

Listening Condition	Story Number	Complexity Level (with Score of at least 75%)	Speed Score (Words per Minute)
1st -	01		
2nd -	02		
3rd -	03		

Penalty Points

Level 10 – do not add any points.
Level 09 – Add 50 points.
Level 08 – Add 100 points.
Level 07 – Add 150 points.
Level 06 – Add 200 points.
Level 05 – Add 250 points.
Level 04 or lower – Add 300 points.

Based on the Complexity Levels recorded above, ADD the penalty points to the left, then record your scores for each condition below. Note that the order below may be different than your order above.

	Score
Control Condition	_____
Instrumental Music Condition	_____
Music with Lyrics Condition	_____

LAB RECORD WORKSHEET FOR STUDY 8A OR 8B

Name: _____ Date: _____

Group Member Names: _____

Purpose _____

Hypothesis _____

_____

Conceptual independent variable _____

Conceptual dependent variable _____

Operational definition of IV (what were the three levels of the IV?)

1) _____

2) _____

3) _____

Operational definition of DV (how did we measure the DV?):

_____

Prediction _____

_____

Participants: _____ *college students enrolled in introductory psychology class participated as part of the course. Age and gender were not recorded, but most participants were between 18 and 22 years old and gender was mixed.*

Method

Materials _____

_____

_____

_____

_____

_____

_____

_____

_____

Procedure_____

_____

_____

_____

_____

_____

_____

_____

_____

Data Handling _____

_____

_____

_____

_____

Results

Provide the means and SDs for each condition, the results of the overall comparison, and the results of pairwise comparisons, if the overall comparison was significant.

_____

_____

_____

Discussion

Explain whether any part of the research hypothesis was supported and discuss the evidence for that claim.

_____

_____

_____

_____

_____

STUDY 8C

EFFECTS OF MINDFULNESS AND ATTENTIVENESS ON SPORT PERFORMANCE[5]

Module 5 introduced true experiments, and Study 5C invited students to test the effect of a mindfulness exercise on working memory. If you completed that research, you probably recall what mindfulness is and the claims that surround it. If not, or if you've forgotten since then, please read the very short introduction to Study 5C and skim Table 5.4 for a gentle reminder of mindfulness research. Stop before "Applying Research Terminology" on the next page, and return to this page to read the rest of this introduction.

Have you read the brief intro to Study 5C or at least reviewed it to refresh your memory? If not, please do; then come back and read the rest of this introduction.

In this two-way experiment, we will take a closer look at the reported relationship between mindfulness and sport performance (Kaufman et al., 2018). To those of us who do not see ourselves as athletes, the idea that athletic performance is our DV (implying that our athletic performance might be measured!) is uncomfortable at best. For some, it is terrifying. Fear not, Those Whose Strengths Lie Elsewhere. It is a reasonable assumption that athleticism includes motor coordination, specifically eye-hand coordination, and we will use this aspect of sport performance as our dependent measure. We will measure mouse-tracking accuracy.

In this study, we have two independent variables. The basic idea of our hypothesis is that a brief mindfulness exercise can improve sport performance. That's one IV (the mindfulness exercise). However, some research suggests that certain personalities are more likely to benefit from mindfulness exercises than others (Norris et al., 2018). This means that we might see an effect of mindfulness training on sport performance in some people, but not in others, based on certain personality traits.

As any teacher can attest, humans vary considerably in their general levels of attentiveness. By some definitions, mindfulness is equivalent to general attentiveness, though not by the definition we will use in this research. Instead, we define mindfulness as we did in Study 5C: It is a trained, meditative effort to nonjudgmentally pay closer attention to one's surroundings and present-moment experiences. However, it makes sense to consider levels of general attentiveness when examining the effect of mindfulness training on any particular outcome. It's possible that those who start out generally attentive will be more strongly influenced by a mindfulness exercise that focuses their natural attentiveness. The opposite is also possible: Those who are usually less attentive might be helped more by a technique designed to increase their attentiveness. Of course, the null hypothesis could also be true—perhaps general attentiveness doesn't matter, and all people are helped (or not helped) equally by a brief mindfulness exercise. To test all of these ideas, we'll do one experiment that tests our simple hypothesis (a brief mindfulness exercise increases sport performance) in two different contexts: those with pre-existing high general attentiveness, and those with low.

The ***interaction hypothesis*** we are testing is that the effectiveness of a brief mindfulness exercise in improving sport performance depends on pre-existing general levels of attentiveness. The only data we have are pilot data, collected by the group of students who very cleverly designed this original research (see Footnote 5). Their data suggested that those who are low in attentiveness might benefit more than those who are high in attentiveness, so let's restate our hypothesis more clearly:

A brief mindfulness exercise improves sport performance more for people who are low in general attentiveness than for those who are highly attentive.

---

[5] This research idea originated with a group of five students at Lafayette College and is included here with their permission and only slight modifications. Credit to (in alphabetical order) Jae Bratskeir, Maddie Colledge, Louie Franzone, Peter Grimmett, and Keon Modeste.

This hypothesis has two IVs: the mindfulness exercise and general attentiveness levels. Because people can be randomly assigned to either practice mindfulness or not (as we did in Study 5C), the mindfulness exercise will be a true experimental variable. However, we cannot randomly assign people to be generally more or less attentive to their surroundings. So general attentiveness will be a quasi-experimental variable, and we will set up groups as we did in Study 6A (the sleepiness study), using a *median split*. If you didn't do Study 6A, don't worry; you can look up the definition and examples of a median split in the glossary for Module 6. Quite simply, we'll measure general attentiveness in everyone, rank everyone (anonymously) by their scores, and place those who scored higher than the median into the High Attentiveness Group (HA) and those who scored lower than the median into the Low Attentiveness Group (LA). Data will be kept anonymous so no one will know which group anyone else is in. Those who score exactly at the median will be allowed to select the category they feel better describes them. (Normally, they would be dropped from the analysis in order to maximize the difference between different levels of attentiveness, for reasons described in Essay 7.2, but that's no fun for those participants and costs data points.)

After the median split, one half of each group (HA and LA) will be randomly assigned to either listen to a brief meditation exercise or listen to a book on tape. We will then measure motor coordination with an online mouse accuracy task. It is important that you use a mouse for this task, not a touchscreen.

We don't know how many people will wind up in each group, but we can describe the group treatments and understand the design better by presenting it as shown in Figure 8.2.

Our predictions for this study are multiple: First, if the mindfulness part of our hypothesis is true, but general attentiveness doesn't play a role, we would predict a *main effect* of mindfulness exercises on mouse accuracy scores. This means the combined mouse accuracy scores of Groups A and B should be higher than the combined mouse accuracy scores of Groups C and D. If general attentiveness strongly affects performance itself, we would predict a *main effect* of general attentiveness on mouse accuracy scores, with higher scores for Groups A and C (combined) than for Groups B and D (combined). If our *interaction hypothesis* as stated above (in italics) is true, we would predict an *interaction effect*: The difference between Groups B and D will be significantly larger than the difference between Groups A and C.

Second IV:
General Attentiveness

		High	Low
Mindfulness Exercise (yes)		**Group A** High Attentive, Mindful Exercise	**Group B** Low Attentive, Mindful Exercise
Control (no)		**Group C** High Attentive, Control	**Group D** Low Attentive, Control

First IV: Mindfulness Exercise

Figure 8.2 Research design for a two-way experiment testing the hypothesis that a brief mindfulness exercise improves sport performance more for people who are low in general attentiveness than for those who are generally highly attentive.

PROCEDURE **8C**

1) All students will take an online or paper version of the MAAS (Brown & Ryan, 2003), which will be used as a measure of general attentiveness. Respond honestly, with no concern for which group you might end up in. There is no evidence that high or low general attentiveness levels are preferable. Also note that your actual score will remain anonymous. If you take the survey online, you'll be given your score. If you take it on paper, total your ratings for each answer. Double-check the accuracy of your calculations. Jot down your score somewhere so you don't forget it. Also record it on a piece of scrap paper, fold it, and place it in the bag provided by your instructor.

2) Your instructor will take a few minutes to enter all scores on an excel or google sheets file, then announce the median. If your score was higher than the median, circle HA on the data sheet; if it was lower, circle LA. If your score was exactly at the median, decide which group better describes your general attentiveness and circle that group on your data sheet.

3) Your instructor will randomly assign half of the students in each group to be in Group 1 (Mindfulness) or Group 2 (Control). Circle your group assignment on the data sheet.

4) Using headphones or earbuds, people in Group 1 should listen to Audio File 1. You'll need your data sheet and a pen or pencil before you begin. It will be a 5-minute mindfulness exercise, with a practice grounding exercise. Before you begin listening, be sure to have your data sheet and pen or pencil ready, silence notifications on your phone and find a comfortable place to sit with both feet on the floor, no crossed arms or legs, and your back straight, but comfortable. People in Group 2 should do exactly the same thing, except that you will listen to Audio File 2, which will be a 5-minute excerpt from an audio book, with a practice writing exercise.

5) After finishing the audio file, proceed to a computer (do not use your phone). Go to the website **mouseaccuracy.com**. You may select your preferred target color and cursor style, but leave all other settings at their default levels. **Make sure the browser window is maximized to use most of the screen, but do not start the game yet.**

6) If you are in Group 1, perform your grounding exercise, using your notes from Audio File 1. If you are in Group 2, perform your writing exercise, using your notes from Audio File 2.

7) Click "Start" and get ready. You'll see a 3-second countdown, after which dots will begin to appear and disappear on the screen in random places. Use your mouse to click on as many dots as you can. The more dots you hit and the sooner you hit them after they appear, the more points you score. Do your best until the game is over (30 seconds). In the last 5 seconds, you will see another countdown letting you know that the task is almost over. Don't give up! Time to really push yourself to get the highest score you can! Your total score will be displayed in the lower left corner. Record your score on the data sheet for Trial 1. Repeat steps 6 and 7 two more times, starting with your grounding or writing exercise each time, and record your scores for Trials 2 and 3.

8) Calculate your average score for all three trials, and submit your data. Your instructor will run a two-way analysis of the data and the whole class will discuss results. In the meantime, begin your Lab Record Worksheet for Study 8C.

STUDY 8C DATA SHEET

While listening to your assigned audio file, take notes as instructed inside this box.

ATTENTIVENESS GROUP: CIRCLE "HA" IF YOU WERE ABOVE THE MEDIAN, "LA" IF BELOW.

HA   LA

CIRCLE RANDOMLY ASSIGNED GROUP NUMBER: 1   2

Mouse Accuracy Test	Score
(Do noted exercise first) Trial 1 Score →	_____
(Do noted exercise again) Trial 2 Score →	_____
(Do noted exercise again) Trial 3 Score →	_____
Average Score (Total Score divided by 3; Use, 2 decimal places)	_____

LAB RECORD WORKSHEET FOR STUDY 8C

Name: _____ Date: _____

Group Member Names: _____

Purpose: *To examine the influence of brief mindfulness meditation on sport performance, and whether it is dependent on general attentiveness levels.*

Interaction Hypothesis _____

_____

Conceptual independent variables

1) _____

2) _____

Operational definitions of each IV (what were the two levels of each IV?):

1) _____

And _____

2) _____

And _____

Conceptual dependent variable _____

Operational definition of DV (how did we measure sport performance?):

_____

Interaction Prediction _____

_____

Method

Participants _____ *college students enrolled in introductory psychology class participated as part of the course. Age and gender were not recorded, but most participants were between 18 and 22 years old and gender was mixed.*

Materials _____

_____

_____

_____

_____

Procedure _____

_____

_____

_____

_____

_____

_____

_____

_____

Data Handling How did we summarize the data for each group? _____

_____

_____

_____

_____

We used a two-way ANOVA to compare scores.

Results

Main Effect of Mindfulness _____

Main Effect of Attentiveness _____

Interaction Effect _____

Discussion

What can we conclude about the effect of a brief mindfulness exercise on sport performance? Include evidence for your conclusion. _____

_____

_____

_____

_____

STUDY **8D**

YOUR OWN RESEARCH

Before each study this semester, you have been given background information, often with references to published articles on the topics we've studied. Those articles and the content of the Essays of this book have provided the context for each research project, illustrating the importance of educating oneself on a topic before attempting to design research.

If your instructor chooses this application, your final project will be designed by you and your group, so the articles to which you will connect your research ideas are (perhaps) yet to be uncovered. Lecture content and lab discussions will provide some context, but you and your group might be asked to use your library's resources to find a few scientific reports that are relevant to your topic of interest, and then formulate a hypothesis and design a way to test it. As a group, you'll prepare all your materials, including an application to the Institutional Review Board. You'll obtain approval, collect data, interpret your results (statistical results will be provided by your instructor), and present the completed project according to certain standards of scientific communication, as outlined in Essay 8.5, Appendix C, and/or in documents provided by your instructor. *Each member of the group might be asked to independently write his or her own full lab report on your research.*

With thousands of psychology-related articles published worldwide, finding the information you want can be overwhelming. A broad Internet search may turn up a few articles, but most of them will not be original research published in peer-reviewed journals, which is what you must use for your research. "Google Scholar" can help, but is limited in its search techniques. To get better, more comprehensive coverage of all published articles, the **PsycInfo database** will be useful. As you find articles that are related, even tangentially, to your topic, you can skim the Introduction and Discussion sections in html format and link easily to other articles that could be more relevant, using the reference lists to find them. Or, you can just skim the reference list for relevant titles, and/or use authors' names to search for more articles on the same topic.

Study 1B includes advice on using PsycInfo. As you sift through research articles in psychology, we hope you will come to realize why we stress standardization in scientific reporting. In so many ways, standardization makes finding the information we need a lot easier! Here are just some of the useful things you may notice about how standardization helps you find the information you need faster:

1) Long, informative, accurate titles make it easier to find relevant information, compared to brief titles that tell you only the main topics and lead you into a dead-end search, chasing down an article that you thought was exactly on your topic, only to find out it was actually a study on hippos or penguins. No kidding. That has happened to me. More than once.

2) Introductions that demonstrate the principle of connectivity (see Essay 8.5) will lead you back to original sources for information and can show you the progress that has been made in testing your hypothesis.

3) A well-written method section will lead you precisely to the information you want about how research related to your topic has been conducted.

4) Results sections that stick to results will give you exactly what you want to know about which differences or comparisons were significant, and will not confuse the numbers with their interpretations. This is purposeful and allows you to make some decisions on your own before you read the author's interpretation.

5) Figures and their captions will be clear and concise, allowing you to visualize the important findings at a glance.

6) Discussion sections with clear, plain language will explain exactly what the authors concluded from their results and the evidence for those conclusions. Using the principle of convergence (Essay 8.5), they will bring together other research and inform you of the status of their hypothesis as of the date their article was written. They will also usually suggest great ideas for future research.

7) Reference lists in APA format will give you all the information you're looking for about how to find related articles, without having to search for missing pieces.

Your Reference Librarians are also likely to be very happy to help you find what you're looking for.

IRB APPROVAL

Before conducting any research using human subjects, we must obtain approval from the Institutional Review Board (IRB). The IRB is a group of at least five members of the institutional community, and must include at least one scientist and one non-scientist. Their purpose is to review proposals for research and make sure they meet the standards for ethical treatment of human subjects. For more information on how IRBs are formed in general, see apa.org/advocacy/research/ defending-research/review-boards. For more information on the IRB at your college or university, go to your school's home webpage and search "Institutional Review Board." For information on how IRB review will be handled for this particular project, ask your instructor. Some schools have blanket approval for classroom projects that meet certain (usually very strict) guidelines, as approved by your professor, while others require approval from a second faculty member, and still others may require full IRB review.

Although IRB approval requirements and protocols may differ slightly for different courses and research programs, the basic idea is the same. In general, researchers write proposals that usually include most or all of the following:

- The title of the work
- The dates by which it will start and finish
- Author names (and usually qualifications)
- A brief summary of the work (one or two paragraphs), including general purpose, specific hypothesis, how it will be tested, what will be measured and compared, and what is predicted.
- The number and a brief description of required participants and how they will be recruited
- Information on procedures for obtaining informed consent of participants
- Explanations of any deceit involved and how it will be corrected after the study
- A copy of the informed consent document that participants will sign
- A copy of a debriefing statement and explanation of debriefing procedures
- A script showing what participants will be told/asked to do
- Copies of any materials participants will see or hear, or links to any online content they will encounter.

In general, this information must be presented to the IRB committee or go through some form of ethics review, and must be approved before any data collection may begin. The IRB has the right and the responsibility to deny any research project that does not, in their opinion, clearly meet high standards for ethical conduct in human subjects research (outlined in Essay 6.2).

If all this sounds overly serious, please know that the seriousness is not exaggerated. When it comes to ethical conduct in the treatment of research participants, psychologists are serious, indeed. For this reason, you should not blame your lab professor for being "overly picky" about the ethics of your research plans. He or she is under a professional obligation to make sure the work meets strict ethical standards.

The forms you need to obtain IRB approval and informed consent will be provided by your lab professor, both in template form and with completed examples so you can see what they should look like when you submit them. If all goes well, conducting your own research will be an exciting and eye-opening experience.

PROCEDURE 8D

<u>More information will be provided by your lab instructor.</u>

This project may span a few weeks, and the variety of ways it can be accomplished makes writing a generally useful procedure difficult. However, there are certain necessary steps to doing your own research in psychology that will probably be folded into whatever plan your instructor provides.

1. As a group, discuss your research ideas and, with the guidance of your instructor or a teaching assistant, decide on a general topic for your final project.

2. Each group member will be responsible for finding and reading relevant research articles for your group's topic, and sharing the information you find with the rest of your group.

3. Your group will discuss the research you've found, brainstorm new hypotheses based on that research, and discuss ways of testing them. The better you connect your new ideas to published findings, the easier it will be to write up your research for your final lab report.

4. As a group, you will complete a preparation sheet describing the basics of your research plan, then transfer that information to some form of IRB proposal or application, to be reviewed by at least one professor to make sure your research project meets ethical guidelines.

5. Your group will then produce the necessary materials to collect data and either collect data on campus or in other sections of your lab class, or in your lecture class.

6. Enter and organize your data in MS Excel or Google Sheets, interpret an analysis of your data, and draw conclusions.

7. As per instructions specific to your class, you may be asked to do one or more of the following:
   a. Present your work as a group in a PowerPoint presentation
   b. Write a group lab report
   c. Write individual lab reports
   d. Create a poster for an open poster session

Image © Cartoonresource/Shutterstock

"When you put it like that, it makes perfect sense."

MODULE 8 GLOSSARY OF TERMS AND EXAMPLES

Applied Research: Research designed to provide useful or practical solutions to specific problems.
   Examples: Cancer research, Animal welfare research, Environmental issues research.
   Where to find this term: Essay 8.4

Basic Research: Research designed to provide information for the sake of better understanding of the natural world. It is important to remember that much, if not most basic research in psychology, as in other sciences, later becomes applicable in unforeseen ways.
   Examples: The Hubble Deep Space telescope. The discovery of quasicrystals (see Essay 6.1). Jane Goodall's studies of chimps and Piaget's studies of children (see Essay 2.1)
   Where to find this term: Essay 8.4

Between-Groups: See Module 7 Glossary

Connectivity: A guiding principle of science, this is the idea that what we learn is connected to what we already know. Therefore, when we plan research, we should examine what is currently known on the topic and explain the context from which our ideas emerged, giving credit to previous researchers for creating that context. This principle is most clearly expressed in the Introduction section of our scientific reports.
   Example: A researcher who wishes to test the hypothesis that pigs can fly would have a hard time establishing connectivity in his or her introduction. Everything—absolutely everything—we currently know suggests pigs cannot fly. There is no biological, evolutionary, psychological, or physical science, nor any logical argument that gives the reader any hope for the hypothesis, barring the inclusion of airplanes or hallucinogens in the hypothesis.
   Where to find this term: Essay 8.5

Convergence: A guiding principle of science, this is the idea that the goal of science is to bring together evidence from multiple perspectives to better understand the natural world. We do not drop our findings into a knowledge vacuum and hope the world will find a use for them; instead, we aim to bring our findings together with the work of others to contribute to everyone's better understanding. This principle is most clearly expressed in the Discussion section of our scientific reports.
   Example: A researcher finds that the correlation coefficient for SAT scores and college GPAs is 0.16. Because the sample was so large, this correlation is statistically significant. In the Discussion, the author should cite other relevant research, keeping in mind that the hypothesis is part of a bigger picture of the truth about the relationship between standardized test scores and college success, and that science is attempting to converge on that truth. For example, there might be some mention of other variables related to GPA, whether GPA is a valid measure of success in college, and whether SAT scores can or should be used to predict individuals' chances of succeeding, with citations of studies that address these questions where available.
   Where to find this term: Essay 8.5

Counterbalanced: See Module 7 Glossary

Inflated Error Rate: The increased chance of accidentally rejecting the null hypothesis when it is, in fact, true, due to making multiple predictions. Normally, with just one prediction (a simple, two-group comparison), we reject the null hypothesis if our observed results have less than a 5% chance of happening when it is true. This means that we have a 5% chance of being wrong, because up to 5% of the time, our results should randomly occur *even though the null hypothesis is true*. If we have a 5% chance of being wrong each time we make a decision about our data, and we make several such decisions, then the odds that we will be accidentally wrong for at least one prediction are increased (inflated).

> *Example:* In an experiment testing the effect of rewards on volunteerism, a researcher predicts that people given money each time they volunteer will volunteer more often than people given no reward. He predicts a difference between the reward and no-reward groups, and has a 5% chance of being wrong to reject the null hypothesis if the difference is significant. If that same experiment is done with three groups (no reward, $10, and $20), he might make three predictions regarding differences between each level of reward (0 vs. $10, 0 vs. $20, and $10 vs. $20). For each prediction, he would have a 5% chance of wrongfully rejecting the null, and the inflated error rate would be *about* 15% (Appendix A explains why it slightly less than 15%).
>
> *Where to find this term:* Essay 8.2

Integrity: A guiding principle of science that says that we seek the truth from all scientists, and that our work should be uncompromised by bias, greed, or other motives. Results should be reported honestly and directly; negative findings should not be withheld and our statistical analyses should be as objective as possible. This principle is most clearly expressed through the Results section of a scientific report, which provides the precise outcomes of our measurements in quantifiable terms, and compares those measurements using statistical tools that, when properly applied, force objective decisions.

> *Example:* In the Results section of a scientific report, the authors are obliged to use and report straight-forward, logical, appropriate statistical tests for their research. Any failure to do so should be detected by reviewers before publication. Indeed, many papers in peer-reviewed journals are rejected from publication on the grounds that the statistics are inappropriate for the method used or type of data collected. Unfortunately, there is little that can be done to assure that negative results are not being left out of a report, but see *replicability*.
>
> *Where to find this term:* Essay 8.5

Interaction Effect: In experiments with more than one IV, this is when there is a "difference between differences," such that the effect of manipulating one IV differs, depending on the manipulation of another IV. If the first IV has two levels, A and B, and the difference between A and B depends on some other factor (another IV that we also manipulate), then we have an interaction effect.

> *Example:* Imagine a study where 20 people are asked to arrive hungry for a party, and 20 other people are asked to please be sure to eat before arriving. Ten hungry and 10 full people from each group are randomly sent to one of two rooms, each with the same buffet; one room offers only small plates, and the other offers only large plates. The amount of food consumed for each person is secretly videotaped and later measured. Now imagine that people who were told to arrive hungry ate about the same amount, regardless of plate size, but people who ate before the party consumed significantly more food in the large-plate room. A significant difference between the way hungry people reacted to small versus large plates and the way full people reacted to small versus large plates would be an interaction effect, because the influence of plate size on the amount consumed significantly differed based on how hungry people were (see *interaction hypothesis*).
>
> *Where to find this term:* Essay 8.3, Study 8C

Interaction hypothesis: A declarative statement about a cause-and-effect relationship, stating that the relationship depends on some other independent variable.

> *Example:* The easiest way to think of an interaction hypothesis is to first start with a simple cause-and-*effect* hypothesis: For example, "Using smaller plates causes people to eat less." Then ask yourself, "Does that depend on something else?" Perhaps hunger mediates whether or not plate size affects consumption. That would be an interaction hypothesis. Hunger would be one IV, and plate size would be another. The amount consumed would be the DV (see example for *interaction effect*).
>
> *Where to find this term:* Essay 8.3, Study 8C

Median Split: See Module 6 Glossary

Main Effect: In experiments with more than one IV (A and B) this describes a comparison between the levels of A while completely ignoring that B was also manipulated. To do this, we combine participants at all levels of variable B, as though B was never manipulated. This is allowed because for each level of A, B was manipulated in the same way, so there are no systematic differences between levels of A due to the manipulation of B.

Example: In the example for *interaction effect*, if we compared all the hungry participants to all the well-fed participants (ignoring what size plates everyone was given), and found that hungry participants ate significantly more than well-fed participants, that would be a main effect of hunger. Similarly, if we ignored whether people were hungry or well-fed, and found that all those who used large plates ate significantly more than those who used small plates, that would be a main effect of plate size.

Where to find this term: Essay 8.3, Study 8C, Figures 8.1 and 8.2

One-way (Experimental Design): An experiment with one IV. The term is reserved for experiments with three or more levels of one IV. Simple two-group comparisons with only one IV are just "experiments."

Example: A driving and distractions study like Study 7B might have one IV (distraction) with only two levels (repeating words vs answering questions), but if a control condition were added that measured reaction time with no talking at all, it would have been a one-way experiment with three levels of the IV.

Where to find this term: Essay 8.3, Studies 8A, 8B

Overall Comparison: A way of partially correcting for *inflated error rate* when we want to make multiple predictions. Rather than comparing each group to each other group with multiple tests, we first predict that there is at least one significant difference somewhere among all the groups. This turns multiple decisions into one decision. If the overall comparison is not significant, we cannot perform more comparisons. If it is significant, we must make specific *pairwise comparisons* to see where the difference is, since an overall comparison will not reveal where the difference is.

Example: In the study described in the example for *inflated error rate*, where the researcher wants to compare volunteerism that was measured among those who had received rewards of 0 versus $10, 0 versus $20, and $10 versus $20, the researcher would first do an overall comparison to test for a significant difference among any of those three comparisons. If the overall comparison is not significant, then the hypothesis that rewards increase volunteerism would not be supported and no further comparisons would be done. If the overall comparison is significant, then there is probably at least one difference among the three comparisons, and *pairwise comparisons* would be used to determine where the difference(s) is(are).

Where to find this term: Essay 8.2, Studies 8A, 8B

Pairwise Comparison: A statistical comparison between a *pair* of groups or conditions. This term is *not* used to describe the comparison in a simple, two-group experiment. It is only used when there are multiple pairs of data sets to be compared, as a way of distinguishing them from other types of comparisons that can be made in the same experiment.

Example: If a researcher sets up an experiment with four groups, and predicts that Groups B, C, and D will each differ from Group A, an *overall comparison* is done first. If that is significant, there will be three **pairwise comparisons**: A to B, A to C, and A to D. There is no need to compare B to C or D to D or B to D, as no differences were predicted, so further pairwise comparisons would not support any hypothesis (however, if they are done *after* our planned comparisons, they might suggest new hypotheses are worthy of testing in the future, but only if logical arguments support the observations).

Where to find this term: Essay 8.2, Studies 8A, 8B

Replicability: A guiding principle of science, this says that authentic scientific findings should be reproducible. This principle is fostered by writing clear and thorough Method sections in our scientific reports. We must provide sufficient detail regarding how our research was conducted so that others who wish to test our hypothesis for themselves have a good chance of reproducing our findings, and so that those who question the details of our manipulations and/or measurements will find answers to relevant questions.

Example: Unfortunately, some studies that found promising treatments for Covid-19 were not replicable, probably for a variety of reasons. Some of these have to do with differences in the populations studied; some might be due to a lack of detail regarding how data were collected; and some, undoubtedly, were due to natural, probability-based errors in rejecting the null hypothesis when it was actually true. It is also possible, unfortunately, that some studies failed to find significant positive effects multiple times, but were successful once, and only the significant findings were reported (but see *integrity*).
Where to find this term: Essay 8.5

Theory: See Module 4 Glossary

Three-way (Experimental Design): An experiment with three IVs. Each IV may have two or more levels.
Example: A researcher hypothesizes that a new drug will decrease alcohol consumption, but only if taken within an hour before alcohol is offered, *and* if taken with food. Three IVs (the drug, the time it is taken, and whether or not it is taken with food) would be systematically manipulated, and alcohol consumption would be measured.
Where to find this term: Essay 8.3

Two-way (Experimental Design): An experiment with two independent variables. Each IV may have two or more levels.
Example: Imagine cognitive therapy is hypothesized to be more effective at preventing panic attacks than psychotherapy, depending on the amount of pre-therapy biofeedback training provided. Participants with panic disorder are randomly assigned to one of the two types of therapy. Each of those groups is randomly split into three more smaller groups, and each of these three groups receives either 0, 1, or 4 hours of biofeedback training before their first therapy session. Frequency and intensity of panic attacks are measured for all participants over the next 10 weeks. This two-way experiment has two IVs (therapy and amount of biofeedback training). Therapy has two levels (cognitive and psychotherapy), and biofeedback training has three levels (0, 1, or 4 hours).
Where to find this term: Essay 8.3, Study 8C

Within-participants: See Module 7 Glossary

Don't become a mere recorder of facts, but try to penetrate the mystery of their origin.
~Ivan Pavlov

THE PROBABILITY OF WRONGLY REJECTING THE NULL HYPOTHESIS FOR MULTIPLE COMPARISONS

In Module 8, the problem of inflated error rate was explained with a simple dice-tossing example which, it was noted, does not exactly apply to hypothesis testing (see Essay 8.2). If the additive probability rule for dice worked for hypothesis-testing, then the probability of accidentally rejecting the null on any of five predictions would be 25% (5% for each prediction). But a different rule applies, and the correct estimate of the inflated error rate would be 23%. This brief essay first explains how the correct error rate was calculated and then explains why it is different.

Every decision we make about whether our data support our prediction has a preset probability that we will be wrong if we reject the null hypothesis. By consensus, this acceptable probability of being wrong is usually set at 5%. If we make multiple predictions about the same data, and our acceptable probability of being wrong for each prediction (i.e., each comparison) is 0.05, then the probability of being wrong for any number of comparisons in the same data set would be calculated as $1 - (1 - 0.05)^c$, where "c" is equal to the number of comparisons we make. For example, when we make two comparisons, the probability of incorrectly rejecting the null hypothesis would be $1 - (1 - 0.05)^2 = 0.0975$. Not quite 10%, but close. If we make 20 comparisons, the chances of being wrong on at least one would be $1 - (1 - 0.05)^{20} = 0.64$, or 64%, not 100%. For the example above, taken from Module 8, $1 - (1 - 0.05)^5 = 0.226$, or about 23%.

Why is this different from the die example? In that example, we were simply illustrating a straightforward additive probability situation, with an exhaustive list of all possible outcomes. One roll of a single, six-sided die must turn up one of six ways. If we predict a 6, we have a one in six chance of being right ($1/6 = 17\%$). If we predict a 5 OR a 6, we have a two in six chance of being right ($2/6 = 33\%$). If we predict that it will be a 1, 2, 3, 4, 5, OR 6, we have a six in six chance of being right, or 100%. We used that example in order to illustrate the basic concept of additive probabilities in the simplest case. However, when testing a hypothesis, we are not choosing from an exhaustive list of all possible outcomes to make our predictions. Instead, each prediction is about an independent event with a 5% chance of occurring. A series of independent events can turn out any number of ways. If we change the rules a little on our dice-tossing example, and say that we predict a 6 on at least one of any number of tosses, each toss would be an independent event. It's easy to see that we could never be 100% certain that we will see a 6, no matter how many times we toss the die. Applying the formula above, each toss would be an independent event with a 0.17 (one in six) chance of occurring. The probability of being right if we predict a 6 on any number of tosses would be $1 - (1 - 0.17)^n$, where "n" is the number of tosses. Therefore, even if we tossed the die 100 times, we would not have a 100% chance of getting a 6. Instead, the probability of getting at least one 6 would be $1 - (1 - 0.17)^{100} = 99.99999919\%$ (close, but still not 100%.)

Isn't probability fun? If you want more information on probability and dice, a good source is: http://mathforum.org/library/drmath/sets/select/dm_dice.html

ANSWERS TO SKILL CHECK QUESTIONS

FROM PAGE 50

1. Piaget's research was *analog*, while Goodall's research was *naturalistic*.
2. Quasi-experimental (people are not randomly assigned to the groups).
3. Descriptive, Case Study
4. True Experiment (the children are randomly assigned to the groups).
5. Correlational

FROM PAGE 52

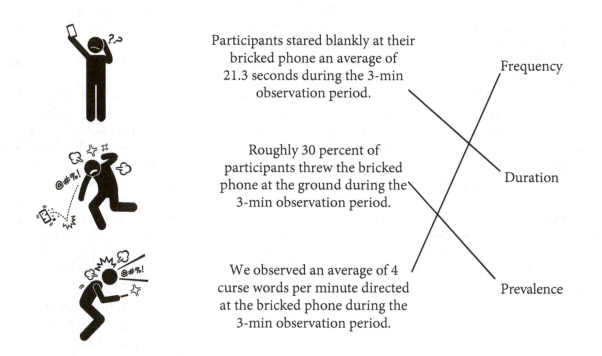

FROM PAGE 53

The operational definition of "friendliness" as "instances of one person walking toward another person to within 2 ft" is probably fairly reliable because it is clearly visible and mostly unambiguous. It's probably not very valid, because people walk closely toward others for a variety of reasons, not all of them friendly. You have to get close to someone to punch them. Also, sometimes people walk closely toward someone else but then brush right past them, which is not friendly.

FROM PAGE 54

These answers will be largely based on opinion and your own experience with each CV. The following answers are not the only correct answers.

Surfing ability—average duration of each ride over five rides. Seems moderately valid. It could also be moderately reliable if the start and end points for each ride are clearly defined.

Thrill-Seeking behavior—number of roller coaster rides over summer vacation. This seems only a little valid, at best, because roller coasters are just one type of thrill-seeking, and opportunities to go on coasters depend on access to them. It would be a moderately reliable definition, though, because it's easy to count accurately.

Smoking Addiction—number of cigarettes smoked in one day. This seems moderately valid, though it might depend on the day (addicted people might smoke more on a very stressful day). It also seems moderately reliable, as it is easy to count, though some people do start a cigarette and then not finish it.

Consumerism—average number of nonfood items bought per day. Seems moderately valid, but should it matter how much money is spent on those items? How necessary the items are? Or how many days are used to calculate that average? This seems only a little reliable because it's not clear enough about what constitutes a "non-food item." For example, if someone buys 7 markers in specific colors, is that more consumerism than someone who buys one box of 20 markers in assorted colors?

Notice that none of the examples are perfectly valid and reliable.

FROM PAGE 57

For Example 1, the CV is "attitude toward children." The operational definition is the proportion of people who select "always terrible, always wonderful," and "sometimes terrible, sometimes wonderful."

For Example 2, the CV is "feelings about the increasing number of electric cars" or "happiness about the increasing number of electric cars." The operational definition is the level of agreement with a statement that one is happy about the increasing number of electric cars, on a scale of 1 (strongly disagree) to 5 (strongly agree).

For Example 3, the CV is "the saddest day of the week." The operational definition is presumably the day that most people name as the day of the week that they feel saddest.

For Example 4, the CV is "age of first romantic kiss." The operational definition would be the average age reported in response to the open question "How old were you when you first kissed someone in a romantic way?"

For Example 5, the CV might be "tendency toward environmental responsibility." The operational definition might be the average agreement (on a 1 to 5 scale from strongly disagree to strongly agree) with a series of statements regarding plans to engage in environmentally responsible behavior.

FROM PAGE 61

You won't see exploratory research among the examples in Study 2A because the goal of exploratory research is to explore the unknown. Once we know enough about something to have a clear operational definition of it, we are moving into descriptive research.

FROM PAGE 89

1. **c)** It is impossible to have a data set with an SD of 0 and a range of 5.
2. **b)** between 2.4 and 3.2 hours

FROM PAGE 159

The conceptual independent variable is *Exposure to classical music*

The conceptual dependent variable is *Children's math performance* (or, just *math performance*).

A few extraneous variables include *children's previous math education, age, willingness to cooperate; also the researcher's mood and demeanor when administering the math test, the time of day when math tests are given, the temperature and lighting in the testing rooms... all these things should be kept the same between groups.*

FROM PAGE 161

Offering ice cream at a dining hall increases the dining hall's popularity.

1. The conceptual IV would be *Ice cream at the dining hall.*
2. The conceptual CV would be *Dining hall popularity*
3. A few extraneous variables might be the dining hall's *pricing, staff, food quality and selection...* (anything that could influence dining hall popularity).
4. You can use as many as you want, but *two would probably be enough to test the hypothesis* as stated.
5. *Ice cream is either available or not available.*
6. *Count the number of students who enter the dining hall during operating hours.*
7. The IV is defined by the *availability of ice cream (available or not available).*
8. The DV is defined by *how many students enter the dining hall during operating hours.*

FROM PAGE 162

The conceptual independent variable is *Ginseng*

The conceptual dependent variable is *Memory (or memory performance)*

A few extraneous variables include *The tea, the belief that the tea might help memory, the age and general memory capabilities of the participants, the amount of time they play video games, the intensity of the video games they play... (anything that could impact memory performance)*

The null hypothesis is that *Ginseng does not affect memory* (or, *Ginseng does not improve memory*).

FROM PAGE 182

The null hypothesis is that *language does not affect thinking.* If true, we would predict *no difference in the time required to complete the task between those who see words while performing the task and those who do not.*

FROM PAGE 206

Asking one group of people to try the medicine and report on whether it works would be a *single-group, posttest only quasi-experiment (with no control over any extraneous variables).*

FROM PAGE 237

The null hypothesis is that *relaxing before exams has no effect on exam performance.*

The conceptual independent variable is *15 minutes of relaxation right before an exam.*

The conceptual dependent variable is *exam performance.*

The levels of the IV are *resting vs studying during the 15 minutes just before the exam.*

The DV is operationally defined as *the score on the exam.*

The prediction is that *those who rest for 15 minutes just before the exam will have higher exam scores than those who study right up to the start of the exam.*

The SDs tell you *how much the majority of the exam scores in each group differ from the mean exam score in that group. In other words, they tell you how much variability there is around the means in each group.*

If the *p*-value is .049, it is less than .05, so *Professor Jackson can conclude that resting just before the exam improved exam performance (the research hypothesis was supported).*

One extraneous variable is t*he amount of time students must wait to take the exam. It is 75 minutes in both groups.* Another extraneous variable is *the amount of time students have available to study during that time, which is 1 hour for both groups.*

A possible confounding variable is that *Group NR had to watch while Group R was allowed to study at the beginning. This might have given Group NR a sense of panic or anxiety that the other group was going to do better on the exam. This anxiety was unlikely to affect Group R, as they got to study as soon as they arrived, and had their studying time behind them while Group NR was still studying at the end. The possible increased anxiety and resentment felt by Group NR but not Group R is a confounding variable because it is different between groups, it is not the IV, and it could affect the DV. One way to control that would be to do the testing in two different rooms, so that Groups R and NR are not aware of differences in how they are treated.*

FROM PAGE 282

1. a. Drug X
   b. Drug X and Placebo
   c. Cholesterol levels (plasma cholesterol test)

2. a. Exercise
   b. Exercise versus No exercise
   c. Cholesterol levels (plasma cholesterol test)

FROM PAGE 283

2. B versus D

3. A versus B

4. C versus D

C APPENDIX

> **NOTE.** "APA-Light" Style is designed for introductory level students based on: (1) The rules of presentation for scientific reports described in *The Publication Manual of the American Psychological Association, 7th Ed.* (American Psychological Association, 2020), and (2) Guiding practice in scientific writing at the introductory level. The goal is to acquaint students with the flow of organized scientific content and to provide some experience with standardized rules of format. The differences between APA Style and APA-Light Style are primarily a matter of leaving some things out, rather than changing the rules. Exceptions: (1) When leaving something out requires a change in a rule to accommodate what is missing, the rule is changed for simplicity's sake. For example, because there is no title page and no abstract, the first page begins with the introduction and is numbered page 1, and each student's name goes on the back of their report. This also facilitates more objective grading. (2) In the interest of saving paper, references do not get their own page. Figures still get their own page at the end of the document, though APA (2020) allows for embedded figures and tables at the authors' or journals' discretion. **All rules that are different from APA are marked with an asterisk (*) and the differences are noted.**

A GUIDE TO WRITING SCIENTIFIC REPORTS: "APA-LIGHT" STYLE

GENERAL RULES FOR WRITING (if there is any disagreement, follow your instructor's rules.)

☐ 1. Express thoughts clearly and precisely, using edited, standard (proper) written English. Make sure each sentence has *useful* information in it. Omit irrelevant information and <u>avoid redundancy</u>. **Shorter is always better, provided no important information is missing.**

☐ 2. * No title page or cover page. Your name goes on the back of the last page only, along with an academic honesty statement and any other information required by your instructor. (Full APA Style has detailed instructions for the title page that you will learn if you go on in Psychology.)

☐ 3. Evenly double space *everything*, even references and figure notes, and use the same font and same size font throughout (a different font within a figure is okay). Start every section just one double-spaced line below the last line of the previous section. There should be no extra spaces between paragraphs, headings or subheadings, **even if a heading title ends up at the bottom of a page with no text after it**. Careful: MS Word automatically adds extra spaces between paragraphs. You must change its default settings. If necessary, ask your instructor or a teaching assistant (TA) for help.

☐ 4. * NO QUOTES ALLOWED. Explain everything *in your own words*, from start to finish. The only exception to this rule is that you may quote your own Materials, e.g., "Our survey asked, "How much do you like cake?"" This is not an APA rule, but is a rule for introductory students, to increase opportunities to practice accurately paraphrasing information from scientific reports.

☐ 5. A running head is a brief version of the title that goes at the top of each printed page in a published article. It is also handy if pages of a manuscript get separated. Include a running head in the top left corner of every page, beginning at the left margin and in ALL CAPS. Use the "insert header" feature of any word processing program. The running head should be a short version of the title, no more than 50 characters, including spaces, and should make sense on its own as a description of the paper.

For example, for a paper entitled, "Role-Playing Games Increase Social Awareness and Confidence," the running head "ROLE-PLAYING INCREASES SOCIAL AWARENESS" would work. Use the same font and font size as the rest of the paper, but USE ALL CAPS. Directly across from the running head, on the same line, insert a page number. The "header" feature of most word processors has an option to insert a page number that will automatically change as you insert new text. Learn to use this feature. Please do not attempt to type in page numbers. Every page of this style guide has a sample running head and* page number at the top so you can see what they should look like. The sample is 45 characters.

☐ **6.** TENSES: In your introduction, use past tense to discuss previous research (e.g., "Smith and Jones reported..."). Also use past tense to describe what you hypothesized, how you tested it, and what you predicted (e.g., "We hypothesized...", "Participants completed...", and "We predicted..."). In Method and Results sections, always use past tense. In the Discussion, use present tense to discuss interpretations, limitations, and implications of your results (e.g., "We conclude that...", "The number of participants limits our ability..." and "This research applies to..."). Avoid future and present tense when referring to the data you are reporting. The data collection part is over, so use past tense. Discuss what you found, not what you "will find" or what you "are finding."

☐ **7.** NUMBERS: For all numbers *10 and above*, use numeric form. Write out all whole numbers nine or lower. *Exceptions*: Always write out a number if it starts a sentence so that you can capitalize your sentence. Always use numeric form if a number provides statistical information (e.g., a mean) precedes a unit of measurement or represents a value on a scale, or is a fraction, decimal, percentage or date. Avoid starting sentences with these because they would have to be written out.

☐ **8.** PRONOUNS: Singular "their" is correct in cases where the gender of the person is unknown or nonbinary. For example, "If a participant hit the target, they were given one point." If this raises any ambiguity (if a group of people other than the participant could earn the point), try rewriting the sentence to eliminate the need for a pronoun: "For each target hit, the participant was given one point."

☐ **9.** Edit for clarity and concise writing. Go on a "Search-and-Destroy Mission" for unnecessary words. A report that has not been edited for clarity is a missed opportunity to practice science writing and will probably earn a lower grade than you expect.

☐ **10.** The elements of the report should be combined in the order they are listed below (a–f), Use fonts and placements as indicated, and remember Item #3 above: Eliminate any extra space that your word processor inserts above or below headings.
  ☐ **a.** The **title of the report** is centered at the top of the first page and **bold**.
  ☐ **b. Method** (heading is centered, **bold**).
     Subsection headings (**Participants, Materials, Procedure**) are flush left and **bold**.
  ☐ **c. Results** (heading is centered, **bold**)
  ☐ **d. Discussion** (heading is centered, **bold**)
  ☐ **e. References** (heading is centered, **bold**)
  ☐ **f.** Figures with titles and notes. (See *How to Format Figures*, items 50–52.

WRITING THE INTRODUCTION – FOCUS ON CONNECTIVITY

☐ **11.** The title is the heading for the introduction section. It should be centered, in bold text, with all major words capitalized. Words that are three or fewer letters (and, if, but, to) should not be capitalized unless they are the first word of the title or the first word after a colon. Make your title as informative and focused as possible, and make sure it mentions your conceptual variables and the relationship between them. Making it "snappy" or fun to read is a plus. Phrases like "A Study of" are not fun to read, add nothing of value, and should be avoided. There is no maximum or minimum number of words, but a good, informative title is usually about 10–15 words.

☐ **12.** Start the text of the introduction immediately after the title (no extra space, just double-space like the entire report). Do not write "Introduction."

☐ **13.** Introduce the problem. In no more than one paragraph, draw the reader's attention to the main topic of the research. State the general purpose of the research you did. What was the point of it all? Provide the big-picture context.

☐ **14.** Develop the background and rationale. Explain what the reader needs to know to understand the research you did. Remember the principle of connectivity: Your research must not sound like a random study that came out of nowhere. Introduce other studies that either tested the same hypothesis in a different setting or presented conclusions that logically lead to the formulation of your hypothesis. Your description of those connections should build a rationale—a persuasive argument that your hypothesis was worthy of testing in the way you tested it. *Only include as much detail as needed to help the reader understand where the hypothesis came from, and/or why it needed new or further testing.* It might help to describe how previous research could be improved, but keep any criticism of other research professional and *only discuss problems with other studies if your own research attempted to fix those problems.* Remember that this is not about you; it's about the research. Avoid references to your own personal journey through this research project. Instead, be direct and concise: Not "We decided to test...", but "We tested..." Not "The studies we read about happiness gave us the idea that..." but "Previous happiness research suggests..."

☐ **15.** State the goals (either together with the hypothesis or as separate ideas). While the rationale is the *reason* for the research, goals are statements about what you (the researchers) tried to do. In other words, a *goal* is *what* you wanted to accomplish; a *rationale* is *why* you wanted to accomplish it.

☐ **16.** In the *last paragraph or two of the introduction*, you must do three things:
   ☐ **a.** Clearly state what was hypothesized. Remember to state it in terms of conceptual variables. The hypothesis itself is a present tense claim, but you hypothesized it in the past. (e.g., "We hypothesiz**ed** that play increas**es** joy.")
   ☐ **b.** Briefly (but logically) describe how the hypothesis was tested. In about one to three sentences, describe what your participants were asked to do and under what conditions. Make the logic of the hypothesis test clear from your description. The operational definition of the IV should be easily understood without actually saying, "our operational definition was...". The same is true for the DV and its measurements. For correlational studies, briefly describe how variables were measured. The most important point here is that the reader sees the *logic* in the way you tested your hypothesis. The details will be in the Method section.
   ☐ **c.** State predicted outcomes. Predictions should be in past tense and in terms of operational definitions, not conceptual variables (see Figure 4.5). If your predictions are not completely obvious, then go back to Item 14 above and make sure that you have thoroughly explained the rationale for your hypothesis, so that the reader is not left wondering "why would you predict THAT?"
   ☐ **d.** Use past tense to state what you predicted, and use "would" rather than "will" or "did" if an auxiliary verb is needed. For example, "We predicted that reaction times *would* increase", not "... *will* increase", or "... *did* increase."

WRITING THE METHOD – FOCUS ON REPLICABILITY

☐ **17.** USE PAST TENSE for ALL SUBSECTIONS (**Participants, Materials** and **Procedure**).
☐ **18.** **Participants** subsection: Describe the people who participated in the study.
   ☐ **a.** Include the number, gender identity (if you have this information. If not, say "mixed genders" or report on "apparent genders"), and age range of participants and any other information pertinent to their performance in this study (for example, that they were students in an introductory level psychology class). Use general terms (e.g., not "Psych 101," but "introductory psychology").

☐ **b.** Describe how participants were recruited. If anyone was excluded, explain why. Tell whether participants were compensated and how. If participation was mandatory for a class grade, that should be clearly stated.

☐ 19. **Materials** subsection: Describe what was used during data collection.

☐ **a.** Describe measurement tools (surveys, inventories, software) and any other materials that were needed to collect data. Describe the **tools**, <u>not</u> what the participants did with them. A good rule of thumb is to avoid even using the word "participants" in the Materials section, but especially avoid using it as the subject of any sentence.

☐ **b.** Avoid exhaustive lists when brief descriptions with a few examples will make the point. If materials can be adequately described in general terms such that a reader could replicate your work, then detailed lists are not needed.

☐ **c.** Do not include obvious things like pens, paper, calculators, or spreadsheet programs used to manage data.

☐ 20. **Procedure** subsection: Describe all relevant aspects of how the study was conducted.

☐ **a.** Provide a summary of the research procedure. Be concise but include enough detail that another researcher could replicate your study.

☐ **b.** Any information or instructions given to participants that could impact their behavior during data collection should be noted. Details of the instructions that would not affect the results of the study should not be included (e.g., leave out that participants "walked to a computer," or "took out a pen").

☐ **c.** Treat this report as real research, ***not a class project***. Do not talk about "the professor" or "the students" within the procedure subsection. Use "we" to refer to people who collected or analyzed data (assuming this was a group project—if not, use "I") and use "participants" to refer to those who provided data.

☐ **d.** Describe the data handling, that is, how the data were summarized and analyzed. See the Module 2 Glossary for some basic examples of "data handling," but don't forget to also add information in your report about the statistical test that was applied to your data.

WRITING THE RESULTS – FOCUS ON INTEGRITY

☐ 21. USE PAST TENSE for all information in this section.

☐ 22. Describe the results <u>in terms of operational definitions and measurements (e.g., frequencies or means), not conceptual variables</u> (see Modules 2 and 4, esp. Figure 4.5). If your results were as predicted, then they should sound a lot like the predictions.

☐ 23. Refer the reader to figures that illustrate the results as "Figure 1," "Figure 2," etc., *in the order they are mentioned* (i.e., don't mention Figure 2 before Figure 1 has been mentioned). Always capitalize "Figure" when you use it as a label (proper noun). For example, "the figure shows…" and "as Figure 1 shows…" are correct, but "as figure 1 shows…" is incorrect.

☐ 24. *Add all your figures to the end of the paper, in consecutive order.* See *How to Format Figures*, Items 50–52. Do not embed them within the text. APA Style leaves this option open so that figures may be embedded or placed at the end, but for APA-Light, please place all figures at the end to avoid word processing complications and spacing errors.

☐ 25. When a mean is reported, it must be accompanied by a standard deviation in parentheses. The subject or object of the sentence can be the mean, but the standard deviation is always parenthetically reported with the mean. For example:

Correct: The mean shoe size was 9.5 ($SD = 1.2$) for men and 7.6 ($SD = 1.1$) for women.

Incorrect: The mean shoe size was 9.5 for men and the standard deviation was 1.2. For women, the mean shoe size was 7.6 and the standard deviation was 1.1.

☐ **26.** When statistical significance is mentioned in a sentence, whether the sentence is saying the result was significant or not, it must be supported mathematically with an additional statistical clause, usually at the end of the same sentence (see Figure C1).

☐ **27.** Means (with SDs) and information about statistical significance may be included in the same sentence, and means may be reported parenthetically, with SDs. If so, place the parenthetical information (M and SD) immediately after the first mention of the group to which it applies. Do not use "M" within the parentheses if it is clear from the sentence. For example:

Correct: Shoe size for men ($M = 9.5$, $SD = 1.2$) was significantly larger than for women ($M = 7.6$, $SD = 1.1$), $t(42) = 3.56$, $p = .004$.

Correct: The mean shoe size for men (9.5, $SD = 1.2$) was significantly larger than the mean for women (7.6, $SD = 1.1$), $t(42) = 3.56$, $p = .004$.

Incorrect: The mean shoe size for men ($M = 9.5$, $SD = 1.2$) was significantly larger than the mean for women ($M = 7.6$, $SD = 1.1$), $t(42) = 3.56$, $p = .004$.

☐ **28.** Italicize letters representing calculated values (M, SD, r, t, F, p), but not the numbers, as shown in the examples Rule 27.

☐ **29.** Report only results, not what they mean or what they imply, nor even whether they support or fail to support the hypothesis. Save those comments for the Discussion section.

Figure C1

Proper Format for a Statement Regarding Significance in the Results Section

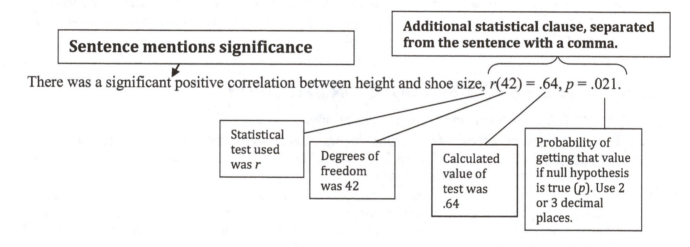

Note. The statistical clause should be added after a comma. Do not put it in parentheses.

WRITING THE DISCUSSION – FOCUS ON CONVERGENCE

☐ **30.** In the first paragraph, the hypothesis must be clearly stated in the context of a discussion of whether it was supported. That discussion should include plain-language evidence: What observations from the current research support or fail to support the hypothesis? Plain language means that anyone can read this paragraph without having read the rest of the paper and can understand your hypothesis and what you observed that supports or fails to support it. Upon first mention, rather than "Group CM" say, "...

children who heard classical music (Group CM)..." Only use acronyms if they make the remaining prose flow more smoothly, and don't mention them if you don't use them later.

☐ 31. * Do not include statistics. APA Style does not prohibit statistics in the Discussion, but in APA-Light, the goal is to practice ways of communicating the *meaning behind* the numbers, rather than repeating them, so statistics are not allowed in your Discussion.

☐ 32. Elaborate on the most meaningful and important observations. Describe <u>*what*</u> was interesting or important, not <u>*that*</u> you (specifically) thought it was interesting or important (focus on the topic, not how *you* feel about it). For example:

Not this: We thought the observed difference in shoe size was interesting because it is useful for the shoe industry.

But this: **The observed difference in shoe size is useful for the shoe industry.**

☐ 33. Where observations disagree with predictions, try to explain why. Use information from your method, past research, or other observations. Try to offer testable explanations for any unexpected results.

☐ 34. Compare the current research to previous research, but stay focused on the hypothesis and the context in which it fits. Try not to compare just for the sake of comparison. Use other studies to help clarify your interpretations or alternative explanations for your results. For example, don't *just* point out that someone else used a different method than your study; if they *came to the same conclusion*, state that clearly, and point out how the combined evidence either supports or refutes the hypothesis. If your results conflict with previous research, differences in methodology can often be used to explain the different results.

☐ 35. * Briefly describe TWO limitations in the design or execution of the study that should be considered when interpreting the results. Choose the *two* most important. APA Style imposes no minimum or maximum on this, but restricting yourself to two limitations for this paper will remind you to think about their relative importance.

☐ 36. <u>Be sure to explain how each limitation might have influenced the outcome or conclusions</u>, even if it seems obvious to you.

☐ 37. * In the last paragraph, answer *at least two* of the following questions: What does the combined evidence (other research plus this study) say about your hypothesis? What is the big-picture importance of these findings? What are the implications and applications, and who should be most helped by these findings? APA Style asks for the same kinds of content in the last paragraph, but has no minimum number of questions you should answer.

☐ 38. Also in the last paragraph, suggest a good direction for future research on this hypothesis or topic. *APA Style is more flexible on this point, but APA-Light is about demonstrating your understanding of the context of your research, so do not simply suggest repetition of the same study without the limitations. Instead, suggest testing your findings in meaningful applications; ideally, these should connect in some way to what you have already presented.

HOW TO FORMAT CITATIONS

Citations are written within the text of your report, mostly in the Introduction and Discussion. Whenever you write about something that is not your own idea or your own work, you must cite the source. Sources can vary from book chapters to government documents to websites, but the most common citations in scientific reports are journal articles. For this class, * cite *only* peer-reviewed journal articles. If your instructor approves the use of other types of sources, it is your responsibility to make sure your citations are in APA Style (for correct format, see American Psychological Association, 2020).

☐ **39.** Unlike MLA Style, there is no page number included in APA-Style citations unless you are using a direct quote. Since you may not use ANY direct quotes (see * Item 4), you should not include page numbers in your citations.

☐ **40.** Refer to the work using *only the last names of the authors* and the *year* of the publication, which should be in parentheses if it is not part of the sentence (see Item 42). Format depends, to some extent, on the number of authors (see Items 44 and 45).

☐ **41.** Citations *should not include*: page numbers, first names or initials, article titles, journal titles, or where the research was done (unless any of this information is relevant to the idea being discussed, for example, when comparing results in one city to results in another).

☐ **42.** Present the author names in one of two ways (a or b below). Notice that when two author names are part of the sentence, we use "and" but when they are parenthetical, we use an ampersand (&):

   ☐ **a.** Cite the authors as part of the sentence in which the citation is made, for example:
   "Craik and Tulving (1975) reported that memory depends on how information is processed."

   ☐ **b.** Cite the authors as parenthetical information, either at the end of the sentence or immediately after the work is first mentioned or described, for example:
   "A study of memory based on information processing (Craik & Tulving, 1975) suggests that..."

☐ **43.** The order of the authors' last names in the citation must match the order given in the References section and in the original publication.

☐ **44.** For sources with one or two authors, always use the name(s) of all authors in the citation.

☐ **45.** For sources with three or more authors, always use the first author's last name with "et al." If two different sources would be cited the same way under this rule, then add only enough author names to clarify the difference.

HOW TO FORMAT REFERENCES

> The "References" list is the list of bibliographic information for all cited sources. It comes immediately <u>after the Discussion, but BEFORE any tables or figures</u>. These instructions focus on how to format a reference to a journal article, as that is the type of source you are most likely to use in a scientific report. If necessary, proper formatting for other types of sources can be looked up in the APA's *Publication Manual* or online at APA.org. Note that some other Internet sites claim to put references into APA format for you but fail to do so accurately. If you use one of them, be sure to check the format against the instructions in this style guide or the APA's *Publication Manual*.

☐ **46.** The entire list of References should be in alphabetical order based on the last names of the first authors of each article. As noted in Item 43, author names for each entry must remain in the same order as the publication.

☐ **47.** Each reference must be cited somewhere in the report, and every citation must be in the References section, and all information (publication dates, spellings, order of names) must match exactly.

☐ **48.** Follow all style points in Figure C2, including using a "hanging indent," double-spaced. A hanging indent means that each source starts flush left, and subsequent lines for that source are indented. The References section of this book shows what APA Style should look like for multiple entries, except that yours will be evenly double-spaced throughout. Be careful to remove extra space between entries that your word processor might insert by default.

☐ **49.** DOI's, if available, may be added after the final period (after page numbers).

Figure C2

Elements of an APA-Style Reference

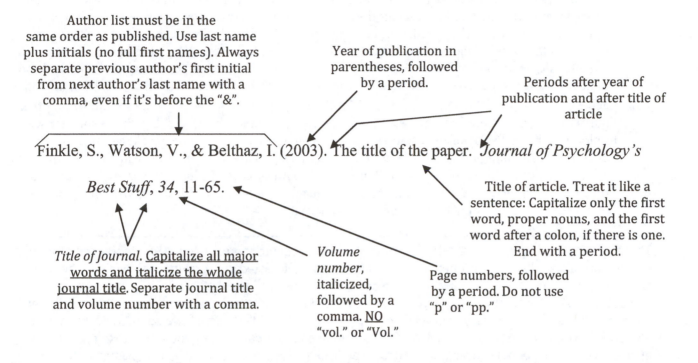

Note. This figure shows the correct style for both APA and APA-Light, except that as a figure, it should be on its own page with no text other than the running head, the figure label (Figure C2), the title (Elements of an APA-Style Reference), and this note (double-spaced). APA Style allows embedded figures like this one, but APA-Light requires that all figures go at the end of your paper.

HOW TO FORMAT FIGURES

☐ 50. *** Every figure has its own page**. Figures should be the last thing in the report, after the References section. This is not required in APA Style, but in APA-Light, we avoid the complications of embedding a figure within text by placing all figures at the end.

☐ 51. Formatting an APA-Style figure:

    ☐ **a.** Most important: Keep it simple and clear. All other rules are based on this one.

    ☐ **b.** Major axis lines are required, and tick marks on the axis lines are acceptable if they make the graph easier to read. Trendlines that clarify relationships in scatterplots are allowed. There should be no other unnecessary lines, no boxes or borders around the chart area or the plot area, and no 3D effects. Include nothing that could distract from the meaning of the graph itself. Clear the plot area of gridlines.

    ☐ **c.** If more than one color is needed, use black, white, gray, or a simple diagonal stripe pattern for columns in charts, and simple squares, dots or diamonds for scatterplots. Make sure scatterplot symbols are large enough to distinguish between different shapes.

    ☐ **d.** Label both axes clearly, but briefly. Use the title and *Notes* to provide more detail on the meaning of labels (see f and g below). Capitalize the first letter of all major words in the axis labels (and legend, if needed).

    ☐ **e.** Write the figure number above the figure, flush left and bold, with no punctuation after it.

    ☐ **f.** One double-spaced line beneath the figure number, write a title for your figure in italics. The figure title should be a short description of the main point of the figure. Capitalize all major words. Use no punctuation at the end of the title.

☐ **g.** One double-spaced line beneath the figure, write the word "*Note.*" (in italics, and include the period.) After the period, write in any notes that will help the reader understand the figure. The notes themselves should be brief and in plain text, not italics (see Figure C3).

☐ **h.** *If a legend is needed* (because there is more than one IV or DV), place it in the most open space within the plot area. By default, MS Excel puts the legend beneath the x-axis, which confuses it with the x-axis labels. Move the legend by selecting and dragging it into the plot area. Resize the box as needed to make it fit, but be careful: if the box is too small, some text might be hidden. When the legend is where you want it, delete the border around it by right-clicking on it and choosing "format legend," "border," and "no line." There should be no box around the legend unless a box is needed to separate it from the data.

☐ **52.** Each figure should be ALONE on its OWN PAGE, as shown in Figure C3. There should be no other figures or text except the running head, Figure label, Figure title, and Notes. Figure C3 shows a scatterplot, which is a display of correlational data. If you have a bar or column chart, the same rules apply but your title should not start with "*Relationship Between...*" Titles for bar charts usually start with the label for the y-axis. For example, "*Math Scores Based on Music Genre*". Notice that there is no punctuation after the figure label or title, but there is a period after "*Note.*" Also, the note is written in complete sentences with normal punctuation and is not italicized.

That's all! Just 10 pages and 52 rules to follow! If it's any comfort, the complete APA *Publication Manual* is over 400 pages! It's an excellent book to read for anyone interested in improving their writing. The rules above, while they might seem overly picky, are designed to make science writing easier to read or skim, and to prepare you for the full set of rules if you go on in psychology or another science. If so, you'll eventually get used to all this structure, just like you've gotten used to other things that might have seemed overwhelming at first (like where the important buildings and classrooms are on campus). If you never take another science course, we hope that this experience has helped you feel better about reading and skimming scientific reports, and confident that you know exactly where to find the information you're looking for.

Figure C3

Relationship Between Shoe Size and Height

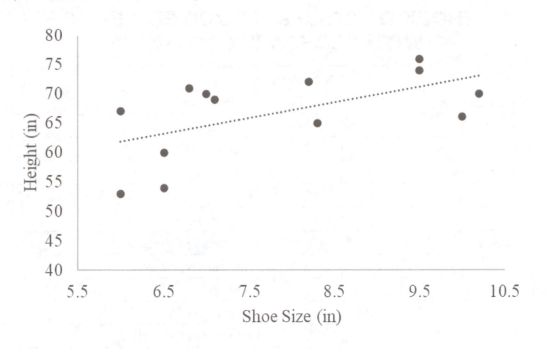

Note. Shoe length was measured heal to toe in flat shoes with no pointy toes. This chart shows fabricated data to illustrate figure format. No shoes or humans were actually measured.

INDEX OF BOLD & ITALICIZED TERMS WITH GLOSSARY LOCATIONS

REFERENCES

Alm, H., & Nilsson, L. (1995). The effect of a mobile telephone task on driver behavior in a car following situation. *Accident Analysis and Prevention, 27*, 707–715.

American Psychological Association. (n.d.). Spurious Correlation. In *APA dictionary of psychology*. Retrieved May 18, 2020, from https://dictionary.apa.org/spurious-correlation

American Psychological Association. (2020). *Publication Manual of the American Psychological Association* (7th ed.). https://doi.org/10.1037/0000165-000

Arch, J. J., Brown, K. W., Goodman, R. J., Della Porta, M. D., Kiken, L. G., & Tillman, S. (2016). Enjoying food without caloric cost: The impact of brief mindfulness on laboratory eating outcomes. *Behaviour Research and Therapy, 79*, 23–34.

Astin, J. (1997). Stress reduction through mindfulness meditation: Effects on psychological symptomatology, sense of control, and spiritual experiences. *Psychotherapy and Psychosomatics, 66*(2), 97–106.

Bamber, M., & Schneider, J., (2016). Mindfulness-based meditation to decrease stress and anxiety in college students: A narrative synthesis of the research. *Educational Research Review, 18*, 1–32.

Bandura, A., Ross, D., & Ross, S. A. (1961). Transmission of aggression through imitation of aggressive models. *The Journal of Abnormal and Social Psychology, 63*, 575–582.

Baron, L., Rouleau, V., Grégoire, S., & Baron, C., (2018). Mindfulness and leadership flexibility. *Journal of Management Development, 37*(2), 165–177.

Beaver, K. M., & Barnes, J. C. (2012). Genetic and nonshared environmental factors affect the likelihood of being charged with driving under the influence (DUI) and driving while intoxicated (DWI). *Addictive Behaviors, 37*(12), 1377–1381.

Beck, K., Yan, F., & Wang, M. (2007). Cell phone users, reported crash risk, unsafe driving behaviors and dispositions: A survey of motorists in Maryland. *Journal of Safety Research, 38*, 683–688.

Bjorvatn, B., Fiske, E., & Pallesen, S. (2011). A self-help book is better than sleep hygiene advice for insomnia: A randomized controlled comparative study. *Scandinavian Journal of Psychology, 52*, 580–585.

Boroditsky, L. (2001). Does language shape thought? Mandarin and English speakers' conceptions of time. *Cognitive Psychology, 43*, 1–22.

Boyack, K. W., Klavans, R., & Börner, K. (2005). Mapping the backbone of science. *Scientometrics, 64*, 351–374.

Brown, K.W., & Ryan, R. M. (2003). The benefits of being present: Mindfulness and its role in psychological well-being. *Journal of Personality and Social Psychology, 84*, 822–848.

Capretz, L., Varona, D., & Raza, A. (2015). Influence of personality types in software tasks choices. *Computers in Human Behavior, 52*, 373–378.

Carskadon, M. A. (Ed.) (2002). *Adolescent sleep patterns: Biological, social, and psychological influences.* Cambridge University Press.

Cattell, R. B. (1965). *The scientific analysis of personality.* Penguin Books.

Clarke, T. C., Barnes, P. M., Black, L. I., Stussman, B. J., & Nahin, R. L. (2014). *Use of yoga, meditation, and chiropractors among U.S. adults aged 18 and over.* National Center for Health Statistics Data Brief No. 325. https://www.cdc.gov/nchs/data/databriefs/db325-h.pdf

Cohen, S., & Hoberman, H. (1983). Positive events and social supports as buffers of life change stress. *Journal of Applied Social Psychology, 13*, 99–125.

Coulter, R. W. S., Bersamin, M., Russell, S. T., & Mair, C. (2018). The effects of gender-and sexuality-based harassment on lesbian, gay, bisexual, and transgender substance use disparities. *Journal of Adolescent Health, 62*, 688–700. http://dx.doi.org/10.1016/j.jadohealth.2017.10 .004

Craik, F., & Tulving, E. (1975). Depth of processing and the retention of words in episodic memory. *Journal of Experimental Psychology: General, 104*, 268–294.

Cramer, S., Mayer, J., & Ryan, S. (2007). College students use cell phones while driving more frequently than found in government study. *Journal of American College Health, 56*, 181–184.

Csibi, S., Griffiths, M., Demetrovics, Z., & Szabo, A. (2019). Analysis of problematic smartphone use across different age groups within the 'components model of addiction.' *International Journal of Mental Health and Addiction.* https://doi.org/10.1007/s11469-019-00095-0

Cunningham, J., Humphreys, K., Koski-Jännes, A., & Cordingley, J. (2005). Internet and paper self-help materials for problem drinking: Is there an additive effect? *Addictive Behaviors, 30*, 1517–1523.

Deary, I., Whiteman, M., Starr, J., Whalley, L., & Fox, H. (2004). The impact of childhood intelligence on later life: Following up the Scottish Mental Surveys of 1932 and 1947. *Journal of Personality and Social Psychology, 86*, 130–147.

Dvorakova, K., Kishida, M., Li, J., Elavsky, S., Broderick, P., Agrusti, M., & Greenberg, M. (2017). Promoting healthy transition to college through mindfulness training with first-year college students: Pilot randomized controlled trial. *Journal of American College Health, 65*(4), 259–267.

Eskine, K. J., Kacinik, N. A., & Prinz, J. J. (2011). A bad taste in the mouth: Gustatory disgust influences moral judgment. *Psychological Science, 22*, 295–299.

Fredrickson, B., & Roberts, T. (1997). Objectification Theory: Toward understanding women's lived experiences and mental health risks. *Psychology of Women Quarterly, 21*, 173–206.

Ghelfi, E., Christopherson, C. D., Urry, H. L., Lenne, R. L., Legate, N., Ann Fischer, M., Wagemans, F. M. A., Wiggins, B., Barrett, T., Bornstein, M., de Haan, B., Guberman, J., Issa, N., Kim, J., Na, E., O'Brien, J., Paulk, A., Peck, T., Sashihara, M., ... Sullivan, D. (2020). Reexamining the effect of gustatory disgust on moral judgment: A multilab direct replication of Eskine, Kacinik, and Prinz (2011). *Advances in Methods and Practices in Psychological Science, 3*(1), 3–23.

Gibson, E. J., & Walk, R. D. (1960). The visual cliff. *Scientific American, 202*(4), 64–71.

Gray-Little, B., & Burks, N. (1983). Power and satisfaction in marriage: A review and critique. *Psychological Bulletin, 93*, 512–538.

Godden, D., & Baddeley, A. (1975). Context-dependent memory in two natural environments: In land and underwater. *British Journal of Psychology, 66*, 325–331.

Haig, B. (2003). What is a spurious correlation? *Understanding Statistics, 2*(2), 125–132.

ICT Data and Statistics Division. (2015). *ICT Facts and Figures.* Geneva: International Telecommunication Union.

IJzerman, H., & Semin, G. R. (2009). The thermometer of social relations: Mapping social proximity on temperature. *Psychological Science, 20*, 1214–1220.

James, W., (1892). *Psychology: Briefer Course (p. 335).* H. Holt & Co.

James, J. E., Baldursdottir, B., Johannsdottir, K. R. Valdimarsdottir, H. B., & Sigfusdottir, I. D. (2018). Adolescent habitual caffeine consumption and hemodynamic reactivity during rest, psychosocial stress, and recovery. *Journal of Psychosomatic Research, 110*, 16–23.

Jung, M., & Hallbeck, M. (2004). Quantification of the effects of instruction type, verbal encouragement, and visual feedback on static and peak handgrip strength. *International Journal of Industrial Ergonomics, 34*, 367–374.

Just, M., Keller T., & Cynkar, J. (2008). A decrease in brain activation associated with driving when listening to someone speak. *Brain Research, 1205*, 70–80.

Kakalios, J. (2011). *The amazing story of quantum mechanics: A math-free exploration of the science that made our world.* Duckworth Publishers.

Kaufman, K. A., Glass, C. R., & Pineau, T. R. (2018). Mindful sport performance enhancement: Mental training for athletes and coaches. *American Psychological Association.* http://dx.doi.org.ezproxy.lafayette.edu/10.1037/0000048-000

Kidwell, B., Hardesty, D., & Childers, T. (2008). Consumer emotional intelligence: Conceptualization, measurement, and the prediction of consumer decision making. *Journal of Consumer Research, 35*, 154–166.

Kiefer, H. M. (2003, March 25). Wake up, sleepy teen. *Gallup News.* https://news.gallup.com/poll/8059/wake-up-sleepy-teen.aspx

Kiefer, H. M. (2005, January 25). Who dreams, perchance to sleep? Mom and dad could use more sleep. *Gallup News.* https://news.gallup.com/poll/14716/who-dreams-perchance-sleep.aspx

Knecht, S., Dräger, B., Deppe, M., Bobe, L., Lohmann, H., Flöel, A., Ringelstein, E. B., & Henningsen, H. (2000). Handedness and hemispheric language dominance in healthy humans. *Brain, 123*, 2512–2518.

Lannin, P. (2011, October 5). Ridiculed crystal work wins Nobel for Israeli. *Reuters.* Retrieved May 31, 2020, from reuters.com/article/us-nobel-chemistry/corrected-ridiculed-crystal-work-wins-nobel-for-israeli-idUS-TRE7941EP20111006

Lund, H., Reider, B., Whiting, A., & Prichard, J. (2010). Sleep patterns and predictors of disturbed sleep in a large population of college students. *Journal of Adolescent Health, 46*(2), 124–132.

Marshal, M. P., Friedman, M. S., Stall, R., King, K. M., Miles, J., Gold, M. A., Bukstein, O. G., & Morse, J. Q. (2008). Sexual orientation and adolescent substance use: A meta-analysis and methodological review. *Addiction, 103*, 546–556. http://dx.doi.org/10.1111/j.1360-0443.2008.02149.x

Martin, R. A., Puhlik-Doris, P., Larsen, G., Gray, J., & Weir, K. (2003). Individual differences in uses of humor and their relation to psychological well-being: Development of the Humor Styles Questionnaire. *Journal of Research in Personality, 37*(1), 48–75.

Massy-Westropp, N., Gill, T., Taylor, A., Bohannon, R., & Hills, C. (2011). Hand grip strength: Age and gender stratified normative data in a population-based study. *BMC Research Notes, 4*, 127–131.

Meehl P. (1978). Theoretical risks and tabular asterisks: Sir Karl., Sir Ronald, and the slow process of soft psychology. *Journal of Consulting and Clinical Psychology, 46*, 806–834.

Mrazek, M., Franklin, M., Phillips, D., Baird, B., & Schooler, J. (2013). Mindfulness training improves working memory capacity and GRE performance while reducing mind wandering. *Psychological Science, 24*(5), 776–781.

Norris, C. Creem, D., Hendler, R., & Kober, H. (2018). Brief mindfulness meditation improves attention in novices: Evidence from ERPs and moderation by neuroticism. *Frontiers in Human Neuroscience, 12*, Article 342.

Oxford University Press. (n.d.) Spurious. In *Oxford English Dictionary (OED Online).* Retrieved May 18, 2020, from https://www-oed-com.ezproxy.lafayette.edu/view/Entry/187980?redirectedFrom =spurious

Piet, J., & Hougaard, E. (2011). The effect of mindfulness-based cognitive therapy for prevention of relapse in recurrent major depressive disorder: A systematic review and meta-analysis. *Clinical Psychology Review, 31*(6), 1032–1040.

Puhl, R. M., Himmelstein, M. S., & Watson, R. J. (2019). Weight-based victimization among sexual and gender minority adolescents: Implications for substance use and mental health. *Health Psychology, 38*(8), 727–737.

Redelmeier, D., & Tibshirani, R. (1997). Association between cellular-telephone calls and motor vehicle collisions. *New England Journal of Medicine, 336*, 453–458.

Reiss, S., Peterson, R., Gursky, D., & McNally, R. (1986). Anxiety sensitivity, anxiety frequency and the prediction of fearfulness. *Behavioral Research Therapy, 24*, 1–8.

Roy, M., & Liersch, M. (2014). I am a better driver than you think: Examining self-enhancement for driving ability. *Journal of Applied Social Psychology, 43*(8), 1648–1659.

Schilder, J., IJzerman, H., & Denissen, J. (2014). Physical warmth and perceptual focus: A replication of IJzerman and Semin (2009). *PLoS ONE, 9*(11). Article e112772.

Schneider, M., Voracek, M., & Tran, U. (2018). "A joke a day keeps the doctor away?" Meta-analytical evidence of differential associations of habitual humor styles with mental health. *Scandinavian Journal of Psychology, 59*, 289–300.

Sherman, P., & Flaxman, S. (2001). Protecting ourselves from food: Spices and morning sickness may shield us from toxins and microorganisms in the diet. *American Scientist, 89*, 142–151.

Skolnick, D., & Bloom, P. (2006). What does Batman think about SpongeBob? Children's understanding of the fantasy/fantasy distinction. *Cognition, 101*(1), B9–B18.

Stoet, G. (2010). PsyToolkit - A software package for programming psychological experiments using Linux. *Behavior Research Methods, 42*(4), 1096–1104.

Stoet, G. (2017). PsyToolkit: A novel web-based method for running online questionnaires and reaction-time experiments. *Teaching of Psychology, 44*(1), 24–31.

Strayer, D., & Drews, F. (2004). Profiles in driver distraction: Effects of cell phone conversations on younger and older drivers. *Human Factors, 46*, 640–649.

Strayer, D., Drews, F., & Johnston, W. (2003). Cell phone-induced failures of visual attention during simulated driving. *Journal of Experimental Psychology: Applied, 9*, 2–23.

Strayer, D., Drews, F., & Crouch, D. (2006). A comparison of the cell phone driver and the drunk driver. *Human Factors, 48*, 381–391.

Strayer, D., & Johnston, W. (2001). Driven to distraction: Dual-task studies of simulated driving and conversing on a cellular telephone. *Psychological Science, 12*, 462–466.

Stroop, J. (1935). Studies of interference in serial verbal reactions. *Journal of Experimental Psychology, 18*, 643–662.

Tapper, K. (2017). Can mindfulness influence weight management related eating behaviors? If so, how? *Clinical Psychology Review, 53*, 122–134.

Vliek, M., & Rotteveel, M. (2012). If time flies, are you more fun? The relative effect of expected exposure duration on the evaluation of social stimuli. *European Journal of Social Psychology, 42*, 327–333.

Sannita, W. G., Narici, L., & Picozza, P. (2006). Positive visual phenomena in space: A scientific case and a safety issue in space travel. *Vision Research, 46*(14), 2159–2165.

Tang, Y., Tang, R., & Posner, M. (2016). Mindfulness meditation improves emotion regulation and reduces drug abuse. *Drug and Alcohol Dependence, 163*(S1), S13–S18.

Veehof, M., Trompetter, H., Bohlmeijer, E., & Schreurs, K. (2016). Acceptance- and mindfulness-based interventions for the treatment of chronic pain: a meta-analytic review. *Cognitive Behaviour Therapy, 45*(1), 5–31.

Villar-Rodríguez, E., Palomar-García, M. Á., Hernández, M., Adrián-Ventura, J., Olcina-Sempere, G., Parcet, M. A., & Ávila, C. (2020). Left-handed musicians show a higher probability of atypical cerebral dominance for language. *Human Brain Mapping, 41*(8), 2048–2058.

Zagorsky, J. (2007). Do you have to be smart to be rich? The impact of IQ on wealth, income and financial distress. *Intelligence, 35*, 489–501.

ABOUT THE AUTHOR

Photo courtesy of Erick Stroudsburg Foto

Books with optical illusions and anatomical drawings of brains and eyes, on loan to a young girl in the 1970's, ignited a life-long interest in the science of brain and behavior. About 10 years later, Carolyn (Chapple) Buckley earned a dual Bachelor of Science degree in Psychology and Education. She went on to complete a Master's degree in Biology, focusing on the neuroscience of learning and memory, and then a PhD in Integrative Biology (Behavioral Neuroscience, focusing on the endocrinology of appetite). Over the past 25 years, she has taught courses in statistics, comparative psychology (animal behavior), and introductory psychology at the community college, four-year college, and university levels. The last 13 years have been devoted to teaching the laboratory course described in this book. If given the choice (lecture or lab), she prefers teaching labs, due to an almost maniacal passion for fostering scientific reasoning through practical experience. She recently made the difficult decision to arrange a semi-retirement from teaching to give her full attention to the book you are now reading. This book is an important part of her mission to promote a future where all college graduates will have a real and lasting appreciation for scientific thinking and will know the joy of doing real science, regardless of their majors.